READING VERGIL'S *AENEID*

OKLAHOMA SERIES IN CLASSICAL CULTURE

Oklahoma Series in Classical Culture

Series Editor

Susan Ford Wiltshire, *Vanderbilt University*

Advisory Board

Alfred S. Bradford, *University of Oklahoma*
Ward W. Briggs, Jr., *University of South Carolina*
Susan Guettel Cole, *State University of New York, Buffalo*
Carolyn J. Dewald, *University of Southern California*
Thomas M. Falkner, *The College of Wooster*
Elaine Fantham, *Princeton University*
Nancy Felson-Rubin, *University of Georgia*
Arther Ferrill, *University of Washington*
Helene P. Foley, *Barnard College*
Ronald J. Leprohon, *University of Toronto*
Thomas R. Martin, *College of the Holy Cross*
A. Geoffrey Woodhead, *Corpus Christi College, Cambridge/Ohio State University*

READING VERGIL'S *AENEID*

An Interpretive Guide

EDITED BY

Christine Perkell

UNIVERSITY OF OKLAHOMA PRESS : NORMAN

Library of Congress Cataloging-in-Publication Data

Reading Vergil's *Aeneid* : an interpretive guide / edited by Christine
  Perkell.
      p.   cm. — (Oklahoma series in classical culture; v. 23)
    Includes bibliographical references.
    1. Virgil. Aeneis.   2. Aeneas (Legendary character) in
  literature.   3. Epic poetry, Latin—History and criticism.   4. Rome—
  In literature.   I. Perkell, Christine G.   II. Series.
  PA6825.R38   1999
  873'.01—dc21   99-18499
                                                                                    CIP

    ISBN 0-8061-3138-1 (cloth)
    ISBN 0-8061-3139-x (paper)

Reading Vergil's Aeneid: *An Interpretive Guide* is Volume 23 in the Oklahoma
Series in Classical Culture.

1   2   3   4   5   6   7   8   9   10

CONTENTS

ACKNOWLEDGMENTS

Many people and institutions played critical roles in bringing this volume to fruition, and it is a great pleasure for me to be able now to acknowledge with gratitude their efforts and commitment.

First I would like to thank the National Endowment for the Humanities for funding the 1994 summer institute "Reading Vergil's *Aeneid* in the Humanities Curriculum," in which this volume found its origin.

The Office of the Dean of Emory College and the Department of Classics hosted the institute and offered generous support of its activities, both formal and informal. David F. Bright, then Vice President for Arts and Sciences and Dean of Emory College, and Peter Bing, Chair of the Classics Department, deserve special thanks.

The University of Oklahoma Press, particularly in the persons of Kimberly Wiar and Alice Stanton, has been admirable in its dedication to seeing the project through to completion. Preparation of this volume, while a gratifying challenge, has been time-consuming. I thank the contributors for their patience and good humor.

Finally, I wish to thank the many generous friends and colleagues who read prior versions of my particular contributions to this volume or gave valuable aid or counsel of other sorts: William S. Anderson, Lowell Edmunds, Joseph Farrell, Helene Foley, Ralph Hexter, Zeph Stewart, Marsha Swislocki, James Tatum, Eric Varner, Susan Ford Wiltshire, Alan Cattier, Adam Lipkin, and Marshall Jones. For shortcomings that remain despite this excellent help, I am, of course, responsible.

READING VERGIL'S *AENEID*

EDITOR'S INTRODUCTION

This volume originated in a 1994 NEH-sponsored summer institute for American college and university faculty entitled "Reading Vergil's *Aeneid* in the Humanities Curriculum." The purpose of the institute was, through fresh and rigorous rereading of the *Aeneid* in English translation, to encourage nonspecialist faculty to read the *Aeneid* in a wide variety of courses in which otherwise it might not have been included. In the institute, we aimed for modern interpretive approaches to the *Aeneid*, focusing on central thematic issues that would illuminate the poem's relationship to great texts of other periods. Our purpose in this volume is analogous: to offer to nonspecialist faculty and the general reader discussions of critical issues in the *Aeneid* from a contemporary perspective.[1] This introduction aims to situate the *Aeneid* in its historical and literary context, thus providing background information to help the reader better understand the issues discussed.

THE LIFE OF VERGIL

The earliest extant biography of Vergil was written by Aelius Donatus, a fourth-century A.D. grammarian and commentator, who thus composed his *Life* some four hundred years after Vergil's death in 19 B.C. Donatus' primary source was probably Suetonius' (born ca. A.D. 69) biography of Vergil in his now lost *De Poetis* (*Lives of the Poets*). Some of the events included in Donatus' life are: Vergil was born in 70 B.C. in a small village near Mantua; his excellent rhetorical education included study in Cremona, Milan, and Rome; he met Pollio, later consul, his first patron; then Maecenas, and, through Maecenas, Octavian, destined to become Caesar Augustus. Pollio's intervention saved Vergil's land from the confiscations that accompanied the civil wars. Vergil composed the *Eclogues* over a course of three years, then the *Georgics* in seven, and the *Aeneid* in eleven. In 19 B.C., he left Italy to travel in Greece and Asia, intending to spend three years revising the *Aeneid*, after which he would devote himself to the study of philosophy. Meeting with Augustus in Athens, however, he was persuaded to change his itinerary and return to Italy. He fell ill in Megara and died in Brundisium on September 21. During his last hours he requested repeatedly that the *Aeneid* be burned. Augustus himself countermanded this request. Varius, Vergil's literary executor, edited and published the poem on Augustus' instruction.

Some assertions of Donatus' *Life* are more credible than others. Similarities that seem too remarkable to be coincidental between this *Life* and lives of other ancient poets, as well as between events ascribed by Donatus to Vergil's life and events represented in Vergil's poetry, have led some scholars to dismiss a number of details of this biography, including some of those mentioned here, as either conventions of the genre, and thus fabrications, or naively biographical readings of Vergil's texts.[2] For example, the *Life* recounts marvelous signs, typical of the genre, at the poet's birth, portending happiness and fruitfulness; similarly, Vergil's assumption of the toga of manhood on the very day that the poet Lucretius died seems a remarkable coincidence, too neatly contrived to mark the passing of greatness from the earlier to the later poet. The *Life*'s assumption that Vergil loved boys may be an inference from the second *Eclogue*, in which the speaker Corydon expresses his passion for the youth Alexis. Yet despite this and other liaisons alluded to in the *Life*, we learn from the same source that the poet acquired the name Parthenias (i.e., maidenly, virginal) because of the moderation of his personal conduct. Again, the lament for Daphnis in *Eclogue* 5 is read by the *Life* as an expression of the poet's lament for the death of his brother Flaccus. His father is said to have been a beekeeper, perhaps because of the extended passage on bees in *Georgics* 4. The *Life* states that Vergil wrote the *Eclogues* particularly to honor Asinius Pollio, Alfenus Varus, and Cornelius Gallus, because they exempted his property from confiscation for returning veterans after Philippi: confiscations are the subjects of *Eclogues* 1 and 9. *Eclogue* 9 includes as well the allusion to a poet, called Menalcas, who quarreled dangerously with an ex-soldier over his land. The *Life* states that Vergil wrote the *Georgics* to honor Maecenas, who had, precisely, saved him from the violence of an ex-soldier with whom he had quarreled over his land.

While the question of whether some parts of the *Life* are accurate may seem to many readers largely inconsequential, Vergil's reported request that the poem be burned is significant. Scholars have given much consideration to what aspects of the poem might have troubled Vergil as he was dying. Fifty or so half lines awaited completion; there were also small discrepancies in matters of detail, such as the difference between the narrator's account of Palinurus' death in Book 5 and Palinurus' own narration in the Underworld in Book 6. Yet these seem insufficient cause for the poet to destroy his life's major work. Was the poem, then, fundamentally incomplete? Lacking, as some scholars have suggested, the ending its author would have written, had he lived? Clearly this last possibility has consequences for interpretation and suggests a solution to some readers' dissatisfaction with the poem's closing scene. Although most scholars today do believe that we have the ending Vergil intended, the persistence of questions points to the problematic nature of the poem's abrupt and, in some respects, unresolved closure.

HISTORICAL CONTEXT

Many scholars believe that the recurrent images of a new golden age reflect the poet's own hopes for a positive future under the regime of the future Augustus. The fourth *Eclogue*, which prophesies the birth of a child whose coming of age will restore a paradisiacal peace, is perhaps the most famous text in which such an image occurs. Other examples are Jupiter's and Anchises' prophecies of a new golden age in *Aeneid* 1 and 6, respectively, to be ushered in by the ascendancy of Caesar Augustus. Whether, in fact, these golden age passages are best read as expressions of genuine optimism or rather as escapist fantasy—or perhaps as something in between—it is important to remember that, during his first forty years, Vergil lived through a time of virtually continuous civil conflict. Although Rome had long been a world power at the time of his birth, the Roman world was undergoing tremendous political and social upheaval, as Romans conducted wars abroad, struggled with their Italian allies at home,[3] and witnessed protracted bloody strife between political rivals. The unresolved problems both of governing an extensive empire as well as of controlling partisan rivalries between ambitious generals revealed the limitations of the senatorial government of the Republic and thus paved the way for the Principate.

Important historical figures for the *Aeneid* are Julius and Augustus Caesar and their primary opponents. Julius Caesar (100–44 B.C.), a brilliant military strategist, charismatic commander, and gifted literary stylist as well, was the conqueror of Gaul. Denied, as he felt, the appropriate advancement and gravely threatened by political enemies in Rome, Caesar crossed the Rubicon into Italy with his troops in 49 B.C., thereby precipitating a constitutional crisis. Many senators fled to Caesar's rival Pompey (106–48 B.C.), whom he pursued and defeated at the battle of Pharsalus in Asia Minor in 48. Caesar's affair with Cleopatra delayed his prompt consolidation of this victory, which came in the battles of Thapsus in North Africa (46) and Munda in Spain (45). Made dictator for life, Caesar appears to have envisioned substantive reforms in the administration of the empire. Although he refused the title *rex* (king), Caesar's wide-ranging ambitions were manifest and represented an intolerable threat to the Republic in the eyes of Brutus and other senators, who conspired to assassinate him in 44 B.C. When the popular support they had anticipated in reward for this action failed to materialize, the assassins fled to Asia Minor, where they were defeated at the battle of Philippi (42 B.C.) by the combined forces of Octavian, Caesar's young (nineteen years old in 44 B.C.) great-nephew and chosen heir, and Caesar's first lieutenant, Mark Antony (83–30 B.C.). The victory of these two at Philippi, however, proved to be only a stage in the fierce military and political competition between them for unchallenged supremacy. To many contemporaries it appeared that Antony, with his superior age, power, and experience, must surely triumph eventually, but Julius Caesar had correctly seen in his young nephew the vision and determination that would allow him to become, as Shakespeare's Cleopatra says, "sole sir o' th' world."[4]

Between 43 and 31 B.C. a series of struggles occurred between Octavian and Antony or his partisans in Italy, followed by uneasy reconciliations, as the two continually maneuvered for advantage in the decisive conflict to come. The first reconciliation saw them, along with Lepidus, appointed triumvirs in 43 B.C., with virtually absolute power, for a five-year term. The orator Cicero was the most famous victim of the proscriptions that followed upon this accord. After their success at the battle of Philippi, Octavian and Antony divided the empire between them, with Octavian taking the West and Antony the East. This was a fateful moment, for Antony made the East the center of his operations, relying on the wealth of Egypt and Cleopatra to pursue his military goals. Octavian was left to consolidate his power and popularity in Italy, while Antony, as Octavian's propaganda made known, consorted with a foreign queen, divorced his Roman wife Octavia (the sister of Octavian), and styled himself the god

Dionysus for his Eastern subjects, who were thus encouraged to see him and Cleopatra as a divine couple united for the interest of Asia. His bequests to his children by Cleopatra and his wish to be buried in Alexandria further shocked Roman sentiment. Octavian's propaganda exploited Antony's actions to develop a consciousness at home of a united Italy, which he would champion against the dangers of the depraved East. After Italy and the Western provinces swore allegiance to him in 32 B.C., Octavian moved against Antony and Cleopatra, whom he defeated in the battle of Actium in 31 B.C. Antony and then Cleopatra committed suicide in Egypt the following year, as Octavian closed in.

Shrewd deployment of force, along with careful observance of republican forms, allowed Octavian to maintain absolute power in Rome. The title of Augustus, created to acknowledge and yet simultaneously to veil his unique status, was awarded to him by a weakened Senate in 27 B.C. Formally the Republic was restored, as Augustus returned certain powers to the Senate, but substantively the Republic had come to an end. A century of devastating civil war had come to an end as well, bringing as a consequence all the possibilities of peace. Although the end of the Republic was regretted by many of the senatorial class, the benefits of peace were ample compensation to most of those who had survived the carnage. For these survivors the question surely was: What would be the future be? What did Octavian's ascendancy really portend?

All this epochal history—the long civil conflicts in Italy, the various passions of the combatants, the cultural opposition between West and East—finds its reflection in the *Aeneid*. As Vergil composed the poem in the years 29–19 B.C., he could not have anticipated that Augustus would rule as emperor until his death in A.D. 14 or that his forty-five year reign would mark the beginning of four hundred years of imperial Roman rule. Conspiracy against the emperor, his serious illnesses in the twenties, the unresolved problems of succession, along with the raw memories of civil war, mean, I suspect, that we cannot overestimate the unease mixed with hope that characterized the period during which the *Aeneid* was composed.

THE LITERARY CONTEXT: GREEK

The most important models for the *Aeneid* were the Homeric epics, the *Iliad* and *Odyssey*. These poems are the perfected products of an oral tradition dating back to at least the eighth century B.C.[5] The usual dating of the texts of the *Iliad* and *Odyssey* as we have them is approximately 750–700 B.C., although the circumstances of the transcription remain unknown. The Homeric poems constituted the major cultural heritage of the Greek, and then of the Roman, world, whose literary sensibility was shaped by the poems' language and whose moral and ethical code was influenced by those of the two poems' respective heroes.[6]

The Trojan War is the setting of the *Iliad*, which narrates some events in the tenth year of the Greek siege of Troy, as the Greeks attempt to recover Helen, Menelaus' wife, who had run off with Paris, the beautiful Trojan prince. While it is Menelaus' brother Agamemnon who commands the Greek forces, the poem's major themes are reflected in the experience of Achilles, the greatest of the Greek warriors, who sustains grievous personal loss through the death of his companion Patroclus. In Achilles' return of the body of the Trojan Hector, slayer of Patroclus, to his father Priam, Homer models a humanity that transcends the enemy/friend dichotomy in favor of a perceived larger community of mortality and loss that joins all people. As the setting of the *Iliad* is war, so the setting of the *Odyssey* is war's aftermath. The *Odyssey* tells of the wanderings of Odysseus after the Trojan War (Books 1–12) and of his homecoming to Ithaca (Books 13–24). Odysseus (Latin Ulysses) is able, after physical and spiritual trials, to resume his place as father, husband, and king. In the last verses of the poem, reconciliation in the city is achieved, even if only by divine intervention.

In both Homeric poems, then, the protagonist moves toward more humane action: Achilles to a transcendent pity and generosity, Odysseus to restoration of civilized order and moral insight following the temptations of military and sexual adventurism. The *Aeneid* is an extended allusion to these two poems, inviting comparison with them throughout. It was suggested in antiquity that the *Aeneid* might be seen as divided into halves, the Odyssean books 1–6 largely focusing on Aeneas' travels toward his new home, and the Iliadic books 7–12 showing him at war.[7] Retrospective self-narration, funeral games, descents to the Underworld, ecphrases (extended descriptions primarily of works of art), catalogues, epic similes, and epithets are other features of the *Aeneid* that find their origin in the Homeric poems. Vergil would have expected his readers to know these texts thoroughly, and thus they provided a structure and meaning he could exploit for his portrait of Aeneas, whose values come to be provocatively at variance with those of Homer's heroes. Vergil allows the Roman mission of conquest and rule to stand in implicit continual contrast to the Homeric heroes' individual purposes. While Odysseus himself achieves his homecoming but loses all his men, Aeneas' mission of founding a new state, by definition, cannot succeed without the group. The requirement for success in this mission is not so much self-discovery as self-abnegation—dedication to a cause larger (or is it narrower?) than personal moral growth.

Some early critics of Vergil called his imitations of Homer plagiarisms or thefts, and discussion of Vergil's use of allusion continues to engage readers. For my part, I would propose that readers understand Vergil's uses of Homer as not narrowly imitative or typological but rather as essentially ironic. That is, Vergil's construction of affinity with his Homeric models allows him to create suggestive, resonant disparities from these models—disparities that open ironic perspectives on traditional heroic values and their relationship to Roman power. Vergil's relationship to Homer is not, I believe, adversarial, as in the Bloomian model of misprision, but rather engaged or dialogic.[8] The better a reader knows the *Iliad* and the *Odyssey*, the richer his or her reading of Vergil's comprehensive engagement with Homer's literary and moral programme.[9]

Another epic model, whose impact on the *Aeneid* has sometimes been underrated, is the *Argonautica* (or Voyage of *Argo*) of Apollonius, born ca. 295 B.C. in Alexandria. "Alexandrian" or "Hellenistic" refers to the refined, even precious, culture of this Greek-speaking empire in the third century B.C., a culture that looked back to the masterworks of Homeric and Classical Greece with awe, but also with a sophisticated detachment. Against this monumental heritage, Hellenistic poets strove for newness, incongruity, brevity, and wit.[10] Significant innovations of Apollonius' epic include the weak hero and the moral ambiguity of success. In the *Argonautica*, Jason and his men set out on a conventionally heroic (as they think) quest for the Golden Fleece, but find themselves instead in an unheroic, seductive world of women and magic spells more powerful than their weapons. In the antihero Jason, we find a beautiful protagonist disdained by his men, seduced and outmaneuvered by Medea, and corrupted in pursuit of his mission. Although the quest for the Fleece is successful, the moral trajectory of Jason is a negative one, as betrayal, murder, and marriage to Medea, whom, by the end, even the narrator fears (4.1669–75), are the conditions of success. Thus the poem brilliantly reveals that Jason's only alternatives are failure in the mission or moral compromise, for honorable heroic feats of strength are obsolete in the world in which he finds himself. In the *Argonautica*, experience of the wider world brings moral implosion rather than, as in the Homeric poems, moral elevation. After

Apollonius, we might say that the genre of epic encompasses questioning of the protagonist and of the traditional heroic ethos. To the degree that readers of the *Aeneid* ultimately see either Aeneas or the Roman mission as put into question, they might find precedents in the *Argonautica*.

THE LITERARY CONTEXT: ROMAN

Vergil's predecessors in Latin epic exist only in fragments, so that our knowledge of their influence on Vergil is limited. Latin epic was created sometime in the third century B.C. when Livius Andronicus, a Greek from Tarentum, who likely arrived in Rome originally as a prisoner of war, composed a Roman adaptation of Homer's *Odyssey* in Latin saturnians, the native Italic meter. His successor in Latin epic, Gnaeus Naevius (died ca. 201 B.C.), took the Punic Wars (between Rome and her commercial and military rival Carthage) as his subject in his *Bellum Punicum*. Naevius, who fought in the first Punic War (264–241 B.C.), elevated this theme to epic status by alternating mythological digressions with contemporary historical events. Ennius (239–169 B.C.), also an army veteran, wrote the *Annales*, a chronicle of Roman history in epic verse. His first book encompassed the Trojans' flight from Troy and the founding of Rome by Romulus. Ennius' technical innovation was his use of the Homeric dactylic hexameter instead of Livius' and Naevius' saturnians, which he considered primitive.

Many scholars have assumed that the early Roman epics were unambiguously militaristic and traditional in their values. A famous verse of Ennius, *moribus antiquis res stat Romana virisque* ("the Roman state stands strong through her ancient traditions and courageous men"), is certainly suggestive of such a reading. Others point out, however, that fragments, as they are often cited without context, may give misleading impressions. It is also useful to note that even some fragments, such as the following, suggest more moral complexity than is often acknowledged:

> pellitur e medio sapientia, vi geritur res;
> spernitur orator bonus, horridus miles amatur.
>   (Ennius 248–49, ed. Skutsch)

> wisdom is exiled, violence rules;
> the honorable speaker is disdained, the fearsome soldier is loved.

This passage may suggest criticism of the use of violence or armed force. A lengthier Ennian fragment, Pyrrhus' speech rejecting a Roman offer to ransom captives after the battle of Heraclea (280 B.C.), apparently portrays the enemy as an honorable adversary, who disdains mere gold, but honors the gods and the courage of men in war. He concludes:

> quorum virtuti belli fortuna pepercit
> eorundem me libertati parcere certum est.
> dono—ducite—doque volentibus cum magnis dis.
>   (183–90, ed. Skutsch)

> Whose courage the fortune of war has spared,
> their freedom I have decided to spare.
> I grant—take [them]—I give [them], as the great gods will.

If only a few verses remained of the *Aeneid*, we could have an imperfect notion of its contents. *Romanos rerum dominos gentemque togatam* ("Romans the masters of the world, the race that wears the toga," 1.282, M 1.394–95), apparently Augustus' favorite line (it occurs in Jupiter's prophecy of Roman power), suggests an unambiguously patriotic poem. On the other hand, *sunt lacrimae rerum et mentem mortalia tangunt* ("There are tears for passing things; here too things mortal touch the mind," 1.462, M 655), spoken by Aeneas as he views a frieze representing the Trojan war, suggests a different sensibility. It is possible, therefore, that Roman epic prior to Vergil, especially as it was conceived initially for private circulation rather than public performance,[11] had a more comprehensive humanity than is generally assumed. Alessandro Barchiesi proposes, indeed, that epic in its very defining conditions of the inequality of god and mortal, enemy and friend, is by necessity filled with pain, and therefore that the sympathy Vergil's poem shows for the defeated may be traditional of epic and not necessarily unique to him.[12]

The so-called (by Cicero) New Poets, the most famous of whom is Catullus (84–54 B.C.), also had a critical influence on the *Aeneid*. In emulation of the Alexandrian poets, these young men pursued a private rather than a public art, aimed at brevity and refinement of style, and characterized by recherché mythological allusion and interest in often pathological love stories. They rejected in particular traditional epic poetry, with its edifying public themes. Catullus is best known for his intense love poems addressed to a woman he called Lesbia, but his "Peleus and

Thetis," an *epyllion* or little epic (408 verses in dactylic hexameter) of Alexandrian sensibility, was very influential among later poets and finds echoes in the *Aeneid*. As the new poetry expressed an esthetic alternative to the epic of Naevius and Ennius, so it also expressed a cultural critique of established public figures and norms of appropriate male behavior. In the poems of Catullus (and later of Tibullus, Propertius, and Ovid) love, not war, and poetry, not political power, are the superior pursuits.

Vergil's first poems, the *Eclogues* and *Georgics*, reflect the esthetic refinement and, in their own fashion (e.g., *Eclogues* 1 and 9), the political critique characteristic of this movement. The Aristaeus epyllion of *Georgics* 4, with its tragic and moving story of Orpheus and Eurydice, owes much to the New Poets' Alexandrian sensibility. That Vergil subsequently wrote a manifestly political epic is a surprising literary development, which perhaps suggests the urgency of the claims of Roman political life. Vergil's great predecessor Lucretius (ca. 94–55 B.C.), author of the *De Rerum Natura* (*On the Nature of Things*), a philosophical/missionary poem in six books, was likely a critical influence on Vergil in his explicitly acknowledged moral purpose. Lucretius expounded an atomic theory of matter and an Epicurean philosophy of life, with the goal of freeing readers from superstitions about an underworld and the gods. The *De Rerum Natura* was a poem of intense ethical commitment, which put into question a range of conventional political and moral assumptions. While the *Aeneid* dispenses neither with gods nor with the underworld, it is pervaded by a comparable moral seriousness. Yet in its haunting and resonant verse, vivid characters, dramatic confrontations, and melancholy memorializing of tragedy and triumph, the *Aeneid* eclipsed its predecessors in epic, becoming immediately *the* Roman poem and—worst of fates—a standard school text. The long established fame of the *Aeneid* inclines us to forget how innovative and comprehensive was Vergil's achievement.

THE AENEAS LEGEND BEFORE VERGIL

Aeneas appears several times in the *Iliad*. Along with Hector he is an important warrior on the Trojan side. He fights Diomedes in Book 5.166–346, Idomeneus in Book 13.458–544, and Achilles himself in Book 20.160–339. In two of these encounters, he requires divine rescue—by Aphrodite and Apollo in 5 and by Poseidon in 20. Crucially for *Aeneid* readers, Poseidon says that Aeneas is fated to escape from Troy and that his descendants will rule over the Trojans (20.307–8).[13] The *Homeric Hymn to Aphrodite* (seventh century B.C.), which recounts the story of Aphrodite's (Latin Venus') seduction of Anchises, includes Aphrodite's prophecy to Anchises of Aeneas' future rule (196–97). The association of Aeneas with what Romans called *pietas* (loyalty, devotion to family, gods, and, by extension, state) is early. Suggested in a general way in the *Iliad*, Aeneas' piety finds its emblematic expression in his carrying his aged father from flaming Troy, an image depicted on vases and seals as early as the sixth century B.C. The story of Aeneas' arrival in Latium can be dated to the fifth century B.C. By 480 B.C., Romans seem to have adopted this legend for their own city and so began to acquire a heroic heritage suited to their political expansion. Naevius appears to have told of Aeneas' departure from Troy, his wanderings, and his arrival in Italy with his father.[14] According to Servius, Naevius represented Romulus, the founder of Rome, as the grandson of Aeneas, thus integrating the independently developing stories of Romulus and Aeneas.[15]

By the time of Vergil, the Aeneas story had become associated primarily with the family of the Julii, which for centuries had claimed descent from Aeneas. Julius Caesar enhanced his stature throughout his career by claiming Venus and Aeneas as ancestors. With Octavian's coming to power and with the *Aeneid*'s status as *the* Roman poem, the legend of Aeneas became national. In sum, Vergil shaped his poem around a protagonist who had the epic provenance to bring distinction to myths of Roman origin. The claimed descent of the Julii from Venus allowed the integration of Augustus into Rome's founding myths and the representation of Augustus as the natural culmination of the movement of Roman history.

It is useful to try to recover Vergil's innovations in the story of Aeneas, for, as suggested above, deviations from tradition are significant. Apparent innovations in Vergil's treatment of Aeneas concern his primary antagonists, Dido and Turnus. While in the common version of Dido's story, she is, as in Vergil, an exile from Tyre who becomes queen of Carthage, she is also famed for chastity and kills herself to avoid a second marriage to a local African king. Aeneas plays no part in her story. (Naevius, however, mentioned Dido and Anna and may, therefore, have included a meeting of Dido and Aeneas. This meeting could have served, as in Vergil, as aetiology for the Punic Wars.) According to Servius, Cato (234–149 B.C.) in his *Origines* made Dido's sister Anna perish for love of Aeneas, but to our knowledge no author before Vergil made *Dido* commit suicide for love of Aeneas.[16] Vergil's implied comparisons between Dido and Cleopatra, as dangerous Eastern seductresses, would also appear to be new. Aspects of Vergil's account of Turnus appear to be original as well. In both Cato (again, as reported in Servius [on 4.620 and 6.760]) and Dionysius of Halicarnassus (*fl.* 30 B.C.), Aeneas is killed or disappears (perhaps drowned, perhaps apotheosized) while fighting the Latins. In Cato, Aeneas kills Turnus; in Dionysius, the killer of Turnus (or Tyrrhenus) is not specified. The Arcadians Evander and Pallas do not figure in the story, for Evander had his own legend (Dion. Hal. 1.31–33, 40; Livy 1.7.4–15). Therefore, the climactic action that concludes the *Aeneid*, Aeneas' slaying of Turnus to avenge Turnus' own slaying of Pallas, is likely a Vergilian innovation.

Finally, representation of the protagonist's mission as conquest and foundation of an empire differs from that of heroic missions in the Greek tradition. In the context of the Homeric tradition, power as a goal that serves as its own legitimation is not necessarily or obviously right or sufficient; yet, as Denis Feeney observes: "The *Aeneid* is preoccupied with power before any other subject."[17] Plato implicitly represents Socrates (as in the *Apology* or *Symposium*) as on a mission comparable to that of Homer's heroes, but Aeneas' mission differs from Socrates' in that its primary purpose is not ethical or philosophical. Naevius' poem may have had a communal ethic, but it lacks a central heroic figure. In sum, Aeneas' heroic Roman mission—as oriented toward the future, divinely inspired, and manifest in power—is likely Vergil's conception.

RECEPTION OF THE AENEID

Although the *Aeneid* has been considered a classic for two thousand years, its fundamental meaning is currently the subject of dispute among scholars. In brief, Vergil critics dispute whether the *Aeneid* is "pro-Augustan" or "anti-Augustan." Although Duncan Kennedy (1992) has gone far to deconstruct the question as so posed, most readers will feel, nevertheless, that the question does invite an answer. Pro-Augustan or, as they are also termed, "optimistic" readers believe that the *Aeneid* endorses (indeed, even propagandizes for) the Roman imperial project of conquest and rule, with its attendant moral values of *pietas*, order, and reason. These values they see symbolized in the poem by Aeneas and embodied in Vergil's time by the regime of Augustus Caesar. H.-P. Stahl summarizes the pro-Augustan, "optimistic" reading of the poem:

> Traditional interpretations of the *Aeneid* . . . draw on program-
> matic passages such as Jove's revelation of Rome's future in
> Book 1, Anchises' prophecy in Book 6, Vulcan's fate-informed
> survey of Roman history in 8. Here Virgil is seen to lend special
> support to Augustus by showing that his rule, equivalent to the
> return of the Golden Age, was fate-ordained all along. The Julians'
> ancestor Aeneas acts in agreement with Jove and Fate. His oppo-
> nents, e.g., the Carthaginian Queen Dido and Rutulian Prince
> Turnus, are clearly wrong and accordingly confess to personal
> guilt. Let us add that moral innocence and suffering without guilt
> are reserved for the Trojan (Julian) party.[18]

Pessimistic readers, on the other hand, believe the *Aeneid*, through, for
example, its varied and pervasive expressions of sympathy for victims of
Roman conquest, challenges imperial values and portrays not the triumph
of reason and order but precisely their dissolution. Aeneas' killing of
Turnus "with furor and anger" (*furiis et ira*, 12.946) exemplifies for them
the triumph of the irrational over reason and compassion; despite Aeneas'
continual aspirations to control and humanity, his virtues are inadequate to
the challenge of what Juno (as *furor*, "disorder," "violence") represents.
(Vergil's earlier poems, the *Eclogues* and *Georgics*, have elicited similarly
ideological and contrary readings.)

The "anti-Augustan" or "pessimistic" reading, though not entirely
new, gained a special currency in the United States during the Viet Nam
War period, when questions about the moral use of military power were
widely debated. More recently, critical dispute about Vergil's texts is
protracted by its implications for current cultural and moral debate.
Because the *Aeneid* (as in the speech of Jupiter in Book 1) prophesies the
triumph of empire, most have read it as an endorsement of traditional
order and values, associated now with cultural conservatives. Alterna-
tively, a "pessimistic" or "anti-Augustan" *Aeneid* could suggest a different
meaning altogether: in its counternarrative that elicits pity for the defeated,
it could be seen as modeling a liberal commitment to human rights and
humane values. Finally, some readers, in this way resembling the "optimists"
described above, understand the *Aeneid* as an endorsement of traditional
values, but see these traditional values as perpetuating modes of oppres-
sion that must be resisted. For these readers, any resistance is to be found
in their own readings and not in the text itself. A goal of this volume, then,
is not only to attempt to read the *Aeneid* with enhanced understanding, but

also to illuminate for readers how it comes about that this poem elicits such varied interpretations.

HOW DID WE GET TO THIS INTERPRETIVE PASS?

Reception of Vergil's *Aeneid* has a long and surprisingly varied history. In order to give an idea of the range of responses, I will summarize readings of some of the poem's most famous readers and then conclude with discussion of some contemporary readings of the poem that provide an idea of where, as I see it, the discussion is currently focused.[19]

The oldest extant commentaries (fourth century A.D.) assert that Vergil had a clear and simple ideological goal in the *Aeneid*, namely, to praise Augustus. The fourth-century grammarian and commentator Servius explicitly states (on *Aeneid* 1.1) that Vergil's purpose was to praise Augustus "by means of his ancestors" (i.e., by telling their story). Servius' virtual contemporary Tiberius Claudius Donatus, in his introduction to *Aeneid* 1, states that Vergil intended to show Aeneas as a worthy (*dignus*) first ancestor of Augustus, in whose honor the poem was written. Nevertheless, we learn from the poet Ovid (43 B.C.–A.D. 17) (*Tristia* 2.533–36) that the Dido episode was the most popular part of the poem. This observation would seem to be corroborated by St. Augustine (A.D. 354–430), who grieves that he spent his youth lamenting over Dido rather than over the loss of his own soul.[20] The poem therefore seems to have exerted a strong pull on early readers in a direction other than that described in the school commentaries as its primary purpose. On the other hand, both Ovid's *Metamorphoses* and Lucan's (A.D. 39–65) *Bellum Civile* with, for example, their unteleological plots, their elimination of any central heroic protagonist, and their variously anti-imperial ideologies, can be read as challenges to an imperial Augustan *Aeneid*. Even in antiquity, then, despite the unanimity of professional commentators, we can see some evidence of competing readings of the *Aeneid*.

Centuries later, Dante, a Christian reader deeply learned in and moved by Vergil's poems, although he did not read the *Aeneid* as "anti-Augustan," did not, nevertheless, read it as an untroubled validation of the order of things. Rather, responding to the poet's pervasive despair about divine justice, Dante read the *Aeneid* as a tragedy (his Vergil refers to the *Aeneid* as "*l'alta mia tragedia*," *Inf.* 20.113), to which he polemically and triumphantly opposed his own *commedia* (e.g., *Inf.* 21.2), predicated on the justice of God, that would or should be reflected on earth in perfected monarchy. As an example of Dante's implied polemic against Vergil, readers may consider Aeneas' bitterly despairing verses about the indifference of the gods who let a certain Rhipeus perish during the sack of Troy. "Rhipeus," recounts Aeneas, was ". . . the first among the Teucrians for justice and observing right; [but] the gods thought otherwise" (. . . *Rhipeus, iustissimus unus / qui fuit in Teucris et servantissimus aequi / (dis aliter visum)*, 2.426–28, M 574–75). Dante "corrects" Vergil and his Aeneas here, asserting the justice of God by placing Rhipeus, exceptionally for a pre-Christian pagan, in *Paradiso* (20.68). The various intimations of Dante's Vergil's deficient faith are most bleakly exemplified in his eternal exclusion from Paradise.

John Dryden, on the other hand, another great poet devoted to Vergil and a monarchist like Dante, is consistently cited as a traditional reader of the *Aeneid*. Indeed, he states in the preface to his translation of the *Aeneid*: "The design of [a heroic poem] is to form the mind to heroic virtue by example."[21] He describes Vergil's purpose as: "to infuse an awful respect into the people towards such a prince [Augustus]: by that respect to confirm their obedience to him, and by that obedience to make them happy. This was the moral of his divine poem."[22] Yet a reading of the whole preface reveals that this summary of Vergil's purpose follows several pages of justification of Vergil's position, based on Dryden's inference that Vergil in fact had "republican," that is, anti-imperial, sentiments. "Yet I may safely affirm for our great author. . . that he was still of republican principles in heart."[23] For Dryden, Vergil is making the best of a difficult situation. "I say that Virgil, having maturely weigh'd the condition of the time in which he liv'd, that an entire liberty was not to be retrieved . . . that this conqueror, tho' of a bad kind, was the very best of it: that the arts of peace flourish'd under him; that all men might be happy, if they would be quiet. . . . these things, I say, being considered by the poet, he concluded it to be in the interest of his country to be so govern'd."[24] This sense that the surface content of the poem is at variance with the poet's real sympathies lies at the heart of contemporary controversy about the poem's meaning. In seeing the *Aeneid*'s support of Augustus as somehow conflicted, Dryden was responding to what we might now call tensions, contradictions, or ideological fissures in the poem.

T. S. Eliot is unusual among poets in not responding to the *Aeneid*'s apparently conflicted purposes. Eliot established a kind of interpretive norm for the poem by lending his considerable authority to the traditional reading. In two famous essays, "What is a Classic?" (1944) and "Virgil and the Christian World" (1951), he presented Vergil as the ultimate exemplar of evolved, stable Western values. "What is a Classic?" starts from the assumption that Vergil *is* the classic, a "universal classic," whose work the definition of classic must primarily encompass.[25] "Virgil acquires the centrality of the unique classic; he is at the centre of European civilisation, in a position which no other poet can share or usurp. The Roman Empire and the Latin language were not any empire and language but an empire and a language with a unique destiny in relation to ourselves; and the poet in whom that Empire and that language came to consciousness and expression is a poet of unique destiny."[26] Eliot's views were apparently derived primarily from Theodor Haecker's *Virgil: Father of the West* (1934), according to Theodore Ziolkowski, who finds that Eliot had little but second-hand knowledge of the *Aeneid* and was, in particular, unfamiliar with the second half of the poem.[27] Eliot's nostalgia for the *ordo* and *pietas* he ascribed to Vergil associated him with conservative thinkers.[28] Haecker, by contrast, was an Austrian Catholic anti-fascist. Reading the *Aeneid* as a proto-Christian text (he focuses on the phrase *sunt lacrimae rerum* ["there are tears of things"]) and Vergil as an *anima naturaliter christiana* ("a soul Christian by nature"),[29] Haecker implicitly exhorted readers to reject the narrow solution of fascism in favor of a transcendent Christian humanism. These antithetical readings show how Vergil's text or, perhaps, any text may be appropriated for opposing ideological purposes.[30]

Eliot's views were harmonious with those of the influential German scholars Richard Heinze (first published 1902; Eng. trans. 1993) and Viktor Pöschl (1950; Eng. trans. 1962), who respectively preceded and succeeded him. Heinze's *Aeneid* praises Roman might and Augustus, and his Aeneas, a Homeric hero reconceived for his contemporary world, develops into the ideal Stoic, following the will of destiny.[31] Pöschl's *Aeneid* has absolute moral clarity, as it enshrines imperial ideology and portrays a parallel triumph of order over chaos in the victories of the Roman god, the Roman hero, and the Roman emperor over their enemies, Juno, Dido/Turnus, and Antony, respectively. "The image of the dark demon of passion in Turnus confronts the shining spiritual and moral power in Aeneas. Roman history is presented as a struggle between two principles, and Rome's victory is seen as the victory of the higher one."[32]

This reading of the *Aeneid* characterizes what W. R. Johnson terms the "optimistic European school" of readers[33] as opposed to the "pessimistic Harvard" school, and epitomizes what he terms Vergil's "role as a maker of the myth of Europe."[34] Ziolkowski observes that newly urgent readings of Vergil emerged in the period of crisis between the two world wars in efforts precisely to save "the myth of Europe." As he puts it: "In the effort to bring meaning into the world of the 1920s and 1930s the Roman poet was invoked, who two thousand years earlier had succeeded in distilling beauty and order from the political and social horror of his own age: civil war, revolution, expropriation, brutal agrarian reform, exile, dictatorship, and imperial aggression."[35] Reading of Vergil led to no political consensus, however, since readers found what they wished in Vergil's texts: "populism or elitism, fascism or democracy, commitment or escapism."[36] To Johnson, it is World War II, "when the center failed to hold disastrously,"[37] more even than the period between the wars, that made urgent the question of what the *Aeneid* is saying about our civilization.

In the United States the "pessimistic" reading gained prominence during the 1960s. Adam Parry began his influential "The Two Voices of Vergil's *Aeneid*" (1963) with the elegiac lines on the death of the priest Umbro (7.759–60), taking them as exemplary of the mourning landscapes and melancholy of the poem's closing books. These, along with the sorrows and failures of Aeneas as hero, created for Parry the poem's "private voice of regret," which is at variance with its "public voice of triumph" as expressed in its explicit Roman epic "message." Wendell Clausen, in "An Interpretation of the *Aeneid*" (1964), illuminating the nostalgia and sorrow of Aeneas, the poem's sympathy for defeat and suffering, and the absence of reconciliation in its conclusion, read the *Aeneid*'s view of Roman history as a "long pyrrhic victory of the human spirit." In *The Poetry of the Aeneid* (1966), Michael C. J. Putnam argued that the *furor* initially associated with the destructive Juno, against which Aeneas struggles throughout the poem, in fact dominates Aeneas in the final scene of the poem as he kills the wounded, suppliant Turnus. The resulting circular movement of the poem from the vengeful *furor* of Juno to the vengeful *furor* of Aeneas thus adumbrates the limitations of the figure of Aeneas and of the imperial project he embodies.

The darkness of these readings was significantly informed by attention to the second half of the poem, rather than exclusively to the more famous earlier books. In addition, the New Criticism, which favored paradox, irony, and ambiguity as the defining virtues of poetry, created an intellectual environment in which it was possible to perceive contrary movements within a text (e.g., a "public" and a "private" voice), assuming these were ultimately resolved into unity.[38] Critical debate among scholars continues to center on Putnam's reading of the poem's closing scene. Later scholars, such as A. J. Boyle and R. O. A. M. Lyne, have developed the pessimistic reading. Lyne (1987) found implicit subversive comment in any perceived discrepancy or deviation from epic convention. Irony created by such discrepancy he termed a "further voice" that through its difference from the norm puts into question the utterances of the epic voice, thereby subverting its implied ideology. For Boyle (1986, 1993), tracing the whole "constellation of *furor* imagery,"[39] Vergil's despair about the violence of politics and the impotence of poetry was revealed as the essential meaning of the *Aeneid*, which has, in his view, been so misread as to be a "failed" poem. For pessimists, then, the oppositional voice, however constituted, delivers authentic criticism of the regime, despite the indirection of its expression. Johnson's *Darkness Visible* (1976), although generally associated by readers with the "pessimistic" critics, in fact argued for an unresolved reading, which acknowledged both the *Aeneid*'s passionate patriotism and its existential doubts. "The *Aeneid* moves constantly in the dialectic of its polysematic configurations between these two poles [of optimism and pessimism]."[40] For Johnson, both the optimistic and the pessimistic readings were reductive, as they failed to acknowledge what he perceived to be the poem's polysemous quality.

Traditional readings have also been published recently, the most often cited being those of Karl Galinsky, Philip R. Hardie (1986),[41] and Francis Cairns. Galinsky in particular accommodates contemporary theoretical debate about the poem in that he acknowledges multiple meanings in the *Aeneid*. However, unlike many Marxist or deconstructionist theorists, he conceives the range of these meanings to be authorially controlled, asserting that "an escape into indeterminacy is to be only a last and rare resort."[42] Therefore, in his most recent writing (1996), we find that the *Aeneid* has an "intentional multiplicity of resonances," "an authorial center [that] exists along with the intended polysemy";[43] readers are asked to respond to this multiplicity of meaning "within the framework of a guiding *auctoritas*."[44] As an illustration of this, he argues that, despite the manifest pathos of deaths in the *Aeneid* or the (to some, disquieting) rage (*furor*) of Aeneas, his is a "pious and just war,"[45] conducted by a man whose changing moods reveal him to be not a deficient but a believable human figure. For Galinsky, then, the *Aeneid* does not evince ideological doubts. "That Vergil shared in the basic values of the Augustan reform is self-evident."[46]

As I see it, the overall result of the last thirty-five years' controversy is that relentless argument for a monologic reading has largely evolved into the current hypothesis that internal contradiction, deemed broadly characteristic of literary texts, characterizes the *Aeneid* as well. For most scholars, I believe, the questions now are: How is one to describe the nature of the felt opposition to the dominant value of the epic? Of what does this opposition actually consist? And what does it mean for interpretation? The attraction and interest of the Dido episode is one kind of opposition. Vergil's sense of despair, as Dante, for example, reads him, is another. While in Dante's reading it is not pursuit of empire that is put into question but rather the nature of God (the gods), the nihilism implicit in Vergil's perceived despair would question not only empire, but any human enterprise. Parry's sense of the poem's pathos and his attribution of this pathos to the poet's private voice is another kind of opposition. Putnam's finding that the *furor* that initially characterizes the destructive Juno drives Aeneas in the last moment of the poem as well is another.

The most important focus of critical controversy concerns precisely Aeneas' killing of Turnus at the end of the poem. This action has been read in many ways: traditionally, as legitimate and closural; "pessimistically," as showing Aeneas' and the empire's moral bankruptcy; more recently, as showing, despite the poem's pathos and other apparent subversions of epic value, the inevitable failure of resistance (cf. Wofford 1992); or, finally, as suggesting the fundamental unknowability of the nature of the Roman imperial story (cf. Quint 1993). These incompatible but not manifestly indefensible readings might lead us to reflect on what constitutes a legitimate basis for interpretation of the *Aeneid* as a whole or of its final scene in particular. Clearly, different readings have resulted from the different interpretive strategies that scholars have pursued. Putnam's intratextual reading, attending to the negative valence of *furor* as it is established in the *Aeneid*'s opening scenes, reads Aeneas' *furor* as moral failure. Barchiesi's 1984 intertextual method of "decoding" (to use his term) the *Aeneid* compares the poem's close, in which Turnus supplicates Aeneas, to its Homeric intertexts, that is, scenes of supplication in the *Iliad* and the *Odyssey*. His study results in a suggestive inconclusiveness, for while warriors' supplications are always denied, Achilles' yielding to Priam's plea constitutes a counterexample. Thus, a kind of interpretive *aporia* is created for readers that—from the perspective of epic tradition—puts into question the rightness of Aeneas' refusal of Turnus' supplication.[47] Gian Biagio Conte (1986) understands genre to be determining of meaning, arguing that genre correlates predictably with ideology and that epic necessarily celebrates its protagonist and his purposes. According to this critical strategy, one must read Aeneas and the imperial project as ultimately endorsed by the poet, even if not without complexity. As a final example, some scholars have considered that what is known of contemporary Roman history, culture, and ethics outside the poem offers the key to the poem's meaning. Pursuing this positivistic approach, Karl Galinsky (1988 and cf. 1994) argues that, despite the negative valence of *furor* throughout the *Aeneid*, Aeneas's own *furor* in the final scene of the poem is legitimate in the context of conventional Roman attitudes toward anger, which he assumes Vergil shared.

Perhaps there is no "correct" way to read the *Aeneid* or its crucial final scene, which Vergil may have left "open," undecidable. The continuing debate about the meaning of the poem suggests that it poses immensely challenging interpretive problems. Critics seek to establish a firm basis for interpretation, but such a basis seems to remain elusive.

WHERE IS AUTHORITY IN THE POEM?

Watson and Crick, when asked, after their epochal discovery of the structure of DNA, what the most important step in making a discovery was, responded that it was recognizing what their assumptions were. In my own reading of critical interpretations of the *Aeneid*, I have noticed how often scholars base their readings on unacknowledged and consequently unargued assumptions external to the text. In that spirit, I wish to call to readers' attention some interpretive assumptions that many or most readers have made about the *Aeneid* throughout the centuries.

1. *Epic as a genre celebrates military heroes; the* Aeneid *in particular celebrates Augustus.*

As we have seen above, this assumption is at least as old as Servius. While its claims may be true in some instances, they are, nevertheless, open to question. Conte (1986) has argued that the Roman epic norm in particular requires authorial endorsement of protagonist and the state, but others have suggested that not enough Latin epic prior to Vergil exists in order to substantiate such a claim. The narrator of the Homeric poems does not endorse every action of his protagonists, who advance unevenly along a moral trajectory that only ultimately brings them into harmony with the narrator.[48] As we have seen, there is precedent in the *Argonautica* for subversion of military heroism and of the epic protagonist.

2. *The three great set pieces that are the heart of the poem's Augustan ideology—Jupiter's prophecy of eternal Roman rule in Book 1, Anchises' pageant of heroes in Book 6, and Vulcan's shield for Aeneas in Book 8— express the moral message of the poem, which in turn reflects Vergil's own convictions.*

As an example of this view, we may cite R. G. Austin (1971) on Jupiter's prophecy: "The speech reflects some of Virgil's deepest feelings . . . his conviction of Rome's imperial power as hers by right of fate. . . . If it is a political manifesto, it is also a spiritual testimony to his love for Italy."[49] As an example of Anchises as speaker for Vergil, one might consider Austin 1977 in his note on 6.724–51: "Here in this speech of visionary beauty and earnest solemnity, it is as if the poet were 'thinking aloud', giving expression to his inmost beliefs." Putnam (1995) and Charles Martindale,[50] along with many others, assume that Anchises' discourse in Book 6 represents the philosophical underpinning of the poem. If one assumes that Jupiter or Anchises or Vulcan speaks for Vergil, then their utterances must necessarily override any seemingly conflicting utterances of other speakers. Feeney and James J. O'Hara, however, have argued that Jupiter is to be read as a speaker like others in the poem, with his own agenda, and not as an authorial voice.[51] Feeney in particular makes the point that Jupiter cannot serve as an impersonal, authoritative vantage point for the reader;[52] indeed, "the narrator is ultimately unable to commit himself to Jupiter's perspective."[53] Analogously, Lyne reads dramatic irony in Anchises' Underworld speech, seeing disparity between the character (for whom the words are appropriate) and the context (which creates ironic perspective on them): "Vergil's context and the irony it produces suggest that Vergil cannot be at one with his character in his view of art, government, and the Roman mission."[54]

These examples illustrate that learned readers vary in their understandings of which characters (if any) speak for Vergil, probably because there is no uncontestable way of arriving at certainty on this question.

3. *Fate is literal and determining.*

Many critics have read fate as literal and legitimizing. Here is an example from Conte: "Fate—the destiny of the world, not of individuals—acts on a plane that is wholly suprapersonal. It consists of a connection and succession of causes held together by a providential, universal overview and is a cosmic necessity that . . . is sanctioned by an unchangeable other world."[55] Conte speaks of the supremacy of divinely ordained

Fate as a distinctive feature in Vergil, a notion whose origin he finds in the Roman epic norm.[56] Gordon Williams, on the other hand, reads fate as a retrospective expression of what happens in history, symbolic and illuminating, but not causal.[57]

4. *Showing victory means endorsing victory.*

According to S. J. Harrison, the traditional view of the *Aeneid* is "that it asserted the values of order and civilization by depicting their eventual victory."[58] This is also the view of, for example, Pöschl, as described above, or Brooks Otis: "We see that Fate is finally on the moral side because the moral forces have in fact already put themselves on the side of Fate."[59] On the other hand, Putnam and Johnson, as we have seen, have questioned whether civilized values are in fact embodied in Aeneas' victory. The *Argonautica*, as was suggested above, would seem, in fact, to offer readers a paradigm of victory achieved through corruption rather than through virtue or any civilized value. Further, study of the motif of victory in the *Aeneid* itself reveals that victory is not consistently associated with moral authority: the triumphant Greeks in Book 2 are morally condemned by Aeneas and the narrator; the games in Book 5, an extended study of victory within the larger poem's action, suggest an imperfect correlation between victory and virtue.

5. *The first person narrator is the real Vergil, speaking frankly and personally to us.*

It has traditionally been assumed that the voice of the narrator, the *Aeneid* poet let us say, is Vergil himself. Servius describes the emotion that the poet intrudes into the narrative as his own or on his own part: *ex affectione sua posuit poeta* or *interiectionem ex sua persona interposuit.* Among more contemporary readers, we find Otis commenting on the narrator's warm apostrophe to dead Nisus and Euryalus in Book 9: "Yet Virgil at this juncture takes occasion to intrude on the narrative *in propria persona* . . . He here shows that he admires their heroism in spite of all the reservations he has so far expressed".[60] On the authorial intrusion at Book 10.501–5, Otis says: "Virgil even intervenes editorially to point the moral."[61] Terry Eagleton, however, has termed "naive" the "notion that the text is just a kind of transcript of the living voice of the real man or woman addressing us,"[62] and some Vergil critics have indeed proposed that the persona of the narrator is a poetic construct, like that of other speakers in the poem. (See discussion of assumption 2 above.) For Susanne L. Wofford (1992) "the speaker whom the poem impersonates" is dramatized as someone unwilling or unable to read the poem's critical counternarrative,[63] as it is expressed both in the various pathetic figures and in the violence of the narrative. In her reading, the "poem" or "text" with its "claims," the narrator, the implied poet, and Vergil are all potential sources of meaning.

It may be useful to note, further, that assertions of the narrator, although on the whole of a consistent sensibility, are not always so. As an example, one might cite the apostrophe to Nisus and Euryalus discussed above, where the slaughter these two carry out might be expected to be at variance with the narrator's usual regret of carnage, Trojan and Italian. The narrator promises fame to the pair as long as the Roman state endures. Given the failure of their mission and Nisus' choice to die with Euryalus, without a thought given to Aeneas or the future Roman state, this endorsement by the narrator seems problematic. Inconsistent prophecies, introduction of events unconventional in epic (e.g., the ships turning into nymphs in *Aeneid* 9), and occasional authorial intrusions at variance with the established ethos of the text undermine the coherence of the persona of the narrator and function as destabilizing features for some readers.

6. *Pathos reflects the personal involvement or private voice of the poet.*

Vergil's famed subjective style, as described by Otis (1964)—his intrusion of adjectives that direct the reader's emotional response, his use of apostrophe, and his representation of characters' internal feelings—is often read as an expression of the poet's own feelings. (This assumption overlaps with assumption 5 above.) Barchiesi (1994), however, as discussed above, has suggested that pathos may be a traditional feature of epic and therefore may not necessarily imply any personal sentiment of the poet's. Certainly pathos is a feature of Homeric epic, and Sander Goldberg's (1995) study of Roman Republican epic reveals pathos in Vergil's earliest Latin predecessors. Hardie (1993), in any case, proposes quite a different reading of pathos. For him the pathos inhering in the death of the young, often interpreted as an expression of the poet's individual sympathy for suffering, can be read as apprehension for survival of empire rather than as opposition of a private voice to war or to the political goals of the principate.[64] Finally, Conte argues that pathos has been misread, since critics have failed to distinguish between the author's *empathy* (attribution of feelings to characters) and his *sympathy* (intrusions in the narrator's voice). The former subverts the unity of the epic, while the latter holds the disparate voices of the poem together.[65] Both empathy and sympathy, for Conte, are rhetorical strategies, and both are essential to Vergil's reconception of epic. Neither is attributed to the poet's personal feelings.

Assumptions 1 through 4 or 5 would tend to affirm a traditional, pro-Augustan reading, while 6 has been the very foundation of the pessimistic reading. I have pointed to these assumptions not necessarily to refute any or all of them, but rather to propose to readers that they are prior to and outside the poem and not uncontested. While we cannot read any text without prior critical assumptions, it is nevertheless salutary to be aware of those that may foreclose fruitful interpretive possibilities.

The Plan of this Volume

This volume contains a chapter on each book of the *Aeneid*, written by a scholar who has published work on Vergil and also has enduring interest in teaching the poem.[66] Contributors to this volume were not assigned specific subjects, but were asked to focus their chapters, from a contemporary perspective, on what they perceived to be major thematic issues and interpretive problems raised by their assigned book. In particular they were asked to discuss, although with a minimum of citation of secondary sources,[67] passages that had elicited critical controversy. The purpose of this latter request was to suggest to instructors subjects that might serve to stimulate class discussion. In my experience, it is preferable to try to engage students in debate about the poem rather than to present them with a magisterial text to which the only appropriate response is awe.

Interpretation of the *Aeneid* has, over time, been distorted by concentration on certain books—especially 2, 4, and 6—and neglect of others. Yet Vergil presumably intended that the poem be read in its entirety and in sequence. Therefore, we offer a book-by-book reading. In my own chapter on Book 1, I consider the initial occurrence of certain conventional epic features (proem, first simile, first speech, and so forth) to show how these establish the poem's themes, while subtly complicating its generic affiliation. W. R. Johnson (Book 2) discusses Vergil's transformation of the conventional *topos* of the hero's self-narration into a questioning of the very assumptions of heroic action. The counter-epical hero,

Aeneas, in his dedication to others and endurance of pain, is a paradigm of humanity, even as the narrator questions the moral meaning of victory and history. Ralph Hexter (Book 3) makes of Aeneas' visit to the derivative and lifeless new Troy created by other Trojan exiles a starting point for discussion of problems of imitation, creation, and innovation, both for Vergil as he composes a Roman epic in the Homeric tradition and for Augustus, as he creates and renews the Roman state. Sarah Spence (Book 4) studies how it comes about and what it means for the poem that Dido is its most compelling, memorable character, and yet also Aeneas' implacable Junonian enemy, the founder of Carthage. Joseph Farrell (Book 5), like Hexter, is interested in problems of literary affiliation; he questions the validity of the Bloomian model for the relationship of Vergil to Homer and the usefulness of conventional formulations of male superiority for the poem as a whole. Eleanor Winsor Leach (Book 6) contextualizes in contemporary Roman life Aeneas' viewing of Daedalus' doors, of the Underworld pageant, and of the Gates of Sleep, reading them as experiences in esthetic and moral acculturation. Book 7, the first book that takes place in Italy, has a large but thus far unremarked number of female characters in both the foreground and background of the action. In her discussion of this book, Sara Mack reveals a subnarrative of female presence below the level of epic plot that complicates and enriches Vergil's portrait of early Italy. Anthony J. Boyle (Book 8) offers a methodical demonstration of how the *Aeneid* invites opposed readings: Hercules' slaying of Cacus and Vulcan's version of Roman history on Aeneas' shield suggest simultaneously opposed ways of reading Roman victory. Susan Ford Wiltshire considers the unepic features of Book 9, in which the leader is absent, ships turn into nymphs, a pair of young men on a military mission die a lover's death, and the lone mother to make the journey laments her son's death. Lament in particular stimulates reflection on the personal costs of war for those who are powerless to affect its outcome. Denis Feeney (Book 10) studies the esthetics of battle books, specifically the attraction of violence for readers of epic; he demonstrates that the poet has given to passages of grotesque deaths care equal to that of presumably more palatable topics. He shows also how Vergil gives unusual meaning to the traditional epic catalogue. William S. Anderson (Book 11) focuses on the Camilla episode, revealing how Vergil has avoided the *topoi* of traditional epic combat and of traditional gender-related behavior. In his reading the poet's respectful portrait of a female warrior suggests a fresh perspective on female figures in the *Aeneid*. Michael C. J. Putnam offers a close reading of Book 12, centering on the exchange of *furor* and sympathy between Aeneas and Turnus, as Turnus moves towards defeat and death. He concludes with some observations on the trajectory of Vergil's literary career as a whole.

Four topic chapters follow those on the text. Gary B. Miles's chapter places the *Aeneid* and its function as a foundation myth in the context of Vergil's world. S. Georgia Nugent's chapter, working from a feminist perspective, focuses centrally on the difference between male and female suffering and moral choice in the *Aeneid*. Charles Rowan Beye's chapter on Apollonius and Vergil sets forth some of the ways in which the *Argonautica*, a text few know well, shaped the *Aeneid*.[68] William S. Anderson's chapter on translations of the *Aeneid* aims to help readers assess biases inherent in any translation, including some of those most easily available today.

As the *Aeneid* has been subject to incomplete readings, so it has also been reduced to anodyne unity. The essays included here have not been edited into uniformity, and attentive readers will find that, while often harmonious, they are variously at odds both with each other's global interpretations of the poem as well as with readings of individual passages. Taken as a whole, they open up for reflection some of the central issues of the *Aeneid*. Notwithstanding its focus on a particular historical time and person, the *Aeneid* has become a classic because of the enduring nature of the questions it engages and because of the dialectical method by which it engages them.[69] It is my hope that the efforts of the volume's contributors will enrich readers' consideration of these questions.[70]

The Latin text of the *Aeneid* is taken from *P. Vergili Maronis Opera*, edited by R. A. B. Mynors (Oxford, 1969), with the exception of printing *v* for Mynors's consonantal *u*. Translations of the *Aeneid*, unless otherwise noted, are those of Allen Mandelbaum, *The Aeneid of Virgil: A Verse Translation* (New York, 1971), indicated as *M*. Translations of Homer are those of Richmond Lattimore, *The Iliad of Homer* (Chicago, 1951) and *The Odyssey of Homer* (New York, 1965).

CHAPTER 1

AENEID 1
An Epic Programme

Christine Perkell

Book 1 introduces the reader to programmatic epic conventions that define the *Aeneid* as heroic epic in the Homeric tradition. Among these are the proem, the episode, the speech, the simile, the prophecy, the ecphrasis, and the bard's song. At the same time Book 1 introduces the reader in various ways to the poem's central subject. This I take, in its largest sense, to be the poet's attempt to understand the moral nature of experience, as it is manifest most obviously in Roman victory and in the actions of the gods. In addition to its narrative function of establishing genre and themes for the poem as a whole, Book 1 has a suggestive structure of its own, which is fully revealed in the book's closing scenes.

THE *AENEID* PROEM: EPIC COMEDY OR EPIC TRAGEDY?

The proem is the opening of an epic poem, in which the poet calls upon the Muse and introduces a version of the poem's central theme. By opening with a proem that recalls in meter and theme both the *Iliad* and the *Odyssey*, Vergil establishes the genre of his poem as heroic epic. Yet while Vergil imitates Homeric models sufficiently to establish a relationship of affinity with them, he also deviates from his models or intertexts, and it is in these suggestive deviations that significant meanings inhere.[1]

Arma virumque cano ("Arms and the man I sing"). These words that open the *Aeneid* are perhaps the most famous in Latin literature. What do they signal to readers? "Classic" as they are now, for Vergil's readers, schooled in the epic tradition as embodied in the Homeric poems, the words represent a departure from as well as an echo of the *Iliad* and the *Odyssey*. The *Iliad* begins: *Menin aeide, thea, Peleiadeo Achileos*. Following the Greek word order we hear or read: "Wrath, sing, goddess, of Peleus' son Achilles." "Wrath," the first word, the object of "sing," thus defines the *Iliad*'s major theme, around which the poet will build his poem. Similarly, the *Odyssey* begins: *Andra moi ennepe Mousa polutropon . . .* ("Man, narrate to me, Muse, the resourceful [man] . . ."). Again a single term, "man" (*andra*), the object of "narrate," defines the subject of the poem and its focus on the figure of Odysseus. While Vergil's statement of themes clearly recalls the openings of the Homeric poems, it also sounds a double, as opposed to single, subject and announces the authority of the poem's singer ("I sing"), as opposed to a prayer to the Muse, which is postponed until line 8. The double subject suggests, I believe, at least two ideas. One is that this new poem, the *Aeneid*, will aim to encompass both of its famed rivals, *arma* being in some sense equivalent thematically to "wrath" and *virum* being precisely equivalent to *andra*. Indeed, ancient commentators recognized this comprehensive nature of the *Aeneid*, referring to its first half, with its male protagonist on a journey filled with obstacles, as Odyssean, and to its second half, in which journey does not figure but rather battles and war, as Iliadic.[2]

A second idea suggested by the double theme is that the *Aeneid* will encompass not only two stories sequentially but also the interrelationship of the "arms" and the "man." The *Aeneid* is the story of Aeneas' movement from defeat in Troy to victory in Italy, from the position of inadvertent leader of a desolate band of exiles to founder, as the poem's prophetic moments assert, of a mighty empire. The poem portrays the difficult discovery of mission and the acquisition of power: "From this have come the Latin race, the lords of Alba, and the walls of mighty Rome" (*genus unde Latinum / Albanique patres atque altae moenia Romae*, 6–7, M 11–12). The poet's anticipation of the hero's triumph marks the *Aeneid* formally as a comedy. By comedy I refer specifically to the model of epic comedy as embodied in the *Odyssey*, which announces from the start that Odysseus, whatever the attendant struggles, will achieve his homecoming, and that his divine antagonist Poseidon will give over his enmity at that time (*Od.* 1.20–21).[3]

Although the *Aeneid* thus declares itself a comedy at the start, the proem also problematizes this formal designation. For an essential part of the comic world view of the *Odyssey* is that divine justice reigns (ultimately if not consistently) and that, while evil is punished, the good also find reward. Such a vision of mortal experience is set forth in the proem to the *Odyssey* (1.7), where the poet attributes the failure of Odysseus' companions to achieve their homecoming to their "own wild recklessness." Similarly, at *Odyssey* 1.31–43, Zeus explains that while mortals blame the gods, it is they who bring troubles on themselves, "beyond what is given." Such a conviction of a just world does not animate the *Aeneid* proem. Rather the poet, through the particular image of Juno's anger, questions the justice of divine action and the suffering of the innocent. Of the higher power he asks *why* Aeneas endures unmerited (since he is distinguished for *pietas*) suffering: "Can such resentments hold the minds of gods?" (*tantaene animis caelestibus irae?*, 11, M 18). By his questions the poet implies his assumption that in a moral universe the pious man would be rewarded by the gods. In Books 1, 10, and 12 the poet questions the justice of the gods; in Books 1 and 2 Aeneas does as well. At first, then, Aeneas and the poet are similar in their questioning of the moral nature of experience, but, unlike Aeneas, the poet continues his questioning until the last book. (One effect of the interaction of arms and man is that the man, as he moves toward victory, stops questioning the gods' justice.)

In this questioning the poet countenances a tragic world. Here by tragedy I refer specifically to the tragic vision embodied in the *Iliad*, of which Achilles becomes the interpreter in *Iliad* 24. In this book Achilles tells two paradigmatic tales. The lesson of the tale of Zeus' two urns is that there is no correlation between human action and divine response: it is at random, as Achilles sees it, that either all grief or a mixture of happiness and grief is allotted to mortals by the gods (24.527–33). The second, the tale of Niobe who boasted that she had more children than Leto, the mother of Apollo and Diana, recounts how these two then killed all of Niobe's children. This second tale suggests that the gods do punish hybris (24.601–17). So if good may go unrewarded (as in the parable of the two urns), bad or hybris may, nevertheless, not go unpunished. This comfortless intelligibility is the tragic insight of Achilles and, as it seems, of the *Iliad* overall. Achilles' compassion for Priam gleams brilliantly against this dark vision.

The *Aeneid* poet also suggests a troubled vision of moral experience, for he depicts a universe continually menaced by irrational evil on the divine, human, and natural levels.[4] The goddess Juno is the poem's primary symbol and agent, through her various minions, of this disruptive force. For the reader Juno is the embodiment of rage, hatred, disorder, and destructiveness; in Juno's own view, however, she is an aggrieved victim. Thus she feels legitimate in her vengefulness, no matter how illegitimate she looks to the poet or reader. To the question "Can such resentment hold the minds of gods?" (11, M 18), there is never an explicit answer. Rather an explanation of suffering is asked of Jove as late as Book 12: "Was it your will that nations destined to eternal peace should have clashed in such tremendous turmoil?" (12.503–4, M 678–80). Readers are invited to note, then, that while the *Aeneid* opens as comic with its anticipation of the fated and divinely willed founding of Rome, it also countenances a tragic vision with its questioning of the gods' justice. In this way the poet puts into question, at the start, the generic affiliation (that is, as comic or as tragic epic) of his own great poem.[5] I suggest that the critical interpretive challenge of the *Aeneid* is to decide whether it is a comedy or a tragedy or instead whether, perhaps deliberately, it evades such categorization.

The *Odyssey* proem suggests a further important theme relevant to the *Aeneid*. Odysseus' wanderings have an explicitly epistemological dimension: "Many were they whose cities he saw, whose minds he learned of . . . struggling for his own life and the homecoming of his companions" (3–5). The *Aeneid* poet, however, does not qualify Aeneas' trials as intellectual. On the contrary Aeneas is often *ignarus* (ignorant) or *nescius* (unknowing). It is not implied that his success is a function of understanding, but rather of faith and endurance. Endurance, as Achilles points out (*Il.* 24.549–51), is the required virtue in a tragic world. The concluding scene of the *Aeneid*, in which Aeneas kills his enemy Turnus, displays his power, but not his philosophical reflection or insight. Unlike Achilles, Aeneas does not, at the close, become the reflective speaker of the poem's moral vision. Rather, by contrast, the poet accords to Aeneas no concluding visionary or interpretive speech but attributes his final action in the poem to "rage and anger" (12.946, cf. M 1264). The poem ends with the killing of Turnus and the descent of his offended spirit to the Underworld, and there is no moral or interpretive summary offered to the reader. Insight remains the goal of the poet, however. Of the Muse he requests not the story but the causes (*causas*) of Aeneas' sufferings on this journey: *Musa mihi causas memora* . . . (8, M 13). Thus the poet and his hero, although parallel in their initial questioning of the divine will, have different intellectual and moral trajectories. In both the *Iliad* and the *Odyssey*, by contrast, poet and hero share an ethical perspective by the poem's conclusion: the *Iliad* endorses the ransoming and burial of Hector; the *Odyssey* endorses Odysseus' homecoming and final reconciliation in Ithaca. The question of whether or not the *Aeneid* endorses the killing of Turnus has become the major interpretive problem for contemporary scholars.

THE FIRST SPEECH

The first speech of the poem is Juno's. As she catches sight of the Trojans making their way to Italy,[6] she voices her frustrated anger, pain, and envy:

> "mene incepto desistere victam
> nec posse Italia Teucrorum avertere regem!
> quippe vetor fatis. Pallasne exurere classem
> Argivum atque ipsos potuit summergere ponto
> unius ob noxam et furias Aiacis Oilei?
> ipsa Iovis rapidum iaculata e nubibus ignem
> disiecitque rates evertitque aequora ventis,
> illum exspirantem transfixo pectore flammas
> turbine corripuit scopuloque infixit acuto;
> ast ego, quae divum incedo regina Iovisque
> et soror et coniunx, una cum gente tot annos
> bella gero. et quisquam numen Iunonis adorat
> praeterea aut supplex aris imponet honorem?"
>
> (37–49)

> "Am I, defeated, simply to stop trying,
> unable to turn back the Trojan king
> from Italy? No doubt, the Fates won't have it.
> But Pallas—was she powerful enough
> to set the Argive fleet on fire, to drown
> the crewmen in the deep, for an outrage done
> by only one infuriated man,
> Ajax, Oileus' son?[7] And she herself
> could fling Jove's racing lightning from the clouds
> and smash their galleys, sweep the sea with tempests.
> Then Ajax' breath was flame from his pierced chest;

> she caught him up within a whirlwind; she
> impaled him on a pointed rock. But I,
> the queen of gods, who stride along as both
> the sister and the wife of Jove, have warred
> so many years against a single nation.
> For after this will anyone adore
> the majesty of Juno or, before
> her altars, pay her honor, pray to her?"
>
>   (M 56–74)

The poet has earlier alluded to reasons for Juno's hatred of the Trojans (25–27, M 40–45): the Judgment of Paris, the abduction of the youthful Trojan Ganymede to be cupbearer of Jupiter, and, in general, the descent of all Trojans from Dardanus, product of one of Jupiter's amours. These griefs of the Iliadic Hera/Juno are of a private nature. The reader may sense a disproportion between the violent depths of Juno's wished for vengeance against the Trojans and the original infractions.[8] Certainly Juno is not represented as a dispassionate agent of justice. This first speech in the poem, as such the first by a divinity, in its recounting of Minerva's punishment of the Locrian Ajax (for *noxa* and *furiae*, "outrage" and "fury," 41, cf. M 61–62), relates a terrifying paradigm of divine wrath. The frightfulness of this initial image of divinity at work may be further appreciated when the reader understands that Juno, this divinity who longs herself to wield Jove's thunderbolt in fiery rages, was, in her manifestation as Tanit, the patron goddess of Carthage and thus the Romans' deadly enemy during the Punic Wars, the greatest historical threat to the survival of Roman power. In the Carthaginian Hannibal, who led his elephants across the Alps to bring war to Italy, the Romans faced their most dangerous enemy. The Romans' fear of Juno is reflected in the many reported propitiatory offerings to her, which succeeded (according to Ennius) only during the Second Punic War in winning the goddess over to the Roman side. The Iliadic motives of the *Aeneid*'s Juno may be depicted as petty, but the political and military consequences of her attachment to and defense of Carthage were of the greatest historical magnitude, for the conflict between Rome and Carthage was perceived to be a question of which of these two great powers would survive to rule the world.[9] In sum, Juno, as the Iliadic Hera, has mythological causes for her hatred of the Trojans; as the Carthaginian goddess Tanit she has historical ones.[10] Although she feels herself to be a victim, most readers do not see her as a sympathetic figure, as her perpetual harassment of the Trojans places her in the role of victimizer and antagonist.[11]

The particular motifs of Juno's speech—private wrath, vengeance— are largely echoed in the poem's last speech, which is Aeneas' just prior to his slaying of Turnus. This similarity of content between the opening and closing speeches may be seen to give a circular structure to the poem. David Quint has described circular structure as characterizing the romance plot, the impotent, digressive movements of history's losers.[12] I would suggest that this structure might, then, also be called tragic. Linear structure, Quint continues, characterizes the victors' plot, the teleological movement of those who have a history. This movement we might also call comic. In having a structure that is, through various means, simultaneously circular and linear, tragic and comic, the *Aeneid* achieves a kind of suspension between traditional paradigms, thus again putting into question its affiliation as either tragic or comic epic.

THE FIRST EPISODE: CHARACTERIZATION OF
PIETAS, *FUROR*, AND *IMPERIUM*

The opening scenes of Book 1 set forth the themes and moral parameters of the poem. The storm instigated by Juno and the calm imposed by Neptune, along with the first simile of the poem that describes the man of "*pietas* and service" calming the raging crowd, are repeated images—on the divine, natural, and political levels—of the maddened, irrational force of *furor* that opposes the values of *pietas* (duty, respect, dedication) and *imperium* (empire, command, or order).[13]

Juno, determined to harass the Trojans despite the dictates of fate, bribes Aeolus, keeper of the winds, to release the storm winds and overwhelm and sink Aeneas' ships and men. The poet pictures the winds circling restlessly in a subterranean prison.[14] When Aeolus opens a passageway in the mountainside, the winds race out, upheaving sea and sky, turning day to night. Aeneas' men vanish from his sight in the mountainous waves and sudden chasms—a fierce picture of nature's violence. Neptune, god of the sea and here antithesis to Juno, abbreviates expression of his own wrath in favor of restoring order expeditiously. The word used recurrently to describe Juno's and then the winds' actions is *furor* (fury, rage). As the description of the winds' prison shows, *furor*, which later becomes manifest in the passion of Dido as well as in the battles between the Trojans and the

Italians of Books 7–12, is always raging—never eliminated, only temporarily contained. Civilization, peace, calm are not the natural state of things at rest, but the result of the temporary constraining of *furor*.[15] The first use of the word *imperium* (order, command, power) refers to Aeolus' constraining of the winds, suggesting the poet's conception of *imperium* as that which contains violence and disorder (54, M 79–80[16]). This word becomes central to the poem's moral vocabulary. When Jupiter predicts everlasting power for the Romans, he says: *imperium sine fine dedi* ("I give them empire without end," 278, M 390); when Anchises in the Underworld of Book 6 reveals to Aeneas the Roman mission of empire, it is: *tu regere imperio populos, Romane, memento* ("You, Roman, remember to rule the peoples with your empire," 6.851, cf. M 1134–35).

Aeneas is characterized by *pietas* (translated as "goodness" by Mandelbaum at 1.16), initially the antithesis of *furor*. *Pius* or "pious," Aeneas' characteristic epithet, is attributed to him both by the poet (e.g., 1.220, 305, 4.393) and by himself: *sum pius Aeneas*, he announces to Venus (1.534, M 378). Ilioneus says the Trojans are a pious people (*generi pio* 1.526); of their king Aeneas he says "no one was more just in piety, nor greater in war and arms" (*Aeneas . . . quo iustior alter / nec pietate fuit, nec bello maior et armis*, 544–45, M 766–68). What is this moral attribute of *pietas* that, as the poet implies in the proem, should protect Aeneas from suffering unjustly? Cicero defines it as "that which urges [us] to carry out responsibility to country or parents or others related by blood" (*quae erga patriam aut parentes aut alios sanguine coniunctos officium conservare moneat, De Inv.* 2.65).[17] Elsewhere he includes the gods and justice (*est enim pietas iustitia adversum deos, De Nat. Deor.* 1.116; cf. 2.153: "*pietas, cui coniuncta iustitia est*"). For Dido, that which epitomizes Aeneas' *pietas* is the story of his carrying his father and his Penates out of burning Troy (4.598–99, M 824–26), because it shows his dedication to his duty to father (male family and tradition) and household gods. She also associates *pietas* with fidelity to sworn oaths (4.597, M 823). W. A. Camps notes that in the majority of cases in which Aeneas is described as *pius* the context is one of ritual observance, burial being the most frequent.[18] *Pietas* can exert contradictory pressures: as examples, Dido feels that Aeneas violates *pietas* in leaving her, since he violates a trust he had sworn; Aeneas feels that he follows the dictates of *pietas* precisely by pursuing his mission of founding Rome. Servius claims that in the last scene of the poem, Aeneas shows *pietas* both when he thinks of sparing Turnus (this would seem in accordance with his father's prescription in Book 6 to spare the vanquished) as well as when he kills him (here he shows piety toward Evander in exacting vengeance for the death of Pallas).[19] In the *Aeneid* overall *pietas* locates correct behavior in a personal or national rather than in a transcendent or universal moral context. R. G. Austin (ad 1.10) perhaps attributes a greater universality to *pietas* than the text supports when he defines it as "duty, devoted service, responsibility, compassion, the full consciousness of what is due to others."[20]

THE FIRST SIMILE

The epic simile, a feature of the Homeric poems, was imitated by all subsequent epic poets and thus became established as a characteristic feature of the genre. The famous first simile of the *Aeneid* likens Neptune's calming of Juno's storm to a political speaker's calming a raging crowd.

> Ac veluti magno in populo cum saepe coorta est
> seditio saevitque animis ignobile vulgus;
> iamque faces et saxa volant, furor arma ministrat;
> tum, pietate gravem ac meritis si forte virum quem
> conspexere, silent arrectisque auribus astant;
> ille regit dictis animos et pectora mulcet;
> sic cunctus pelagi cecidit fragor, aequora postquam
> prospiciens genitor caeloque invectus aperto
> flectit equos curruque volans dat lora secundo.
>
> (148–56)

> And just as, often, when a crowd of people
> is rocked by a rebellion, and the rabble
> rage in their minds, and firebrands and stones
> fly fast—for fury finds its weapons—if,
> by chance, they see a man remarkable
> for righteousness and service, they are silent
> and stand attentively; and he controls
> their passion by his words and cools their spirits:
> so all the clamor of the sea subsided
> after the Father, gazing on the waters
> and riding under the cloudless skies, had guided
> his horses, let his willing chariot run.
>
> (M 209–20)

In Homeric similes the convention is to compare human events to those in the natural world.[21] For instance, the first simile of the *Iliad* (2.87–93) compares the many nations of men who respond to Agamemnon's summons to swarming bees. The first simile of the *Odyssey* compares Odysseus among the suitors to a lion among deer (4.335–40). For a Roman reader a striking feature of Vergil's simile is its inversion of Homeric practice. In likening the calming of the storm to a speaker's calming of a seditious crowd, the poet suggests by contrast the emphatically political[22] subject of the *Aeneid*. As Aeneas' *pietas* opposed the *furor* of Juno in the proem, so in the simile the moral authority of the man of *pietas* (translated "righteousness") and service opposes the *furor* of the mob. *Pietas* and *imperium*, as characteristic Roman values, are in this book ranged against *furor*, on the divine (Juno), natural (storm), and political (the raging mob) level. Viktor Pöschl inferred a specific set of analogous oppositions (good/bad, Jupiter/Juno, Aeneas/Dido, Carthage/Rome, Augustus/Cleopatra and a symbolic equivalence between the Roman god, the Roman hero, and the Roman emperor, whose triumph over their enemies was unambiguously morally edifying.[23]

Pöschl's important insights into the symbolic oppositions of the opening scenes are critical to reading the poem. Nevertheless, as the poem progresses, the clarity of these oppositions is lost: male characters also are described as *furentes*, and *pietas* and *imperium* are achieved not through transcendence of *furor* but rather precisely through its exercise.[24] As Hercules kills the monstrous furious Cacus and thereby allows Roman/Latin civilization to advance by means of his own greater *furor*, so Aeneas, infuriated by grief, breaks the Italian siege and rescues his men.[25] Most famously, at the end of the poem, it is with "fury and anger" (12.946, cf. M 1264) that Aeneas slays Turnus, thus winning his war in Italy and, as the poem's prophecies have it, founding the Roman empire. The reader must note that it is only in this Book 1 simile and never in narrated action of the poem that *furor* is contained without even greater *furor*. There is no model in the *Aeneid* of the control of *furor* other than through *furor*. The two figures in the poem's action who do attempt, like the pious statesman of Book 1, to calm a raging crowd by force of moral authority (Galaesus in 7.535–39 [M 704–11] and Aeneas himself in 12.311–23 [M 423–37]) both fail. Galaesus, the "most just" man, is killed in the melee that follows his vain exhortation for peaceful reflection, and Aeneas, wounded by the arrow of an unseen assailant, is forced to leave the field as fighting resumes around him. Destructive as *furor* appears in those characters opposed to the Roman mission (Juno, Dido, Allecto, Amata, Turnus), it is also the force that makes possible the triumph of civilization over Cacus and of Aeneas over Turnus.

THE FIRST SPEECHES OF THE ROMAN HERO AENEAS

In his first speech Aeneas wishes he were dead—a remarkable entrance into the poem for an epic hero in the tradition of Achilles and Odysseus. In the midst of the heaving ocean, Aeneas throws out his first words to the whirling storm:

> "o terque quaterque beati,
> quis ante ora patrum Troiae sub moenibus altis
> contigit oppetere! o Danaum fortissime gentis
> Tydide! mene Iliacis occumbere campis
> non potuisse tuaque animam hanc effundere dextra,
> saevus ubi Aeacidae telo iacet Hector, ubi ingens
> Sarpedon, ubi tot Simois correpta sub undis
> scuta virum galeasque et fortia corpora volvit!"
>
> (94–101)

> "O, three and four times blessed
> were those who died before their fathers' eyes
> beneath the walls of Troy. Strongest of all
> the Danaans, o Diomedes, why
> did your right hand not spill my lifeblood, why
> did I not fall upon the Ilian fields,
> there where ferocious Hector lies, pierced by
> Achilles' javelin, where the enormous
> Sarpedon now is still, and Simois
> has seized and sweeps beneath its waves so many
> helmets and bodies of the brave!"
>
> (M 133–43)

Aeneas' first speeches show him in despair. A missed moment to have died, he thinks, was that passage in *Iliad* 5.297 ff., where he was in danger of being killed by the great Greek fighter Diomedes. His divine mother Aphrodite whisked him out of the battle, for Homer's Aeneas is destined to found a mighty people. Why does Vergil's Aeneas say that those are blessed who die before their fathers' eyes? One might fill this "gap" in several ways, and many readers assume that Aeneas is speaking of honorable burial. Again the Homeric intertext enhances one's reading of Vergil's introduction of his hero.[26] Odysseus, when in similar straits, makes precisely this point about burial. Also caught in a storm at sea, Odysseus fears anonymous death:

> Three and four times blessed those Danaans were who died then
> in wide Troy land, bringing favor to the sons of Atreus,
> as I wish I too had died at that time and met my destiny
> on the day when the greatest number of Trojans threw their bronze-headed
> weapons upon me, over the body of the perished Achilles,
> and I would have had my rites and the Achaians given me glory.
> Now it is by a dismal death I must be taken.
>
> (5.306–12)

For Odysseus, death at sea means no burial rites, no publicly acknowledged honor. In comparing Aeneas' speech to this one, commentators, seduced by the manifest similarities, put Odysseus' words in Aeneas' mouth.[27] It is, however, necessary to remember that "this [difference] is the meaning of the allusion."[28] Aeneas, in fact, says nothing of burial. Rather, precisely by means of this omission he appears to be speaking of sentiment: those are lucky who die before their fathers' eyes, that is, where people see their sacrifice, where they are known and loved. Aeneas' concern with sentiment is illuminated by his mention of the particular Trojans Hector and Sarpedon. Although Hector is the major Trojan warrior in the *Iliad*, Sarpedon is not even a major character in the poem. What unites these characters is the melancholy, haunting apprehension of death that shapes their great speeches (*Il.* 6.440–65, 12.318–28). Therefore, Aeneas' allusion to these particular figures suggests that it is melancholy attachment to persons of worth and sensitivity, to family and place, that inspires Aeneas' first speech, not the practical or self-serving issue of burial. Where Odysseus is pragmatic and goal-oriented, Aeneas is sentimental and despairing. Vergil's portrayal in this speech of his hero's sentiment and of his indifference to burial and honor thus significantly and polemically distinguishes Aeneas from Homer's heroic Odysseus figure.[29] While some *Aeneid* scholars have felt a need to explain away Aeneas' irresolute spirit here, I read his deviation from the Homeric model as suggestive of Vergil's reimagining of the heroic protagonist and his gradual discovery of the value of his mission.

Aeneas' second speech reveals the same melancholy character. Those of his men who have escaped the storm are safe on the beach. Many men and ships have seemingly perished. Upon Aeneas as leader it falls to rally the men despite this further grievous loss:

> "O socii (neque enim ignari sumus ante malorum)
> o passi graviora, dabit deus his quoque finem.
> vos et Scyllaeam rabiem penitusque sonantis
> accestis scopulos, vos et Cyclopia saxa
> experti; revocate animos maestumque timorem
> mittite; forsan et haec olim meminisse iuvabit.
> per varios casus, per tot discrimina rerum
> tendimus in Latium, sedes ubi fata quietas
> ostendunt. illic fas regna resurgere Troiae.
> durate, et vosmet rebus servate secundis."
>
> (198–207)

> "O comrades—surely we're not ignorant
> of earlier disasters, we who have suffered
> things heavier than this—our god will give
> an end to this as well. You have neared the rage
> of Scylla and her caves' resounding rocks;
> and you have known the Cyclops' crags; call back
> your courage, send away your grieving fear.
> Perhaps you will one day remember even
> these our adversities with pleasure. Through
> so many crises and calamities
> we make for Latium, where fates have promised
> a peaceful settlement. It is decreed
> that there the realm of Troy will rise again.
> Hold out, and save yourselves for kinder days."
>
> (M 276–89)

For his men Aeneas pretends to confidence that he does not have, feigning hope on his face while feeling despair in his heart (208–9, M 290–92). Generous and reflective, he affirms the quality and courage of his men, who have endured so much: they are to have realistic hopes based on their own virtues. This speech too has an Odyssean intertext that helps us shape an understanding of Aeneas here. Odysseus also addresses his men in crisis. At the point they must attempt to make a safe passage between the dangers of Scylla and Charybdis, he says to them:

> Dear friends, surely we are not unlearned in evils.
> This is no greater evil now than it was when the Cyclops
> had us cooped in his hollow cave by force and violence,
> but even there, by my courage and counsel and my intelligence,
> we escaped away. I think that all this will be remembered
> some day too. Then do as I say, let us all be won over.
>
> (12.208–12)

With high confidence in his own intelligence, Odysseus exhorts his men to rely on his demonstrated resourcefulness—he cites examples—to save them. In contrast, Vergil suggests his own hero's despair and lack of confidence in his fortunes, but also his modesty and his selflessness on behalf of a cause larger than himself. For me this is a seductive portrait that renders Aeneas powerfully sympathetic—not, like Jason in the *Argonautica*, contemptible in his weakness.[30] Nevertheless, Vergil's strategy here is risky and has resulted in controversy, for how we read these first speeches is critical to how we read the overall trajectory of the character of Aeneas in the poem. If Aeneas, in his desire to die, is read as weak in his first speech, but as strong in his last when he kills another, then the slaying of Turnus represents a moral achievement. If, on the other hand, Aeneas is read as sympathetic in his weakness in the opening, but as pitiless and vengeful in the closing, then the slaying of Turnus may be seen as a moral failure. Both these—contradictory—readings suggest themselves to readers and thus epitomize in brief the essential critical question of the poem.

THE FIRST PROPHECY

The first prophecy, spoken by Jupiter, is the poem's grandest statement of Roman military power (257–96, M 357–417). The sole audience for this prophecy is an anxious Venus, who solicits assurance from her father that, despite Aeneas' seemingly serious troubles, his previous pronouncements of positive intention toward the Trojans and their future

remain unchanged. To comfort her, Jupiter prophesies Rome's future suc-
cesses in history: Aeneas, having waged huge war in Italy and crushed
fierce peoples, will establish customs and walls and ultimately ascend into
heaven. His son Ascanius, to be called Ilus, will rule for thirty years; their
race will rule for three hundred years until the priestess Rhea Silvia,
pregnant by Mars, will give birth to the twins Romulus and Remus.[31]
Romulus will found Rome (Jupiter omits the death of Remus), naming the
Roman people after himself. Later Augustus, a descendant of Venus
through adoption by Julius Caesar, will extend his power to the ocean and
his fame to the stars; he too will be elevated to heaven and worshipped as
a god. Jupiter's most stirring and grand line—"I set no limits to their for-
tunes and no time: I give them empire without end" (*His ego nec metas
rerum nec tempora pono: imperium sine fine dedi*, 278–79, M 389–90)—
expresses the conviction of (at least some) Romans that their remarkable
military successes must reflect divine will.[32] In integrating Augustus,
through this prophecy of Jupiter, into the originary myths of the Roman
state and envisioning its power as eternal, Vergil thus constructs a reading
of Roman history as a coherent whole under divine direction.

In the conclusion of his prophecy Jupiter reiterates the image of
imperium constraining *furor* that predominated in the book's opening
scenes. *Furor* here—*Furor impius* ("Unholy Rage"), as Jupiter terms it—
refers primarily to civil conflict. The term *Furor impius* implies, as
linguists would point out, the existence of a *Furor pius* or "pious rage."
In fact, however, there is no such formulation in the *Aeneid*; closest is
the one instance of *furiis iustis*, "just rage" (8.494), where Evander
speaks of Etrurian uprising against Mezentius. In the great preponderance
of its occurrences in the *Aeneid*, *furor* is unqualified and unarguably nega-
tive. As was noted earlier, the poem depicts no benign approach to victory
and power, even for a legitimate cause. Universal Roman conquest will
bring an era of peace or, as Erich Gruen puts it more precisely,
"pacification,"[33] which will be achieved when all enemies are defeated. At
that time traditional Roman values such as *Fides* (holy faith, a virtue on
which Romans prided themselves) and *Vesta* (the goddess of the hearth,
here the sacred hearth fire in Rome to be always kept burning by the
Vestal virgins) will shape the peace. Unwriting Romulus' murder of
Remus, Jupiter promises that Romulus (*Quirinus*) and Remus will give
laws—an image of the cessation of civil conflict.[34] Readers may be
tempted to equate the peace foretold in this prophecy with Isaiah's
prophecy of the lion lying down with the lamb. Yet it is to be noted that

Jupiter does not prophesy, even in his extravagance, that all enmities—
even the most inveterate and innate—will vanish. Rather he prophesies
that *Furor impius*,[35] still roaring from bloody mouth, vital and dangerous,
will be—not destroyed—but constrained by chains behind bolted gates.
The poem never envisages the passing of *furor*.

Jupiter's prophecy is emphatic in placement and scope. Many readers,
thrilled by its patriotism and confidence, attribute to it a positive signifi-
cance that radiates throughout the poem, validating the Roman mission.[36]
The traditional reading of the *Aeneid* assumes that Jupiter's utterance here
and elsewhere expresses the poet's own patriotic pride.[37] On the other hand,
in assessing this speech, readers may want to consider the representation of
the figure of Jupiter in a larger context. Some recent scholars have read
Vergil's Jupiter not as the embodiment of a transcendent moral authority,
but rather as one speaker in the poem, whom they characterize as morally
inconsistent and politically parochial.[38] If this kind of reading is legitimate,
it would, of course, affect our overall evaluation of Jupiter's authority as a
speaker. In this speech in particular, Jupiter, if read as a character with his
own agenda, could be seen to be acting in accordance with a consolatory
purpose that likely shapes his prophetic visions.[39] Further, the validity of the
poem's prophecies as a whole has been questioned, largely because of
discrepancies between this first prophecy and those that come after. In the
Aeneid, prophecies characteristically have a delusive dimension, becoming
true in ways that differ from their apparent meaning. James O'Hara has
observed that optimistic prophecies consistently omit the significant deaths
that their fulfillment will entail.[40] Of course, prophecies traditionally have a
delusive character, yet the *Aeneid*'s prophecies also diminish in scope and
frequency as the Trojans approach Italy. These patterns are, of course, sus-
ceptible, to multiple interpretations; for some readers they undermine the
authority of prophecy in the poem as a whole, and hence of Jupiter here.
Although Jupiter is referred to in the poem as the father of gods and men, in
fact he does not express transcendent moral purposes that embrace all
peoples. In the *Aeneid* overall Vergil does not represent the Olympian gods
as concerned with morality as much as with power. On the other hand, some
of the human characters do have large notions of right and wrong and wish
for ethical action to be rewarded by the gods.

However a reader decides to construe the authority of Jupiter, neither
Aeneas nor any other human character hears his prophecy of eternal power
and worldwide dominion for Rome. The dreams and visions through
which Aeneas' mission is revealed to him (largely in Books 2 and 3) set

narrower goals than universal empire and imposition of law; instead they
center on the salvation of the Trojan people. Aeneas, as an individual actor
in history, is—perhaps inevitably—represented as limited in his under-
standing of the future consequences of his actions.

THE FIRST ECPHRASIS

As Aeneas advances through Carthage he comes upon a grove with an
imposing temple in which he sees a frieze representing scenes from the
Trojan War, in one of which he himself figures. Such an ecphrasis, a
description characteristically of a work of art, is an epic convention. In *Iliad*
18.478–612 Hephaestus makes a shield for Achilles on which are depicted
scenes that suggest a whole world otherwise absent from the *Iliad*. The
ecphrasis of Jason's cloak in Apollonius' *Argonautica* depicts scenes that
revolve around the poem's themes of power, eroticism, and betrayal, con-
cluding with a final representation of Phrixus and the ram (1.763–67), char-
acters who play a part in the action of the *Argonautica* itself. Vergil includes
several ecphrases in the *Aeneid*, the most elaborate being this first one in
Book 1, the description of the doors of Apollo's temple in Book 6, and the
shield that Vulcan makes for Aeneas in Book 8.[41] Aeneas interprets the
frieze as demonstrating respect for failed heroism and pity for mortality, a
reading that persuades him to abandon fear and to hope again.

> constitit et lacrimans, "quis iam locus," inquit, "Achate,
> quae regio in terris nostri non plena laboris?
> en Priamus! sunt hic etiam sua praemia laudi,
> sunt lacrimae rerum et mentem mortalia tangunt.
> solve metus; feret haec aliquam tibi fama salutem."
>
> (459–63)

> As he wept he cried: "Achates,
> where on this earth is there a land, a place
> that does not know our sorrows? Look! There is Priam!
> Here too the honorable finds its due
> and there are tears for passing things; here, too,
> things mortal touch the mind. Forget your fears;
> this fame will bring you some deliverance."
>
> (M 651–59)

Aeneas' reading in the frieze of "tears of things" reveals much about his own values at this point in his life but not necessarily about the "true" meaning of the frieze itself. Many scholars argue that Aeneas misreads the frieze, for its location in a temple dedicated to Juno must in all probability suggest that it celebrates the triumph of Juno's favored Greeks rather than lamenting the fate of her despised Trojans or, more universally, expressing sorrow for mortal suffering.[42] Further complicating interpretation for the reader is Aeneas' merely partial viewing of the frieze. Of the panels that he sees, all but one appear to him to represent Trojan tragedy. There are two apparently matched panels, one of Greeks fleeing, the other of Trojans fleeing. The other panels that catch Aeneas' attention represent the death of Rhesus and the loss of his horses before they could taste the Xanthus river and thereby presage Troy's survival; the death of young Troilus at Achilles' hands, his spear dragging uselessly in the dust behind his chariot; Minerva turning away from the suppliant Trojan women; and Achilles dragging Hector's body around the walls of Troy and selling his lifeless body to Priam for gold.[43] Finally, and ominously, just as Dido enters the temple and the poem, Aeneas sees the Amazon Penthesilea, "soldier-virgin and queen, daring to war with men" (M 696–97), doomed to be killed—in the next panel?—by Achilles.

What, then, is the "correct" reading of this incompletely read frieze? Aeneas' interpretation of the frieze as an expression of pity and not celebration appears validated in what immediately follows, for Dido does receive Aeneas and his men with whole-hearted generosity, because, as she says, her own suffering has taught her compassion. But perhaps the major significance of this scene is that Vergil has placed in paradigmatic position the possibility (or even the fact) of misreading art that, in subject matter, is very much like this poem we are reading. And the interpretive question here is precisely the one that confronts critics of the *Aeneid*'s ending as well: what is the authorially endorsed reading of the violence depicted there?

CLOSING MOVEMENTS OF BOOK 1

The Dido narrative of Book 1 is marked throughout with intimations of tragedy for her. On first sight Dido embodies all that is good: magnanimity, generosity, dignity, responsible exercise of power with judgment and commitment.[44] Yet she is also associated with Juno's favored city and temple and subsequently with her *furor* as well. The simile with which the poet describes Dido on her entrance into the poem (496–504, M 702–11) hints at the disparity between what seems and what is. This simile is based on *Odyssey* 6.102–9, which describes Odysseus' first sight of the youthful beauty Nausicaa with her companions, who are playing on the shore. Nausicaa, in appearance and stage of life, resembles the virgin goddess Diana with her naiad escort dancing in the mountains. In antiquity Vergil's adaptation of this simile was criticized for its inappropriateness to Dido, but inappropriateness may be its very point. As applied to Dido, the simile misleads, for Dido is neither a goddess nor a virgin, but a young and, in the event, passionate widow; furthermore, since she is head of state, her responsibilities are other than leading mountain dances. Pöschl suggests plausibly that the simile is to be understood as expressing Aeneas' vision. If this is indeed how Dido looks to Aeneas, then he fails to see much other truth and may again, as with the frieze, be misreading a "text." Seduced by Dido's youth and beauty, Aeneas misreads her passion, high ideals, and pride.

Dido's future tragedy is variously intimated: her characteristic epithet is *infelix* ("unhappy" or "unlucky"), and her entrance into the poem implies some deathly outcome. As Aeneas is studying the Trojan war frieze his gaze fixes on a representation of Penthesilea (490–92, M 693–97), the Amazon warrior killed by Achilles. Vergil leaves unspoken Penthesilea's death and its particular pathos,[45] but suggests her vulnerability, as she is bare-breasted, a young woman, yet mad (*furens*) for war, leading her ranks of Amazons into battle, daring to contest with men (*audetque viris concurrere virgo*). (One recalls Venus' analogous anomalous conjunction of *dux femina facti* [1.364], something akin to "female general," to describe Dido.) As the reader's imagination inevitably conjures up Penthesilea's death by the sword thrust of Achilles, Dido, also a woman who dares to contest with men, enters the temple and fills Aeneas' sight. Ominous as well is Aeneas' first speech to Dido (595–610, M 838–55), which, in its delicate allusion to funeral epigram,[46] implies parting and even death. Dido, the victim of passion contrived by goddesses conspiring at cross purposes and with obscure relation (in the case of Venus) to the announced will of Jupiter, is represented as the victim of powerful irrational forces.

THE SONG OF IOPAS

Dido marks her peaceful reception of the Trojans with a luxurious feast: night darkens, torches blaze, gold glitters, and wine flows amidst prayers to the gods for a happy future for their two peoples. The prayers and joy of the moment highlight the tragic inversion of human hopes and divine purposes. Dido's worldly achievements, destined to imminent destruction, find expression in the luxury and high culture of her court, which are signaled not only by the gold artifacts so plentiful at the banquet, but also by the presence of the bard Iopas who sings for the court's entertainment. The presence of a bard is a feature of epic courts. In the *Odyssey* we find the bard Phemius at the home of Odysseus, and the bard Demodocus at the court of king Alcinous in Phaeacia. Here again Vergil is following Homeric precedent, but—as always—with a difference. The bards in the *Odyssey* sing epic songs celebrating the fames of men (*klea andron*). Their songs (with one exception) are heroic songs like Homer's own. Yet Iopas does not sing heroic song; instead he sings commonplaces of the didactic genre, which include the risings and settings of the sun and moon, the origin of men and beasts, storm and lightning, the constellations, and how the days' length shortens with the winter season (742–46). His song recalls Vergil's own earlier *Georgics* and its major models, Lucretius' *De Rerum Natura* and Hesiod's *Works and Days*. Perhaps Iopas' song's closest antecedent in epic, although found in a substantively different context, is the didactic song of Orpheus in the *Argonautica* (1.496–511), sung to pacify the unruly Argonauts who have fallen into a dangerously belligerent mood.

Why does Vergil give Iopas such a song?[47] To this question various answers have been suggested: to provide a chaste topic for a chaste (thus far) queen (Servius, Pöschl); to discredit the opulence of the Carthaginian court (Segal); to allude indirectly to predictions of storm and thus to induce Aeneas to stay in Carthage (Kinsey).[48] All these are resonant suggestions, and I would propose a further one. In the *Georgics*, Vergil opposes the gradual acquisition of scientific knowledge as derived from study of the fixed laws of nature to poetic knowledge as expressed in myth and in inspiration from the Muses. In my reading of this work, scientific insights are shown to embody a more limited truth than the truth that comes from revelation, myth, and symbol.[49] Iopas' song suggests the same opposition. One of Iopas' topics is storms; presumably he sings, as did Vergil in the *Georgics*, of storms and of the signs that presage their coming (*G.* 1.311–34), and of the seasons in which farmers or sailors might expect them (e.g., *G.* 1.351–92). Didactic literature is optimistic in that it presumes the possibility of learning through study and therefore of dealing with forces of nature, of controlling outcomes to some degree, of shaping our own destiny. Yet Book 1 begins precisely with a wild storm that arises without signs and from no humanly predictable sequence of events. In Book 1 the true, demonic nature of human experience, defying logical deduction and study, escapes the potential of human knowledge. Thus Iopas could not be more wrong about the causes of storms, since his song includes neither Juno's *furor* nor Aeolus' consequent losing of the wild winds. Indeed, Iopas' song omits the gods altogether.[50] Through these omissions Vergil suggests the limitations of human knowledge, rationality, and good intentions. To an observer ignorant of Juno's vengefulness and of Venus' machinations—ignorant, in short, of the divine purposes that circumscribe human lives—this banquet, with its opulence and its art, would seem to epitomize ordered, rational control and high civilization. It would appear that reason and decorum reign. We see a queen so unsensual, so abstemious, that she only touches her lips to the toasting cup. But this image is soon revealed as delusive, for Dido is, like the winds in Aeolus' prison, a portrait of *furor* only temporarily contained.

Infelix (unhappy) Dido, preferring Aeneas' heroic epic to Iopas' didactic epic, importunes Aeneas to tell the story of Troy's fall (749–50). For Dido, heroic epic is a more seductive song, and she would rather hear of Aeneas' wanderings (*errores*, 755) than of the moon's (*errantem*, 742). But as Aeneas perhaps misreads the temple frieze and surely misreads Dido, so Dido tragically misreads Aeneas' tale of Troy's fall, in which she sees only the appeal of Aeneas' heroic sufferings, not the unrelenting dedication to mission of the future imperial Romans.

In sum, Book 1 establishes the epic identity of the *Aeneid*, introduces the poem's protagonist, and suggests the central moral values around which its action circles. That the *Aeneid* is epic in the Homeric tradition is signaled by, for example, its meter, epithets, similes, and gods. That it is also contemporary and Roman is signaled from the first verse of the proem and, as another example, emphatically as well in the first simile and in Jupiter's prophecy. The poem encompasses, as the first book reveals, some ambiguity as to the nature of the epic universe it portrays, since comedy for Aeneas and tragedy for Dido are intimately commingled, within a larger frame of gods' unknowable and often malign purposes. There will be a Roman empire, readers know, but how it will be achieved, according to which epic model or with what moral valence, is an open question as Book 1 closes.

CHAPTER 2

DIS ALITER VISUM
Self-Telling and Theodicy in *Aeneid* 2

W. R. Johnson

At the end of Book 2, with the Greeks triumphant and Troy in flames, Aeneas was in despair because his father, Anchises, refused to leave his homeland and join his son in escape and exile. When Jupiter's omen changed Anchises' mind, Aeneas said to him:

> "ergo age, care pater, cervici imponere nostrae;
> ipse subibo umeris, nec me labor iste gravabit.
> quo res cumque cadent, unum et commune periclum,
> una salus ambobus erit. mihi parvus Iulus
> sit comes, et longe servet vestigia coniunx."
>
> (707–11)

> "Come then, dear father, mount upon my neck;
> I'll bear you on my shoulders. That is not
> too much for me. Whatever waits for us,
> we both shall share one danger, one salvation.
> Let young Iulus come with me, and let
> My wife Creusa follow at a distance."
>
> (M 956–61)

Having said this, Aeneas took his family and left their home. As they moved through the darkness (*per opaca locorum*), Aeneas now remembers, he was surprised to find himself frightened, he who had recently faced Greek weapons fearlessly:

> "et me, quem dudum non ulla iniecta movebant
> tela neque adverso glomerati ex agmine Grai,
> nunc omnes terrent aurae, sonus excitat omnis
> suspensum et pariter comitique onerique timentem."
>
> (726–29)

> "and I, who just before could not be stirred
> by any weapons cast at me or by
> the crowds of Greeks in charging columns, now
> am terrified by all the breezes, startled
> by every sound, in fear for son and father."
>
> (M 980–84)

There are moments in Vergil's epic as famous as this one perhaps, but none surpasses it for the resonance it has both inside and outside the poem. This cardinal moment in Aeneas' self-narration at Dido's court defines with vivid economy both Aeneas' mission and his feelings about it and himself. He is, here and usually elsewhere, but supremely here, a mere vessel of history, its transparent instrument; he is, in a manner that accords perfectly with Roman ideology of empire, the selfless agent of history, the vanishing present that fuses the sacred past with the sacred future; he incarnates the just power that, obedient to tradition and to the common good, labors to accomplish what duty and providence command him to accomplish. But in this "eternal moment" he is also, simultaneously and paradoxically, *profugus* (fugitive, runaway slave), an icon of the world's dispossessed, of the wandering outcast; he is a figure of diaspora, he is the courageous vanquished, down but not out, because required to survive and thrive elsewhere. Finally, he is also, in this image of his self-representation (and here one thinks inevitably of Theodor Haecker's *Vergil: Father of the West* and of the astonishing mileage T. S. Eliot managed to get from the fuel that book gave him) the bright phoenix of humane culture that the forces of darkness and barbarism cannot annihilate.

This complex figure, though borrowed from Homer's epics and constantly clothed in their conventions, distorts his models so radically that one is tempted to speak not so much of epic alteration (in the manner, say, of Gian Biagio Conte, for whom genre is a sort of glacial flow that, unchanged itself, changes all the matter, all the content, that it touches) as of epic transformation (in the manner of Mikhail Bakhtin, for whom massive distortions of the generic model transform the model utterly, irreversibly). In this scene and in the self-narration of Book 2 that it crowns, Aeneas is less an epic warrior than a baffled, anguished, and compassionate human being, a man whose concerns as a son, a father and, more ambiguously, as a husband shape his identity; he is, to be sure, a brave warrior when he finds it necessary to fight (see, for example, 433), he is never a coward here or elsewhere, but here and elsewhere the glory of killing and being killed is low among his priorities. One way of examining how this subversion works would be to try to rewrite Book 2 (and Book 3) in standard epic third-person narrative. In this context, the epic narrator would be the omniscient narrator, or, better, Gérard Genette's zero-degree narrator.[1]

It becomes rapidly apparent, when one conducts such an experiment, that the epic narrator cannot do much with this hero's complexities and superb self-contradictions In a third-person version this character soon disintegrates, his hesitations, doubts, and clouded self-esteem combine to make him appear not merely unheroic but also ridiculous, and "the illusion of reality" that epic conventions provide when they are efficiently and faithfully observed completely deserts him. The epic narrator could tell us that his hero felt confused or frightened briefly, even that he was tempted to run away perhaps, but he could not continue to present him in that manner for very long.

When Homer allows Odysseus to replace Demodocus (*Od.* 8.536 ff.), the self-narrating, self-fashioning narrator represents himself exquisitely framed in an intricate pattern of large but plausible virtues offset with some small vices: he hesitates, he doubts, he even (almost) despairs both of heaven and of himself. But he always surmounts his difficulties and himself as well. As he tells it, the cunning that reinforces his courage (or compensates for courage that has been mislaid) never really fails him. In point of fact the picture the hero gives us of himself differs little from the picture his epic narrator gives of him. The "impartial" narrator loves the con-man almost as much as the con-man loves himself. What Odysseus' self-narration adds is the spice of watching this "originary" picaro enjoy himself performing himself.[2] Odysseus' "advertisements for myself" enact the huge gusto and self-satisfaction of the hero with his belly and brain (his *gaster* and *metis*) that are elsewhere vividly narrated in the third person, but they hardly alter our sense of *this* hero (even if this poem's dissection of the *Iliad* complicates our understanding of the epical and the heroic, even if, in a sense, it makes new *Iliads* impossible).[3]

Aeneas' borrowing, so early in his poem, of the Odyssean mode accomplishes the essential thing that Vergil's refiguration of epic requires. It allows an untypical, counter-epical hero to enter into traditional epic form, it allows perspectives on moral worth that are contrary to both the Iliadic and the Odyssean perspectives to be dissonantly juxtaposed with them, and it dramatizes (Aeneas challenging Odysseus as self-narrator) the subversion of Homeric forms and Homeric content and values. This tormented, self-critical, abject voice (of the vanquished) replaces both the voice of Achilles and the voice of Odysseus. This is a new hero for a new epic. Later Aeneas will be, at certain moments, almost as courageous and forceful as any fan of high epic could wish him to be, he will take on (randomly?) some of the styles and some of the power of the Iliadic heroic, but his complexities and his limitations and his humane, "modern" virtues, as they have been defined in Book 2 (and will be, somewhat differently, in Book 3), will continue to reverberate later whenever he is represented, will continue to tinge what he says and what he does. Early in Book 2 he may flirt with the notion of grasping for himself some of the aesthetic splendor that defines the glorious deaths in Homer's poems, the imperishable *kleos* that a great hero's confrontation with mortality confers on him and on his heirs, but what he chooses in Book 2 is responsibility, one that is so pure and so immense that mere identity is swallowed up into it: there is no room here for Homeric (or Greek) individualism.

This reinvention of the heroic could not have been accomplished if the hero's speeches, actions, feelings, and thoughts had been presented throughout in traditional third-person style. By positioning Aeneas at one of his most helpless moments, saved from his latest disaster by a woman, then asked by her to recite for her and her court the story of his city's destruction and the loss of his wife, Vergil's narrator forces his surrogate narrator to reveal himself in a way that is almost unimaginable for the Homeric Odysseus. He must tell more, reveal more, about his fears and hopes, than he wishes to reveal, lay bare the dark corners of his mind, where, unconsciously, his dreamwork has caused his fears and his self-hatred to manifest themselves in the uncanny and recurrent symbols that various critics have detected in Book 2.[4] Caught at a less vulnerable moment, Aeneas might have presented himself in a more traditionally epic manner. By placing Aeneas' self-narration early in the poem, at Dido's court, Vergil emphasizes the novelty of his heroic figure and of his distortion of genre, not just for purposes of literary display (that is, in order to underscore his challenge to Homer) but also for the purpose of drama-

tizing the nature of that novelty. At the instant when Aeneas shoulders his
father and the Penates of his clan and his "nation," he, the vanished hero
(no Homeric hero could endure, could survive, the destruction of his
native city) enters into a new life, he becomes a new man. Furthermore,
when the hero, fresh from his latest catastrophe in Book 1, the loss of so
many of his ships and comrades, comes to Carthage, still feeling guilty
and still feeling himself a failure, in exactly the mood and the state to
recount what Vergil needs him to recount about defeat and escape and
diasporic sorrows, he is, though he does not know it, poised to enter upon
a crucial new stage of his new life; for from Carthage he will finally begin
the last movement of his journey to his goal, to the Italy that has been
promised him in the welter of omens, dreams, and prophecies that have
led him on, as he sometimes thinks, obscurely, almost cruelly, from the
moment Troy fell and he escaped from it.

It is, then, a feat of elegant plotting that combines the just rescued
and still abject narrator whom Dido listens to as he recollects (*recherche*)
the origin of his flight (and quest), the beginnings of his rebirth as
hero, from disjointed memories of the destruction of his city, from
nightmarish pictures of his terror and humiliation, from the sour ruins
of his selfhood:

> "hic mihi nescio quod trepido male numen amicum
> confusam eripuit mentem. namque avia cursu
> dum sequor et nota excedo regione viarum,
> heu misero coniunx fatone erepta Creusa
> substitit? erravitne via seu lassa resedit?
> incertum: nec post oculis est reddita nostris,
> nec prius amissam respexi animumque reflexi,
> quam tumulum antiquae Cereris sedemque sacratam
> venimus . . .
>
> (735–43)

> "At this alarm I panicked: some unfriendly
> god's power ripped away my tangled mind.
> For while I take a trackless path, deserting
> the customary roads, fate tears from me
> my wife Creusa in my misery.
> I cannot say if she had halted or
> had wandered off the road or slumped down, weary.

> My eyes have never had her back again.
> I did not look behind for her, astray,
> or think of her before we reached the mound
> and ancient, sacred shrine of Ceres."
>
> (M 991–1001)

As Aeneas persists in trying to reconstruct Troy's last night, then to construct his experiences of that horror into a linear, logical, sequential order, the "narrating I" becomes more and more decentered, more and more prey to the vehement swirl of his confused, confusing "memories" and of the emotions they image.[5] At this moment of the poem, he and what is left of his immediate family and the small band of Trojans who have somehow joined them are just nearing the gates of the city, are just about to escape into the wildness and its safety. But suddenly he hears the tramp of feet, and his father, from his point of vantage, sees ahead of them the flash of shields in the flames that are destroying the city. So they turn and run in another direction, down unfamiliar streets. And when they pause Aeneas discovers that Creusa is missing.

What Aeneas feels mostly, perhaps, is guilt, a guilt he will feel again in Book 6 (450–76) when he reencounters in hell the kind woman whom he now addresses and who has taken pity on him in his desolation, a guilt not dissimilar to the feelings of Orpheus (*Georgics* 4.499–502; cf. *Aen.* 2.790–94) when he loses Eurydice. But compact with that guilt are grief and loneliness. He has his father and his son, he has his companions, but the loss of his wife (one thinks here perhaps of how Hector feels toward Andromache) is unbearable and (almost) unspeakable. And he cannot say what needs saying, cannot bring himself to shape and respond to the question that we want to ask him, that he needs to ask himself: Why did you/I allow this to happen?

In panic he rushed off without thinking where he was going, his father on his back, his son clutching his hand, the rest of them, Creusa included, left to scramble after him as they could. In that confusion, she stopped running somehow, or she got lost, or she was too worn out to continue. She was, then, in any case, somehow at fault, even though he admits that he never looked back at her, that he had been giving her no thought: "when all were gathered" at the temple of Ceres, "she alone / was missing—gone from husband, son, companions" (*collectis omnibus una / defuit, et comites natumque virumque fefellit*, 743–44, M 1002–3). "Was missing" in Latin is *fefellit*, which in this context means literally "had escaped the notice,"

"eluded the observation of," that is to say, "none of us could remember
when he had last had a glimpse of her (because we did not have her in
mind, on our minds)." But it also means, "to cheat," to delude," or "to
disappoint." He knows the fault is his, he knows that she is innocent, but
his tongue, even here, tries to find an indeterminacy that can mitigate his
failure of her. Or better yet, neither of them is guilty. It is a god's fault (or,
in a slight variation of the displacement), a god's will.

"What men, what gods did I in madness not / accuse? Did I see any-
thing more cruel / within the fallen city?" (*quem non accusavi amens
hominumque deorumque, / aut quid in everso vidi crudelius urbe?*,
745–46, M 1004–5). The "narrating I" can, and indeed must, rebuke the
"narrated I" for his/my blasphemy in cursing the gods at this worst of
bitter moments in this long nightmare of that night, can call him(self)
once again (see also 314) *amens* (in madness), but by this time the
"narrated I" has been so maddened, so broken and so numbed by all he
saw as his city was being destroyed, has become himself so unselved, that
the curse called down on gods and men seems a mere reflex, seems less
an act of impiety than a gesture of self-defense, an arm lifted against the
face to shield it, a healthy attempt to ward off annihilation. Aeneas as
abject narrator may chastise Aeneas as abject hero, but for all the miles
and years that separate them, despite the fact that this Aeneas knows so
much more about self and world than that Aeneas knew back then and
there, the teller to Dido of his own tale cannot erase from his/their story of
salvation and renewal the broken faith in men and the gods that tinges it
with a special shade of religious dubiety. Earlier, at 735, Aeneas remarked
that when he bolted in panic just before reaching the city gates it was
because "some unfriendly / god's power ripped away my tangled mind"
(*hic mihi nescio quod trepido male numen amicum / confusam eripuit
mentem*, M 991–92).

In the original Latin the phrase is *male numen amicum*, which means,
literally, "a divinity badly friendly." Piecing together his faded and fading
recollections of the tangled fragments of his perceptions of his earlier self
in that appalling moment, Aeneas means by this phrase that what he
hoped for at this instant of wanhope was a guiding divine hand that was
sympathetic to his situation and his needs. After his mother had appeared
to him and persuaded him to return to his home and attend to his family,
after the omen of the fire in Ascanius' hair and after the answered prayer
of his father to *Iuppiter Omnipotens*, it was surely not unreasonable of
him, once he had accepted (at least temporarily) the inevitable truth of

these portents, to believe that his going would be unhindered and unharmed. (*Nusquam abero*, 620, "in no place will I be absent," his mother had said, and true to her word she had led him, *ducente deo*, 632, back to his family. Is it possible that the son chides his goddess mother with *male numen amicum* for her unconscionable absence when he was most beset and thereby lost his wife? And if he cannot trust her, what deity can he trust?)

When Aeneas leaves Ceres' temple and goes back to search for her in the horrors of what is left of Troy, the ghost of Creusa appears to him and assures him that her loss and his "long exile" and eventual arrival in Hesperia are fixed by the will of Jupiter and that confirmation of divine favor, of a bitter exile that will gradually transform itself into a world-historical mission, will be further validated in Book 3 by more omens, more prophecies (some less obscure and less conflicting than others).[6] The "narrating I" knows about these later confirmations, knows a bit more about the will of Jupiter, about how the designs of providence are achieved than does the "narrated I" of Book 2 in the last moments of his experiences of Troy's fall, and he could be using that increase in knowledge to soften his presentation of his earlier self's anxiety and doubt. He fails to soften it, however, not because of his desire for mimetic accuracy ("I describe myself as I was then as faithfully as I can"), not, probably, because he has no sense that he should be trying, in the Odyssean manner, to embellish his self-portrait, but because, different though he is from the man he was before, he resembles him still in his mistrust of men and gods, because the divinities that claim to be friendly to him are seldom disposed to show that friendliness with great clarity, because even here, in Dido's court, safe for now from the perils of the angry sea (where so many of his companions have just perished), the memory of old disasters, intensified by new ones, takes hold of his imagination and causes him to identify with the older self, his hero, who is more ignorant than he, the teller of the tale, is of newer griefs that await him.

To get at the mounting anguish of the self-narration of Book 2, at a quality in it that approaches hysteria as it moves toward the closing scenes and their condensation of theodicean paradox, imagine how this text would be read, first by its author when he read it to friendly critics with a view to improving it, then by its later first readers when, after his death, his first editors released the fruits of their labor. Whether alone or (maybe more likely) in a small group of friends, the reader would enact the text, would perform it. For the couple of hours his or her performance of Book

2 requires, this reader/performer/reproducer of this text must render (as a pianist, say, renders a Beethoven sonata) not just the words of the text and the events it evokes in his mind and mouth, in his hearers' ears (and eyes, for they are watching him, too), but also the peculiar, unstable fusion of the narrating/narrated hero of the text. What are the complexities that this reader/narrator confronts as he or she renders this composition?

Vergil the narrator has been effaced by the "narrating I," so at one level at least and for the time being, the performer can "forget" (or seem to) what he or she knows from that omniscient narrator of Book 1 about Aeneas and his world and his poem (he can also, at almost the same level and for the time being, "forget" all he knows about and from the omniscient narrator of Books 4–12). The central difficulty will be to try to find a way of performing the text's tensions between the narrating and the narrated Aeneas, between what that Aeneas knew about himself and the gods and men he curses and what he, this narrating Aeneas, now knows (has learned in his wanderings) about himself and them and the world. The narrating Aeneas of Book 2 has begun to understand, though he still has serious doubts about, what Creusa's dark words to him signify— about what happened to her and to Troy, about him and about his mysterious fate and mysterious duties. He knows, in ways that the narrated Aeneas of Book 2 never could, that somewhere in the twists and turns of his misfortunes and (seemingly) aimless wandering there lies maybe meaning and maybe salvation for him and for the remnants of his city. He does not know what the Vergilian narrator has told us in Book 1 (254–96) where he represents Jupiter himself reassuring Venus that her son will triumph over his troubles and will found a new Troy that will, as the centuries pass, triumph over the world (*imperium sine fine dedi*, 1.279); but he is well along in the process of becoming, by the time he reaches Carthage, a walking and breathing Roman theodicy: that is, in his story, part of which he knows, is here beginning to know, and part of which he will never really know, he is the incarnation of a question, of the question that in his cursing of gods and men he attempted both to enunciate and to obliterate.

That question takes various forms. But in what are perhaps its most haunting versions it appears at the very beginning of the poem (1.11) when the Vergilian narrator asks his Muses whether gods are capable of human anger, whether gods intervene in the affairs of humankind and so cause suffering and destruction. And finally and much more violently, it reappears at a crucial juncture toward the end of the poem, just before the

final conflicts between the Trojans and the Latins, before Aeneas meets
Turnus in combat, when the Vergilian narrator asks:

> quis mihi nunc tot acerba deus, quis carmine caedes
> diversas obitumque ducum, quos aequore toto
> inque vicem nunc Turnus agit, nunc Troius heros,
> expediat? tanton placuit concurrere motu,
> Iuppiter, aeterna gentis in pace futuras?
>
> (12.500–504)

> What god can now unfold for me in song
> all of the bitterness and butchery
> and deaths of chieftains—driven now by Turnus,
> now by the Trojan hero, each in turn
> throughout that field? O Jupiter, was it
> your will that nations destined to eternal
> peace should have clashed in such tremendous turmoil?
>
> (M 674–80)

The Vergilian narrator looks at the pictures he is about to represent in
words and feels (the rhetorical figure is that of aporia) inadequate to the
task. He doubts that his muse or even some other god could do what he
quails at attempting. So he asks the author (the author of these pictures, of
that text, the story that his poem condenses) the question that this poem,
like the society in which and for which it was produced, kept trying to
forget, kept trying to exclude from its final version of all these pictures
and what they meant. The pictures we are about to see are of Aeneas' war
in Latium, which are also pictures of Rome's wars with the Italians from
its beginning down to Augustus' unification of *tota Italia*, achieved (sym-
bolically at least) just about the time this poem was begun.[7] The question
the narrator fails to suppress, the question he asks about those pictures is:
Why do these terrible things have to happen? Or, more precisely, Why did
you let them happen?

In Homeric epic the anger of the god in question and its aftermath are
usually knowable and become known, and the recipient of that anger,
having learned its origin, is either successful or not in expiating his trans-
gression, then in being restored (or not) to the god's favor or indifference.
When it is communities that are implicated in the divine displeasure,
when it is Achaeans and Trojans battling one another, the supreme god

among the gods is Zeus, the god of all alike, impartial in bestowing his benefits, impartial in executing the design of Fate. Sometimes you win and sometimes you do not. The gaze is, behind the celestial apparatus that supports the plot, already almost Herodotean (*Histories* 1.5): Communities that were once huge and thriving dwindle to insignificance while a place that once was not even shown on the map becomes a metropolis; human felicity doesn't stay long in the same place. On both the personal level, then, and on the political level, the ways of God can be justified to man by demonstrating his/its even-handedness: wrongs will be righted, rights and wrongs will be balanced by the hand of justice, mysteriously balanced perhaps, but balanced none the less. This is not always a comfortable explanation but it is an intelligible one, and in hearing it we do not have the sense that we are listening to the Wizard of Oz executing a fumbling explanation of himself over his loud-speaker. But it works less well when it begins to be used, as it must be in the society Vergil produced his poem in and for, as it must be in this poem, to explain "what happens in history."

History's god, unlike the gods of Homer and Herodotus, does not deal with mere specific incidents, one by one and one at a time; it (history, its god) concerns itself with a pattern of incidents that do not exist in and of themselves in their spacetimes but are rather shaped from their source toward a particular purpose, and at this point in the making of this theodicy (Rome's) the figure of justice has been transformed into the figure of providence.[8] Yet if here the picture of the balancing hand has been subsumed by (and has disappeared into) the benevolent eye whose gaze creates future felicity, the rhetoric of justice is still essential to this process: winners win because they should win and losers lose because they should lose, winners are good and losers are not. God's ways (and history's) are justified in this mechanism of producing meaning by the vices and virtues of those who are caught up into the story of how we came to be masters of this world. It goes without saying that losers are either too ashamed to tell how they lost or, if they brazenly attempt to explain their defeat, their tales of how things went against them, tend, for obvious reasons, to get mislaid and eventually to disappear altogether: we have no Punic history or Gallic history of their wars with Rome, and we do not even have much of anyone's version, a fact of some interest for our reading of Vergil's epic, of the Social Wars—the last of the Italian wars with Rome. In history it is tribe against tribe, and the gods of the tribe against the gods of the tribe: if one's tribe wins, it is because its god was more powerful than the opposing god, if one's tribe loses it is because its god was weak(er).

Or, in a more sophisticated version of tribal history: the god of the winners was better able to see the future, better able to plan for victory than the stupider, weaker god who opposed him and his. In the *Aeneid*, on one of its levels, Jupiter, the supreme god of Roman ideology and of Vergil's epic, is the old tribal god (Aeneas his grandson, Romulus also his grandson) who has (somehow) been transformed into a universal god, one like the Homeric highest god in that he is the god of all alike, except that in this new world-historical context "all" means not just "my tribe" and "your tribe" and "the tribes nearby us" but "everyone in the wide world"; it means "the universal and eternal god," but this god, unlike the Homeric highest god, is impartial and just only in the sense that by virtue of his infallible, unpersuadable providence he has designed the game of the world, how it will be played and what its end will be, who will win and who will lose (that is, they win who should win, they lose who should lose). If you are a winner, this version of god is likely to satisfy you well enough, but if you happen to be on the losing side, it may occur to you to wonder whether the tribal god has in fact become universal (and impartial and providential) or if he has merely disguised himself in a more cosmopolitan and philosophically sophisticated costume, whether he has, though remaining as biased and as aggressive as he ever was, put on the mask of eternity and universality.[9]

With these images of theodicy in our minds, if we look again at the "situation of discourse" of this storyteller (or, better, of these multiple and iridescent storytellers, Vergil, the man and the poet, his narrator, the "narrating I" of Books 2 and 3), we may decide that few narrators—not even Milton, perhaps not even Dostoyevsky, perhaps not even the writers of the Old Testament—have undertaken a heavier, more cumbersome project of theodicy.

The Vergilian narrator and his narrating/narrated Aeneas must adapt their Homeric models to the requirements of a providentialist world-historical vision, they must accommodate the existential anxieties of the individual warrior in his struggle with his enemies both human and divine to the transcendental (yet immanent) designs of universal salvation. It is no longer a question of this warrior dying here or not, dying gloriously or not. All that matters in this new epic mode is this servant's obedience to and compatibility with the Benevolent Fate he shares with the world— what is at stake is how he behaves, weighed down as he is by the past he carries on his back and responsible, utterly, for the future whose hand clutches his. All that is asked of him is that, once he regains his nerve, he move steadily on (*"perge modo,"* says his incomparable mother, 1.389), that he trudge on, impervious alike to the dangers without and to what besets him from within: his grief for the lost wife and all the coming losses, his near despair, and, above all, his all too reasonable mistrust of the justice of heaven. More than anything it is this mistrust that shapes the "narrating I"'s representation of "himself" as he was back then, experiencing in the flesh the fierce paradox of Jupiter's partisan impartiality and tribal universality (*dis aliter visum,* "the gods thought otherwise," 428, vs. *imperium sine fine dedi,* "I set no limits to their fortunes and no time," 1.279) and that also shapes, with no less conflict and no less anguish, his own self-representation as Dido's narrator.[10]

In the performance of his worst nightmare, of his memories of Troy's last night, the narrating hero tells his hostess, who is herself an exile and herself the founder of an empire, how, fleeing from the sight of Troy's king being butchered, alone and frightened, he stumbled upon Helen, origin of Troy's destruction and was stopped from slaying her only by his mother's appearance to him ("more clearly visible to me than ever before," *non ante oculis tam clara,* 589, M 794–95). Having saved Helen, she then directs her son to return to his family and save them, underscoring her request with a gesture: she points to the cityscape which is being violently dismantled—by Neptune and Juno and Athena (*apparent dirae facies,* 622, "these fiendish shapes of gods," says R. G. Austin, ad loc., "who have become near-devils"). And with them, in spirit, is Jupiter himself, who, as Venus tells her son, "furnishes the Greeks with force" and "goads on the gods."[11]

That demonic collage of divine machinery shows the tribal deity wearing his international mask at his ugliest. When the "narrated I" flees that vision of hellfire he may think (but "the narrating I" knows better) that he has seen the worst, but in a very short time, having heard and seen more to hearten him, to spur him on as he travels his long path to Duty Performed, he will see the ghost of Creusa and other visions as bad as that or worse (if "worse," after a while, still has meaning for him). At each stage of this process/progress Aeneas may learn a bit more, but the poem's central (almost hidden) question never becomes less anguished or more nearly answerable. In that sense the "narrated I" that is constructed in Book 2 (Aeneas at his most abject, most confused, least conventionally heroic) becomes the enduring, irremediable image of the hero, becomes the essential Aeneas that will haunt the poem until its end and past it. The "narrating I" (and behind him Vergil's narrator and behind him us, the current performers of all these performers and their performances) takes on the person of that forlorn Aeneas, and takes on with it all his terror, all his suppressed fury with heaven and himself. And so, even when we have come to that final verse of Book 2, "Then I gave way / and, lifting up my father, made for the mountains" (*cessi et sublato montis genitore petivi*) even then, knowing all that the "narrating I" knows (in Book 2) and all that Vergil's narrator knows (in Book 1 and the rest of the poem), knowing all the text can tell us of this strange new hero-as-exile and of the tragic migrations of his counter-Homeric world, we are not surprised, we may even be strangely relieved, when Vergil (or someone or the political unconscious of the time in which the poem was produced and people began their renderings of it), when a voice explodes from the poem to ask again what made this suffering (in Book 12 but also in Book 2 and all through the poem), what made this suffering necessary.[12]

CHAPTER 3

IMITATING TROY
A Reading of *Aeneid* 3

Ralph Hexter

Book 3, while rich in beauties and interpretive challenges, has never been a favorite among readers or critics of the *Aeneid*. Many a first course in Latin, while prescribing selections solely from the first half of the *Aeneid*, avoids Book 3 as assiduously as it does Book 5, preferring the storm and arrival in Carthage of Book 1, the dramatic fall of Troy in Book 2, the personal drama of Dido and Aeneas in Book 4, and the sublimity of Golden Bough and Underworld in Book 6. More objectively, not a few critics note the particularly unfinished state of Book 3, notable even in the context of an *Aeneid* left at Vergil's death without the final polishing its poet planned. Both Books 2 and 3 are narrated by Aeneas to Dido, but Book 3 displays signs that it was placed by Vergil into this inner narrative frame at a later stage in his work, and eminent Vergilians such as Gordon Williams, for example, judge that it has not been completely adjusted to its place in Vergil's fully evolved narrative and representational strategies.[1]

These are important observations. Students of the poem cannot ignore the fact that poems are made, not begotten, and that we presumably do not have the poem Vergil himself would have presented to Augustus had he lived to the point where he could declare himself satisfied with this, his most ambitious undertaking. We can, however, only read the poem we have, saved from the flames to which ancient biographies claim Vergil wished it to be given, just as Aeneas, his father, son, and the Penates are saved from the flames of Ilium in Book 2. Even as we acknowledge the poem's and the book's incompletion,[2] we can neither refuse to respond to it nor read in its place some scholar's version of what it "would" (i.e., might, but of course equally might not) have been. In my view, if Book 3 was still "in progress" later, or more obviously so, than some of the other

portions of the poem, or if it was transferred to its place within Aeneas'
narrative after its episodes had been cast as the poet's own narrative, this
suggests that Vergil's attention to Book 3 and to the issues it addresses
was, if anything, greater and certainly no less than in the other, more
polished books.

Now our explicit practice in this volume, to grasp the poem bookwise
or bookmeal, so to speak, however well established in the traditions of
Vergilian exegesis and teaching, raises methodological concerns. How
separable are the books in terms of interpretive issues and concerns? How
does our tendency to characterize, even individualize books and groups of
books, affect our understanding of the whole epic? There are no simple
answers to these questions. What is fair to observe is that Vergil himself
worked in an epic tradition already textual. At the same time as we con-
sider the way in which classical Roman reading practices differed from
modern technologies and thus constituted readers in some sense different
from us,[3] we know that Vergil and his peers read and studied the works of
Homer and Apollonius of Rhodes, among others, as "booked" epics. Book
division was a formal element several hundred times less frequent than
verse ending, but equally capable of signifying. Likewise, just as portions
of the narrative can change in tonality, so books can vary in tone, tempo,
and topic, even if, in both cases, it is only the reflecting reader who can
devise and attach labels. Thus it is not wrong of R. D. Williams to charac-
terize Book 3 as a "breathing space between two books of great dramatic
power."[4] Certainly, this kind of rhythm makes sense in terms of readers'
experience of the book.

Williams makes a further point to explain our response to Book 3:
"Emotionally . . . we rest; intellectually, however, our interest is main-
tained in the unfolding of the major themes of the poem."[5] Certainly, in a
poem as complex and polyphonic as the *Aeneid*, it is helpful to think of
certain themes as more prominent in some parts, others in other parts.
Indeed, it may be that it is only possible to think about themes by isolating
them, and in each of his books Vergil offers readers (as he would have
listeners to the poem, declaimed in portions) an opportunity to meditate on
certain issues. Given that the "plot" of Book 3 could be described as the
stepwise realization on the Trojans' part that the new homeland promised
them lies in Italy, a revelation or realization communicated to them and to
us via both a series of prophecies and a series of failed attempts at "new
Troys," I would characterize Book 3 as an opportunity to meditate on issues
of interpretation and imitation, with examples of each both good and bad,

failed and successful. Certainly, I hope by the end of this chapter to reduce whatever surprise at or suspicion of the terms "interpretation" and "imitation" my readers have, but already at the outset I want to make quite clear that my claims are contingent and personal. No list of themes could ever be exhaustive or definitive, and different scholars would respond to and thus emphasize different issues. More subtly, one must be aware that the precise formulation of any summary or paraphrase itself sets up a certain interpretation.

Even as I identify central themes for intellectual meditation, I am less certain than Williams about the ability so neatly to distinguish between readers' emotional and intellectual responses. Tensions between public and personal are thematized throughout the poem (to the point where one must acknowledge their inseparability), and one valid reading of the *Aeneid* sees Aeneas himself learning to subordinate the emotional and personal to the political and historical. This could itself be inflected as Roman/Western discipline over Greek/Eastern hysterics. In this context, even the emotional outpourings of Andromache, which Williams identifies as the one scene in Book 3 where Vergil "aim[s] at the pathos elsewhere so characteristic of him,"[6] however affecting, may be dangerous and seductive. As readers we should critique even our own responses, for their arousal may well be a calculated feature of the poem.

The dangers of misreading and misinterpreting are presented in the *Aeneid* itself. Successive prophecies and oracles and revised interpretations are needed because earlier clues are missed or misconstrued. Although most of the prophecies in Book 3 are concerned with first getting Aeneas to Italy and then to the right spot in Latium, Book 3 is likewise a history of false starts and failed attempts to found a new Troy. While the Trojans constitute the audience for the oracles and prophecies and must interpret all they see and hear, even revising their opinion of their own actions, Dido is the book's intended listener and model interpreter. A less-than-perfect model, for while the Trojans fitfully correct their misprisions, Dido becomes the archetypal misreader of Book 3 (and thus of the *Aeneid*), placing personal interest above political calculation. Aeneas' mission, as he understands ever more clearly in this very book, is to find a new home in Italy for his people. Even the harpy Celaeno understands that the Trojans must reach Italy, however much it is hateful to her (see especially 253–54, with *Italiam* twice). Helenus' lengthy and detailed instructions (374–462) make no mention of a stop, much less a permanent stay in Carthage. Quite the contrary. Yet Dido listening to

Book 3 must have paid very little attention to its specific insistence on Aeneas' destiny in Italy. The words of the text notwithstanding, Dido exercises her freedom, a terrible freedom, to make false inferences: that having been dissatisfied to date, Aeneas might stay with her, rather than move on, defying or ignoring oracular and prophetic pronouncements. Dido is the first, but not the last, listener of Books 2 and 3 who preferred the emotional to the intellectual, derring-do to patience and study. Readers of Book 3 must attend to it as Dido does not, not least because Vergil gives us in Dido so spectacular a cautionary counter-example of the interested misreader.[7]

The very narrative placement of Book 3, as the second of the two books narrated by Aeneas to Dido, leads us to an important aspect of the theme of imitation. This inset narrative is the grandest of gestures to Vergil's Homeric intertext, the *Odyssey* in particular.[8] In the *Odyssey*, Odysseus recounts to the Phaeacians his travels, his narration forming books 9–12 of the epic. Even the ratios correspond, each inset section comprising one-sixth of the whole of which it is a part ($4/24 = 2/12 = 1/6$). If Book 2 is in some sense "Iliadic," set at Troy, featuring not a few of the *Iliad*'s dramatis personae and showcasing armed conflict, Book 3 is the most "Odyssean" in the voyaging of the hero to many lands and places.[9] But Book 2 is also non-Iliadic in an important sense: it very much does not retell the *Iliad*. The fall of Troy, even the episode of the Trojan horse, comes after the end of the Homeric *Iliad*. Vergil had multiple sources, of course, the cyclic poems among them, but significantly he did not take up plot segments first treated by Homer.

This principle is particularly interesting as it plays out in Book 3, where, in a similar way, Vergil has Aeneas' itinerary conspicuously not coincide with Odysseus', as it might well have, for both took place (fictionally, of course) in the decade immediately following the fall of Ilium. We are meant to imagine a Mediterranean in which Homer's and Vergil's traveling heroes are crisscrossing each other's paths, but never meeting. The point is that Aeneas is not only like Odysseus in a merely trivial sense—he travels, he is "much tossed about on land and sea" (1.3)—but he is more deeply and significantly unlike Odysseus. Without denying that Homer's Odysseus is often a model of patience and perseverance, nonetheless, whether his own or the gods' fault, he fails to bring his companions safely to their homes in Ithaca. He comes home alone. This would obviously not do for the *Aeneid*, but that Vergil has Aeneas lead men—and women (though we are reminded of this only occasionally, e.g., 3.65, 5.613 ff.,

9.284)—to settle in Latium, and get the bulk of them there alive, is no mere plot necessity. Vergil emphasizes Aeneas' responsibility for others over Odysseus' loss of companions.

In one of the most significant episodes in this context, at the conclusion of Book 3, Vergil brings Aeneas to a spot Odysseus visited in the *Odyssey*—the land of the Cyclopes—and has him rescue one of Odysseus' own companions. Vergil invents—I will return to this in my concluding section—a character, Achaemenides, whom he makes into a named survivor of the nameless Greeks Homer describes as eaten by Polyphemus. This has consequences both for the image of Aeneas as hero and Vergil as poet. Not only is Aeneas shown to be responsible where Odysseus was least so—for if there was any episode in the *Odyssey* where even by Odysseus' own account he was foolhardy, it is the Cyclopes episode—but he assumes responsibility for one of Odysseus' followers in addition to all his own.

By retelling the story in this way, Vergil manages to suggest that *he* got it right as a poet, Homer wrong. One need not invoke the theories of Harold Bloom (*The Anxiety of Influence* [1973]), *A Map of Misreading* [1975]), which may be anachronistic when applied to Augustan poetry (I leave that an open question), to see this as some sort of poetic rivalry. That it was understood as at the very least one-upmanship by Vergil's contemporaries is established by Ovid's own revision and completion of Vergil's revision and completion of Homer: showing he well appreciates the "trick" Vergil played on Homer, Ovid joins the game and has the Trojans encounter—and Achaemenides recognize—yet another invented character, Macareus, one of Odysseus' comrades who is supposed to have stayed behind on Circe's island (*Met.* 14.159 ff.).

Though they would need to be elaborated across a greater expanse of text than just one book, there are correspondences, even conflicts in Book 3 that operate on multiple levels: Aeneas is contrasted with Odysseus, Vergil vies with Homer, and the reader is free to surpass Dido in careful reading. The text itself insists on our making comparisons nowhere more clearly than in the series of what I call "mini-" or "mock Troys": Aeneas and his band found several settlements they hope will be their new home, the new Troy, only to discover that they are wrong; these settlements will not do. They then visit the settlement of Helenus and Andromache, successful in some regards, clearly not in others, with its theme-park Ilium. This is also not the right home for Aeneas. It seems obvious that while Vergil is telling us primarily that Rome needs to be a new Troy on its own terms, a new creation, he is also letting us share in his hard-fought battle as a poet to write an updated Homeric epic. For as Rome is to Troy, so the *Aeneid* is to the Homeric poems. Of the one, Vergil says prominently at the conclusion of the proem, "It was so hard to found the race of Rome" (*tantae molis erat Romanam condere gentem*, 1.33, M 50). We could understand *Romanum poema* as well.

Before I offer interpretive soundings in support of these observations, a brief overview of the entire book, with special attention to its organization and patterning, is in order. Aeneas' journey as narrated in Book 3 can be fit into three groups of three[10] with a few lines before, after, and between the episodes and some admitted fudging in reducing the multiple stops and sailings in the third part. This simplified articulation of the book's 718 Latin hexameters is helpful as a conspectus, and can be laid out graphically as follows:

Aeneas' proem (1–12)

I.   Aegean (13–191):
        Thrace (13–68). Aeneadae; Polydorus.
        Delos (69–123). Apollo's oracle (*antiquam matrem*, 96).
        Crete (124–91). Build "Pergamum"; plague; Penates offer correction.
    Storm (192–208).

II.   Greece (209–505):
        Strophades (209–69). Kill cattle; Harpies; Celaeno's prophecy.
        Excursus: Skirting Odysseus' homeland, Ithaca (270–74).
        Actium (275–88). Leucate/Actium; Apollo's shrine;games.
        Buthrotum (289–505). Helenus and Andromache.
    Calm sea passage (506–20).

III. Italy/Sicily (521–715):
        Castrum Minervae (521–47). First landfall on Italian soil; good
           omens.
        Etna—Cyclopes (548–681). Achaemenides; Cyclopes.
        Voyage around Sicily (682–715).
           Conclusion (716–18). Vergil's own words.

It has been argued for the structurally parallel narrative in the *Odyssey* (Books 9–12) that its many and more varied episodes are unified to some degree because Odysseus is presenting a series of exemplary accounts of hospitality, both positive and negative, monstrous and divine, as part of one sustained attempt to persuade the listening Phaeacians to host him well but not so extravagantly that his homecoming in Ithaca would be delayed.[11] While one might consider whether a similar intention underlies Aeneas' narrative, one cannot fail to note that the theme itself is presented more subtly and is subordinated to one considerably more important for the *Aeneid*, namely, Aeneas' and the Trojans' discovery of their true goal: a homeland in Italy. It is entirely fitting that the theme of the journey's purpose overshadow any message Aeneas might want to convey to the narrative's first listener, for though Dido is that first listener and though it is in Aeneas' interests that she be moved to offer hospitality, in many ways she can only "overhear" or "listen in on" Aeneas' destiny and the course of Roman history, to which she is fated to remain an outsider.[12]

More could be said about the book's organization. For example, throughout this episodic book there are two competing structures, one, a rising movement toward climax (Italian landfall, the horrifying tale of Achaemenides), the other, a rising followed by a falling movement (rising toward and falling away from Buthrotum, with the pathetic Andromache and the prophetic Helenus). In many ways, the second part (II) is the book's center of gravity. It is by far the largest of the three major blocks, and its own third and capping member—the stop at Buthrotum—itself comprises a virtual third of the whole book. The final section exemplifies a rising and falling movement, offering a quiet ending for the book.

To organize my observations most economically, I will open with a selective review of the events of the first section, highlighting examples of hospitality and successive prophecies and interpretations. I will then focus my discussion of imitation and renovation on two episodes, that of Buthrotum from the second stage of the voyage, and that of Achaemenides from the third stage, where the issue of outdoing Homer is particularly pronounced.

I. Aegean Travels

Having lifted his father on his shoulders, as the final words of Book 2 describe, exemplifying the essence of Aeneas' *pietas* in its most basic Roman sense, Aeneas opens the part of his narrative Vergil labels Book 3 with references to the gods, references that suggest what we more readily understand by piety.[13] Already in the first sentence of Book 3 Aeneas attributes the destruction of Priam's realm to the gods (*superis*, 2) and emphasizes the fact that the whole course of exiled journeys is directed by omens from the gods (*auguriis agimur divum*, 5). It has long been taken as one of the imperfections of Book 3 that even though, as Aeneas has reported to Dido, Creusa foretold his wanderings and goal with some specificity—

> longa tibi exsilia et vastum maris aequor arandum,
> et terram Hesperiam venies, ubi Lydius arva
> inter opima virum leni fluit agmine Thybris.
>
> (2.780–82)

> Along your way lie long exile, vast plains
> of sea that you must plow; but you will reach
> Hesperia, where Lydian Tiber flows,
> a tranquil stream, through farmer's fruitful fields.
>
> (M 1052–55)

neither Aeneas nor the Trojans start out in Book 3 betraying any awareness of this prophecy. I will not rehearse the various suggestions that have been made to excuse the seeming inconsistency, nor will I deny categorically the possibility that Vergil would have revised the "problem" away at some future date. But the premise of Book 3 as we have it is that Aeneas must grope his way until his understanding catches up with these words. Faced with prophecies, some ambiguous, some contradictory, Vergil's characters have no way of knowing in advance which are true, which are false, or rather, no way of knowing by what interpretation any given prophecy is true. Indeed, without knowledge of the referents behind Creusa's words, Aeneas could have no more sense of their actual meaning than he does of the scenes on the shield presented him at the end of Book 8, where Vergil strikingly exploits Aeneas' ignorance (esp. *rerumque ignarus imagine gaudet,* "and he is glad / for all these images, though he does not / know what they mean, 8.730, M 952–54).

The first stop on Aeneas' voyage is Thrace. No sooner are the Thracians mentioned (14) than the theme of hospitality is explicitly present (*hospitium,* 15). Aeneas narrates how he founded a city, Aeneadae, which he named after himself (*meo nomen de nomine fingo,* 18). He mentions the foundation almost in passing, for the real interest of this first episode is the story of Polydorus, and the most memorable image is the blood and voice that emerge from the plant Aeneas attempts to uproot. This "omen" (*monstrum,* 26) clearly bodes ill, and the voice of Polydorus confirms that Thrace is a violently inhospitable land, a land of treachery and death (44).

As Aeneas explains to Dido and us (49 ff.), Polydorus was sent as a guest to the Thracian king, Lycurgus, to be raised away from the besieged Troy, a sort of insurance policy to guarantee that, come what might, Priam's male line would not die out and some treasure would be saved. A worthless calculation, in the event, for as soon as the king learned of the Greek victory, he went back on his word, killed Polydorus, and seized the money. If Lycurgus' greed and bloodlust remind Dido of her own brother, Pygmalion, who killed her rich husband, Sychaeus, so much more will she be moved by this exemplum of monstrous inhospitality—such is the narrative calculation.[14] Aeneas repeats the word *hospitium* (61) as he rounds out the episode by describing the tomb he now raises to his murdered brother-in-law.

The Trojans next stop on Delos to learn the advice of Apollo's famous oracle. King Anius is a model of positive hospitality (*hospitio*, 83), though it is in the nature of such things that even the best hospitality is rarely as memorable as grotesque inhospitality such as Lycurgus' or Celaeno's (the latter a frightening figure for Dido). Our interest here, however, is more in the oracle, which, in response to Aeneas' request that Apollo "preserve the second citadel of Troy" (86–87, M 114), tells him to seek "your ancient mother" (*antiquam exquirite matrem*, 96, M 128), the land that first bore the Dardan line. It is traditional for oracles, certainly the oracles we know from literary accounts as far back as Herodotus, to couch their pronouncements in language that is enigmatic, at times deviously deceptive, and at the very least figurative—like much poetry, come to think of it.[15] It is Anchises, the spiritual leader of the Trojans, as it were, until his death, who believes he understands the meaning of this metaphor: the ancient mother, he explains, is Crete (103 ff.).

In Book 3, Aeneas presents Dido, and Vergil presents us, with both positive and negative exempla of hosts, but when it comes to the series of new Troys, all the images are negative. This is basically a tautology: if it is not Rome, Rome it cannot be. It is no surprise, then, that Crete proves the wrong solution to the "ancient mother" riddle. Plague indicates that something is wrong (137–46), and in a vision (147–71) the Penates appear and speak, correcting Anchises' mistake and specifying that the Trojans are to head westward to Italy (*Hesperiam*, 163; *Oenotri*, 165; *Italiam*, 166; *Ausonias*, 171). Indeed, acknowledging his own error, Anchises admits that he too had more than once heard that the Trojans would go to Italy, and in so many words. Incredible it was, for Cassandra, fated never to be believed, was the mouthpiece of the god speaking of Hesperia and Italy

(185). If Anchises had heard these words more than once and not credited them, should we blame Aeneas if he heard Creusa say "Hesperia" but once and not caught and retained its meaning?

II. BUTHROTUM

Already the unthinking speed with which Aeneas built his city on Crete might have given one pause:

> "et tandem antiquis Curetum adlabimur oris.
> ergo avidus muros optatae molior urbis
> Pergameamque voco, et laetam cognomine gentem
> hortor amare focos arcemque attollere tectis.
> Iamque fere sicco subductae litore puppes,
> conubiis arvisque novis operata iuventus,
> iura domosque dabam, subito cum . . ."
>
> (131–37)

> "At length we glide
> on to the ancient coasts of the Curetes.
> There eagerly I raise the longed-for city's
> walls, and I call it Pergamum. I spur
> my people, happy in that name, to love
> their home, to build a citadel on high.
> And now our boats had just been drawn up on
> dry beaches, with our young men busy at
> new weddings and new plowings—I was giving
> us laws, assigning dwellings—when a sudden . . ."
>
> (M 175–84)

Yes, this is a summary. Aeneas wants to suggest that everything was going swimmingly until suddenly (the plague came). The building of the walls and the naming, the rejoicing, the establishment of new institutions within the walls—everything came too quickly, too easily, without deliberation. The way the passage is ordered, it almost seems as if a good part of the building occurred before the ships were drawn up on land. While the primary problem is that the Trojans are in the wrong place, note the particular reason for rejoicing: "and I call it Pergamum. . . . my people, happy in that name." The great late-antique commentator of Vergil's works, Servius, explains that the people are "'happy' on account of Pergama restored."[16] Desire to see Troy restored may be understandable, but excessive zeal and haste may be dangerous. Simple-minded transfer of old names to a new site is not sufficient. (Recall here the tautological imitation of that first settlement, Aeneadae, and especially the polyptotonic repetition of *nomen* in line 18, cited above.)

This principle does not bode well for Buthrotum, the new home of Helenus and Andromache and the most extensive example of a rebuilt Troy in Book 3. Aeneas' visit there comprises the final and most significant episode of the second stage of his travels and in many ways the most significant segment of the entire book. Like Dido's Carthage, this new settlement is not the work of Aeneas and his followers. While the tale and the sight is a cause for wonder, wonder may not prove the best recommendation for clear-headed interpretation.[17] Buthrotum is, I would argue, the most thoroughly negative example of a new Troy in part because it is so seductively familiar.

For the interpreter, everything is of potential significance in Vergil's poetry, but we should note in particular that the two episodes preceding Aeneas' arrival in Epirus are (1) a calculated skirting of Ulysses' realm Ithaca (*effugimus scopulos Ithacae, Laertia regna, et terram altricem saevi exsecramur Ulixi*, "We shun the shoals / of Ithaca, Laertes' land, and curse / the earth that once had nursed the fierce Ulysses," 272–73, M 351–53), and (2) games and the dedication of a shield to Apollo's shrine at this composite of Leucate and Actium (274–88). Thus immediately before we reach Buthrotum two other major fields of imitation or renovation are juxtaposed: first, the poetic, with a nod to Homer,[18] and, then, the political, particularly the refoundation of the Roman polity, since Actium will be—"will be" from Aeneas' perspective, "was" from that of Vergil's readers—the site of Octavius' decisive victory over Cleopatra and Antony in 31 B.C. Octavius and Vergil were both specialists in the theater of restoration, and Vergil links himself and his work with that of the poet of the Roman state (I mean Augustus) by not only mentioning Actium but by having Aeneas stage games there. This provides a post eventum precursor to Augustus' restoration of a temple to Apollo and his establishment of celebratory games at Actium not long after the naval battle in which he vanquished his foes.

Having landed in Epirus and heading for "the steep city of Buthrotum," Aeneas hears the "rumor of incredible events" that so "amazed" him (3.293, 294, 298; M 379, 380, 386):

"Priamiden Helenum Graias regnare per urbis
coniugio Aeacidae Pyrrhi sceptrisque potitum,
et patrio Andromachen iterum cessisse marito.
. . . .
progredior portu classis et litora linquens,
sollemnis cum forte dapes et tristia dona
ante urbem in luco falsi Simoentis ad undam
libabat cineri Andromache manisque vocabat
Hectoreum ad tumulum, viridi quem caespite inanem
et geminas, causam lacrimis, sacraverat aras"

(295–97, 300–305)

". . . that Helenus, the son
of Priam, is a king of Grecian cities,
that he has won the wife and scepter of
Pyrrhus, Achilles' son; that once again
Andromache is given to a husband
of her own country. . . .
. . . .
Just then—when I had left the harbor and
my boat, drawn up along the beaches—there,
within a grove that stood before the city,
alongside waves that mimed the Simois,
Andromache was offering to the ashes
a solemn banquet and sad gifts, imploring
the Shade of Hector's empty tomb that she
had raised out of green turf with double altars
and consecrated as a cause for tears."[19]

(M 381–86, 389–97)

Two key words are *falsi* and *inanem*. This is not Hector's tomb, for his body is not here: this is but a cenotaph, an "empty tomb."[20] By "false Simois" (a more literal rendering than Mandelbaum's) Vergil means that Helenus' Trojans *pretended*[21] that the river was called "Simois," the name of a river that flowed down from Mount Ida and into the river Scamander at Troy. The Epirote river, whatever its name—and it is significant that it remains nameless—is merely a screen on which the displaced Trojans project their impotent nostalgia.[22] It is as little the Simois as the cenotaph is the tomb of Hector. Or, Aeneas or someone may think, as little as

Helenus is Hector. We sense already that Buthrotum is a place of pretense and make-believe.

Such suspicions and uneasy feelings are shown to be well founded when Aeneas arrives at the city itself.

> "procedo et parvam Troiam simulataque magnis
> Pergama et arentem Xanthi cognomine rivum
> agnosco. Scaeaeque amplector limina portae"
>
> (349–51)

> "As I advance,
> I see a little Troy, a Pergamus
> that mimes the great one, and a dried-up stream
> that takes its name from Xanthus. I embrace
> the portals of the Scaean gates."
>
> (M 453–57)

This is a mock Troy, far different from the original, as the contrast little/great (*parua/magnis*) makes perfectly clear.[23] If before, further outside the city, there was a river of indeterminate size called Simois, here, instead of a roiling Xanthus[24] we have not even a real river (*flumen, fluvius, amnis*) but a dried-up (*arentem*) stream bed, gulch, or perhaps even artificial channel (*rivum*). What better way to convey the fact that Helenus' Ilium is nothing but a sterile replica?

Let us note that these images had significant overtones in ancient aesthetics. As symbolized by the spring Hippocrene on Helicon, the traditional Greek source of poetic inspiration, water was linked with poetic creation, and although the Alexandrian scholar-poet Callimachus, to whom most of the notable first-century B.C. Roman poets looked for instruction, advised his contemporaries to avoid common and impure watercourses, he (probably) and his followers (certainly) would not have denied that the great poets of the past had the force of swiftly flowing streams, whether they liked the comparison on not.[25] Horace compares Pindar to a rushing mountain stream,[26] and Homer was compared to an ocean.[27] In terms of the Homeric succession, the words *parua Troia* ("little Troy") take on particular significance. One of the poems in the epic cycle that followed the *Iliad* was known as the "Little Iliad," *Ilias Mikra* in Greek, *parua Ilias* in Latin.[28] In a famous section of his *Ars Poetica* (*Art of Poetry*) Horace describes how far short of his own promise, much less of Homer's achievements, the cyclic poet is bound to fall (136–39). Vergil suggests agreement with Horace's principles. Whatever type of Homeric imitation Vergil is engaged in, he indicates, it will be far different from that of a cyclic poet, the archetypal continuator and epigone.

The issue of imitation of things Greek is underscored in Book 3 by the peculiar circumstances of Helenus and Andromache. Andromache herself tells the story (321–36). Pyrrhus had taken Andromache as part of his war booty and had made her his concubine. Helenus, a priest, was not killed but enslaved. When Pyrrhus decided to marry Helen's daughter Hermione, he gave Andromache to Helenus, "a slave to a slave" (*me famulo famulamque Heleno transmisit habendam*, 3.329, M 428).[29] But Hermione had earlier been betrothed to Orestes, and the jilted and enraged Orestes murdered Pyrrhus, according to Andromache, "beside his [Pyrrhus'] father's altars" (*patrias . . . ad aras*, 332, M 432).[30] Before he died, however, the childless Pyrrhus made Helenus his successor in at least part of his realm.[31]

In other words, Andromache and Helenus owe everything they now have, everything they now are, to a Greek. While we should not despise the two Trojan survivors for their misfortunes, we are not supposed to be reacting to the fates of real individuals but considering them as examples or counter-examples for Aeneas and the Romans. In the context of imitation, their enterprise can hardly be admirable. They have simply renamed a Greek landscape and its features and built their citadels on Greek foundations.[32] Moreover, their Greek benefactor is himself third-rate. He is the son indeed of the archetypally Homeric Greek, Achilles, but what a falling off is there! Even Priam can draw the distinction between the murderer of Hector, noble and the "best of the Achaeans" for all that, and Pyrrhus (2.540–41). An alternate name, Neoptolemus, marks him as the epigone or successor *par excellence*. Working with material left over from Greeks already belated, what Helenus and Andromache create with their literally servile imaginations can hardly thrive or satisfy.

III. ACHAEMENIDES

Just as the actual fall of Troy lies outside the scope of the Homeric *Iliad*, so the founding of Rome is beyond the *Aeneid*. However many improperly reconstructed Troys are presented, the proper manner of refounding Troy is only suggested gradually, partially, and proleptically. Of one thing we can be sure: a more thorough-going renewal or restitution than that effected at Buthrotum will be required. The idea of renewal or restitution is one that obviously resonated in Vergil's Rome, for Augustus did more than restore temples and rededicate altars: the principate itself was supposed to be thought of as a *res publica restituta*—a "restoration" of the republic.

A possible model of restoration and renovation does occur in Book 3 at the level of poetic imitation or renovation.[33] Vergil renews Homer the way the Rome that will be built renews Troy. It is significant that the name "Roma" bears no relation to any name or part of Troy—not Ilium, not Pergamum. Neither is it a repeat of the doomed Thracian *Aeneadae*, a formulation that recalls the many Alexandrias Alexander left in the wake of his conquests, nor is it "New City," like Vergil's chosen residence, Neapolis (our Naples), or Dido's Karthago, both of which mean "new city" or "new town," the one in Greek, the other in Phoenician.

I take as a prime model of this more creative imitation the appearance of the character Achaemenides within the episode of the Trojans' visit to the land of the Cyclopes. These one-eyed, man-eating giants are known of course from the *Odyssey*, indeed from Odysseus' own narration (*Od.* 9.166–566). We are on Homeric ground here, as every reader in Vergil's day would have recognized. We hear of Polyphemus' cave and his sheep. Polyphemus appears, now missing the eye (658) whose destruction Odysseus himself describes with gruesome precision (*Od.* 9.316ff.). One could enumerate more details, but the point is clear: the Vergilian text gestures unmistakably to Homer's, making of *Odyssey* 9 this episode's preeminent intertext.

Against this backdrop of intertextuality, Vergil's innovation stands out clearly. Vergil interpolates a character, not merely inventing a name[34] but creating a character left behind uneaten, an event unreported by Homer. As mentioned above, this underscores the fact that as hero and expedition leader, Aeneas is considerably more responsible than Odysseus. His surpassing of Odysseus is all the more telling, even necessary, given the existence of Greek traditions that connected Odysseus, directly or via descendants, with the founding of Rome itself, and in one account in cooperation with Aeneas.[35] But unlike his own hero, who earlier in the book had taken characteristically prudent pains to avoid Ithaca so as not to risk a confrontation with an old enemy—ironically, for as we "know" from the *Odyssey*, Odysseus was not (yet) back home—Vergil in his poetic journey confronts Homer. When he describes some of the same figures and locales that occur in the *Odyssey*, he risks comparison with the

Greek poet. And by introducing a character whose very existence the Odyssean account excludes, Vergil is telling a "corrected" version of *Odyssey* 9. From the perspective of *Aeneid* 3, Odysseus—and Homer—overlooked a survivor left behind in Polyphemus' cave. Just as Aeneas and his crew save Achaemenides by stopping and picking him up, so Vergil revisits this particular spot of Homeric landscape and revises the original, thereby showing us, from within the microcosm of the poem, what true renovation is.

Ancient criticism assumed that writers would be schooled in and would school themselves in the imitation of their predecessors, but the wisest practitioners from Cicero, Horace, Seneca, and Quintilian to Petrarch and Erasmus knew that the writer who comes later must not aim just to equal his model, for then he is doomed to fall short. Rather, the ambitious writer must aim to surpass his precursor.[36] And to achieve this aim is no easy task, especially if your predecessor is the incomparable Homer. The first generations of Vergil's readers, even though Romans and partisans of Latin literature, often felt that Vergil had fallen short of Homer's achievements.[37] In this particular instance, Homer's description of Polyphemus and his gory gorgings will likely continue to hold our attention over Vergil's later, Latin account. We are, however, not here to hand out prizes or adjudicate a contest, not even to determine whose is the canonical description of Polyphemus. The point is to recognize and appreciate Vergil's revisionary strategies and ideals—imitation that involves augmentation and correction, reformulation and reframing. Such is Vergilian renovation.

While the path is only presented prophetically in the *Aeneid*, it is by comparably transformative means that Troy becomes Rome—after the mixing of Trojans and Latins and the transfer of traditions through Alba Longa. Juno exacts Jupiter's word that the name "Troy" itself will pass away (12.808 ff., esp. 828). Only after it is rendered almost unrecognizable is New Troy ready to become Rome. Again, it may be that the Achaemenides episode is only partially successful in achieving these grand ambitions.[38] Set against the evident shortcomings of the many mock Troys of Book 3, however, it can still represent Vergil's ideas, a freer mode of imitation and recreation that expands upon its original as it aspires to become greater.

CHAPTER 4

VARIUM ET MUTABILE
Voices of Authority in *Aeneid* 4

Sarah Spence

Of all the books in the *Aeneid*, Book 4 is the most famous. Not only have most people heard of its main character, Dido, but every reader of Vergil, from Augustine to Dante, Shakespeare to Chateaubriand, has a firmly held opinion about the story of Dido and Aeneas. While Book 4 belongs to Dido, then, Dido, in turn, belongs to every reader; this fact alone makes the prospect of writing an interpretive essay on the book a daunting task. Ironically, however, while Dido occupies center stage during the book, by the end of the epic she fails to control or even seriously divert its plot. This paradox of centrality and insignificance lies, I would suggest, at the very core of the book and offers a productive angle for critical study. While the fourth book is, indeed, the story of Dido and her demise, its authority and, consequently, *her* authority—by which I mean her ability to control, either politically, morally, or textually, the focus of attention—seem to be consistently undermined by the rest of the poem as she is eliminated from the main plot. My purpose here will not be to rehearse the most famous issues that have repeatedly vexed critics of the poem—although I will try to explicate these briefly for readers of this volume. Rather, I will focus on the events of the book from a particular perspective, namely how Book 4 engages the reader's attention through setting itself apart from the rest of the epic in terms of genre and theme.[1]

Broadly speaking, Book 4 is a tragic story about love and, as such, digresses from the rest of the poem even as it draws us toward it. Dido as a political figure (as she is first introduced) is replaced (or at least supplemented) by Dido as a romantic figure. The book opens with a scene in which Dido reveals her infatuation with Aeneas as she recognizes the "signs

of the old flame" (*veteris vestigia flammae*, 23, M 27) and her assertion that
she ought not break the oath she made to her first husband Sychaeus.[2] The
story unfolds on two planes, mortal and divine, as Dido's growing interest
in Aeneas is supported by her sister Anna (and, one may or may not infer,
Aeneas) and the gods who first encourage the affair (Juno and Venus
conspire to unite the two) then discourage it (Jupiter sends Mercury to
remind Aeneas that his true fate is to found Rome). The turning point of
the book occurs when Dido and Aeneas are brought together by Juno and
Venus to consummate their love in a cave. From this moment on, Dido
assumes they are married; Aeneas' beliefs are not made explicit. Dido's
attempts to talk to Aeneas about his seeming change of heart following
Mercury's visit form the book's central section, and the book ends with
Dido leveling a curse on Aeneas and his heirs, and committing suicide as
Aeneas sails away from Carthage toward Sicily and Rome.

Discussion of Book 4 usually revolves around the question of guilt[3]:
Who is guilty, and of what does that guilt consist? Where does the fault
lie, with Dido or Aeneas? Is it with Dido, who betrays her sworn vow to
her first husband, Sychaeus? (as first described in 1–29, M 1–37, and then
again, with the return of this theme in her final monologue before she
ascends the pyre, in 590–629, M 814–68); or is it with Aeneas who is, at
best, unclear in his intentions and, at worst, downright misleading, espe-
cially when behavior suitable to a Roman marriage is considered.[4] The
central scene at the cave serves as focus (160–72, M 213–28) as well as
the descriptions given of Aeneas by Iarbas and Mercury (213–18, M
285–92; 264–76, M 353–69). Francis Cairns suggests that the relationship
of Dido and Aeneas be understood in terms of the paradigm of the bad
king (in this case Dido) who suffers from a "spiritual disease" and the
good king (here Aeneas) who is not afflicted;[5] Kenneth Quinn similarly
argues that Dido surrenders pride and fame to passion while Aeneas does
not; Brooks Otis concludes that Aeneas is "finally and rightly the moral
superior of Dido" because he does not lose his humanity as a consequence
of their acquaintance.[6] According to Otis, Aeneas may have his flaws, yet
Book 4 demonstrates how his *pietas* enables him to overcome them and
so prove himself Dido's superior.

Christine Perkell, by contrast, argues, in tacit response to Otis, that it is
Aeneas, not Dido, who demonstrates "incomplete humanity."[7] Along similar
lines, R. C. Monti shows how Dido serves to highlight Aeneas' fall from
pietas.[8] In the present essay I will build on these readings by suggesting that

the equivalence between *pietas* and moral superiority found by Otis in Book 4 is precisely what the book fails to establish. On the contrary, the book causes the reader to identify with Dido, the enemy and the victim, despite her symbolic opposition to much that is Roman; it succeeds in doing this through both generic and thematic means that draw our attention to issues and concerns the rest of the epic often downplays. As a result, Book 4 demonstrates how Vergil consistently undermines readers' conventional assumptions and sympathies. My argument will focus not on the voices, per se, that resonate in and through Book 4 but rather on the ways in which those voices are granted or denied authority.[9] With this approach one can also utilize many of the standard readings of the book that tend to polarize the argument into one that either supports Dido in her love for Aeneas or criticizes her for distracting Aeneas from the larger task of founding Rome.[10]

I

However we approach it, Book 4 is a book apart. Even the Dido we get to know here is significantly different from the Dido we first meet in Book 1 or the Dido we see one last time in Book 6. The book can, therefore, serve us well in teaching since it can stand as a cohesive unit, while its integration into the epic overall poses important problems.[11] It is easy to get a sense of just how anomalous Book 4 is merely by looking at the introduction of Dido in Book 1. Here the description makes her parallel to Aeneas—a future Aeneas—as she rules and dispenses justice:

> tum foribus divae, media testudine templi,
> saepta armis solioque alte subnixa resedit.
> iura dabat legesque viris, operumque laborem
> partibus aequabat iustis aut sorte trahebat.
>
> (1.505–8)

> And then below the temple's central dome—
> facing the doorway of the goddess, guarded
> by arms—she took her place on a high throne.
> Dido was dealing judgments to her people
> and giving laws, apportioning the work
> of each with fairness or by drawing lots.
>
> (M 712–17)

Like Aeneas, Dido is a generous leader; like him, she too is an exile, widowed, an accidental leader of her people. The literary echoes evoked by her entrance in the lines that immediately precede these reinforce as well her role in supporting Aeneas: like Nausicaa in the *Odyssey* (*Od.* 6.102–9) Dido and her people are likened to Diana's naiad band (1.496–502). This introduction is highly positive, suggesting parallels between Dido and Aeneas, and granting to Dido a strong sense of power rendered benign by her resemblance to the youthful Nausicaa.

But the beginning of Book 4, the next time we see Dido at any length, tells another story. Intimations of change occur at the end of Book 1, where Dido is inflamed with love of Aeneas. By the start of Book 4 we have moved from observing her at some distance to watching her up close, and that change in our position as audience, with the accompanying shift in focus, is significant.[12] From the opening word *at* ("but") we know we are in a different, oppositional scenario. When *at* is coupled with the second word, *regina*, the text creates a temporary confusion, elaborated as the book proceeds, by suggesting an association between Dido and Juno. In the first book, Juno describes herself precisely as queen ("*Ast ego . . . regina*," 1.46); she is, by definition, the embodiment of the adversative, that is to say of *furor* as established in Book 1, standing as she does for conflict and disagreement with everything Aeneas comes to represent. The metaphor that follows to finish out the first sentence of Book 4, "She feeds the wound within her veins; she is eaten by a secret flame" (*vulnus alit venis et caeco carpitur igni*, M 2–3), only heightens this new parallel between Dido and Juno, as it suggests that even as Juno harbors old hurts within (*alta mente*, 1.26), so Dido now is being destroyed from the same inner place. Dido has changed from being parallel to Aeneas to being parallel to his antagonist, as is suggested to us by these few words at the start of Book 4.

And yet Book 4 shows the reader Dido's perspective; we see the story from her point of view. The first simile of the book suggests just this change in focus:

> uritur infelix Dido totaque vagatur
> urbe furens, qualis coniecta cerva sagitta,
> quam procul incautam nemora inter Cresia fixit
> pastor agens telis liquitque volatile ferrum
> nescius: illa fuga silvas saltusque peragrat
> Dictaeos; haeret lateri letalis harundo.
>
> (68–73)

Unhappy Dido burns. Across the city
she wanders in her frenzy—even as
a heedless hind hit by an arrow when
a shepherd drives for game with darts among
the Cretan woods and, unawares, from far
leaves winging steel inside her flesh; she roams
the forests and the wooded slopes of Dicte,
the shaft of death still clinging to her side.

(M 90–97)

Dido's suffering is visibly portrayed through the wording of the simile. How we are to understand the implicit equation between Aeneas and the shepherd is not obvious: the shepherd's unknowingness (nescius) for some readers makes him pitiable, for others, criminal. There is no easy reading of this image; yet the parallelism between Dido and Aeneas that existed in Book 1 is clearly gone, and Dido, as the victim, becomes the focus of sympathy while Aeneas becomes morally enigmatic.[13]

Images of Dido as a victim of sacrifice reinforce such a confusion. Introduced in the second line of the book, the image of love's poison as a consuming inner fire is strongly suggestive of sacrificial imagery, a connection underscored by Vergil as he juxtaposes the image in lines 60–66 with Dido's performance of just such a sacrifice:

ipsa tenens dextra pateram pulcherrima Dido
candentis vaccae media inter cornua fundit,
aut ante ora deum pinguis spatiatur ad aras,
instauratque diem donis, pecudumque reclusis
pectoribus inhians spirantia consulit exta.
heu vatum ignarae mentes! quid vota furentem,
quid delubra iuvant? est mollis flamma medullas
interea et tacitum vivit sub pectore vulnus.

(60–66)

Lovely
Dido holds the cup in her right hand;
she pours the offering herself, midway
between a milk-white heifer's horns. She studies
slit breasts of beasts and reads their throbbing guts.
But oh the ignorance of augurs! How

> can vows and altars help one wild with love?
> Meanwhile the supple flame devours her marrow;
> within her breast the silent wound lives on.
>
> (M 81–89)

The verses are strikingly ambiguous. Line 65 reintroduces the image of the inner fire that is destroying Dido (*mollis flamma*, "a supple flame") as if to suggest that the fire is also that of the sacrifice she is performing. It is not until the end of the next line that the reader can be sure that the fire is metaphoric, not literal. This ambiguity suggests that Dido is, herself, the sacrificial victim. But this in turn raises the question of what Dido is being sacrificed to, and to this question, again, there is no easy answer. Is she a sacrifice to the Roman mission and so to Venus' cause? Or is she a sacrifice, instead, to Juno's purpose, as Iris' clipping of the lock at the end of the book would suggest?[14]

The text also encourages us to side with Dido as it forces us to stay with her long after Aeneas himself has left. Slightly beyond the halfway point of the book (line 396 out of 705) we are told that Aeneas, though wanting to comfort Dido, reluctantly decides to "turn back to his fleet" (*revisit classem*, 396, M 545); it is at this point that he turns away from Dido for the last time. As a result, we, not he, attend to her while she dies. Not only are we privy to her final curse on Aeneas and his heirs (590–629, M 814–68), but we are present throughout the final scene as she climbs on the funeral pyre and commits suicide; even her nurse and her sister Anna, while present at her death, are not as faithful to her as we as readers are forced to be.

Even if some readers withhold sympathy from Dido, all must acknowledge the change in narrative tack taken by Vergil and address its significance. Two interrelated rhetorical strategies can be helpful in this discussion: the use of tragic form and the use of allusion, both textual and historic. These factors work to position the audience differently from anywhere else in the text, forcing us to acknowledge a shift in perspective from that of the earlier books, and thereby putting into question the locus of power and authority.

II

The allusion to and use of tragedy noted by many readers of Book 4 create a form of generic interference that sets this book in a different place from the rest of the epic and causes the reader to sympathize further with Dido. Richard Heinze, Kenneth Quinn, Viktor Pöschl, J. L. Moles, and Frances Muecke all argue that the structure of Book 4 invokes an Aristotelian understanding of tragedy since it is ordered so that it functions, for the audience, much as tragedy was thought to, forcing that audience into an ironic, even cathartic, relationship with the text.[15] In *Poetics* 6, Aristotle gives the following definition of tragedy:

> Tragedy is a representation of a serious, complete action which has magnitude, in embellished speech, with each of its elements [used] separately in the [various] parts [of the play]; [represented] by people acting and not by narration; accomplishing by means of pity and terror the catharsis of such emotions. . . . But the most important of these is the structure of the incidents. . . . Consequently the incidents, i.e. the plot, are the end of tragedy, and the end is the most important of all . . . the most important things with which a tragedy enthralls [us] are parts of plot—reversals and recognitions. . . . So plot is the origin and as it were the soul of tragedy, and the characters are secondary. (6.1449b25–50b1)[16]

Comparing Dido to specific figures from tragedy, Muecke argues that Book 4 fits the tragic mold in its employment of foreshadowing, dramatic irony, and use of tragic figures. Moreover, the book can be divided into five acts (without a prologue), it focuses on a tragic hero that fits Aristotle's description, the plot is of the best type, complex, "where the change of fortune is accompanied by *peripeteia* or recognition or both" (*Poetics* 10.1452a16 ff.) since "recognition accompanied by peripeteia will involve either pity or fear and tragedy is by definition a mimesis of actions that rouse these emotions" (*Poetics* 11.1452b32 ff.). The plot suffers a *peripeteia* after Mercury visits Aeneas and announces that he must leave; the speeches in lines 305–87 (M 410–532) make clear that the action has shifted dramatically from one *telos* to another. In addition, discussions of Dido's guilt often suggest that it is seen as tragic *hamartia*, or moral flaw.[17] In sum, Book 4 has all of the features of an Aristotelian tragedy, from *hamartia* (*Poetics* xiii.4) to *peripeteia* (xi.1–6) to *anagnorisis* (x.3), the whole achieving *katharsis* (vi.2) through pity and fear.

These formal features of tragedy in relation to Book 4 have been much studied. I will therefore focus instead on the many allusions that contribute to the reader's tragic anticipation. The most salient elements of tragedy are the text's references and allusions to actual tragic dramas; even allusions to nontragic texts help to establish a sense of terrible foreknowledge on the part of the audience, as the place assumed by the audience in the interpretation of such allusion is more that of the involved audience of tragedy than the observing audience of epic. This use of allusion functions both within and outside the poem itself. Within the poem, parallels are set up that create anticipation on the part of the audience. For example, the language of Book 4 makes it clear that the fall of Dido is comparable to the fall of Troy as described in Book 2. Both burn, both are destroyed by an outsider, both are left by Aeneas. Even as the rhetorical prowess of Sinon enabled the Trojan horse to be admitted to the city, and thus caused the final, nocturnal destruction, so it is Aeneas' long saga of his trials at Troy and after in Books 2 and 3 that causes Dido to fall more and more in love with him and allows him to "infiltrate" further and further into her soul and city. Textual echoes implicitly equate the Trojan horse that opens to reveal a destructive force with the effect of love on Dido; specific connection between the destruction of Troy and of Dido and Carthage is made at 669–71 (M 921–24).

But this parallel is not sustained. That is, while Aeneas, in his version of the story of the last night of Troy in Book 2, is the victim of Greek guile, he becomes, in the metaphorical replay in Book 4, the very exemplar of that Greek guile, and Dido becomes his victim. We as readers recognize the allusions to Book 2 and, therefore, know long before Dido does that she and her city, like Troy, will burn. How we are to interpret the fact that Aeneas has become the aggressor rather than the defender is left enigmatic; what is made perfectly clear through the intratextual allusion is that Dido is to be read as the victim. We in the audience can do nothing but watch the tragedy unfold.

Such patterns of allusion lead to intellectual apprehension of the tragedy on the part of the audience that extends, in some cases, to a tragic catharsis. Within Book 4 Dido is initially likened to female characters from epic (Helen, Calypso, Circe, Arete, Penelope), and when echoes of her strongest model, Medea, arise, it is as Apollonius' Medea that she first appears. Vergil's use of Apollonius' *Argonautica*, though epic, is also important in establishing the tragic context. The scene from the *Argonautica* (3.1–110) in which the three goddesses, Hera, Athena, and Aphrodite, conspire to inflame Medea with love in order to help Jason, is alluded to by Vergil as he has the two lead goddesses of the text, Venus and Juno, conspire in a similar way to use Dido. The difference here is that Venus and

Juno have conflicting agendas, while in the *Argonautica* all three goddesses share the single hope of helping Jason. Our recognition of the source leads to a form of anticipation best described in dramatic terms.

Another comparable example of the use Vergil makes of allusion, also from Apollonius, comes in the critical scene in which Dido and Aeneas carry out the goddesses' schemes and venture into the countryside for a hunt that ends with the consummation of their love in a cave. Jason and Medea likewise have a rushed and ill-omened marriage ceremony in a cave, agreed to by both sides as a strategy to save Medea's life from her Colchian pursuers (*Arg.* 4.1128–69). The context of this scene in the *Argonautica* goes back even further to Homer's *Odyssey*. The cave is on the island of the Phaeacians, the same island where Odysseus flirted with Nausicaa and from which he was sent safely to his homeland. Not only has Vergil introduced Dido as a second Nausicaa in Book 1, but even as she prepares to head out for this hunt she is likened to a naive and halting maiden, as Charles Segal has pointed out, hesitating at the threshold of her marriage chamber.[18]

> reginam thalamo cunctantem ad limina primi
> Poenorum exspectant, ostroque insignis et auro
> stat sonipes ac frena ferox spumantia mandit.
>
> (133–35)

> But while the chieftains
> of Carthage wait at Dido's threshold, she
> still lingers in her room. Her splendid stallion,
> in gold and purple, prances, proudly champing
> his foaming bit.
>
> (M 177–81)

If Dido starts the poem as Nausicaa, she ends it as Apollonius' Medea, and, like Nausicaa and Medea both, she too will be disappointed by a stranger with whom she has fallen in love. Through the intertextual overlays of both Homer and Apollonius we know what will happen to Dido by the end of the hunt long before she does; as a result, we are put in the position described by Aristotle of the tragic audience, of feeling pity and fear.[19]

Allusions to specific tragedies occur mostly toward the end of the book. The comparisons of Dido to the maddened Orestes of Aeschylus' *Oresteia* (specifically *The Libation Bearers*) and Pentheus of Euripides'

Bacchae (Aen. 4.469, 471; M 647, 650) have long baffled critics. Certainly these comparisons fit the tragic quality of Book 4. But why these two figures in particular? Vergil's asserted goal for his protagonist is to found the city of Rome, and the founding of the city is opposed throughout the Aeneid by furor in various guises (Juno, Dido, Turnus, among others). Significantly, both the Oresteia and the Bacchae deal, if in opposite ways, with the relationship between furor and the city. Through the suffering of the hero, the audience of these plays learns about the power of furor. In the Bacchae Agave and the audience learn this at Pentheus' expense. Pentheus learns only too late that Dionysus' power cannot be denied. Orestes' murder of his mother, Clytemnestra, provides a context for the institution of Athenian justice. He avoids certain death through the intervention of Athena, and it is she, not Orestes himself, who acknowledges, with the audience, the critical social importance of the Furies-turned-Eumenides. Even as the Oresteia uses mythopoetic elements of tragedy to explain the moral basis for Athens, so Book 4 of the Aeneid uses intertextuality and repetition to involve the audience in a tragic reinterpretation of the moral construction of Augustan Rome. If Dido's city perishes through her furor, the role of furor in the fate of Aeneas' city remains still undetermined. Vergil's references to tragic figures in Book 4 clarify the dangerous but seemingly inevitable role of furor in the founding of a city.

The historic context of Dido's tragedy makes the story even more entrapping for the audience. While the love between Dido and Aeneas is historically unfounded, the animosity between Dido's city of Carthage and Aeneas' of Rome, and the destruction of Carthage by Rome, set the fictional interaction between these two leaders in a historic context. Given the outcome of the Punic Wars and Augustus' armed opposition to Cleopatra and Antony, this story would seem to fit into that kind of mold: tragic, yes, because the woman will die, but a necessary event, much less significant than the journey it allows the hero to complete. Taken historically, also, the reference to a regina will recall yet another queen, Cleopatra, who will be specifically referred to as such in Book 8 and who, for a Roman audience, represented a genuine menace. The entire text of Book 4 can then be discussed in this context, with reference to the mention of Carthage in the opening lines of Book 1 and the fact that the poem as a whole seems to hover not between Troy and Latium but between Troy, Latium, and Carthage. The double beginning granted the poem suggests that the Troy to Latium journey is better understood as a Latium/Carthage opposition, personified in the characters of Aeneas and Juno, and understood historically through the events

of the Punic Wars, in which Rome conquers Carthage, and the battle of
Actium, in which Octavian's victory over Antony is presented as a replay
of the Punic Wars.[20] Historic precedents, then, for siding with Rome over
its enemies are clearly evoked in the opening of the epic and alluded to as
Dido recalls the figure of Cleopatra. In its introduction of Dido as the per-
sonification of Carthage, in other words, the text insists that Aeneas must
and will destroy her.[21] By introducing her as a romantic involvement,
however, Vergil complicates our reading of that history. From the start of
the poem she is cast in a tragic position from which she cannot escape,
and we, as audience, are cast in an equally dubious position of identifying
with the enemy.[22] The destruction of a city by a city bears little pathos
compared to the destruction of a woman by a man.

At the least, the tragic elements of Book 4 cause an awareness of a
change in perspective. Moreover, I would argue that the changes they
signal force us as readers into a new relationship with Dido and, as a result,
with Aeneas. At the same time issues related to the moral purpose of the
epic as a whole are raised as the question of the role of *furor* is introduced.
As tragic hero Dido would seem to embody that *furor*; as tragic audience
we would seem to be sympathetic to it as a force that arouses pity and fear.

III

Perhaps the most powerful example of the quality of difference fore-
grounded by Book 4 is the way in which paradigms established earlier in
the epic are overturned through the course of Dido's story. What Book 4
succeeds in doing is establishing a stance that marks it as different, while
simultaneously asserting certain thematic continuities with the rest of the
epic.[23] A brief comparison of some telling speeches will clarify this seeming
paradox. At the start of the epic Juno's opening speech is pitted in numer-
ous ways against the speeches that immediately follow, and even though
hers is the first speech of the epic it is not granted authority. Juno complains
of a lack of power, and her speech demonstrates the accuracy of her com-
plaint since the storm she initiates—which brings Aeneas to Carthage—is
immediately quieted through the speech and action of Neptune, as he rises
from the waves and silences the storm. Neptune's power through speech
is, in the first simile of the work, likened to that of an orator, and that
image is then used to inform our readings of the speeches of both Aeneas
and Jupiter that immediately follow. In these instances, the male figure is

aligned with a power that is exercised through the use of language that can order and control emotions.[24] The association of reason with power through language is diametrically opposed to the *furor* and powerlessness associated with Juno's speech.

In Book 4 there occurs a series of speeches in which the source of authority is not so easily determined. As in Book 1, we see male authority figures at first associated with speech and power, a power reinforced by their physical superiority: Jupiter "turned his eyes upon the royal walls" (*oculos . . . ad moenia torsit / regia*, 220–21, M 294–95) when he hears Iarbas' prayer; Mercury, immediately following, flies down to talk to Aeneas, and the descent of his flight is emphasized in the route he takes by Atlas "who props up heaven with his crest," (*caelum qui vertice fulcit*, 247, M 331) until, "like a bird" (*avi similis*), he lands "headlong" (*praeceps*) in the waters near Carthage.[25] By contrast, the emotional speech of Rumor (*Fama*) reaches from earth to heaven:

> Fama, malum qua non aliud velocius ullum:
> mobilitate viget virisque adquirit eundo,
> parva metu primo, mox sese attollit in auras
> ingrediturque solo et caput inter nubila condit.
>
> (174–77)

> Then, swiftest of all evils, Rumor runs
> straightway through Libya's mighty cities—Rumor,
> whose life is speed, whose going gives her force.
> Timid and small at first, she soon lifts up
> her body in the air. She stalks the ground;
> her head is hidden in the clouds.
>
> (M 229–34)

Yet there is no denying the effectiveness of Rumor's speech. Moreover, the most powerful speech in the book, Dido's curse against Aeneas, is also highly emotional and all the more powerful because of it.[26] Once again drawing on Aristotle, in this case the *Rhetoric*, one could argue that the speeches in Book 4 show the effectiveness of pathos; in other words, the power of a speech does not reside only in its logos.[27] In order to be effective, the emotions of the audience and the moral integrity of the speaker must both be brought to bear. The authority the text grants to a speech devoid of emotional affect, such as that of Neptune or Jupiter in Book 1, is questioned by the powerful impact allotted the speeches in Book 4 that arouse the readers' emotions. As a consequence, Aeneas' farewell speech contrasts hollowly with Dido's.[28] His speech is comparable to that of Neptune in Book 1, but its effect is of weakness, not of authority, since it fails to engage the emotions of the audience and raises questions about the moral integrity of the speaker. Commentators such as R. G. Austin, therefore, find themselves constrained in their efforts to defend the speech.[29]

Power, such as it is here, is associated in this book with emotional force and, as far as the speeches are concerned, that power is linked with the unsanctioned emotions stirred up by speakers like Rumor (*Fama*) and Dido. Most strikingly, the author enters into this debate by introducing his own voice in lines 401 and 408 (M 551,561), first to address the reader, then to address Dido herself. In each case the authorial intrusion suggests a sympathy with Dido that enlists the emotions of the reader, since we are encouraged to see the Trojans as mere ants in the distance, while Dido, the victim of cruel love, is brought close to us by apostrophe:[30]

> migrantis cernas totaque ex urbe ruentis:
> ac velut ingentem formicae farris acervum
> cum populant hiemis memores tectoque reponunt,
> it nigrum campis agmen praedamque per herbas
> convectant calle angusto; pars grandia trudunt
> obnixae frumenta umeris, pars agmina cogunt
> castigantque moras, opere omnis semita fervet.
> quis tibi tum, Dido, cernenti talia sensus,
> quosve dabas gemitus, cum litora fervere late
> prospiceres arce ex summa, totumque videres
> misceri ante oculos tantis clamoribus aequor!
>
> (401–11)

> And one could see them
> as, streaming, they rushed down from all the city:
> even as ants, remembering the winter,
> when they attack a giant stack of spelt
> to store it in their homes; the black file swarms
> across the fields; they haul the plunder through
> the grass on narrow tracks; some strain against
> the great grains with their shoulders, heaving hard;
> some keep the columns orderly and chide

the loiterers; the whole trail boils with work.
What were your feelings, Dido, then? What were
the sighs you uttered at that sight, when far
and wide, from your high citadel, you saw
the beaches boil and turmoil take the waters,
with such a vast uproar before your eyes?

(M 551–65)

The comparison between the Trojans and the ants as seen through our eyes makes the Trojans seem diminished and inconsequential. Moreover, Dido is explicitly described as looking down at the Trojans. Dido, the audience, and the emotional are each granted the superior position associated in the rest of the epic with power.[31] In conclusion, Dido's speeches have power through an alternative source, *furor*, rather than through *imperium* and *pietas*, which are granted power in Book 1.

IV

Dido's "last word" occurs in Book 6 where her power, this time, resides in silence. In this coda to Book 4, speech and its authority are again at issue, and Dido's final appearance here summarizes themes Vergil introduced in the earlier book. Here, in a scene modeled on the meeting between Ajax and Odysseus in *Odyssey* 11 (noted as early as Servius, ad *Aen.* 6.468), Dido, like Ajax, remains silent. In the *Odyssey*, Ajax stands at a remove from Odysseus as he speaks to the heroes in the Underworld.[32] Even when addressed directly Ajax refuses to answer:

> but went off after
> the other souls of the perished dead men, into the darkness.
> There, despite his anger, he might have spoken, or I might
> have spoken to him. (*Od.* 11.563–66)

Similarly, as Aeneas pleads, Dido merely stares:

> "quem fugis? extremum fato quod te adloquor hoc est."
> talibus Aeneas ardentem et torva tuentem
> lenibat dictis animum lacrimasque ciebat.
> illa solo fixos oculos aversa tenebat

ne magis incepto vultum sermone movetur
quam si dura silex aut stet Marpesia cautes.
                    (6.466–71)

                Whom do you flee?
This is the last time fate will let us speak."
These were the words Aeneas, weeping, used,
.trying to soothe the burning, fierce-eyed Shade.
She turned away, eyes to the ground, her face
no more moved by his speech than if she stood
as stubborn flint or some Marpessan crag.
                    (M 613–19)

This Odyssean intertext profits from being coupled with another, internal text, as the phrase *solo fixos oculos aversa tenebat* is used of Minerva in Book 1, when she denies the appeals of the Trojan women (1.482). In each case, despite silence (or indeed because of it), a tremendous power is projected. Ajax represents the one unresolved relationship for Odysseus; Minerva will not be appeased. Dido, too, stands silently, powerfully, in her refusal to respond to Aeneas.

In Dido's first appearance she is likened to Nausicaa and Diana; in her last to Ajax and Minerva. Comparison of these descriptions is revealing. Although Dido is observed at a distance in both, her authority nonetheless has grown, if we judge solely from the intertexts used to describe her. As Minerva is alluded to throughout the *Aeneid*, yet remains strikingly elusive, so she exerts much silent power.[33] Dido, too, is now silent, but the text suggests that, like Minerva, she does have power. Even though the perspective shifts at Dido's death back to the epic angle of the other books, Dido's appearance in Book 6 suggests that the power granted her in Book 4 has made an enduring, if enigmatic, impact. What the story of Dido problematizes is the moral quality and authority associated with the power of *furor*. Dido, initially "good," becomes the embodiment of *furor*; it is perhaps for this reason that she is characterized as *infelix* ("unlucky"). But her capitulation to *furor* is not, as we might expect, aligned with alienation from the audience. On the contrary, we are drawn along with her, and our sympathy forces us to reconsider the implied analogy between good and bad, *pietas* and *furor*.

Vergil constructs his text in such a way as to make Book 4, when seen from certain angles, narratologically excisable. Book 3 ends in Sicily, Book

5 picks up en route to Sicily, where Book 3 left off. The detour caused by Juno that leads to Aeneas' trip to Carthage is as much of a digression as is his love for Dido. The text comes full circle as Aeneas returns to Sicily to celebrate the anniversary of the death of his father who died there the year before, and the work, to a large extent, closes over the whole affair with Dido, as Aeneas gets back on track. Except, of course, that this is exactly the opposite of how the work is read. Books 3 and 5 make nothing of the impact made by Book 4, for the reasons I have sketched above. Like a memory that refuses to fade, Book 4 insists on being remembered throughout the text. Memory, of course, and wounds of memory, are the domain of Juno, who represents the antagonistic level of the text because of the wrongs done to her in the past.[34] Although the predominant narrative suggests that Book 4 has no lasting authority, a reading of the whole poem reveals that it does. Book 4 grants voice to the cause of *furor* but, more than that, to the degree that it enlists sympathy for Dido, it engages us as audience on the side of difference and against the cause of empire, even if only temporarily. It suggests that the voices of the text, and the power that goes with those voices, are many, not one. On every level Book 4 represents conflict with the rest of the text—a conflict that cannot be easily resolved.[35]

In sum, the voices in Book 4 are many and varied and their interaction and authority are even more so. Book 4 grants power to a voice denigrated elsewhere in the epic, a voice associated more with Juno than with Jupiter. In this book Vergil gives a hearing to Dido's voice and in so doing permits the question of shifting perspectives and authority to be addressed. Dido remains the *Aeneid*'s most compelling character, as even Augustine acknowledges in his *Confessions*. While the saint explicitly regrets that he wept over Dido's death in his youth (*Conf.* 1.xiii.22), he nonetheless models a scene in Book 5 on the parting of Dido and Aeneas, likening his own mother to Dido through a series of allusions to the fourth book of the *Aeneid* (*Conf.* 5.viii.15). If even Augustine cannot write Dido off, or out, it is of little wonder that few other readers can either.

CHAPTER 5

AENEID 5
Poetry and Parenthood

Joseph Farrell

The main events and themes of Book 5 relate powerfully to the motif of generations. The hero holds memorial celebrations on the anniversary of his father's death; in the games that mark these celebrations, Trojan contestants are linked by their names and characters to the prominent Roman families that they will found; and the hero's son leads the other boys, who recall by name and appearance their distinguished Trojan ancestors, in a performance of what future Roman generations will call the "Troy game." The games of Book 5 are also notable for having occasioned at least one classic critical assessment in modern times of Vergil's epic technique vis à vis that of his greatest model, Homer; and in recent years, students of epic have come almost reflexively to figure the relationship between Homer and Vergil as one between father and son, full of anxiety and Oedipal overtones. Thus the dominant theme of the poetry itself finds its parallel in a leading theme of the critical discourse that has grown up around it. As a result, the fifth book of the *Aeneid* offers an ideal opportunity to study the mutually defining relationship between poetry and interpretation.

We may begin by inquiring into the relationship between the hero and the father whose death these games commemorate. How do these games, this poetry, illuminate that relationship?

It is no secret that Aeneas has been viewed by many readers as, shall we say, heroically challenged. This is particularly the case in the first half of the poem, in which we are introduced to a hero who longs to have died at Troy (1.92–101, M 131–43), who narrates a long sequence of debilitating experiences beginning with the traumatic final night of his native city and continuing with an erroneous sequence of wanderings lasting seven years[1] and taking him throughout the Mediterranean in search of a new home. Instead of a home Aeneas finds himself in a foreign country and becomes involved in a love affair from which he extracts himself with difficulty, precipitating the suicide of a woman who had generously received him and his people into her own city. These events, the narrative of Books 1–4, paint the picture not of a commanding figure who would, by establishing a revised pattern of heroism, call into being a new world order and give his name to the Roman national epic, but rather of a helpless refugee unable to escape from a home world that has irrevocably vanished and to find his way in the unfamiliar lands beyond.

It is in Book 5 that Aeneas begins to reassemble the pieces of his shattered life and to come into his own as the leader that he must be. He does so, significantly, by returning to the point from which he had departed just before the poem opens, that is, by retracing his steps to Sicily, the last stop before the storm at sea that takes the Trojans to Carthage in Book 1.[2] The narrative thus, and in a rather obvious way, "starts over" in Book 5, and, in the process, sets Aeneas moving, though not without obstacle, in the direction that fate requires.

He moves, moreover, under his own leadership. Previously in the poem Aeneas had relied heavily on his father, Anchises, for moral support and practical guidance as he labored to take his Trojans to a new home. Anchises, of course, both in his initial refusal to leave Troy at all and in his frustrated efforts subsequently to understand the will of the gods, often failed to provide his son with the guidance he needed; but it is after and in fact immediately upon Anchises' death that Aeneas involves himself in the most grievous error of all, his Carthaginian sojourn. The return to Anchises' grave must, then, represent an effort on Aeneas' part to reestablish some connection with the father who had been his moral compass or, alternatively, to come to terms with and to assume the mantle of leadership that has awaited him since his father's death.

Aeneas' growth as a leader is made clear, tragically and painfully, by definite tokens. In Book 3 when his pilot, Palinurus, is named for the first time, he and his band are unable to find their way in bad weather.

> "continuo venti voluunt mare magnaque surgunt
> aequora, dispersi iactamur gurgite vasto;
> involvere diem nimbi et nox umida caelum
> abstulit, ingeminant abruptis nubibus ignes,

> excutimur cursu et caecis erramus in undis.
> ipse diem noctemque negat discernere caelo
> nec meminisse viae media Palinurus in unda."
>
> (3.196–202)

> "And we are scattered, tossed upon the vast
> abyss; clouds cloak the day; damp night annuls
> the heavens; frequent lightning fires flash
> through the tattered clouds; cast from our course, we wander
> across the blind waves. Even Palinurus
> can not tell day from night upon the heavens,
> can not recall our way among the waters."
>
> (M 260–66)

Palinurus' frustration follows and is of a piece with Anchises' confused inability just a few lines previously to interpret an oracle. Apollo of Delos had commanded the Trojans to "seek out [their] ancient mother" (*antiquam exquirite matrem*, 3.96, M 128)—a command that should steer the Trojans toward Italy, but that Anchises wrongly interprets as indicating Crete. In these cases neither of the hero's principal guides, his helmsman and his father, can provide the direction that he needs. At the beginning of Book 5, however, Palinurus reappears to state confidently in the face of another storm that he can indeed find his way back to Sicily, which he successfully does; and in the main episode of the book, Aeneas himself begins to take on the role of father that has been symbolically vacant since Anchises' death. This apparently cheering development ends tragically, however, as Aeneas' succession to roles of leadership real and symbolic, is completed at the end of the book. Just as his accession to the role of father required Anchises' death, so must the reader witness the death of Palinurus before Aeneas himself can occupy the helmsman's position in the stern of the ship for the final passage to Italy (827–71, M 1093–152).

If such symbols mean anything, then whatever has happened in Book 5 seems to have imbued the hero for the first time with an ability to dispense with the support of lesser figures, to lay the ghost of his father to rest, and to lead under his own auspices. Certainly the emphasis placed by Book 5 on Aeneas' paternity, real and symbolic, appears in many forms. As is often noted, the word "father" occurs more often in this book than in any other part of the poem.[3] It is equally clear, however, that whatever success Aeneas may enjoy in the safe and restricted play world of Anchises' memorial games, the son does not manage to supplant his dead father altogether. The games end abruptly when the Trojan women—themselves repeatedly designated as "mothers"—are goaded by Juno through her minion Iris to set fire to the ships in an effort to prevent the last leg of the Trojans' journey to Italy. This event plunges Aeneas into depression and indecision, revealing that he is still so unready for leadership he cannot even recognize as such the good advice given him by Nautes, one of the Trojan elders—namely, to leave behind any who are unwilling to face the rigors of the Italian wars that lie ahead, but to press on with only the hardiest members of his band. Only when Anchises himself appears in a dream and gives Aeneas precisely the same advice is the hero confirmed in the course he will follow. When Anchises adds that his son should undertake a journey to the Underworld to confer with him about the challenges he will face in Italy, we understand that the symbolic processes of expiation, reconciliation, and growth that inform Book 5 have not been enough—that the death of the father still weighs on the son, that he can successfully contend with this loss only by overcoming it in fact, which he does in the katabasis episode of Book 6.

Thus the relationship between Aeneas and Anchises is fraught with contradictions. The hero's father is both a comfort and a burden to him, a source of guidance and inspiration as well as an insurmountable challenge. Comfort is what Aeneas remembers most when he briefly tells Dido about Anchises' death:

> "hinc Drepani me portus et inlaetabilis ora
> accipit. hic pelagi tot tempestatibus actus
> heu, genitorem, omnis curae casusque levamen,
> amitto Anchisen. hic me, pater optime, fessum
> deseris, heu, tantis nequiquam erepte periclis!"
>   (3.707–18)

> "Then Drepanum's unhappy coast and harbor
> receive me. It is here—after all
> the tempests of the sea—I lose my father,
> Anchises, stay in every care and crisis.
> For here, o best of fathers, you first left
> me to my weariness, alone—Anchises,
> you who were saved in vain from dreadful dangers."
>   (M 915–21)

But later, in taking his leave of Dido, Aeneas reveals (what the reader has not been shown) that he also regards his father in a more frightening aspect:

> "me patris Anchisae, quotiens umentibus umbris
> nox operit terras, quotiens astra ignea surgunt,
> admonet in somnis et turbida terret imago"
>
> (4.351–53)

> "For often as the night conceals the earth
> with dew and shadows, often as the stars
> ascend, afire, my father's anxious[4] image
> approaches me in dreams. Anchises warns
> and terrifies . . ."
>
> (M 477–81)

And, of course, the image of the hero carrying the crippled old man out of the burning city, with the boy Ascanius struggling along beside, is perhaps the most potent expression of Aeneas' position as father and son, gifted and burdened with responsibility and leadership.[5]

Turning from these literary contradictions to the metaliterary relationship between Vergil and Homer, we find that similar patterns can be discerned. If indeed we see Aeneas as a hero manqué, we are judging him by the standard not of Anchises, but of Odysseus and Achilles; and if we find Vergil wanting as an epic poet, we are judging him in comparison to Homer. Aeneas, unlike the Greek heroes on whom he is modeled, is the social hero par excellence—which to some has meant he is no hero at all. By the same token Vergil is, so to speak, the imitative poet par excellence—which to some has meant he is no poet at all, or at any rate a severely impaired one. Neither Aeneas nor Vergil truly stands on his own: each depends on some important predecessor against whom we are invited to measure the success of both hero and poet. In contrast Homer, like his heroes, appears to us in splendid isolation. Just as Odysseus and, even more so, Achilles win undying fame alone and on their own terms, Homer too stands apart. To insist that Homer's isolation is only apparent because we can know hardly anything about the long tradition from which he descends, about the names or qualities of his poetic fathers, is beside the point; for these conditions can never change enough to alter our basic conception of Homer as an, and in some sense the, "original" poet. Vergil is, on the other hand, frankly derivative, and recognition of this fact has long been one of the defining parameters with which all readers of the *Aeneid* have had to contend.

The parallel experiences of Aeneas, the derivative hero, and of Vergil, the derivative poet, speak to the inherent ambivalences of the father/son relationship. It is no accident that Book 5's extensive imitation of a Homeric episode involves a series of contests.[6] Aeneas' succession of Anchises is a far from uncomplicated matter. One infers that the motif of the games signals that "pater Aeneas" is in some sense competing with "pater Anchises." By the same token Vergil's decision to try his hand at an episode of games signals not merely homage to, but competition with, Homer as well. Servius, the most important of Vergil's surviving ancient critics, begins his commentary on the *Aeneid* by stating that Vergil's intention in composing it was "to imitate Homer and to praise Augustus through his ancestors." This remark does not explicitly represent imitation of Homer as simply paying homage to a literary ancestor, nor do Servius' comments elsewhere suggest that he viewed literary paternity and filiation as an uncomplicated relationship. In fact, along with other ancient critics, he more readily speaks in terms of rivalry, and judges Homer as beyond even Vergil's reach. Of Book 5 in particular he states that "the greater part of this book is taken from Homer, for everything that our poet mentions can be seen happening around the tomb of Patroclus [i.e., in *Iliad* 23], except there you have a chariot race, here a boat race." It is difficult not to infer from such a remark that Servius regarded Vergil's dependence on Homer in this book as transparent, somewhat excessive, and perhaps even unsuccessful.

This opinion has played a dominant role in the assessment of Book 5 and of the poem as a whole. To be sure, the passage of time has involved some critical ebb and flow; certainly Vergil has occasionally enjoyed the ascendancy over Homer that Servius denies him. This ascendancy, however, has tended to coincide with periods when Homer's poetry was not well known in the West, and it is generally correct to state that Vergil has most often been viewed as Homer's not altogether successful imitator. In fact, Book 5—possibly because it is so openly imitative of Homer—has often been felt to be one of the less successful books of the poem.[7]

Early in this century, however, Richard Heinze in his epoch-making study of Vergil's epic technique subjected Anchises' memorial games to a detailed scrutiny vis à vis Homer's funeral games for Patroclus in order to illuminate what is most distinctive about Vergil's style.[8] For Heinze, Vergil departs from Homer in order to impose a classical aesthetic canon on the exuberance of earlier epic. Thus the eight events of Homer's games are trimmed to four; Homer's simple arrangement of contests, which moves from longer to shorter episodes, becomes a more elaborate, interlocking sequence of major and minor events; and the entire narrative moves to a more powerful climax in the archery contest. Even the individual events become more complex, as in the case of the boxing match.[9] In Homer's contest, Epeius boasts that he will defeat any challenger, and then proceeds to do just that. Dares in *Aeneid* 5 is clearly modeled on this character, but he is further endowed with a degree of psychological complexity (though young and powerful, he is also inexperienced and overconfident) that is lacking in the Homeric "original." Vergil allows Dares to start strong, but after a fall, his aged challenger, Entellus, pupil of the hero Eryx, rises and beats the braggart senseless, forcing Aeneas to intervene to save Dares' life:

> Tum pater Aeneas procedere longius iras
> et saevire animis Entellum haud passus acerbis,
> sed finem imposuit pugnae fessumque Dareta
> eripuit mulcens dictis ac talia fatur:
> "infelix, quae tanta animum dementia cepit?
> non viris alias conversaque numina sentis?
> cede deo."
>
> (461–67)

> But then father Aeneas would not let
> such fury go unchecked; he would not have
> Entellus rage in bitterness. He stopped
> the boxing, snatched away exhausted Dares,
> and when he spoke to him, used soothing words:
> "Poor man, what madness has possessed your mind?
> Your forces are not matched—can't you see that?—
> The gods have shifted to the other side.
> Give way to heaven."
>
> (M 611–19)

This peripeteia points to another crucial difference in the Vergilian games: their emphasis on the piety of the victors as the basis of their physical or technical prowess. The change in emphasis is related to a difference in style. Heinze's arguments were extended by Brooks Otis, who characterizes Homer's narrative style as "objective," or concerned to describe things, events, and people from an external perspective, as against Vergil's "subjective" style, which in Otis's view allows the reader to enter into the poem as if from the perspective of a participant.[10] Thus Vergil's narrative is about the inner lives of the contestants—about Sergestus' recklessness, Nisus' love for Euryalus, Dares' arrogance, Acestes' favored relationship with the gods. Heinze and Otis carefully avoid arguing openly that these differences prove Vergil's superiority to Homer (although Otis, especially when celebrating Vergil's more "civilized" qualities, comes close). Nevertheless, it is difficult not to see in the work of these scholars an effort to read Vergil as succeeding in his struggle with a powerful poetic father, and in this sense as being engaged in a metaliterary struggle that closely resembles the hero's efforts to assimilate and to revise for his own purposes a paternal legacy that simultaneously sustains and threatens to oppress him.

In this respect, *Aeneid* 5 appears to be an ideal instantiation of everything Harold Bloom means when he speaks of literary influence as a process closely akin to Freud's notion of what takes place in the mind of a son trying to imagine himself as a father.[11] Nevertheless, the validity of reading Book 5 in these terms only is very much open to question. We must consider from a different perspective the generational relationships developed within the book and ask not just what has been written into the history of these relations but what critics have written out. If we return for a moment to Servius' statement that "the greater part of the book is taken from Homer, except that Homer has a chariot race, Vergil a boat race," it should be obvious both how inadequate and, in both senses, how partial this analysis is. If we realize this much, it becomes equally obvious that those critics who have labored to establish Vergil's equality with or superiority to Homer by arguing for his originality even in these extraordinarily imitative games are at bottom simply accepting and reinforcing the terms that the ancient commentator laid down. Rather than doing the same, we should at least ask the question: Is "the greater part" of the book in fact a literary and metaliterary agon between pairs of fathers and sons, Anchises and Aeneas, Homer and Vergil? Or does this formulation leave something out?

Servius' position is far from unassailable. To be sure, by a crude form of measurement, the memorial games for Anchises occupy more than half the book: Aeneas assembles his followers for the first sacrifice to his father's spirit at line 43 (M 57); the climax of the celebration, the Troy game, concludes at line 603 (M 793–94) with the words *hac celebrata tenus sancto certamina patri* ("Such were the competitions they observed / in honor of Aeneas' holy father.") But neither the sacrifice (which actually takes place several days before the games themselves) nor the pageant of the Troy game owes anything to the Homeric games narrative, imitation of which is confined to lines 104–545 (M 144–715). The remaining Homeric sequence is still substantial, but the exemplary status of the games in the critical literature tends to obscure the fact that Book 5 comprises two additional major episodes: the burning of the ships and the death of Palinurus. Neither of these episodes involves a contest or owes much to Homer, and neither is greatly elucidated by the assumption that writing poetry is an agonistic pursuit carried out by wayward and rebellious sons against powerful, controlling fathers.

In the final episode involving Palinurus' death, the symbolism of Aeneas' replacing the lost helmsman seems both clear enough and perfectly consonant with the dominant motif of the son succeeding to the role of father. Michael Putnam, however, in his masterly discussion of Book 5, actually inverts the relationship between these motifs, making the theme of sacrifice as represented by the death of Palinurus into the chief unifying element of the book.[12] Anchises on this reading is not so much Aeneas' father as yet another in a series of individuals whom the hero loses on his way to Italy. Putnam thus reads the episode—and, in the terms of his argument, all of Book 5—as essentially independent of the anxious Homeric influence that other critics find in the games and infer throughout the entire book. This is a powerful, liberating reading that, in my opinion, is obviously right. At the same time, it does not obviate Homer entirely. Indeed, if one insists on reading the sacrificial motif against a Homeric background, there may be a satisfying irony at work. From the un-Homeric episode of Palinurus' death emerges the theme of lost companions, which in fact will be anchored to Homer through the very figure of Palinurus in Book 6, where the helmsman plays the role of the Odyssean Elpenor. Thus Aeneas, the social hero who in Book 1 contrasts so strongly with the isolated Odysseus even as he (unwittingly) quotes the very words of his Greek prototype—"O, three and four times blessed / were those who died before their fathers' eyes / beneath the walls of Troy" (*"o terque quaterque beati, / quis ante ora patrum Troiae sub moenibus altis / contigit oppetere!"*, 1.94–96, M 133–35)—is revealed to be like Odysseus after all, repeatedly sacrificing companions on the altar of his own success. Not dissimilarly Vergil, leaving behind his Homeric model in Palinurus' death scene, constructs one of his most memorable and moving episodes and, here if anywhere, shows the distinctive qualities that make him a true rival (or companion) to Homer as a writer of tremendous emotional and intellectual richness and complexity, and as a poet for the ages.

The central episode of the book, the burning of the ships, presents a rather different interpretive challenge. Like the Palinurus episode it stands in dark contrast to the sunny celebration of the games and (à la Putnam) relates closely to the theme of sacrifice and lost companions. Unlike either the games or the loss of the helmsman, however, this episode represents the book's greatest challenge to Aeneas' leadership. Indeed, the hero's helpless response to this disaster must be felt to gainsay the optimistic reading that understands Aeneas' performance as president of the memorial games or his act of occupying his lost helmsman's place in the stern of his (now rudderless) ship as marking him as a mature, successful leader at last.

The burning of the ships can be related to the hero's succession of his father as a leader, but not without a certain amount of special pleading. The loss of several ships leaves Aeneas uncertain how to proceed and necessitates a more direct reestablishment of contact with his dead father than the games could effect. It has been suggested that this destruction actually strengthens Aeneas. In response to the loss of the ships, the hero follows Nautes' (and then Anchises') advice to establish a city on Sicily under Acestes and to leave there the women, the old, the feeble, and any others who lack the courage to face the challenges that Italy holds. Aeneas is thus able to enter the Iliadic half of the poem heroically accompanied by a quasi-Homeric *Männerbund* instead of by the sorrowful collection of refugees he has dragged along up to this point. Similarly, the hero's momentary indecision in the wake of the disaster motivates the appearance of Anchises in a dream bidding that Aeneas descend to Elysium, where father and son meet again at last and from which meeting the hero emerges able to face any challenge that may arise.

Thus the burning of the ships does advance Aeneas' mission, though the deed is perhaps better characterized as a *felix culpa* rather than as an actual contribution. Beyond this, however, the episode is generally taken as a textbook illustration of the strong dichotomy between male and female elements in the *Aeneid*: the Trojan women "burn" under Juno's influence with a passionate unreason that leads them literally to burn their ships in order to prevent the crossing to Italy. The women are, as I noted above, repeatedly called "mothers," and this coloration is felt to contrast sharply with the theme of fathers and sons in the memorial games. The full implications of this dichotomy are most clearly viewed from a feminist perspective: the master narrative of western patriarchy figures the succession of generations as a sequence of sons struggling to prove themselves worthy of heroic fathers, to become fathers in their own right, and to beget sons worthy of themselves and of their ancestors. Mothers have no place in this succession, or a small one; whatever role they play after giving birth threatens to retard the ephebe's progress and threaten his maturation as a hero.

A powerful critique along just these lines has been mounted by S. Georgia Nugent.[13] Accepting the idea that the games narrative "is strongly determined by the father/son relation"[14] and reading Vergil's imitation of Homeric material in explicitly Bloomian terms,[15] Nugent goes on to argue that "the Trojan women are constructed here as the quintessential Other."[16] In support of this claim, she notes, the women are segregated from the men, treated as a collective entity, and misrepresented through the ventriloquism of a patriarchal text.

Nugent's commentary on the role of the Trojan women is forceful and important. Certainly relegation of female characters to futile oppositional roles is a familiar trope of *Aeneid* criticism, borne out by abundant textual evidence. But there is even in such a committedly feminist argument a high degree of unwarranted complicity with the narrowly paternalistic readings that have dominated *Aeneid* criticism. To argue that Vergil's treatment of the Trojan mothers is utterly consistent with a starkly androcentric ideology of gender is very much at odds with many contrasting gestures present throughout the poem and by no means absent from Book 5. Specifically, the Trojan women are not the only mothers, nor is Anchises the only parent whose influence is felt in this book. In fact, it is Venus who furthers her son's cause far more than does his father. Through her powerful symbolic presence and behind-the-scenes machinations against his enemies, she provides assistance not by endowing Aeneas with a greater capacity to lead, but by working against his enemies herself, making sure of his supporters in the world of the divine.

Venus' presence is quietly established at several points in the narrative of Book 5 where critics have been quicker to see the mark of Anchises. If we view the action of the book from the perspective of the narrative moment, which is the anniversary of Anchises' death, then he will indeed appear as the dominant figure. But if on the other hand we adopt a larger perspective, we will understand Anchises' much more limited place in a hierarchy that begins on Olympus and shapes the narrative of the poem in ways that overwhelm the individual importance of Anchises and Aeneas as fathers or leaders. From this perspective, the pervasive importance of Venus relegates Anchises to a clearly inferior role.

Earlier I adduced Palinurus' first appearance in Book 5 to examine a motif that makes of him an analogue to Anchises and of the return to Sicily a gesture of filial piety. But looking up at a threatening sky, the helmsman asks the ominous question, "Father Neptune / what are you preparing?" (*"quidve, pater Neptune, paras?"*, 5.14, M 17–18). It is the immediate danger of inclement weather that Palinurus fears, of course, never dreaming that on the next leg of the journey to Italy he himself will become the one sacrifice Neptune demands to insure the safe passage of the many. And it is no accident that Palinurus addresses this threatening Neptune as a "father" who brings the Trojans neither aid nor comfort. But in these circumstances more welcome familial ties suggest themselves: Sicily is at hand, and Palinurus is sure he can steer a course to landfall there that same day:

> "superat quoniam Fortuna, sequamur,
> quoque vocat vertamus iter. nec litora longe
> fida reor fraterna Erycis portusque Sicanos,
> si modo rite memor servata remetior astra."
>
> (22–25)

> "Since Fortune has the better of us now,
> let us obey and turn aside where she
> has called. I think the faithful shores of Eryx,
> your brother, and Sicilian ports are not
> far off, if only I remember right
> and can retrace the stars I watched before."
>
> (M 30–35)

These "faithful shores of Eryx, your brother" take their name from the son of Venus and Butes, who is therefore half-brother to Aeneas. It is this connection on the mother's side that Palinurus cites when he recommends a return to Sicily. Aeneas accepts Palinurus' suggestion; but, as if in rejoinder, he accepts on the grounds that Anchises, not Eryx, is buried there and, shortly after landing, determines that his father should receive cult. Aeneas' celebration seems almost an attempt to establish Anchises as a local hero alongside or in place of Eryx. But Palinurus' mention of fraternal shores proves to be only the first in a series of references to Eryx throughout Book 5. The memory of this hero and legendary boxer inspires his pupil, Entellus, to answer the challenge issued by the braggart Dares (392, M 518), and it is to him that Entellus sacrifices his victor's prize (483–84, M 639–41).

Because they are in Eryx' homeland where Acestes rules, Iris/Beroe can convince the Trojan mothers that it would be an appropriate place for them to make their settlement (630, M 830).[17] Upon founding this new city, Acestes establishes a cult to Venus on the peak of Mount Eryx, with a grove nearby in honor of her consort, the hero Anchises (759–61, M 1000–1003). Finally, the Trojans at their departure sacrifice to Eryx and to the Tempests to ensure safe passage to Italy (772–73, M 1016–18). Finally, the power behind the hero is disclosed in the scene that immediately follows as mother Venus procures safe passage for Aeneas by bartering Palinurus' life to father Neptune.

These references to Eryx, Aeneas' maternal half-brother, and to Venus, his mother, occur at significant moments throughout Book 5 and establish a counterpoint to the theme of paternity represented by Anchises. At the very least, the role of Eryx as epichoric hero should prevent us from regarding Aeneas' return to Sicily exclusively or even primarily as a move into paternal space.[18] Furthermore, Eryx' identity as Aeneas' half-brother ought to remind us that Venus' (let us say) sphere of influence is much larger than that of Anchises. The motif of the half-brother has appeared earlier in the person of Cupid: in addressing the god of love, Venus actually refers to Aeneas as his brother (1.667, M 934). Later, in Book 8, when Venus brings the full force of her sexual power to bear on her wedded husband, Vulcan, she does not hesitate to cite parental concern as the force that moves her to request new arms for Aeneas—despite the fact that, from Vulcan's point of view, Aeneas is simply the result of the goddess' infidelity to him, an aspect of their marriage to which he has evidently become accustomed. Aeneas' father is but one of Venus' consorts; Butes, father of Eryx, is another. Butes is a nobody, but Eryx, son of Venus, is an important hero in this part of the world. The same line of reasoning applies to Anchises and Aeneas as well. By casting Anchises not so much as Aeneas' father but as just one of Venus' many consorts, the subtext of Book 5 tends to inscribe paternity within a more dominant theme of motherhood.

It is of course not wrong to see paternity as the theme that at crucial moments receives the greater stress: the hero is obviously obsessed with his father and troubled by his own paternal obligations. It seems evident that he must resolve this issue before he can get on with his mission. At the same time, while Aeneas' obsession with Anchises is clearly an important element of Vergil's interest in the psychology of the poem's main character, it is not at all clear that "solving" this problem per se materially advances the hero's cause. Anchises is in all practical respects a hopeless guide to Aeneas, and whatever strategic counsel he bestows on his son in the Underworld pales in comparison to the apocalyptic pep talk that precedes it. Once again, however, the impression that this scene of revelation makes on the reader in its immediate context does not suggest how utterly the entire experience seems to be forgotten by the hero as he moves through the subsequent narrative. The emphasis of the moment often enough does not reflect the forces that shape the longer view. And time and again it is Venus, the hero's mother, who intervenes in the narrative to make sure that the hero, sometimes despite his will, stays on course. She does so not only by her bargaining with Neptune in Book 5 and with Vulcan in Book 8, but through other interventions as well: at Carthage in Book 1, where she conspires with Juno to insure the Trojans a hospitable reception at Dido's court; at Troy in Book 2, where she reveals to her son the active hostility of the other gods to the falling city; in Book 6, when "his mother's birds" (*maternas . . . avis*, 193, M 262) lead the hero through a grove by Lake Avernus directly to the tree that bears the Golden Bough; and in Book 12, when she rescues Aeneas from a wound dealt "by hand / that is unknown" (*incertum qua pulsa manu*, 12.320, M 433–34). In terms of efficacy, it is consistently not his father who helps Aeneas toward his goal, but rather his mother. *Venus genetrix*, not *pater Anchises*, is the parent who insures her son's success.

Obviously the relationship between Aeneas' parents, and his own relationship to each of them, is wildly asymmetrical. Venus is a goddess and the ancestress of the Roman people; Anchises is but one of many consorts and thus much less important to the goddess than the fruit of their union. Aeneas' obsession with his father may blind him to the fact that it is his mother who helps him at every turn, who actually controls his destiny. Many critics of differing persuasions have inherited this obsession, to the point that the *Aeneid* is often read as the embodiment par excellence of the epic genre as constituted by the relationship between father and son. But the *Aeneid* is a poem of many voices, and the maternal voice is prominent among them.

In sum, attention to the theme of parenthood in *Aeneid* 5 is instructive (as in many other ways) on two particular counts. First, a reading that focuses on the issue of paternity brings out an important aspect of Aeneas' development as a hero. Having lost his own father, who was in some sense a burden to him, he has lost his bearings as well. His task in this book is to bury his father's ghost once and for all and to take upon himself the role of father to his people. Though he does not wholly complete this task, as the necessity of subsequently visiting Anchises in the Underworld shows, he nevertheless makes some progress. But what progress he makes occurs mainly under the auspices of his mother. It thereby becomes clear that the theme of parenthood is larger than that of paternity, and that the hero's obsession with his father turns his attention from the real source of his success: the sponsorship of his mission and the machinations on his behalf by his divine patroness and mother, Venus. Similarly, the reader's— or better, perhaps, the critic's—obsession with the hero's paternity and with the poet's Oedipal agon against his literary "father" has obscured the importance of feminine elements in the narrative. These elements may well be in tension with their corresponding masculine elements, but exclusive emphasis on one or the other side can only result in a failure to understand what are, after all, mutually defining aspects of the poem's thematic structure.

CHAPTER 6

VIEWING THE *SPECTACULA* OF *AENEID* 6

Eleanor Winsor Leach

As Aeneas stands before the doors of Apollo's temple at Cumae contemplating a series of narrative images referring to the history of Daedalus and the Cretan Minotaur, the Sibyl, Apollo's priestess, chides him, "The occasion does not call for spectacles of this kind" (*"non hoc ista sibi tempus spectacula poscit,"* 37, M 53), and she hurries the Trojans into the god's lofty temple to perform the first of many sacrifices to be offered at Cumae as preliminaries to Aeneas' journey into the Underworld.

As features of the temple that Daedalus has consecrated to Apollo in consequence of his safe landing at Cumae, the narrative images carved here are votive dedications. Their fictive embodiment constitutes a master craftsman's rendition of such pictorial *tabellae* as commonly were offered by persons who attributed their preservation amidst perils to one or another god. Frequently the perils of travel figured among such events.[1] In application to such pictorial *ex votivis*, however, the Sibyl's word *spectacula* might seem surprising since its customary point of reference is to live actions staged with a certain theatrical panoply, rather than installations of the graphic arts. Vergil's only other use of the word, in *Georgics* 4.3–5, carries such implications; commending to Maecenas his ethnography of the bee-kingdom in mock-epic dress, the poet announces:[2]

> admiranda tibi levium spectacula rerum
> magnanimosque duces totiusque ordine gentis
> mores et studia et populos et proelia dicam.

> I shall set forth to stir your amazement the
> theatrics of trifling affairs and great-souled leaders,

and in order the customs, the desires, the people, and
battles of all the race.

The rubric emphasizes a response to seeing. Although the Sibyl's admoni-
tion imposes the opposite condition of *not* seeing, the reader should not
miss implications of contrast in her words *ista spectacula* ("spectacles of
this kind"), which distance the temple pictures in favor of some open-
ended alternative yet unknown. Other spectacles do in fact await Aeneas.
His underworld journey will display a series of scenes and encounters,
some, like Daedalus' personal history, appealing to memory and others
oriented toward a historical future for the Romans.

Because of Aeneas' analogous revisitations of past experience scholars
have frequently construed Daedalus' autobiographical narratives as an
anticipatory paradigm for the action of Book 6.[3] But what, we must ask, is
anticipated? Is Aeneas' journey a psychological turning point at which his
sympathies come at last to be fully aligned with his mission? The sugges-
tion, advanced by Brooks Otis in 1963, that Aeneas' review of past exper-
ience effects a cure for nostalgia preliminary to a new missionary sense of
commitment has provided impetus for three decades of controversy that
have left the issues far more complex than when the discussion began.[4] One
current way of approaching the controversy is to ask whether Vergil has
indeed encoded a clear answer in his narrative or left its possibilities open to
the reader's determination. By introducing the idea of the Underworld
scenes as *spectacula* I wish to frame this question within a discursive con-
text of spectacles and viewing, which were so great a part of Roman cul-
tural experience.[5]

The larger outlines of Book 6 can be sketched according to a struc-
tural model. Three large segments pattern the action: 1) Aeneas' arrival at
Cumae and his dealings with the Sibyl; 2) the descent and the Underworld
journey; 3) the interview with Anchises in the Elysian Fields and the
vision of future Roman heroes that, from the reader's standpoint, com-
prises a pageant of the Roman historical past. Aspects of the journey have
been twice anticipated in events leading up to this moment, yet each of
these anticipations is partial, the emphasis being placed upon prophecy. At
Buthrotum Helenus had given Aeneas explicit instructions for obtaining a
viable prophecy from the frequently elusive Sibyl (3.453–57), while
Anchises in a dream called him to the Elysian Fields to obtain his knowl-
edge of the future race and the walls granted to him (5.737). Hearing his
father's mandate, Aeneas does not respond with the same kind of imme-

diate despair as does Odysseus who weeps as for his own death when Circe instructs him to visit Hades (*Od.* 10). When Aeneas repeats Anchises' order to the Sibyl, he seems confident that his credentials are equivalent to those of other heroes who have journeyed into the Underworld and returned (119–23).[6]

What has not all the same been broached in these instructions and warnings is the manner in which the journey itself might be accomplished. Considering how this uncertainty might arouse the interest of a Roman reader should remind present-day readers how often Vergil's fictive inventions in the *Aeneid* unite us with the hero in shared suspense. Here, more than in any other place, Aeneas is a spectator dependent upon guidance through unknown regions and is only partially prepared for what he will see. Beyond this, a notable passivity is imposed upon him insofar as his responses to what he sees become subject to certain restraints that check emotion and heroic action.

For the reader this condition of spectatorship as enacted by a divinely favored hero offers an unusual vantage point. In the prospective visit to Avernus and to the Underworld can be anticipated a voyeuristic gratification of curiosity concerning the fate common to all men that plays upon all their fears. The Sibyl speaks to Aeneas of the extraordinary craving that must drive a person to undergo this dire journey more than once:

> quod si tantus amor menti, si tanta cupido est
> bis Stygiis innare lacus, bis nigra videre
> Tartara et insana iuvat indulgere labori . . .
> (132–35)

> But if your mind is moved by such a love,
> So great a longing twice to swim the lake
> of Styx and twice to see black Tartarus
> And you are pleased to try this mad attempt . . .
> (M 185–88)

But this craving is scarcely extraordinary; it is only human. To experience the Underworld twice, to glimpse the categories of punishment and reward in the afterlife and to understand the nature of the judgments by which spirits of the dead are assigned to these categories is an experience that must surely be bound up with the reader's own apprehensions and with his or her self-evaluations. Even more, to see and escape is an extraordinary opportunity given only to those whom the gods favor; this opportunity is the adventure now vicariously promised the reader courtesy of the legendary national founder. Indeed the living status of the hero even occasions humor, as when Charon the boatman grumbles over the trouble caused by the last fully fleshed mortals he had seen—Hercules who made off with Cerberus, and Perithous who grabbed Persephone herself (392–97)—or when Charon's creaky old boat realistically admits water under the unaccustomed living weight (413–14). Similarly the reader can laugh when Aeneas reaches the far fields that are home to former warriors and sees his former Greek enemies run in terror to their ships (491–92). Such levity amidst grim circumstances might be called comic relief, but its effect is to endow readers with a sense of superiority at being included within the number of those who can experience the Underworld with impunity, temporarily able to evade judgment upon their individual lives.

Judgment, however, is the essence of the Underworld, and the mythological retrospective thus obtained renders Aeneas' underworld journey as a survey of cultural history that constructs an eschatological framework for the poem and its vision of the Roman world. But viewing mythological figures will not be the only exercise in spectatorship to engage the reader here. In addition, the reader will find that certain moments of the journey will recall events previously enacted within the poem, thereby activating his or her own reading memories. For instance, the reader will recall how Palinurus died or what Aeneas' intentions toward Dido may have been. Thus the narrative itself invites our judgments. Finally, the pageant of heroes that closes the book will also make demands upon memory insofar as it involves Roman national history. In sum, the sixth book of the *Aeneid* demands of the reader a new kind of involvement suitable to the transition that Aeneas himself will be making from the old world to the new, from the literary past to a world that is of close concern to himself.

The travelogue wants background. To the Roman of Vergil's time, Cumae and the territory called the Campi Phlegreii surrounding it would have offered an unusual blend of modernity and legend to make it a place well worth visiting. An account complementary to the *Aeneid* in reinforcing the mystique of its atmosphere can be found in the geographical treatise of Strabo, a Greek living in Augustan Rome. Investing places with their proper mythological associations is one of Strabo's purposes in writing because he makes the point that geographical knowledge aids our understanding of myths, which ought to be regarded as a kind of instructive language that can teach people new things (*Geography* 1.2.3–5).

Strabo recounts the tradition that the shores of Lake Avernus were the setting of Homer's *nekuia* in the *Odyssey*. On these shores had once been located the Oracle of the Dead that Odysseus visited (*Geography* 5.4.5). Strabo explains that the landscape of earlier times had been wild and untrodden, thickly covered with a forest of trees that, reinforcing superstitions, made the gulf a darkly shaded place. In recent years, however, the forest had been cut by Agrippa, the tracts of land built up with houses and a tunnel constructed from Avernus to Cumae (5.4.5). The reason for this transformation was military. During the war waged in the mid-thirties against Sextus Pompey as a pirate commander, Agrippa had chosen the two lakes of the Gulf at Baiae, Lucrinus and Avernus, for his naval base. From Vergil's description in the *Georgics* of the artificial constructions that held back the indignant sea, we can be certain he was aware how greatly military operations had altered this coastal landscape (*G.* 2.160–64):

> an memorem portus Lucrinoque addita claustra
> atque indignatum magnis stridoribus aequor
> Iulia qua ponto longe sonat unda refuso
> Tyrrhenusque fretis immittitur aestus Avernis?

> Or should I recall the harbor and enclosures added
> to the Lucrine Lake and the ocean protesting with
> clamorous might where the Julian surf sounds far off
> amidst the poured-back sea and the Tyrennian tide is
> let into the narrow straits of Avernus?

Thus Strabo through his informative contrast between ancient and contemporary topography helps us to understand the particular effort of imaginative reconstruction by which Vergil restored its primitive aspect to the territory of the Campi Phlegrei.

Likewise Vergil reconstructs an older Cumae, a city whose long history did indeed begin as a Greek colony, although Vergil is the first to have brought Daedalus to the site.[7] The presence there of a prophetic Sibyl, one of twelve such in the Mediterranean world, must belong to the Greek history of the town that came to an end with a Samnite conquest in 420.[8] A hundred years later Samnite Cumae entered into an alliance with Rome. Finally, in the second century, the town became Romanized. Like Avernus, Cumae had figured in the Augustan/Agrippan building program. One of the series of impressively engineered tunnels that linked the city with Avernus and the shore ran from the foot of the Acropolis directly into the lower town where an extensive program had updated the Forum, basilica, and other parts of the town. For our purposes it is most important to know that Augustus had also rebuilt the ancient Greek temple to Apollo on the Acropolis, completely reorienting the structure upon its old foundations so that its facade overlooked the town. This rebuilding of 28 B.C. parallels the dedication of the Apollo temple of comparable date on the Palatine at Rome. That temple, vowed in 36 B.C., celebrated Octavian's victory over Sextus Pompey at Naulochus, but also his later victory at Actium. Here at Cumae the victory over Sextus Pompey was the paramount connection.

Of course the temple doors Aeneas inspects are not to be taken for an authentic feature of either building, but, as a fictive reconstruction, they are wholly in keeping with the contemporary reader's experience. Citizens of Augustan Rome would have been long accustomed to seeing figurative art deployed in decoration with a purpose at once commemorative and symbolic. Perhaps the closest analogue to Daedalus' Cretan scenes would have been the doors of the Palatine temple whose large ivory panels showed the Slaughter of the Niobids and the defeat of the Gauls at Parnassus (Propertius, *Elegies*, 2.31.12–14). By the time Vergil left off the *Aeneid*, Augustus and Agrippa had already put into place an extensive, and according to many scholars, cohesive program of new artifactual messages embodied in monuments, temples, and statues, in which Romans might read the ideology of the post-Republican state.[9] As one scholar has phrased it, Augustus had virtually rewritten the urban narrative that comprised the historical memory of the city.[10] Iconographers have given much attention to investigating the symbolic intermeshes procured by such art.

Such is the contemporary material context, but the scenes of Daedalus' doors have an equally important literary background, inasmuch as they participate in a tradition of describing art objects that extends backwards to Homer and is, for that reason, closely associated with epic narrative. The *Aeneid* contains six ecphrases, three descriptions of minor objects and three that are more extensive,[11] including in addition to this one, the series of Trojan War pictures on Juno's temple in Book 1 and the Shield of Aeneas in Book 8. Since the three differ considerably in their presentational technique as well as in their content, the Cumean doors become most meaningful when seen by contrast and comparison with other members of this series. A few general words about the phenomenon are in order.

While older studies of Latin literature looked unfavorably upon ecphrasis as gratuitous digression, and G. E. Lessing, the eighteenth-century German critic, denigrated the Shield of Aeneas as a perfunctory Homeric imitation,[12] the same discursive qualities that once turned readers away have now become a source of attraction. Occurring in narrative contexts, ecphrasis creates a pause in the action. Its visual self-consciousness seems to demand a different kind of attention from the reader and even a different response from that which the central narrative demands.[13] Classical New Critics began giving respectful attention to ecphrasis on the basis of content when they noticed how the subjects or actions thus incorporated might function in the manner of figures of speech or allusions reaching outside narrative context to add thematic reinforcement by means of contrast or comparison.[14] But if thematic reinforcement were all that counted, then the specific focusing of ecphrases in epic narrative upon the perception of a material object would still appear curiously redundant. While the content of ecphrasis may be extraneous to the story line, its communicative operations remain within the narrative framework, constructing a set of interrelationships between maker, object, and receiver. Simulation of the viewer's experience, that is to say the contribution of ecphrasis to the ongoing narrative, is what differentiates it from all other forms of rhetorical *enargeia* or "vivid description" that turn the hearer into a spectator.[15] From artifactual ecphrasis we capture a double vision uniting both the subject matter and the interpretive process within the same frame; we watch the forces that enact persuasion at play within a context of culturally defined experience. As vicarious spectators we must be alert to the point of view through which our experience of seeing has been channeled. To focus on ecphrasis as paradigmatic of viewing or participating in a visual text is not to deny the thematic potential of its content, but rather to understand the thematic value in terms of the location of interpretive authority that gives it meaning.

Locating interpretive authority is particularly important in the case of the three major *Aeneid* ecphrases because of the manner in which each one exercises selectivity concerning what figures or events to represent. Rather than presenting obscure stories whose relevance might tax the reader's knowledge, these artifacts present scenes from well known stories with which the reader is likely to be familiar, even in multiple versions, so that he or she can judge not only the relevance but also the bias of the presentation. Beyond this, however, are major differences among the ways in which the descriptive rhetoric configures the relationship between narrator, viewer, and reader and thus in the degree of knowledge or emotion brought into play. In viewing the scenes of the Trojan War in Book 1, Aeneas is so fully a participant that the images are shown vicariously through his eyes. We see them by being told what he sees. This mediation is made clear through his spontaneous affective response to the images as he cries to Achates, "*En Priamus*" (1.461). Recognition lends life. When Vergil proceeds to animate the narrative as a revelation of Aeneas' response to experience, he engages the reader in a sharing of subjective recognition. Not to sympathize with a hero undergoing so painful a series of reflections would be unthinkable.

Almost the opposite effect is given by the Roman historical vignettes on Aeneas' shield. Here the hero is *inscius*, able to admire the complex workmanship of the artifact but without understanding its points of reference. Rather it is Vulcan the maker "who is not without knowledge of coming events and ages" (*haud vatum ignarus venturique inscius aevi*, 628, cf. M 812–13), and his figuratively embodied knowledge is what the narrator reports. This ecphrasis takes its communicative task seriously, presenting the images with a fullness adapted to the hero's lack of knowledge. Rather than leaving details to be imagined, it shows the wolf-nurse licking the "fearless twins," the blood of Mettius Fufetius spattered on thorn-bushes, the bristling thatched roof of Romulus' hut. We sense an intensity about the narrator's engagement in this description when he directly addresses two characters in the panorama: the treacherous Fufetius and Catiline. But he also reaches out across time to engage the reader with a series of directives in the intimate second person: *aspiceres* ("you would perceive"), *videres* ("you would see"), *credas* ("you would believe"). This writing of the spectator into the image highlights mimesis but also reminds us that our own historical knowledge is the context within which these images are to be rationalized—all the more so because the narrator has told us by way of introduction that the images shown are only a selection from a fuller account that Vulcan has incorporated into the shield.

Looking backward, then, from the shield to Daedalus' images, we can see how an absence of narrative preparation makes the location of interpretive authority uncertain. The context into which this descriptive passage enters contains neither any hint of the mind-set that Aeneas brings to the pictures nor any direct indication of the viewpoint from which they will be shown. Many have interpreted this indefiniteness to indicate that the control of meaning lies by default with Daedalus as maker since this ecphrasis is the only one known in Latin literature where the story that the artist depicts is his own.[16] But the reader should not accept his telling of the story as definitive without noticing that the visual rubrics of this ecphrasis are the most elliptical of all three in the poem. In rhetorical terms one might say that the description lacks *enargeia*, that it does not show but merely tells, even though this happens under the rubric of showing. Conflations of action and image are the result. A phrase such as *crudelis amor tauri* ("cruel love of the bull," 24, cf. M 34) leaves the reader uncertain as to exactly what he or she should be visualizing, and also how far to go in drawing upon independent knowledge, including the full extent of Daedalus' own participation in the story he tells, to fill out the lacunae of the text.

This failure of mimesis in the description brings us finally to an empty panel concerning which the narrator intervenes directly to address the absent subject by name with apparently privileged information concerning the act of creation:

> tu quoque magnam
> partem opere in tanto, sineret dolor, Icare, haberes.
> bis conatus erat casus effingere in auro,
> bis patriae cecidere manus.
>
> (30–33)

> And Icarus, you also would have played
> great part in such work, had his grief allowed;
> twice he had tried to carve your trials in gold,
> and twice a father's hands had failed.
>
> (M 44–47)

No matter how one reads this panel, whether sympathetically as Otis and Charles Segal, or more ironically as later interpreters who have noted how the suppression of articulation also suppresses guilt,[17] it is crucial to the paradigmatic function of the ecphrasis to notice how the narrator has arbitrarily taken over for the artist in order to make emptiness an index of emotional content.[18] Also worth noting is the way that this preemptive interpretation precludes any response that Aeneas himself might have made to the pictures. In view of the Sibyl's injunction to hasten and the use of the verb *perlegerent* ("would have been reading") in a contrary-to-fact condition, it is not even certain whether he has had time to contemplate them carefully at all.[19] This model sets up a tension between seeing and interpretation that may apply to other moments of the journey conveyed by reported description, such as the Sibyl's account of legendary criminals punished within Tartarus and the procession of heroes that Aeneas witnesses in the Elysian Fields. But we might also apply this paradigm to the two great conundra of Book 6 whose meaning is so often sought with reference to external sources: the Golden Bough that gives entrance to the Underworld and the Gates of Horn and Ivory that allow egress. Insofar as its internal reference is concerned, the first of these two tests the truth of the Sibyl, but by the same token, tests Aeneas' chance of success, while the second sets up a set of polyvalent references that might be thought to test the truth of the episode itself.

The journey proper begins when the earth gapes and Aeneas and the Sibyl begin their supposedly "easy" descent on a track compared to a road through the forest in uncertain nocturnal light. Periodic recurrences of the word *iter* ("route") remind us that Aeneas is progressing through a territory. Around his path the Underworld possesses a concrete spatial extension that might be charted on a map. This map will be characterized by a series of definite locations: by architecture, by fields, and by groves, some of these laced with divergent paths leading often into unseen depths of trees. Since Vergil is the first to give such an extended topography to the Underworld, as a framework for Aeneas' viewing and our own, we might first consider what are its ties and its divergences from previous accounts. Multiple intertextualities quickly come to mind.

Readers familiar with the *Odyssey* will readily see how Vergil's landscape differs from the Homeric. Although the seat of Pluto is indeed called a house (*domos Aidos*, e.g., *Od.* 11.69, 150), Odysseus never fully enters it. His interviews take place at the threshold where the shades approach to drink sacrificial blood that empowers their speech. Thus one is never quite certain whether the "halls of Dis" are a metaphorical expression or one meant to conjure up a physical presence.[20] Later Odysseus' vision allows one to see further into an interior space where heroes inhabit meadows clothed with asphodel (11.538–39), while the famous sinners undergoing their endless punitive tasks appear to be distributed over space (11.576 ff.). In rendering Homer's descriptive landscapes as a visual panorama, an artist of the late Republic brought out the natural imagery, showing the entrance beside the ocean as a great cavernous mouth.[21] Within this visual frame the spectator is positioned to look directly at the underworld rivers edged with willows and at the figures of Odysseus and the shades he interviews. Beyond, in another panel, are cliffs and fields—

no doubt the Homeric "meadows of asphodel." Inspiration for the craggy shoreline features of these landscapes has often been referred to the traditional connection between Odysseus' wanderings and the coastline of Campania, as Strabo, for example, relates it, while the compositional patterns employ a Roman mode of aerial perspective to realize gradations of spatial depth. These landscapes decorated a house on the Esquiline. Given Vergil's own familiarity with the Esquiline, it is possible that the paintings figured in the artistic background he brought to his poetic creation.

But the topography of Vergil's Underworld differs even from the scenery of the *Odyssey* landscapes because it allows the reader together with Aeneas and the Sibyl to move through it in sequential stages. The sequence makes possible the various divisions of Underworld inhabitants Aeneas views. No seat is assigned without judgment (431–32), the narrator tells us, calling Minos by the Roman title *quaesitor* (judge) and showing the process of judgment more explicitly than does Homer. But Vergil has added other touches of unsettling familiarity to his Hades by remaking Homer's shadowy "domus of Pluto" with features common to the Roman house. The entrance is characterized as a *vestibulum*. In the vocabulary of domestic architecture this is the protected exterior space before a doorway separating the house from the street. In this area clients of prestigious aristocrats gathered each morning to await admission to their patron's presence. But the crowd gathered outside Pluto's dwelling is not the everyday Roman assemblage of petitioners and dependents, but rather a sinister collection of personifications: diseases, debilities, and deprivations besetting human life. Mythical monsters stable in the doorway. In confrontation with these monsters Aeneas obeys the heroic impulse to draw his sword. Here for the first time the Sibyl imposes a restraint when she warns him that the images have no substance, to which the narrator adds that he might otherwise have beaten his sword against shadows in vain (294).

This *vestibulum* is the first of two within the Underworld landscape; the second is that of Tartarus whose exterior prospect alone is visible to Aeneas: the threefold walls beneath a cliff surrounded by fiery Phlegethon, and the doorway flanked by columns of adamant. Tisiphone guards the threshold, from which dreadful sounds emerge: groans, blows, and creaking chains. Confronted with these incitements to curiosity, Aeneas does not disappoint us but asks the questions any person would want to ask: "Who is inside there and what have they done?" Nor does the Sibyl's answer disappoint. As an ecphrasis of spectacle her account intermingles the crimes and punishments of legendary sinners with those of everyday criminals by Roman definition (562–627). Some items of the description echo those Lucretius had invoked when he banished the physical reality of the Underworld in his Epicurean argument against fear of death (*De Rerum Natura*, 3.997–1002). A reader who recalls that passage can find here, for better or worse, a restoration of belief in the effects of life upon afterlife.

Between these two locations architecturally defined as *vestibula* lies a territory conceived in natural terms by uniting the proverbial underworld rivers with surroundings of groves and forests, seemingly Vergil's own creation, which might be seen as an extension of the Avernian landscape from the upper into the lower world. Finally come the remote fields where warriors, primarily those of the Theban and the Trojan wars, continue to play out replicas of their battles fought in life.

As Aeneas crosses this territory his view of the categories is focused by a series of personal encounters that serve, as Otis puts it, to "represent his past in a reverse of the temporal order."[22] This reading recognizes the evocative power of the past as a challenge to self-discipline and the conquest of emotions. What Aeneas cannot alter must be forgotten. Segal has commented on the emotional complexity of these encounters, pointing out how the immutability of the Underworld enforces Aeneas' passivity by holding him back from desired interactions: from lending a hand to aid Palinurus across the Styx, from wringing a word of forgiveness from Dido, and from comforting Deiphobus, whose sadly mutilated body is a final witness to the sordid disgrace of Troy.[23]

Beyond this, however, the encounters incorporate previously unrevealed information that makes them appear almost as alternative versions of their stories and may cause the reader to reflect upon what had really happened before. Otis takes a traditionally philological view that such contradictions are symptomatic of the unfinished state of the poem at Vergil's death and would surely have been rectified in revision.[24] Whether or not this might be true, more recent readers have interested themselves in the discrepancies as suggesting the inevitable hiatus between event and interpretation. Here as with the narrator's elliptical report of Daedalus' autobiographical votives we may sense a tension between the energy that drives the narrative and our own readerly insistence on knowing all.

When finally Aeneas reaches his goal in Elysium, the prophecy meant to inspire him with zeal for his mission comes to him also in visual form as a parade of individuals embodying the future glory of his race. Since these heroes of the future are, in fact, the purified spirits of those who have lived previously, the prophecy challenges one conclusion that our preliminary views of the Underworld seemed to imply: that of absolute bondage to the conduct of a former life. Rather it will be seen that the Underworld involves process; that the majority even of the spirits who have entered the Elysian Fields will not be allowed to remain there but must leave under the impetus of an active desire for the upper world. This philosophical grounding that Vergil has given to his pageant rationalizes the driving force of Roman ambition, a point to which I will shortly return, but a few more preliminary words are in order because the prophecy Aeneas receives forms the context for the most controversial lines in the *Aeneid*: lines that are controversial not only in their reflection upon Roman culture, but also in their bearing on the final action of the poem and the reader's evaluation of it.

Underlying the rhetoric of this passage is the form of *recusatio*, a species of disclaimer frequently used by Augustan poets, in which the speaker calls attention to one literary course of action ostensibly being rejected in favor of another more suitable or desirable course elected instead. Anchises' disclaimer, however, is not personal but cultural. Abruptly interrupting his presentation of certain heroes of the Carthaginian period—the Gracchi, the Scipios, Fabricius, Regulus (under the less familiar name Serraneus), and Fabius—he utters a pronouncement for all Romans:

> "excudent alii spirantia mollius aera
> (credo equidem), vivos ducent de marmore vultus,
> orabunt causas melius, caelique meatus
> describent radio et surgentia sidera dicent:
> tu regere imperio populos, Romane, memento
> (hae tibi erunt artes), pacique imponere morem,
> parcere subiectis et debellare superbos."
>
> (847–54)

> "For other peoples will, I do not doubt
> still cast their bronze to breathe with softer features
> or draw out of the marble living lines,
> plead causes better, trace the ways of heaven
> with wands and tell the rising constellations;
> but yours will be the rulership of nations,
> remember, Roman, these will be your arts:
> to teach the ways of peace to those you conquer,
> to spare defeated peoples, tame the proud."
>
> (M 1129–37)

Many details in this passage raise questions. When viewed as an evaluation of Roman cultural achievement, its judgments can seem harsh and even unfair. Although any reader might grant that superiority in bronze artistry may not be a Roman attainment, still the Roman art of marble portrait sculpture might be allowed, on the basis of the sophistication and originality it had already developed both in the late Republican and more recent Augustan years, a serious claim to preeminence in "bringing living countenances out of marble" (848). Assuredly astronomy is no Roman science, but oratory is rather a different matter, and the pronouncement "others will plead cases better" has caused some to ask whether Vergil consciously implied a slight to Cicero's preeminence. Far more controversial, however, is Anchises' specification of Roman *artes*, apparently justifying Roman hegemony when structured in the name of peace yet appending the exhortation, scarcely incompatible with peace, to "spare the fallen and put down the proud."[25] The fact that Aeneas' own father says this will naturally count for much when Aeneas, caught in a complex of paternal/ filial inter-relationships, will deliver his final unpitying blow to Turnus.[26]

Rather than pursuing this matter that is better left to its proper occurrence in the poem, let us turn back to the pageant that forms its context and consider how its particular conditions of spectatorship may position the reader in this final Underworld viewing of a history at once future and past.

What Anchises wants to tell Aeneas derives from his own particular situation in the Elysian Fields and also marks a division between mythology and philosophy in the eschatology of the poem. When Aeneas and the Sibyl enter the region they first see heroes who are pursuing occupations they followed during life. Like the sinners in Tartarus, these are persons with strong mythological identities—Trojan founders and legendary singers—whose occupations of athletics, warfare, and choral performance attach a certain archaic, indeed Pindaric, coloring (642–63, M 850–53). As Aeneas will soon learn, these persons are enjoying their state after purification. Their stable condition is the positive counterpart to the perpetual punishments suffered by the great criminals of Tartarus. Anchises, however, stands apart from these figures within a secluded valley where he gains his particular pleasure from counting over the number and the glory of his descendants of the Roman race. To Aeneas these persons first appear, as did the Carthaginians building their city, like bees in a joyously flourishing meadow.[27]

In introducing the sight of these *innumerae gentes et populi* ("number-less races and peoples," 706, M 931–32), Vergil reuses language and images that the poem has previously made familiar. Previously Aeneas had asked the Sibyl what the crowds on the banks of the Styx were seeking (318–20). Now he sees souls apparently no less desirous of further progress drinking the waters of oblivion in final preparation for their return to the upper world (703–15). Once their actual essence has been revealed to him, Aeneas asks a quite poignant question concerning the cupidinous compulsion that might drive free souls back into dull bodies: "Why this wild longing for the light of earth?" (*"Quae lucis miseris tam dira cupido?"*, 721, M 952).

In the answer that Anchises gives to explain how these spirits lose memory of their past, scholars have recognized a rich intertext drawing upon Plato, Lucretius, Orphic literature, and Cicero, to mention the most conspicuous. One may cut quickly to the essence of this passage with the assistance of Thomas Habinek's identification of a conceptual dichotomy between two recognized manners of discourse: the first a didactic that proceeds upon principles or precepts and the other a hortatory that makes use of examples corresponding to the theme of knowledge versus action.[28] This makes Cicero's *Somnium Scipionis* the most pertinent model both for Anchises' familial framing of his presentational mode and for his epitomizing of Roman ideals concerning civic virtue and its rewards.

In the long run these points reinforce a fundamental difference between Vergil and Plato that turns upon the two items of forgetfulness and choice. While the spirits in the Myth of Er select new forms on the basis of residual character tendencies, those of the *Aeneid*, once purified, appear to have no choice as to what identities they will assume within the pageant of Roman history. These are the identities that Anchises now proceeds to disclose. His presentation follows the same ecphrastic mode as the previous descriptions and catalogues of the book. Like Aeneas before the doors of Daedalus, he is said to be "reading" (*legere*) the pageant as he translates (*expediam dictis*, M 999–1003) *gloria* (756) and *illustris animas* ("distinguished spirits," 757) into words. The difference, of course, is that this mediation stands between Aeneas and the images, and the recital is punctuated by various forms of second person address—hortatory imperatives and descriptive questions—bringing details into view.

Again it is worth reconstructing a Roman cultural context for this exposition. A link has often been proposed with the Roman funeral ceremony in which the masks of distinguished ancestors and their noteworthy achievements are paraded.[29] This analogy covers the active character of Anchises' procession but not its inclusive scope since the ancestors reanimated by the funeral procession represent the line of only one house while

Aeneas' future descendants comprise the ancestors of all Rome. Surely
also the series would have evoked for a Roman spectator some reminder of
the great assemblages of sculpted portraits on view in many parts of the
city: the piazza called the Area Capitolina, which was crowded with
statues, the Library of Asinius Pollio, parts of the Campus Martius.[30] If in
fact the catalogue can be seen to remind readers of such actual displays in
their experience, we might see it as an appropriate context in which to
mention the artistry of bronze and marble portraits since many of these old
faces in the public sphere would have preserved the styles and crafts-
manship of earlier centuries. These public portraits also carried words to
commend their subjects to the viewer: words that, while not always
explicit, would fit the subject into place.[31] In this context we might imagine
the scene between Anchises and Aeneas as one reenacted many times when
noble fathers explained to their sons the deeds behind the faces of marble
and bronze.

As explanations, Anchises' remarks are more allusive than informa-
tive, but they are also iconographical in their tendency to fix often upon
visible signs. If there is a certain consistency about the details to which
Anchises calls attention, it is their significance as tokens of honor: the
civic crowns of oak that shade the foreheads of the Alban fathers,
including Aeneas Silvius (772); the twin-crested helmet of Romulus and
the visible marks of divine honor bestowed by Jove (779–80); the olive
branches and the sacra carried by the law-giver Numa (808–11); the
fasces of the Tarquins appropriated by Brutus (818) and the *signa* earned
by Torquatus and Camillus (825); the *spolia opima* of Marcellus (855).
Along with this highlighting, another kind of personal address enters into
the catalogue in the two instances when Anchises breaks through his
recital to protest the future fates of his descendants. Seeing Pompey and
Caesar dressed with equal arms and still united in spirit (*concordes
animas*) while wrapped in shadow, he is stirred to remake the future,
reducing the mature figures of *socer* and *gener* (father- and son-in-law) to
pueri (boys), and calling upon Caesar as his own descendent to be first in
casting his weapons away. The second occurs when Aeneas himself asks
why dark shadows surround young Marcellus (883). In these passages,
Anchises' authority falters, or rather it becomes the subject of regret. The
interventions impose a model of hindsight upon this past-become-future
as he recognizes that he too is an enforced spectator of prospects he would
like to change. But Anchises' injunction *parcere subiectis* ("to spare those
subdued," 853, M 1137) enters into this category of rhetorical interven-

tions. It is ambiguously addressed, one might say, to *Romane*, whether by this token counting Aeneas himself among the number of Romans, or speaking only to his descendants.[32]

Toward what kind of conclusion should Anchises' words point us? Does he successfully as the text seems to tell us "through such details set Aeneas' spirit on fire with a great love of coming glory" (*"per singula / incenditque animum famae venientis amore*," 888–89, M 1185–87)? Or, to pursue a recent critical suggestion, is his role paradigmatic of constructive forgetfulness, the necessary preliminary to the Trojans' escape from the repeated failures of the past.[33] Or again, is the problem one of Aeneas' forgetting so that the entire experience of descent and prophecy assumes the value of an evanescent dream?[34] Thus we come to the gates, where one might pause to wonder just which are "these words" (*his dictis*) with which Anchises "accompanies" (*prosequitur*) (898–99, M 1197–99) Aeneas and the Sibyl before he dismisses them through the Ivory Gate of False Dreams? Do they refer to his exhortations and advice or possibly to the actual ecphrasis of the Gates?[35] Does Aeneas himself know through what gate he is passing or is this information entrusted to the reader alone?[36] Every reader may have his or her individual answer to these questions which, when regarded in the light of the underworld journey as *spectacula* for interpretation, unite the intangible that escapes representation with the specificity of images.

CHAPTER 7

THE BIRTH OF WAR
A Reading of *Aeneid* 7

Sara Mack

In this essay I will touch on aspects of Book 7 that readers are likely either to have trouble with (the Muse Erato, for one) or not to notice at all (the founding of Ardea is a prime example), rather than on major elements of plot. I will also look at some of the intertexts suggested by Vergil's allusions to other poets and to his own poetry. We know that Vergil wrote with immense care, finishing fewer than three verses a day over a ten-year period, and we know that he is one of the most allusive (and elusive) of Roman poets, all of whom wrote with an eye and an ear on their Greek and Roman predecessors. We twentieth-century readers do not have in our heads what Vergil seems to have expected his Augustan readers to have in theirs (Homer, Aeschylus, Euripides, Apollonius, Lucretius, and Catullus, to name just a few); reading the *Aeneid* with an eye to what Vergil has "stolen" from others can enhance our enjoyment of the poem.

Book 7 is a new beginning. So the Erato invocation, parallel to the invocation of the Muse in Book 1, seems to indicate. I shall begin my discussion of the book with an extended look at some of the implications of the Erato passage. These difficult lines make a good introduction to the themes of the book as a whole (to the themes of the whole second half of the poem, in fact). Erato herself suitably introduces the main subject of this essay: Vergil's focus, throughout the book, on female characters, from Caieta at the beginning to Camilla at the end.

ERATO

A new day is at hand (or so it seems) as the Trojans finally arrive in the promised land, and Vergil marks the occasion grandly with a new invocation:

Nunc age, qui reges, Erato, quae tempora rerum,
quis Latio antiquo fuerit status, advena classem
cum primum Ausoniis exercitus appulit oris,
expediam, et primae revocabo exordia pugnae.
tu vatem, tu, diva, mone. dicam horrida bella,
dicam acies actosque animis in funera reges,
Tyrrhenamque manum totamque sub arma coactam
Hesperiam. maior rerum mihi nascitur ordo,
maius opus moveo.

                                            (37–45)

Now, Erato, be with me, and let me sing
of kings and times and of the state of things
in ancient Latium when the invaders
first beached their boats upon Ausonia's coasts,
and how it was that they began to battle.
O goddess, help your poet. I shall tell
of dreadful wars, of men who struggle, tell
of chieftains goaded to the grave by passion,
of Tuscan troops and all Hesperia
in arms. A greater theme is born for me;
I try a greater labor.

                                            (M 45–55)

The first question thinking readers are likely to ask on reaching this passage is, "Why Erato?" Any undergraduate who knows anything at all about the Muses knows that Clio (history), Calliope (epic), or maybe even Melpomene (tragedy) would be a better choice than Erato to help out an epic poet in need of inspiration. Indeed, in the most famous ancient depiction of Vergil, the third-century A.D. mosaic from Tunis, the poet is depicted with a tablet on his lap on which *Musa mihi causas memora* ("Tell me the reason, Muse," 1.8, M 13) can be read, with Clio on one side and Melpomene on the other. Why does Vergil call on Erato?

Obviously Erato's name suggests love or desire, and it makes a kind of sense for her to head a book which is infused from beginning to end with Vergil's love for his native land, expressed again and again as he gives one area after another its moment in the sun.[1] Vergil includes most of the Italian countryside in Book 7, mainly but not exclusively through the catalogue of warriors at the end. The book opens with a lovely evocation of the beautiful grove at Ostia full of brightly colored birds "caressing the

heavens with their song" (*aethera mulcebant cantu*, 7.34, my translation).
Vergil has chosen not to follow the tradition that brought the Trojans in
further south by the river Numicus (the river where Aeneas is traditionally
supposed to have died); instead he lands them right at Ostia, which was
later to be Rome's busy maritime emporium, full of businesses announcing
their trade in grand mosaics, full of houses and temples and eating places,
as the visitor today can still see in the very impressive ruins.[2] Thinking this
bustling Roman settlement out of existence, Vergil creates, as Aeneas' first
stop in Italy, a deserted place of natural beauty and peace. (The moment,
like all peaceful moments in the *Aeneid*, is brief—only 120 lines later
Aeneas begins to transform the landscape by building Ostia's very first
settlement—a military camp.)

The warriors described in the catalogue come from all over Italy: from
Caere in Etruria, from various parts of Latium, from the Sabine territory,
from all over Campania, from among the Aequians, the Marsians, the
Rutulians, and the Volscians. What is more, Vergil turns geographical fea-
tures into people and makes them leaders of armies from areas that have no
connection with their own.[3] This tactic allows him to cover most of the
map of Italy, as Professor Louise Adams Holland told my college Vergil
class years ago. Almo and Galaesus, the first casualties of the war, are
rivers, the Almo a tributary of the Tiber, the Galaesus a river in Calabria.
Vergil gives each an identity in his death: Almo, the oldest son of Tyrrhus;
Galaesus, a man as just as he is rich. Messapus, who is clearly to be
connected with Messapia in the toe of Italy, is made the leader of forces
from Southern Etruria; Ufens is a Volscian river turned into the leader of
Aequians from Nersa. Halaesus, the traditional founder of Falerii, comes
from Campania. Modern students find all catalogues boring, it seems;
Italians of Vergil's day were no doubt pleased to hear of their little piece
of the country playing a role all those years ago when Aeneas arrived
from Troy.[4] Surely Erato helped Vergil express his affection for all these
places, some of them no longer in existence, others no longer of any
importance in the twenties B.C.

Erato must have been hard at work when Vergil created one of the
most exquisite pathetic fallacies in Latin literature in his lament for Umbro
near the end of the book. Umbro—priest, snake charmer, and healer from
Marruvia—was unable to "heal the hurt of Dardan steel" (*Dardaniae
medicari cuspidis ictum*, 756, M 994) despite his skill, and his homeland
mourned for him (all this before the battle really even begins): "For you
Angitia's forest wept, the crystal / wave of the Fucinus, for you bright

lakes" (*te nemus Angitiae, vitrea te Fucinus unda, / te liquidi flevere lacus*, 759–60, M 997–98). I feel sure that Erato inspired that lovely coupling of person and place and tragedy.

A first-time reader of the *Aeneid* is not likely to connect Erato with the poet's task, as I have just done, however. Whatever else it may suggest, the call on Erato indicates that the poet needs fresh creative force and new momentum to tackle what lies before him. (Similar is his invocation of the Muse in Book 1 when he gets to the difficult task of trying to understand the *causas*, the "reasons," for Juno's hatred.) Who better than Erato to keep him from flagging now as he begins the second movement of his epic? The language throughout the invocation suggests toil, ordering, and creation: *expediam* ("I will disentangle"); *revocabo* ("I will recall or call back into being"); *exordia* ("beginnings"). The word *exordium* is a term from weaving: the warp that will form the basis of the woven fabric. Sound and meaning connect *exordia* with *ordo* (ordering, arrangement) in the last line. Erato is to preside over a new birth (*nascitur ordo*); a new order is coming into being in history and in poetry, firmly linked with Italy. And the *maior ordo* (grander, more significant ordering or order of things) requires a *maius opus* (greater work, construction, epic poem). The subject matter of the second part of the poem will be grander, the events more significant; something new is coming into being, and the birth process is difficult. It is easy to imagine that the prospect of getting the second half of the poem right was daunting to Vergil. How was he to create a worthy prehistory for Rome? How to express his love of Italy while showing its ambiguous nature? How to paint the Trojan arrival as both a return home and an invasion? The war in Latium as at once a civil war, a replay of the Trojan war, and a pre-enactment of historical Rome's fifth- and fourth-century Latin wars as well as the civil wars of the poet's own day?[5] Erato has a big job ahead of her.

In the triumphantly climactic words: *maior rerum mihi nascitur ordo* ("a greater theme is born for me"), a Roman would hear the ringing opening of Vergil's *Eclogue* 4: *magnus ab integro saeclorum nascitur ordo* ("the great order of generations is being born anew"). In the *Eclogue*, the poet is proclaiming the beginning of a new golden age. Here in Book 7, he reminds us of that earlier golden-age dream, now that Roman history is about to begin with Aeneas' arrival in Latium, the very place where Saturn presided over the original golden age (8.319–25, M 18–26). Vergil is not just marking the end of Aeneas' *Odyssey*, he is marking the mythological-historical moment when Troy can begin the process of merging with Italy to become Rome.[6] Aeneas is just about to meet with King Latinus, Saturn's direct descendant and so heir to the golden age of the past. Augustus is, so Anchises claimed in Book 6, the ruler "who will renew a golden age in Latium, / in fields where Saturn was once king" (*Latio regnata per arva / Saturno quondam*, 6.793–94, M 1050–51). There is, however, no golden age in store for the protagonists of Book 7. Any golden age is firmly in the past, and the Latins who think of themselves as golden-age people are sorely mistaken. The young men are playing war games when the Trojan embassy arrives, the entrance to the palace is decorated with spoils of war, and Turnus has been fighting Latinus' wars for him—hardly golden-age activities. In fact, the end of the poet's statement of intent in the Erato invocation hooks the wars of Aeneas' day specifically onto the wars of Vergil's own day. A Roman reader hearing *totamque sub arma coactam Hesperiam* ("all Hesperia in arms") could hardly fail to be reminded of the battle of Actium only twelve years before Vergil's death, when, according to Augustus' own propaganda, *tota Italia* (all Italy) voluntarily swore an oath of allegiance to him against Antony. So intricate are the links between past and future.

Vergil speaks here as an inspired prophet, putting himself in the same category as Helenus in Book 3 and the Sibyl in Book 6. It is clear that this invocation should be connected both with those prophecies (which also predict the war in Latium) and with the poet's first invocation of the Muse at 1.8–11, M 13–18. The opening statement about times and things (*tempora rerum*) is certain to remind us of Jupiter's grand prophecy to Venus when he said of the Romans who will be descended from Aeneas' line: "I set no limits to their fortunes and no time" (*nec metas rerum nec tempora pono*, 1.278, M 389–90). How sharply Vergil has limited the scope of Jupiter's promise. Jupiter offered limitless possibilities, this seer establishes a place and a time for war. Again and again Book 7 at once parallels and contracts or darkens the hopes of Book 1.

Modern readers who know Aeneas' story are likely to connect Erato with the "love story" of Lavinia and Turnus and Aeneas, and rightly so. Lavinia is, in a sense, a second Helen, and the war that breaks out between Latins and Trojans is at least in part a replay of the Trojan war, with the Trojans coming out this time on top. The Sibyl predicted it as such back in Book 6, and Juno will, in just a few lines, call Aeneas a second Paris. What Augustan readers would have perceived in addition is the very suggestive echo of the *Argonautica*.[7] At the beginning of Book 3, the halfway point in his four-book epic, Apollonius calls on Erato for help. The Argonauts have reached their goal, the home of the Golden Fleece. At the beginning of Book 7, the halfway point of *his* epic, Vergil calls on Erato for help. The Trojans have reached *their* goal, the place where the Roman future can begin, and Vergil begins his invocation of the Muse with a literal translation of Apollonius' opening words: "Come now Erato." Apollonius asks how Medea's passion helped Jason bring home the Fleece, making it clear that his Erato is Muse for a love story. But Vergil's story is not a love story; it is the story of war. Note the way Vergil connects Erato specifically with war by introducing his subject matter, war, in the same line as, almost as the conclusion to, his request for the muse's help—a terrible difference from Apollonius' plea. Note too that he has just called Aeneas' men a foreign army (*advena . . . exercitus*), even though they are also peace-seeking exiles returning to their homeland. And because the Trojan force is really an army, it should perhaps not surprise us that Aeneas' first settlement, begun just over a hundred lines after the Erato invocation, is a military camp, not a town.

Parallels with Apollonius bring Jason and Medea into the second half of Vergil's poem in a new guise. As Walter Moskalew demonstrates, Vergil creates elaborate parallels between the events of Book 7 and the events of Books 1 and 4, directly, and also indirectly through Apollonius.[8] The Erato invocation suggests that Aeneas is a new Jason and Lavinia a new Medea. Vergil fits Lavinia into the Jason and Medea story in another, rather sinister way by drawing on Euripides. One of the most vivid pictures in the excursus into Laurentum's recent past introduced by the Erato invocation is the description of Lavinia's flaming hair, one of the portents of her glorious and deadly destiny (73–77, M 93–98). The words come straight from Euripides' *Medea* (1186 f.) describing the lethal effects of Medea's "gift" on Jason's new young bride. By implication, then, in Vergil's linkage of Apollonius and Euripides, Lavinia is at once Apollonius' Medea and Medea's nameless victim in Euripides' play, while Aeneas is both Apollonius' Jason who wins Medea and Euripides' Jason who deserts Medea. The Aeneas/Lavinia connection is, through allusion, ill-omened indeed.

Furthermore, since Vergil had already equated Dido with Medea in *Aeneid* 1–4, by bringing Medea into his new story he brings back Dido. Vergil makes us aware throughout his poem that we mortals can never leave anything behind. Whatever people do is part of what they are, and whatever the individuals who make up a civilization do is part of what that civilization is. Aeneas deserted Dido in Book 4, but the flames of her pyre follow him into Book 5, he meets her again in the Underworld in

Book 6, and her curse (4.612–20, M 845–56) is pretty well fulfilled in the last half of the poem, while her summoning of an avenger from her bones embroils all of Roman history, for Hannibal, the hero of the second Punic War, is clearly the avenger Dido calls up, and the Punic Wars are, in Vergil's representation of history, the direct result of *Aeneid* 1–4.

THE WOMEN OF BOOK 7

All things considered, Erato seems the perfect Muse to introduce the birth of Roman history, which, in Vergil's picture of things, is the birth of war.[9] What remains is for the poet to set the scene for the war by giving his readers a sense of early Italy in all its variety and to orchestrate the outbreak of the war. This Vergil does in large measure through a cast of female characters. Whatever we are to make of it, it is a fact that female characters predominate in Book 7. It is also a fact that the women of Book 7 play such varied roles in the poem that they cannot be grouped generically, as, for example, sacrifices to Rome's destiny, or irrational forces that must be suppressed in the name of masculine order.[10] Perhaps it does not mean anything that Juno, Allecto, Amata, Lavinia, Silvia, and Camilla, all of whom play major roles, and Caieta, Circe, Erato, Celaeno, and Danaë, who play bit parts in the book, are female.[11] Quite possibly Vergil never thought about the matter at all. Quite possibly he did. Vergil includes Danaë, a woman readers cannot have expected to find in Italy, and gives her a story that is significantly different from the usual version. I shall begin my discussion of the women of Book 7 with Danaë, even though she does not appear until halfway through the book, because her presence suggests that Vergil was indeed aware of the central role he was giving to women in this section of the poem.

DANAË

As Allecto flies toward Ardea to infect Turnus with her venom, Vergil interrupts his narrative to give a thumbnail sketch of the city where the action will take place:

> quam dicitur urbem
> Acrisioneis Danaë fundasse colonis

praecipiti delata Noto. locus Ardea quondam
dictus avis, et nunc magnum manet Ardea nomen,
sed fortuna fuit.

(409–13)

the city built by Danaë when, carried
upon the swift south wind, she founded it
as home for her Acrisian colonists.
Our fathers used to call it Ardea;
and Ardea is still a mighty name,
but its great days are done.

(M 545–50)

Vergil has changed the traditional story. Normally Danaë and Perseus arrive
in Seriphos in a chest, set adrift by Danaë's father Acrisius who heard that
he would be killed by Danaë's child. Mother and son are rescued by the
king in a fairly typical story of helpless female rescued by a man, and the
real concern is the fate of the baby hero Perseus. Vergil's Danaë arrives in
Italy in a ship, and there she founds a city for her fellow travelers, just as
Dido did. Many commentators, including C. J. Fordyce, T. E. Page, and R.
D. Williams, say (ad 372) she marries Pilumnus, Turnus' ancestor, but
Vergil does not mention this; his sketch suggests a Dido unencumbered by
an Aeneas. Danaë's part in Book 7 may be small—not even a walk-on—but
it is, I think, significant that Vergil has created any part at all for a woman
who, like Dido and like Camilla, plays a man's role in a man's world, a
woman who is successful, as they are not. Furthermore, there is not a word
of Perseus; the story hinted at is a *woman's* foundation story, not an account
of the birth of a male hero.

CAIETA

With Caieta Vergil begins his portrayal of the collision between Troy
and Italy as a series of moments featuring women. He suggestively begins
the second half of his poem, even before the Erato invocation, with death,
a final tie with old Troy broken as Aeneas buries his nurse, and a first
connection in Latium between the old and the new, as a character from the
Trojan past becomes a piece of Italian geography. Vergil could easily have
attached Caieta to Book 6, or left her out entirely. Her presence in the first

four lines of his *maius opus* tells us that there is not going to be a truly new beginning in Latium. The last figure Aeneas saw in Book 6 was Marcellus, Augustus' nephew, son-in-law, and chosen successor: heir to the promised new golden age. Marcellus dies in 23 B.C. (Vergil makes us think of the actual time of his death by alluding to his funeral); Caieta dies a few lines later, some one thousand years earlier—death at the beginning of the Trojan/Roman future, death at the end.

Caieta seems to me to have further significance. In Book 5 the women (750, M 988) were left behind in Sicily along with the less enterprising men, in an episode that furnishes good ammunition for a gender-based reading of the *Aeneid*: passionate irrational females (who just tried to incinerate the Trojan fleet, after all) must be left behind or sacrificed to masculine imperial destiny. But Caieta was not left behind; she pressed on with the stalwarts despite her gender and her presumably advanced age and, although she dies before reaching the promised land, she is not presented as a sacrifice to Aeneas' mission in the way that Dido and Palinurus are. What is more, she is memorialized in the Italian landscape, the only Trojan woman to be so honored. Caieta has only a bit part in Vergil's tragedy, but it is an important part.

CIRCE

The second female presence in Latium is Circe (7.10–24, M 12–30), a much more ominous presence than Caieta, as we find out gradually.[12] In Book 3 Helenus warned the Trojans of Circe, identifying her as one of the dangers that had to be encountered before they could found their city. She seems threatening indeed as the Trojans approach her territory. The alluring sounds and smells Vergil mentions connect her both with Homer's Calypso and his Circe; the howls and groans of her victims connect her with the Underworld. But Helenus' warning seems to have been unnecessary: Circe is not a threat to the Trojans at this moment, Neptune is on the alert to keep them safe, and they sail on to the beautiful wood at Ostia where lovely birdsong replaces the eerie sounds of Circe's kingdom. We may wonder in passing about the nature of a promised land that contains such threats to people's humanity, but the lovely dawn scene at the Tiber mouth is likely to drive Circe from most readers' thoughts, at least for a while.

Circe returns twice in the next three hundred lines. Aeneas does not meet her, but in a way her presence in Italy is even more sinister because he does not get to confront and defeat her as Odysseus did. One of the statues in Latinus' palace is that of Picus, King Latinus' grandfather. He is portrayed wearing the dress of an augur, with a staff, striped toga, and sacred shield (all nice anachronisms connecting Roman times with primitive Italy). Vergil suggests a bizarre relationship between Picus and Circe:

> Picus, equum domitor, quem capta cupidine coniunx
> aurea percussum virga versumque venenis
> fecit avem Circe sparsitque coloribus alas.
>
> (189–91)

> . . . Picus himself,
> trainer of horses, sat: he whom his bride,
> Circe, within the clutch of lust had struck
> with her gold rod, transforming him by drugs
> [literally, poisons]
> into a bird with wings of speckled colors.
>
> (M 248–52)

Whatever we are to make of this, it is clear that Aeneas, who is supposed to marry into this family to create the Roman race, is not safely remote from Circe at all.

The last major Circaean intrusion into the poem connects her directly with Aeneas. Things still look good, on the surface. Latinus has received the Trojans handsomely, he has accepted Aeneas in absentia as his son-in-law to be (father-in-law and son-in-law, as Juno will say (317, M 419), reminding every Augustan reader of the deadliness to Rome of a more recent father-, son-in-law pair, Caesar and Pompey (6.826–35, M 1095–109). Now Latinus and Ilioneus exchange gifts (243–48, M 319–26; 274–83, M 362–76). Latinus wins the prize for the most ill-omened gift of all in a poem in which presents tend to have deadly implications. The stallions he sends to Aeneas are bastards that Circe bred on the sly from the immortal stallions of her father, the Sun. In Book 3 Helenus gave Aeneas the armor of Achilles' son Neoptolemus as a departure present (3.467–69, M 611–13). This gift has always seemed to me to make a deadly connection between Aeneas and Achilles; now Aeneas will be carried into battle by bastard offspring of the horses of the Sun. The fact that Aeneas will have direct contact, through the horses, with Circe the monster-maker, from whom he was so carefully protected at the beginning of the book, is bad enough; still worse is the additional suggested parallel with the *Odyssey*. Horses of the Sun remind us of the Cattle of the Sun, and, as every Roman would remember, all of Odysseus' men lost their lives because they killed and ate these cattle. The *Odyssey* allusion fits perfectly with Juno's prophetic threat a few lines later:

> hac gener atque socer coeant mercede suorum:
> sanguine Troiano et Rutulo dotabere, virgo.
>
> (317–18)

> Then let the son- and father-in-law pay
> for peace with their own people's death. Virgin,
> your dowry will be Latin blood and Trojan.
>
> (M 419–21)

The cost of the leaders' quarrel will be high.

In the *Odyssey* Odysseus is able to outwit Circe and win her help thanks to Hermes. In the *Aeneid* Circe infiltrates the Trojan ranks without Aeneas even knowing it. As Kenneth J. Reckford asks in connection with Aeneas' possession of this "gift": "Once war commences, will he keep control of his passions?"[13] Books 10 and 12 give us the answers to that question. Two more brief allusions to Circe ensure that she will never be far from our minds. Angitia, mentioned at 759, is either Circe herself or her niece, possibly Medea, and Circe's ridge is mentioned less than twenty lines from the end of the book. So the dangerous goddess hangs over the book from beginning to end.

LAVINIA

Lavinia is the central figure in Vergil's flashback into recent Laurentian history (45–106, M 55–134), since she is the bride promised by Creusa (2.783–84, M 1056–57). It does not matter what *Lavinia* thinks of the proposal; it does not matter what *Aeneas* thinks of it either—their union is part of the great plan, and fate has taken pains to ensure that Latinus will not marry his daughter off to the wrong man before Aeneas comes on the scene. Lavinia is often adduced to show the cost of Aeneas' mission to himself. Pale Lavinia cannot compare with loving Creusa or passionate

Dido—not surprisingly, since she is really only a city turned into a woman by inflection. (Take the neuter noun *Lavinium*, give it a feminine ending and, behold, you have a woman![14]) Lavinia can equally well be seen as another sacrifice to male imperialism. So, of course, is Aeneas.

We have observed the connection of Lavinia with Medea, with Dido, and with Helen. In addition, she is a typical upper-class Roman daughter whose marriage is arranged for her for political reasons by her father. As far as I can make out she never even meets Aeneas.[15] She is rushed off and hidden in the woods by her mother in a faked Bacchic frenzy after Amata has been infected by Allecto. What does Lavinia think about any of this? We do not know. She never speaks, she never acts. After her brief part in Book 7 she vanishes from the poem until Book 12, where she makes two appearances, in each case reacting to a situation in which her mother is involved. At 12.64–70 (M 88–94) Lavinia blushes after her mother has told Turnus that she will die if he dies and that she will never accept Aeneas as son-in-law. (What does this mysterious blush suggest? Lavinia's embarrassment at her mother's excessive regard for Turnus? Her own love for Turnus? Vergil does not tell us.) The last time Lavinia appears is as a silent mourner after Amata's suicide. She is the first to tear her hair and cheeks in lamentation (12.605–6, M 812–14).

The poem does not ask us to imagine the kind of marriage Aeneas and Lavinia will have after the poem ends, for Vergil says nothing of it, and Augustan Romans certainly did not look for happiness in political marriages anyway. To a modern reader, however, the omens do not look good for a union between a woman who was perhaps in love with another man and the man who is responsible for the moral collapse of her father, for the burning of her city, for the suicide of her mother, and for the death of her cousin (or fiancé, if she thought as her mother did). Vergil throws out one tantalizing detail in Book 6, though. According to Anchises, Lavinia will raise Aeneas' late-born son Silvius in the woods (6.764–65, M 1009–10).[16] Obviously this is one of Vergil's many aetiological etymologies designed at once to explain a family name and to connect present day Latium (where we will shortly meet Silvia) with later Trojan-Latin history; perhaps it is only meant to imply a well-wooded spot in Italy, but it does seem suggestive, in a poem that is full of dysfunctional families, beginning with Aeneas' own, that Lavinia should rear Aeneas' child in the woods. And, of course, the woodland domicile connects the future child of Aeneas with the present-day Camilla, raised in the woods by her father Metabus

who was, like Mezentius, thrown out of his city by his subjects
(11.539–42, M 707–10).

CELAENO

Virgil connects his digression into recent Laurentian history with
Aeneas' story by restating the Trojans' arrival at Ostia:

> sed circum late volitans iam Fama per urbes
> Ausonias tulerat, cum Laomedontia pubes
> gramineo ripae religavit ab aggere classem.
>
> (104–6)

> But racing wide across Ausonia's cities,
> swift Rumor had already carried them [warnings],
> just at the time the Trojan crewmen fastened
> their fleet along the grassy riverbank.
>
> (M 131–34)

Laomedontius, "Laomedon's" or "Laomedontian," is much more specific
and much more negative than Mandelbaum's "Trojan," as we can see if we
look at *Georgics* 1.501–2: "long since we have paid with our blood for
Laomedontian perjuries" (*satis iam pridem sanguine nostro / Laomedonteae
luimus periuria Troiae*). Vergil could have used the more neutral "Trojan"
or "Dardanian." He chooses, instead, to remind us of King Laomedon,
Priam's father, who tricked the gods and perjured himself twice causing the
destruction of the first Troy. This is the legacy Vergil reminds us of just as
the Trojans arrive to found their own city.[17] Dido was the person who last
used the word, and she knew exactly what she meant when she asked, "do
you not yet know, not feel, the treason of the breed of Laomedon?" (*nescis
heu, perdita, necdum / Laomedonteae sentis periuria gentis?*, 4.541–42, M
749–50). Is it to remind us of this, perhaps, that Vergil refers to Fama
(described so graphically in Book 4) in the line before he mentions Laome-
don? In any case, the Harpy Celaeno used the adjective when she was
cursing the Trojans in Book 3 (248, M 321). So it seems safe to assume that
Vergil meant something specific and negative when he chose the word here.

   This brings us to Celaeno's reappearance in Book 7. For once a pro-
phecy turns out (or so it seems initially) to be much less dire than it

sounded. The Fury's prediction that the Trojans would have to eat their tables before they could found their city terrified them (3.259–62, M 337–40). In Book 7 it seems to be a joke. "Hey, we're eating our tables," laughs Ascanius, when the Trojans eat the wheat cakes they had been using as plates. We remember Celaeno, Aeneas does not. We remember that the Celaeno episode was modeled on the Cattle of the Sun episode in *Odyssey* 12; Aeneas remembers a totally different occasion, one we know nothing of: Anchises apparently told him that when hunger forced the Trojans to eat their tables on an unknown shore they would be able to build their city. Certainly Aeneas' interpretation is auspicious, and it is clear that he is right in one sense at least—this is the place they will build the new Troy. Vergil's description of the table-eating is strange, however:

> consumptis hic forte aliis, *ut vertere morsus*
> exiguam in Cererem penuria adegit edendi,
> *et violare manu malisque audacibus* orbem
> *fatalis* crusti patulis nec *parcere* quadris:
> "heus, etiam mensas consumimus?" inquit Iulus.
>
> (112–16)

> . . . they *turned upon*
> the thin cakes *with their teeth*; they *dared profane*
> *and crack and gnaw* the *fated* circles of
> their crusts *with hand and jaw*; they did not *spare*
> the quartered surfaces of their flat loaves.
> "We have consumed our tables after all,"
> Iulus laughed . . .
>
> (142–48)

The language suggests profanation; it reminds us of Odysseus' men killing the cattle of the Sun and so recalls our memory of Celaeno's prophecy, the polluted feast and her terrifying words. In Aeneas' remembered version, Anchises told his son the table eating would be a sign that they should start to build; his own interpretation of the hunger is that it is their last hurdle, the end of their misfortunes. He is so wrong. What is to come is worse than anything the Trojans have suffered before. Thus Celaeno is an ominous presence in *Aeneid* 7 even though she seems to be absent. The *Odyssey* continues to be present in a sinister way in

Vergil's *Iliad*, and the Trojans' past misdeeds (after all, they went against all standards of proper behavior when they killed someone else's cattle and then tried to drive off the rightful owners) follow them into the new world.

OUTBREAK OF WAR: JUNO, ALLECTO, AMATA, AND SILVIA

Vergil concludes the first movement of Book 7, the Trojan arrival in Latium and alliance with Latinus, with the words "bringing back peace" (*pacemque reportant*, 285, M 377), as Ilioneus and his embassy return from Laurentum. The next verse shows us Juno, a more sinister and powerful force than she was in Book 1. Appropriately enough, she seems to be en route from Greece to Carthage. In the light of this book her machinations in Book 1 seem almost innocuous. There she bribed Aeolus, a minor godling, to do her bidding, creating the storm that brought the Trojans in to Carthage. One Trojan ship was lost but this damage was relatively minor, and it seems slight indeed when we think that in the Odyssean prototype all Odysseus' men are killed. And Poseidon/Neptune, instead of creating the storm, puts an end to it. Aeolus and a storm cannot compare in horror (or in the magnitude of disastrous effect) with Allecto and civil war. True, the storm brought Aeneas to Carthage and changed the course of Roman history (if we assume that the Punic Wars are the direct result of the meeting of Dido and Aeneas). The war that is Juno's handiwork in Book 7 results, by the end of the poem, in irredeemable loss. Nearly every character we care about is killed and Roman history seems compromised beyond repair. It is no wonder that many readers find the ending of the poem profoundly disturbing.[18]

Allecto is one of Vergil's most powerful (in all senses) female characters.[19] She is a Fury, a denizen of the Underworld, one of many creatures Aeneas was protected from in Book 6 that are let loose to make trouble for Trojans and Italians in Book 7. In Book 6 the Furies (Vergil does not name them but they are traditionally called Tisiphone, Megaera, and Allecto) reside between War and Discord, *Bellum* and *Discordia*, on the threshold of the Underworld (279–81, M 370–72). Later in Book 6 Tisiphone the avenger (*ultrix*), whose very name suggests vengeance (*tisis* in Greek being the equivalent of *ultio* in Latin), is depicted calling her sisters to punish the guilty in Tartarus:

continuo sontis ultrix accincta flagello
Tisiphone quatit insultans, torvosque sinistra
intentans anguis vocat agmina saeva sororum.

(6.570–72)

Tisiphone
at once is the avenger, armed with whips;
she leaps upon the guilty, lashing them;
in her left hand she grips her gruesome vipers
and calls her savage company of sisters.

(M 755–59)

She is playing the role we would expect of a Fury. Furies are, as any reader of the *Oresteia* knows very well, closely connected with blood guilt and vengeance. It is clear from the many allusions to Aeschylus' trilogy in Vergil's Allecto episode that he has that aspect of the Furies' function very much in mind. But he has added something new for his Allecto. In fact he prepared us for it when he initially stationed the bedrooms of the Furies between War and Discord and gave Discord the snaky hair of a Fury. Vergil's Allecto is not an avenger, she is discord personified: "in [her] heart are gruesome wars and violence and fraud and injuries" (*cui tristia bella / iraeque insidiaeque et crimina noxia cordi*, 325–26, M 431–32). She is hated by her own father and sisters, can turn brother against brother, wreck homes and kill. She has a thousand names and a thousand ways of doing harm. Juno does not need to bribe Allecto, as she bribed Aeolus; she does not even have to tell her what to do.

Allecto knows just where to go to cause trouble. She heads for the queen who wants Turnus to marry her daughter. Amata (the loved one, an odd and suggestive name for a proto-Roman matron) is strangely involved with her nephew and hoped for son-in-law Turnus: *adiungi generum miro properabat amore* (57), "she was, with strange passion, pushing for Turnus to be joined as son-in-law" (my translation: Mandelbaum's "wished to see him as her son-in-law," 72, does not get the force of the Latin).[20] Amata is a perfect target for Allecto because of her passionate nature, her strange love for Turnus, her hostility to an outsider as husband for her daughter, and (one imagines) her distress at the dangerous precedent set if mothers have no say at all in the choice of their daughter's spouse. (After all, as Catullus wrote in poem 62 [lines 63–64], a girl's virginity has three parts: one third belongs to her father, one to her mother, one to herself. Latinus is taking more than his share.) The Latin women agree, apparently, since they follow the queen when she says, "if care for a mother's rights still gnaws at you" (*si iuris materni cura remordet*, 402, M 535). By working on the queen, Allecto foments dissension not only in the royal family but in the city at large. Following Amata's lead, the Laurentian women take to the hills in a pseudo-Bacchic frenzy and hide Lavinia from her father. Dissension in the royal household is the first cause of the war; from there it spreads to others. (At 580–82, M 763–69, the husbands of the women who left home demand war.) Allecto knows her business; she has created the sort of rift between the sexes we know from Aeschylus' *Oresteia*, a split that could destroy Laurentian society.

Allecto's attack on Amata is reminiscent of Venus' plan, carried out by Cupid, to infect Dido with love for Aeneas in Book 1: "inflame / the queen to madness and insinuate / a fire in Dido's very bones" (*furentem / incendat reginam atque ossibus implicet ignem*, 1.659–60, M 921–23). Vergil uses language drawn right from Book 4 when he describes how Allecto's venomous snake, now a disease, coils Amata's bones with fire: "entwined her bones / in fire" (*ossibus implicat ignem*, 355, M 469–70).[21] Love, hate, war—they are fatally linked in the world of the *Aeneid*.

Allecto's next stop is Ardea and Turnus. We do not get to know Turnus until Amata has infected him, as one of the teachers at the NEH Institute pointed out, so we cannot really tell what he might have been like otherwise. Presumably he was the sort of person who would be susceptible to fury, but all we know about Turnus before his meeting with Allecto is that he is the handsomest of Lavinia's suitors, well-descended, and, in Amata's view at any rate, Lavinia's betrothed. He does not seem unduly upset about the Trojans when Allecto arrives in his bedroom masquerading as a priestess of Juno. In response to Allecto's inflammatory speech he laughs and tells her in effect to go mind her knitting, as any young man might do when confronted with an old woman interfering in what he regards as men's affairs. Only after Allecto reveals herself and hurls her torch at him does he become the fiery warrior he is in the rest of the poem. Turnus and Amata are to be the Dido of this half of the poem; her passion for him and his *amor ferri* ("passion for iron," 461; M 609: "lust for the sword") are the equivalent of Dido's all-consuming love for Aeneas: the madness of all three god-inspired.

Allecto's second target is as well chosen as her first. The sphere of discord has widened. When the Trojans arrived in Latium, Turnus and

Latinus were allies. Then Latinus allied himself with Aeneas, with the result that Turnus now sees himself as the enemy of both Trojans and Laurentians. Latinus has, in his view, "polluted the peace" (*polluta pace*, 467, my translation). It will take Allecto's next move to ally Latinus and Turnus *against* the Trojans. Vergil has changed the story found in other authors including Livy; instead of having the Trojans allied *with* Latinus *against* Turnus, he has allied against *Aeneas* all the peoples of Italy except for Mezentius' Etruscan enemies. Rome's history begins with common hostility against Trojan invaders.

Meanwhile Allecto moves on to her next target, Ascanius' hunting dogs, in order to make the Trojans guilty both of the deed that actually begins the war and of spilling first blood. Ascanius loves to hunt, as we remember from Book 4. Hunting is ambiguous in the *Aeneid*, as many scholars have noted. It can be seen positively, as after the Trojans' arrival in Libya when Aeneas brings back seven deer for his men, but it frequently has negative tones, as in the Carthaginian hunt and the Dido/deer simile. The last time the Trojans hunted in an unknown land without permission was in Book 3 on Celaeno's island. The Trojans do not seem to learn from their mistakes. Aeneas seems to use poor judgment when he starts to build his city before hearing the result of his embassy to the king. It is equally poor judgment on Ascanius' part to go hunting in someone else's land without asking, particularly after what happened in Book 3.[22] Allecto makes sure the dogs' canine instincts are directed against the target that will do the greatest damage possible and move the conflict to a still larger sphere.

And what are we to make of Silvia's deer? Like so much in Italy, it is a strange mixture of the wild and the tame. It is the special care of Silvia, whose name connects her with Aeneas' own descendants, the Alban dynasty. Vergil seems to ask us once again to think of the conflict as a civil war. Appropriately, the first human victim of the conflict will be one of Silvia's brothers. (The second, Galaesus, is not only the richest and most just of Italians of that day, he is killed while trying to make peace.) Ascanius goes after the tame stag "inflamed with love of praise" (*eximiae laudis succensus amore*, 496, M 655). *Amor*, "love" or "desire," is always dangerous in the *Aeneid*, as indeed it is here. Vergil makes the significance of this attack clear in words that bring back Dido, "this hunting was the first cause of the troubles" (*quae prima laborum / causa fuit*, 481–82, M 636–37).[23] Once again love and war seem intimately related.

Ascanius' shot, so an undergraduate told me, is the worst kind of shot a hunter can make, a "gut shot." There is a terrible irony in Vergil's *nec dextrae erranti deus afuit* ("some god / did not allow his faltering hand to fail," 498, M 656–57). In other words, Allecto did not let him miss, but his hit was an error and caused not only suffering to the deer, which would have died painfully, my student informed me, but to the whole world of Latium.

After Allecto sounds the trumpet call that brings the farmers to the rescue and sheds the first blood so that there can be no going back, she reports to her boss in heaven that she can get neighboring cities involved through rumors (shades of Fama in Book 4?) and "fire hearts with love for insane Mars . . . and sow arms through the fields" (*accendamque animos insani Martis amore / . . . spargam arma per agros*, 550–51, M 722–26). Juno sends her back to the Underworld; she herself will put the finishing touches on the war. Heaven will replace Hell in the final stage of bringing to birth a forbidden war (as Jupiter tells the gods in the council of the gods at the beginning of Book 10). For Juno's final touch Vergil invents for Laurentum gates of war traditionally associated with Rome and imagines the Roman consul ritually opening the gates after the Senate has decided on war. In Book 7, since Latinus refuses to declare war on the Trojans, Juno flings them open herself. Everyone knows that the Gates of War were closed only three times in Rome's history, twice during Augustus' lifetime. Vergil seems to have invented this Laurentian ritual to make a connection between the closing of the Gates in Rome (1.293–94, M 412–14) and the present war. In other words, Juno opens the Gates of War in Laurentum in Book 7 to announce a sequence of wars that will not end until a distant day in Rome's future (that is, if we believe Jupiter when he is trying to cheer up his daughter in Book 1). That original Roman prophecy is so compromised by the end of the poem that the chance of Furor being (and/or staying) bound seems slim indeed. In any case, Juno has shown herself to be as much a fury from Hell as is her handmaiden Allecto.[24]

CAMILLA

We come now to our final section of the book and the mysterious female with which it closes.[25] Camilla comes as a surprise; no reader would, I think, expect to find a woman included in a catalogue of warriors. There is no woman in the equivalent passages in the *Iliad* or Apollonius' *Argonautica*. Camilla's name would no doubt remind a Roman both of the great Camillus who saved Rome in the dark days of the Gallic invasion in 390

B.C. and of Roman religious ritual (a *camillus* being a boy attendant to a priest), in each case an equation of a female with a male figure. Camilla is similar to Dido in that she ignores traditional female roles. Vergil's characters do not seem to hold this against her—both young men and older women admire her (812–13, M 1066–68), and it is clear from Book 11 that Turnus thinks of her as his equal. Unlike Dido, Camilla is not a civilizer; quite the opposite. And, as we will learn in Book 11, she is a virginal devotee of the goddess Diana, the goddess Dido resembled but, unfortunately for her, was not (1.498–504, M 702–11). Camilla is a free spirit, like Harpalyce who can outstrip the river Hebrus (1.316–17, M 448–50). Camilla can outrun the winds; she could, it seems, even run over fields without bruising the grain and over water without wetting her feet (808–11, M 1062–65). This comparison between Harpalyce and Camilla is disturbing because it was Venus who was compared with Harpalyce in Book 1 when she was masquerading as a Diana figure in order to set her son up for Dido in Carthage. Once again we see how Carthage casts a long shadow over the *Aeneid*.

Camilla gets the last word in a book that, as we have seen, uses an extraordinary array of women characters to paint the portrait of pre-Roman Italy and Troy's impact on it. I believe Camilla, huntress turned warrior, represents Italy as it is when Aeneas arrives—its youthful energy and its paradoxical mixture of pastoral peace and militarism. The final verse in the book perverts the pastoral into the military before our eyes: *pastoralem/ praefixa cuspide/myrtum* ("pastoral"/"tipped with a spear point"/"myrtle"); before we even get to the myrtle wood of the shepherd's staff, we find that it has been transformed into an implement of war. When the Trojans arrived in Latium Italy seemed to be at peace, though hedged round by war (in the past, in the distance, in the future). By the end of Book 7 war is here to stay.

The war that Book 7 introduces is, as we have seen, the first of Rome's civil wars; it is also a second Trojan war. But this Trojan war will have no *Iliad* 24, no meeting of two enemy chiefs who can—for a night, at least— rise above their mutual hatred as Priam and Achilles do. Book 7 is also the beginning of Vergil's *Oresteia*, with Furies loose in the house of Latinus, in the city of Laurentum, and in the cities connected with Laurentum that will become Roman Italy. But this *Oresteia* will have no transformation of Furies into Kindly Ones who will confer peace and prosperity on Italy. Allecto may be sent back to hell, but Juno can do the job without her, and even Jupiter has a Dira (another kind of Fury) up his sleeve for Book 12. Maybe Furor will one day be bound, as Jupiter claims in Book 1, but, as I read the poem, it will not happen soon.

CHAPTER 8

AENEID 8
Images of Rome

Anthony J. Boyle

What persuades men and women to mistake each other
from time to time for gods or vermin is ideology.

Terry Eagleton

We share the same biology
Regardless of ideology.
What might save us, me and you,
Is if the Russians love their children too.

Sting

Just before the end of Book 8 Venus presents Aeneas with the arms made
by Vulcan:

dixit, et amplexus nati Cytherea petivit,
arma sub adversa posuit radiantia quercu.

(615–16)

These were Cytherea's words.
She sought her son's embraces, then set up
his glittering arms beneath a facing oak.

(M 796–98)

This is the first and only time in Vergil's epic that the divine ancestress of
the Julian family and goddess of imperial Rome, whose great temple
dominated the forum of Caesar, embraces her son. It signals the completion
of the Romanizing of Aeneas begun by Aeneas' father in Book 6:

> tu regere imperio populos, Romane, memento
> (hae tibi erunt artes), pacique imponere morem,
> parcere subiectis et debellare superbos.
>
> > (6.851–53)

> but yours will be the rulership of nations,
> remember, Roman, these will be your arts:
> to teach the ways of peace to those you conquer,
> to spare defeated peoples, tame the proud.
>
> > (M 1134–37)

That *tu . . . Romane* (literally "you . . . Roman"), addressed to Aeneas in the singular, is the pretext of Book 8, the main subject of which is the refashioning of Aeneas through contact with images, practices, ideologies, and values of imperial Rome. Of all the books of the *Aeneid* this is the one that most defines Augustan Rome's self-image, its projected place in history. Vergil's text and Vergil's world closely and problematically intersect.

From the Sow to Actium

Italy is in arms and Aeneas dreams, and the dream becomes the reality (1–85, M 1–110). Portent follows prophecy as in Book 6. Like the Golden Bough, the white sow with its thirty piglets underscores the divine teleology of Aeneas' mission and presages the splendor to come. Prophesied by Helenus in Book 3 (389–93, M 505–11) and reconfirmed by the river god of Rome, the portent of the gleaming sow (*candida sus*, 82 f.) foreshadows "shining" Alba, "gleaming" Venus (*candida*, 608), and the Augustan trumph emblazoned on the shield (*niveo candentis limine Phoebi*, 720). The sacrifice to Juno (84 f.) may make the reader pause. But not Aeneas. He seeks Evander at Pallanteum. Replaying Ilioneus' embassy to Latinus in Book 7 with added urgency and purpose, Aeneas reenacts too his experiences of Book 6. Once again a portent sacred to Juno (cf. 6.138) leads to a journey and a meeting, to a review of the past and a contemplation of the future. Evander not only responds favorably to Aeneas' solicitations; he introduces him to the values of Arcadia, to the site and origins of Rome, and despatches him to Etruria, where he will receive from his other parent another but more literal imaging of future glory.

The two Evandrian sections of Book 8 (102–369, 454–607; M 131–484, 552–787), which occupy the substance of the book, are remark-

able for their fusion of Roman history, Vergilian and Augustan ideology, and
narrative fantasy. Evander is originally from Arcadia, a remote area of the
Peloponnese transformed by Vergil in his *Eclogues* into an idealized land-
scape of peace, simplicity, friendship, and human creativity. He is intro-
duced to the reader in a way that both attends to his Arcadian origins and
presents his community as itself an embryonic Rome:

> Forte die sollemnem illo rex Arcas honorem
> Amphitryoniadae magno divisque ferebat
> ante urbem in luco. Pallas huic filius una,
> una omnes iuvenum primi pauperque senatus
> tura dabant, tepidusque cruor fumabat ad aras.
>
> (102–6)

> That very day the king of the Arcadians
> happened to hold an anniversary feast
> in honor of Amphitryon's great son
> and all the other gods, within a grove
> before the city. With Evander were
> Pallas, his son, young chieftains, and his senate
> (there was no wealth among them) offering incense;
> the warm blood was still smoking on the altars.
>
> (M 131–38)

Rome's political and religious institutions are fused with Arcadian values.
The Arcadians are even sacrificing to Hercules, as was done annually in
Rome at the Great Altar or Ara Maxima in the Forum Boarium (Cattle-
Market). The sacrifice was performed on August 12, which in 29 B.C. was
the day preceding Augustus' entry into Rome to celebrate his triumph over
Egypt and Cleopatra. To underscore this relationship Vergil draws attention
in the Evandrian scene to the chief priest Potitius (8.269, 281), whose
family together with the Pinarii (8.270) had charge of the cult until 312 B.C.
(Livy 1.7.12–15) and were prominent in Augustan times. Specifically a
member of the Potitii, Valerius Potitus was consul *suffectus* in 29 B.C., the
year of the Actian triumph described later on the shield. There is a direct
line from Evander to Actium.

There are models of behavior too. Told to Aeneas on the day before he
receives the "Actian" shield (185–275), the story of Hercules' victory over
Cacus (= Greek "Bad Man") recited by Evander (= Greek "Good Man")

sets up a paradigm for both Aeneas' and Augustus' subsequent victories. The comparison of Augustus' achievements to those of Hercules is not a new one in the *Aeneid*; it was made earlier by Anchises in Book 6 (801 ff., M 1061–65), where the issue was the extent of territory conquered. Here what is at stake is the morality of conquest itself. Hercules' triumph over the monstrous Cacus (*monstro*, 8.198) involves the use of violence to remove moral evil and danger and to protect the established community; Hercules is literally—to use a Greek title accorded him elsewhere (e.g., Lucian, *Alexander* 4)—*alexikakos*, a "defender from evil." His victory over barbarism prefigures typologically Augustus' triumph over the monstrous gods of the East (*monstra*, 698), and foreshadows Aeneas' killing of Mezentius (whose description at 8.483 ff. replays that of Cacus) and Turnus. And like Hercules' "labors" (*labores*, 291), Aeneas' own "labors" (*labores*, 1.10) are caused by Juno's wrath. Hercules is also the "great avenger" (*maximus ultor*, 201), and, as such, both anticipates the poem's terminating vendetta and reflects in myth the Caesarian avenger at Rome (*Caesaris ultor*, Horace, *Odes* 1.2.44). And like the name of Augustus (*Res Gestae* 10, Dio Cassius 51.20.1) that of Hercules is accorded divine celebration in a Salian hymn (285 ff.).

Other Herculean values include humility and contempt for wealth.

> ut ventum ad sedes, "haec" inquit "limina uictor
> Alcides subiit, haec illum regia cepit.
> aude, hospes, contemnere opes et te quoque dignum
> finge deo, rebusque veni non asper egenis."
>
> (362–65)

> When they reached his doorway
> Evander said: "The victor Hercules
> has stooped to cross these thresholds; even he
> has found a welcome in this royal house:
> my guest, dare to despise riches and try—
> as he did—to deserve divinity;
> do not be sullen, seeing our poor things."
>
> (M 474–80)

In a passage modeled on the traditional theoxeny (wherein a god is entertained as the guest of a mortal) and redolent of Odysseus' reception by Eumaeus in *Odyssey* 14 (for there is a clear sense in which Aeneas' arrival at Rome is a homecoming), Evander invites Aeneas into his humble house on the Palatine, a manifest precursor of Augustus' own self-consciously humble abode on the same hill (Suetonius, *Augustus* 72). The *luxuria* of Dido, Cleopatra, and Antony are implicitly condemned as non-Roman and antithetic to the establishment of a moral, civilized community. That Evander's words here serve to express canonic Roman values is dictated not only by the analogy with Augustus' Palatine house. Evander's famous advocation of humility is delivered after conducting Aeneas through the site of early Rome (306–61, M 401–74). The poet's and Evander's description of the site juxtaposes anachronistic place-names ("Carmental gate," "Lupercal," "Argiletum," "Tarpeian" house, "Capitol," "Janiculum," "Carinae," "Roman Forum") with pastoral and religious description to present an image of future Rome as the fusion of urban monuments, pastoral values, and antique religiosity. This future Rome is the one of Augustan ideology, imaged and rhetoricized by the first *princeps*. Evander is even referred to with blatant anachronism as *Romanae conditor arcis* ("founder of Rome's stronghold," 313). This is the only occasion in the poem where the word *conditor*, "founder" (which occurs frequently in Livy's first pentad), is used; it marks Evander as a clear precursor of Aeneas, Romulus, and Augustus himself, who is to refound (*condet*, 6.792) the Saturnian golden age described to Aeneas by Evander (*aurea saecula*, 6.792 f., 8.324 f.). Aeneas is not simply being Romanized, but Augustanized. Indeed the two notions subtly fuse.

After the Venus-Vulcan interlude (370–453, M 485–591), Aeneas is ready for departure. He accepts the assistance promised by Evander, including Evander's son Pallas, and departs for Etruria with him. He is met by Venus who embraces him and presents the armor made by Vulcan. Most important of all is the great shield with "its texture indescribable" (*non enarrabile textum*, 625):

> illic res Italas Romanorumque triumphos
> haud vatum ignarus venturique inscius aevi
> fecerat ignipotens, illic genus omne futurae
> stirpis ab Ascanio pugnataque in ordine bella.
>   (626–29)

> For there the Lord of Fire had wrought the story
> of Italy, the Romans' victories,
> since he was not unskilled in prophecy
> or one who cannot tell the times to come.

> There he had set the generations of
> Ascanius, and all their wars, in order.
> (M 810–15)

The ecphrasis of the shield constitutes the third of a quartet of ideological passages (1.257–96, M 358–417; 6.756–899, M 999–1199; 8.626–731, M 810–955; 12.830–40, M 1101–19), articulating at crucial points in the epic an idealized vision of Rome, in which Rome's history, values, and empire are presented as those of a triumphant moral force. The focus in this ecphrasis—an appropriate one, since the battle books (Books 9–12) are about to begin—is upon the achievement of civilization through warfare. Roman history from Romulus through the Sabine rape, the banishment of Tarquin, the defeat of the Gauls, the crushing of Catiline, Augustus' victory over Antony and Cleopatra at Actium (to which almost half the ecphrasis is devoted: 671–713) is presented as a movement from pastoral origins to world empire through a succession of wars, in which the manifestation of Roman *virtus, iustitia,* and *pietas* prove triumphant over the barbarous, criminal, and monstrous enemies of civilization. In Jupiter's prophecy and Anchises' revelation Romulus and Augustus were conjoined (1.286 ff., 6.777 ff.); here the progression from the first to the second *Quirinus* (the name for Romulus at *Aen.* 1.292 and for Augustus at *Georgic* 3.27 and Propertius, *Elegies* 4.6.21) is presented as the teleological completion of Rome's history. The rivalry with Livy's first pentad is overt. Overt too is the display of specific Augustan values on the shield. For in 27 B.C. the Senate and People of Rome had presented Octavian both with the name Augustus and with a golden shield precisely commemorating his *virtus, clementia, iustitia,* and *pietas* (*Res Gestae* 34). Aeneas' "golden" shield (for gold is by far its most prominent metal and used to denote the shield in 10.243, 271, 884) is its narrative reflection. That reflection becomes self-reflection when the shield's narrative climaxes in Augustus' Actian triumph (714–28), even as it folds into that climax the imagery of radiance and gold and the themes of Herculean *virtus* and civilizing violence that preceded. Aeneas' Augustanization is now complete. It will not surprise the reader to find that when Aeneas first enters battle in Book 10 bearing the "glowing shield," its "golden boss" spouting flames, Vergil makes the description echo the appearance of Augustus at Actium (cf. 8.680 f.; 10.261, 270 f.). The historical association of Aeneas with Augustus, evidenced as early as 42 B.C. on coins minted at Rome, becomes narrative fact.

But contemporary history is not everything. Also significant is the relationship to Homer. In *Iliad* 18 Thetis persuades Hephaestus to make armor for Achilles, since his own armor has been stripped by Hector from the body of Patroclus. What Hephaestus forges onto Achilles' shield (*Il.* 18.483 ff.) is a vision of the entire Homeric world, in which weddings, festivals, law courts, warfare, death, plowing, reaping, gathering, singing, herding, and dancing are juxtaposed within a large cosmic frame. When Achilles goes into battle he bears with him the image of a world now lost. Vergil inverts this relationship. The world imaged on Vulcan's shield is the Roman future at which Aeneas marvels and in which he rejoices; it is the Atlantean burden of this world that he accepts as his own.

> Talia per clipeum Volcani, dona parentis,
> miratur rerumque ignarus imagine gaudet
> attollens umero famamque et fata nepotum.
>> (729–31)

> At such scenes on Vulcan's shield, his mother's gift,
> He marvels, and ignorant of things joys in the image,
> Lifting on his shoulder his descendants' fame and fate.
>> (my translation)

The semiotic value of images was well appreciated in the world of late Republican and early Imperial Rome, in which paintings, coins, sculptural reliefs, busts, statues, and statuary groups functioned as a common language between the literate aristocratic elite and the illiterate many, and were widely used for political effect. The affective and instrumental power of such images, their ability to arouse emotion and generate behavior, is well attested: "Things admitted through the ear stir the mind more faintly than those which are set before the reliable witness of the eyes and which the *spectator* sees for himself" (Horace, *Ars Poetica* 180–82). Here *spectator* Aeneas responds both emotionally and behaviorally to the *imago* of the shield. Instructed by his father in Book 6, embraced and confirmed by his mother in Book 8 in an almost identical landscape (cf. 6.703–5, 8.597, 599, 609 f.), Aeneas marvels and rejoices in an ideological representation of the historical process in which he is involved, and, lifting the shield onto his shoulders, takes into the battle books an *imago* for whose realization he is responsible. Augustan self-imaging and Augustan reality are to be tested.

READING THE PROBLEMATICS

Few critics would disagree with the substance of the above account. But many leave it at that, viewing the progress from the prodigy that opens the book to the shield that closes it as an essentially unproblematic narrative of Augustanization. Brooks Otis's description of Aeneas at the end of this process is worth citing: "He [Aeneas] has become, after Hercules and before Augustus, the divine man of Roman destiny, the divine opponent of Allecto and all that she symbolises."[1] Similarly K. W. Gransden: "In Dido's bed, in her grand palace, Aeneas reverted to his 'Asiatic' origins, Paris not Hector, the type of Antony not Augustus. From the bed of Evander, in a primitive hut, he arises refreshed, ready to put on the armour of the *theios aner* to emerge as the 'Iliadic' victor and Roman *triumphator*, the type of the stoic and of the Christian hero."[2] Neither Otis nor Gransden sees anything in Book 8 that might make a reader question this reading of the book's surface rhetoric. Even Michael C. J. Putnam's more sophisticated analysis yields a triumphalist conclusion: "From the description of Augustus' return in triple triumph, with all races and nations in abject surrender at his feet, one feels that Virgil too felt himself keenly admiring, at least for the moment, that peace gained through might which was the glory of the regime he felt called upon to eulogise and which forms so important a theme in *Aeneid* VIII."[3]

Other interpretive possibilities present themselves, starting with Hercules. The narrative of his defeat of Cacus, the monstrous offspring of Vulcan, operates supertextually as a victory of civilizing force over barbarism, and Hercules' mythic status as a hero of civilization underscores this. But the narrative itself takes care to present Hercules and Cacus as doublets: both are proud, haughty (*superbis*, 196; *superbus*, 202), fiery (199, 219), and prone to *furor* (205, 219, 228); violence dissolves rather than confirms distinctions between them. The reader is presented with the victory of *furor* over *furor*, not the triumph of civilizing values. There is a further point. Hercules ("Herakles" in Greek) means "glory of Hera/Juno," and Juno is the *Aeneid*'s chief embodiment of anger and *furor*, the principal narrative and ideological opponent of Rome. The triumph of Hercules' wrath (*ira*, 230) consequent upon Aeneas' sacrifice to overcome Juno's wrath (59–61, 84 f.) problematizes that sacrifice's meaning and success. As the Herculean wrath and fury with which Aeneas concludes this epic's action will reveal (cf. 8.219, 230, 12.946, 951), Juno's wrath seems placated only when Aeneas becomes its agent.

The principal divine supporter of Aeneas' mission is his mother, Venus, who has an important role to play in Book 8. She presents her son with the divine armor and the shield, and completes his Romanization. Like Achilles' mother Thetis in *Iliad* 18, she approaches the fire-god Vulcan/Hephaestus and solicits his labor. Venus, who is Vulcan's wife, goes further, and in an extraordinary scene (387 ff.) overcomes Vulcan's hesitation with her erotic charms, arousing sexual desire and imprisoning him in "eternal love" (*aeterno amore*, 394). Throughout the seduction scene Venus is conscious of her beauty and her tricks (393). What Vergil has done here is to combine the *Iliad* 18 passage with Hera's seduction of Zeus in *Iliad* 14 (153–351) and with a precise evocation of Mars' projected erotic imprisonment by Venus in the proem to Lucretius 1 (1.34; cf. *Aen.* 8.394). Several problems arise. One of the effects of the *Iliad* 14 intertext is to emphasize Venus' use of trickery (*Aen.* 8.393), for trickery and deception are the defining features of Hera's erotic beguilement of Zeus (*Il.* 14.160, 197, 215, 300, 329). Venus' *dolus* (393) recalls directly Hera's repeated epithet, *dolophroneousa* ("purposing trickery," *Il.* 14.197, 300, 329); and trickery (*fraus ac dolus*) is, as Livy remarks (1.53.4), not the Roman way: *minime ars Romana*. It is important to notice that Vulcan is initially resistant to Venus' charms: unlike either Zeus in *Iliad* 14 or Hephaestus in *Iliad* 18, he "hesitates" (*cunctantem*, 388). But like the other attempts to resist the movement toward Rome—that of Dido in Book 4 (*cunctantem*, 4.133), Palinurus in Book 5 (*cunctanti*, 5.856), the Golden Bough in Book 6 (*cunctantem*, 6.211), Turnus in Books 7 and 12 (*cunctantem*, 7.449, *cunctanti*, 12.919), and Aeneas himself in the final scene of the epic (*cunctantem*, 12.940)—that of Vulcan is futile; in each case opposition is overcome by violence, passion, mindlessness, and *furor*. When Aeneas fails to resist the impulse to kill the suppliant Turnus (12.940 ff., M 1255 ff.), he not only enacts the triumph of Juno and of *furor*, he reenacts and embodies all the failed resistance that the narrative has displayed, including that of Vulcan. Appropriately it is with the sword made by Vulcan that he terminates both the epic and Turnus with a foundational act of bloodshed, "sinking" the steel (*condere* means to "found" as well as to "sink" or "bury") in Turnus' flesh.

The inversion of Lucretius is also telling. In the invocation to Venus as "mother of the children of Aeneas" (*Aeneadum genetrix*) Venus is asked to seduce her lover, Mars, to generate peace (Lucr. 1.38–40); here she seduces her husband to generate war. And her husband is described, in a way that has puzzled critics, as "father," *pater* (394). The puzzle seems less than accidental. His fatherhood was mentioned earlier in connection with Cacus (198), and only in Vergil (later to be followed by Ovid) is Vulcan represented as the fire-monster's father. In Livy, for example, Cacus is simply a shepherd (*pastor*, 1.7.5). Is this intercourse with Venus, herself underscored as "mother" (370), to generate another fire-monster? The reader awaits what this mating will produce.

There is also a paradox—which the Hera-Zeus scene of *Iliad* 14 does not really mitigate—in a female's use of her body, her "snow-white arms" and "soft embrace" (387 f.), to generate war. For the female voice in Homeric and Vergilian epic—Amata and Camilla notwithstanding—is more typically the voice of war's deprivation, suffering, and pain: the voice of peace. Hence the plangent presentation of war in Dido's frescoes of Book 1; hence the rush by the Trojan women to burn the ships in Book 5; hence the unendurable wailing of Euryalus' mother in Book 9, which numbs the warriors and stops the battle (9.498 f.)—for a moment. Hence too the sharp observation of female anxiety, as the glorious horsemen leave Pallanteum in Book 8:

> stant pavidae in muris matres oculisque sequuntur
> pulveream nubem et fulgentis aere catervas.
>
> (8.592–93)

> The mothers tremble, standing on the walls,
> and watch the cloud of dust, the gleaming brass.
>
> (M 770–71)

The narrative's predominant ideology of warfare is suddenly bracketed as male and paradoxically supported by the softness of Venus' flesh.

The paradoxes of the shield's production are embodied in its description. Its prevalent and overt ideology is problematized by aspects of its "texture indescribable." The "immoral" (*sine more*, 635, M 823) Sabine rape, the death-horror of Mettus (642–45, M 832–37), the Cacus-like portrayal of Augustus at Actium (678–81, M 878–83), the sympathetic tableau of the defeated Cleopatra (709–13, M 923–29) with its clear traces of Dido (cf. 8.709, 4.644) are deviant markers in an ideological landscape. Even the presence of "slaughtered steers" (*caesi iuvenci*, 719, M 936) at Augustus' post-Actium triumph might give a Vergilian reader pause. For "slaughtered steers" are not only involved in the second *Georgic*'s paradigm of postlapsarian man (*G.* 2.537); they signal the end of the Saturnian golden age that Augustus is proclaimed to be refounding (*Aen.* 6.792–94, M 1049–51; *G.* 2.538). One word more than any other in the shield-text threatens the imposed worldview: *Antonius* (685). Noticeably omitted from the accounts of Horace (*Odes* 1.37) and Propertius (*Elegies* 4.6), as if from Rome's collective memory, the naming of Antony is as pointed as it is audacious. For the conceptual framework of the shield's narrative of Actium—civilized, controlled, pious Roman West against decadent, monstrous, barbaric Egyptian East—risks disintegration at the recollection of that other dynast and the half of the Roman world whose allegiance he commanded. It risks disintegration too through the Cacus paradigm, whose operation in the representation of Augustus is not restricted to the vomiting of flames (680 f., cf. 199, 256); like Cacus, Augustus fixes trophies to "proud" doors (*superbis*, 196, 721). The "Lord of Fire" and father of Cacus seems to have fathered again. And what has been produced does not sit easily with the Roman imperative of Aeneas' own father in Book 6 ("spare defeated peoples, tame the proud"), nor with the humility exhibited by Hercules in Evander's earlier injunctions. The analogies between Augustus at Actium and Aeneas as he enters battle in Book 10 question both the former's and the latter's embodiment of Rome's imperial self-image.

Not to be forgotten is the analogy with Achilles. The shadow of Achilles has dogged Aeneas throughout the journey from Troy to Rome. The Venus-Jupiter colloquy in Book 1 (223 ff.) (recalling Thetis' visit to Zeus on behalf of Achilles at *Iliad* 1.493 ff.), the association with Achilles' son Pyrrhus in Book 2 (379 ff., 471 ff.) and 3 (469), the funeral games of Book 5 (modeled on those held for Patroclus by Achilles in *Iliad* 23), the enigmatic prophecy of "a new Achilles" by the Sibyl in Book 6 (89 f.) prepared the reader for Aeneas' representation of Achilles in the second half of the *Aeneid*, Vergil's own *Iliad*. Ironically Aeneas had groaned at savage Achilles (*saevum Achillem*, 1.458) and the suffering he had caused, when he confronted their depiction on the walls of Dido's temple at Carthage:

> . . . videt Iliacas ex ordine pugnas
> bellaque iam fama totum vulgata per orbem,
> Atridas Priamumque et saevum ambobus Achillem,
> constitit et lacrimans "quis iam locus," inquit, "Achate,
> quae regio in terris nostri non plena laboris?"
>
> (1.456–60)

He sees the wars of Troy set out in order:
the battles famous now through all the world,
the sons of Atreus and of Priam, and
Achilles, savage enemy to both.
He halted. As he wept, he cried: "Achates,
where on this earth is there a land, a place
that does not know our sorrows?"

(M 647–54)

Aeneas' immediate behavior at Carthage, his suspension of the mission and movement from *Roma* to its inversion, *Amor*, seemed to reflect his understanding of an imbalance between fame and its cost, evident in the frescoes and its figures. But eventually Aeneas leaves Carthage and embraces implicitly in Book 5 the example of Achilles. And when Vergil in Book 8 concludes Aeneas' Romanization with an extended allusion to the Achilles of *Iliad* 18, he raises the question of whether the example of the old Achilles is to be repeated by the "new." Is Aeneas to remodel heroism for a new era and a new world, as Otis believes?[4] Or are the savagery and violence indispensable to Achillean heroism and its unstoppable pursuit of fame to manifest themselves once more as the major motor of history? The detailed analogies between Aeneas and Achilles that dominate Books 10–12, culminating in the final scene itself, underscore Aeneas as the "new Achilles," and reveal savagery, anger, and flesh-dissolving fury as the prime instruments of Rome's success. The shield's imaging of Roman history as the triumph of civilizing *virtus* over barbarian *furor* is problematized by its own literary allusion. It exhibits itself as an *imago* only, to match empire's false dream (6.896, M 1195).

The presentation of the shield as constructed image is undisguised (626–726, M 810–947): "had wrought . . . had set . . . had made . . . he made . . . he set . . . You might have seen . . . Carved . . . in relief were carved . . . Vulcan added . . . set apart . . . he carved a golden image . . . were shown . . . you might have seen . . . you could believe . . . engraved in steel . . . was seen . . . had fashioned . . . he set . . . had modeled . . . he showed." And it is on the notion of representation and image that the book closes:

Talia per clipeum Volcani, dona parentis,
miratur rerumque ignarus imagine gaudet
attollens umero famamque et fata nepotum.

(729–31)

At such scenes on Vulcan's shield, his mother's gift,
He marvels, and ignorant of things joys in the image,
Lifting on his shoulder his descendants' fame and fate.

(my translation)

Achilles too rejoices (*terpeto, Il.* 19.18) but not in the image. And he is ignorant of nothing. At the end of the *Aeneid*'s second tetrad the reader is left to contemplate the relationship between the "image," *imago*, in which Aeneas rejoices and the "things" or "reality," *res*, of which he is ignorant. The opening line of the final tetrad is as follows: *Atque ea diversa penitus dum parte geruntur* ("And while far off these things were happening," 9.1, M 1). That is to say, the action of Book 9 is to be thought of as taking place at the same time as Aeneas receives the imperial *imago* of Book 8. Are the events of Book 9, the mindless butchery there displayed (esp. 9.324 ff., M 430 ff.), the "things" of which Aeneas is ignorant? Or is his ignorance rather of *res Romanae*, the "true" history of Rome? Or is it of *res* in that general sense, the realities of experience, "things," the way the world works? Or are all these the reality of which the Trojan hero is ignorant and which the reader is invited to compare to the fire-god's imaging? As Aeneas lifts on his shoulders the "fame and fate/death" of his descendants (for *fata* means both "fate" and "death"), he seems to be projected as a joyful, motivated but deluded reader of the *Aeneid*'s prime Augustan text. Only through ignorance of *res* can the pleasure of such reading and the pursuit of fame and death be sustained, and history endlessly repeated.

But if Aeneas offers a paradigm of reading, the shield offers a paradigm of art, one that reflects on the *Aeneid* itself. The description of the great shield is the third major ecphrasis of the *Aeneid* and, like the epic's initial ecphrasis, the frescoes on Dido's temple in Book 1 (453 ff.), it sets up a paradigm of a commissioned work. But not only are Dido's frescoes and the shield commissioned works, they are antithetical ones: the former, commissioned by the queen of Carthage, are seen initially to embody both "tears," *lacrimae*, and "fame," *fama* (1.453–63), but then focus exclusively on "tears" (1.464 ff.); the latter, commissioned by the imperial ancestress Venus, elevates *fama* over *lacrimae*. The *Aeneid* invites a comparison between the two formally commissioned works and its own status. The comparison intrigues. For the compassion evident in the Carthaginian frescoes' treatment of the Trojan War and their implicit criticism of the imbalance between fame and its cost are evidenced in the *Aeneid*'s own account of the fall of Troy in Book 2, in the early underworld scenes of Book 6, and in the battle books of 9–12, where the Trojan War is resurrected as Aeneas' war in Italy and the Trojan hero becomes Achilles reborn. On the other hand, the shield's ideological rhetoric seems undermined by the events of the *Aeneid*'s narrative and in a way that draws attention to the gap between the *Aeneid* and the shield as instances of the commissioned work. When Aeneas accepts the shield from his goddess mother and takes it with him into battle, he recalls not only the Achilles of *Iliad* 18 but the paradigm of brutality that in Dido's temple he had deplored. The end of *Aeneid* 8 reminds the reader not only that the frescoes have been forgotten, but that the human dissolution there depicted is about to be repeated, exemplifying history's tragic cycle. The battle books of the *Aeneid* inscribe not empire's golden image, but Dido's lachrymose frescoes. And as those frescoes were seen to constitute but a *pictura inanis*, an "empty picture," one that failed to nourish the "feeding" Aeneas (*pictura pascit inani*, 1.464), to alter his values, motivation, or behavior, so the *Aeneid* exhibits its own account of *lacrimae* and empire's cost, its own cognitive revaluation of history, as an exercise in art's futility. The only *imago* that moves the world is ideological misrepresentation.[5]

CHAPTER 9

THE MAN WHO WAS NOT THERE
Aeneas and Absence in *Aeneid* 9

Susan Ford Wiltshire

I have long suspected that the *Aeneid* is not "about" Aeneas but rather about Vergil, his poetic sensibility and his clear-eyed comprehension of the impossible paradoxes of his times and his task. Nowhere is this more apparent than in Book 9, the only book of the epic from which the person of Aeneas is altogether absent. As if verbally to underscore the absence of the hero, forms of the term *absens*, "absent," appear more frequently in Book 9 than in any other book of the *Aeneid*—four times, including once in a simile, while there are three occurrences in Book 4 (from which the hero is also busy absenting himself), and only two in the other ten books of the *Aeneid* combined. At the same time, the abiding presence of Vergil's larger concerns in the *Aeneid* is underscored by repeated allusions in Book 9 to *arma virumque*, "arms and a man."[1]

In the absence of Aeneas, we may discern in greater detail three Vergilian themes that interweave the epic and transcend the poem's protagonist: 1) Vergil's legacy from Homer, especially in this and the remaining books of the *Aeneid*, including imaginative leaps so swooping as to transform ships into nymphs; 2) the poet's awareness of the power of sexual, possibly homoerotic, possessiveness, a power that arguably draws into question the very meaning of traditional epic heroism; and finally, 3) his prescient and unheroic compassion for mothers—who, he seems to show, pay most dearly the costs of war.

Such unconventional, curiously unepic events have elicited a wide array of critical approaches to Book 9. After some initial comments about the structure of the book and its place in the epic, I will address various treatments of these three major themes and suggest ways that each may enlarge our reading of the *Aeneid*.

STRUCTURE AND PLACEMENT

Internally, the structure of Book 9 falls into three parts: lines 1–167, the attack of the Rutulians on the Trojan camp and the burning of the ships; lines 168–502, the story of Nisus and Euryalus; and lines 503–818, the first full-scale battle of the war. Notably absent from Book 9, in addition to Aeneas, is the young prince Pallas, so critically important in Books 8, 10, and 12. Vergil emphasizes Aeneas' absence by deliberate parallels in the timing of the events of Books 8 and 9, signaled in the opening line of Book 9: "While these things were happening at a far distant place . . ." (*Atque ea diversa penitus dum parte geruntur*). While Aeneas is making his way to Evander's town, the battle at the Trojan ships is so fierce that an observer might think all was lost for the Trojans. While Aeneas is sleeping in Evander's hut and Vulcan is making new armor for his use, Nisus and Euryalus are embarking on a disastrous nighttime expedition to summon him home. While on the second day Aeneas is touring the site of the Rome he is destined to found, Turnus is all but in possession of Aeneas' present encampment.

In addition to the two Homeric halves of the poem, with Books 1–6 modeled on the *Odyssey* and 7–12 on the *Iliad*, the *Aeneid* may be seen as constructed on a "wave" pattern, in which the odd-numbered books alternate with the more emotionally intense even-numbered ones. Within this scheme, Book 9 is bracketed by Aeneas' luminous visit to the future site of Rome in Book 8 and by the horrors of war, culminating in the death of Pallas, in Book 10.

In Book 8 Aeneas is the admiring guest of King Evander, a modest and kindly host. The book is filled with wonderment—forms of the word *miror* ("wonder") appear four times more frequently in this book than in the rest of the *Aeneid* all together—and the future site of Rome is painted with a glow of pastoral simplicity. The greatness of Rome's future people materializes in the scenes emblazoned on Aeneas' new shield at the end of the book. All here points to a hopeful future.

Book 10 in contrast contains some of the most violent descriptions of warfare in any ancient epic, including Homer's. Aeneas is maddened in his lust for battle, and in some twenty-five scenes Vergil paints the physical horrors of war in ways that surpass the most gruesome modern action films.[2] It is difficult to see how the Vergil who is said to have studied the peaceful ways of Epicureanism in Siro's school at Naples could bring himself to write in such grisly detail about body parts. R. D.

Williams offers one possible explanation: "It would have been easier for Virgil to pretend that even in wild grief his hero would show the self-control and humanity that we all admire; but it was truer to what Virgil knew of real human behaviour to present Aeneas otherwise."[3]

In the wave structure of the *Aeneid*, Book 9 lacks both the allure of the peaceful future in the book preceding it and the mayhem seemingly required to secure that peace in Book 10. Book 9 is thus an odd book in more ways than one, especially when we consider a third overall structure according to which the book can be read.

The *Aeneid* is also composed as a triptych of four books each, with Books 1–4 recounting the wanderings of Aeneas; 5–8, his entry to Italy and the future site of Rome; and 9–12, the war with Turnus and the Latins. In this reading, Book 9 initiates the climax of the epic, the account of the war and the portion of the poem that Vergil declares his more significant: "a greater order of things is born for me, I begin a greater task" (*maior rerum mihi nascitur ordo, maius opus moveo*, 7.43–44, M 54–55).[4] It is therefore puzzling that Vergil starts the war—and what is for him the most important section of the epic—in the absence of his hero.

VERGIL AND HOMER: THE TRANSFORMATION OF THE SHIPS

In the book's first episode, Turnus and his Rutulians, prompted by Juno to attack the Trojan camp in the absence of Aeneas, find it tightly closed on Aeneas' orders. Turnus determines to smoke the defenders out of the camp into battle by laying fire to the Trojan ships anchored nearby. This leads to the story of how Cybele, the Magna Mater, great mother of the gods, once sought a promise from Jupiter that her trees used to make Aeneas' ships would someday be saved from destruction. Jupiter fulfills his promise now by turning the ships into sea-nymphs just as they are about to be burned by Turnus' Rutulians.

This passage is easier to summarize than to understand, primarily because the tone of the event described seems at variance with conventional standards of epic decorum. As a consequence, readers from Servius on have troubled over how to interpret its place in the *Aeneid*. For Servius it is *vituperabile*, "worthy of censure," for a poet to invent something so far from the truth as Vergil's turning the ships into nymphs.[5] Recent scholars have, on the other hand, attempted to justify the incident precisely in terms of epic convention. Philip R. Hardie (ad loc.) discusses how, on one level, the episode recalls Homer's tale in *Odyssey* 13.125–64 of Poseidon's turning the ship of the Phaeacians into stone.[6] He points out further that while most of the rest of the Homeric models for Book 9, some dozen in all, come from the *Iliad*,[7] one does find the spirit of the *Odyssey* present in these final books as well.[8] The episode of the ships may corroborate, therefore, his observation that the war in Italy is, from the point of view of Turnus, another *Iliad*, a last stand in defense of home, while for Aeneas it is also an *Odyssey*: a homecoming, a battle with suitors, and the winning of a bride.[9] Elaine Fantham takes another tack, contextualizing the incident in what she shows to be a long tradition in Greek and Roman literature of supernaturally endowed ships. She demonstrates through close verbal analysis how carefully Vergil prepares the way for Aeneas to learn later of the strange transformation of his fleet, as the nymphs intervene in Book 10.219 ff. to lead him back to his mission. In Fantham's reading, the departure of the ships, transformed into nymphs, enables Aeneas to put away his sea-going past and to embrace his loyalty to a Roman future on Italian soil. "Vergil embarked," she argues, "on a dangerous poetic enterprise in order both to bring Aeneas' fleet to a worthy ending and to recall for the last time the adventures at sea that Aeneas had abandoned to establish his community on Italian soil."[10]

There is yet another explanation, the simplest of all, that might account for the ship-nymph metamorphosis in Book 9: Vergil liked it. Vergil was an "imaginary" poet—as a young child in the present day said of her writer mother[11]—possessed of such imaginative power that the sheer poetics of this scene might have pleased him more than any mere rationale.

If centuries of readers do not know how to "read" this event, neither does Turnus, who seems to misread it—quite disastrously—as a positive portent for himself and his army.[12] Thus the motif of misreading a difficult "text" recurs throughout the poem. Turnus' reaction, as Brooks Otis emphasizes, is markedly different from the despair of Aeneas when the latter's ships are in fact actually burning in Book 5.[13] (This contrast is even more precise when one recalls that in a tripartite reading of the *Aeneid*, Books 5 and 9 introduce new sections of the poem.) At 5.685–86, Aeneas tears his clothing from his shoulders upon learning the news; at 5.700–703, he is overwhelmed: "Aeneas is stunned by his bitter disaster" (*At Aeneas casu concussus acerbo*).

In the ship episode of Book 9, however, Turnus loses none of his supreme self-confidence: "but Turnus' bold bravado does not fail him" (*at non audaci Turno fiducia cessit*, 126, M 164). Always the leader, he interprets the strange disappearance of the ships as favorable to himself because the hope of escape is now lost to Aeneas. He sees his own strength growing with the coming reinforcements of Etruscan allies. Furthermore, he adds, *his* men do not need to hide in the belly of a horse or sneak into the citadel by night but will fight on the next day in broad daylight. He then urges them to get some well-deserved rest and to gather hope for the battle to come (128–58).

In the broader Homeric context, Turnus is the new Achilles, arch-foe of Aeneas, seen by some readers to be the new Hector of the renascent Trojan race. Here, however, Turnus is at the center of the fighting at the ships while Aeneas is away—very much as Achilles was away in his tent while the Trojans were threatening the ships of the Greeks in the *Iliad.* This puts Aeneas rather than Turnus in the role of Achilles, while it can be argued that Turnus is defending his homeland as Hector defended Troy while Achilles sulked in his tent. This difficulty of deciding which of the two, Turnus or Aeneas, is the new Achilles (prophesied by the Sibyl in Book 6) is another one of the interpretive puzzles the text seems continually to set for readers.[14]

SEXUAL POSSESSIVENESS: THE EPISODE OF NISUS AND EURYALUS

The more I read of war, in other times as well as our own, the more I am persuaded that battle-lust is closely akin to sexuality. The central episode of Book 9, the story of Nisus and Euryalus, comprises a compelling tale of young ambition eager to be tried, together with the perils and heartbreaks always ready to thwart such endeavor. Along with the conclusion of the epic, the episode also presents one of the most overt examples of sexual possessiveness in the *Aeneid.*

In this passage, Nisus, the older of the inseparable pair of Trojans, longs to do some glorious thing. He proclaims his determination to set out on a mission to bring Aeneas from Pallanteum back to the Trojan camp, sure that he can find a path through the camp of the sleeping, wine-sodden enemy. Nisus prefaces his intentions with a question that suggests even at this moment a certain Vergilian ambiguity about passion for martial heroism: "Is it / a god that instills such passion in human minds, / Euryalus, or does each one's terrifying desire / become his own divinity?" ("*dine hunc ardorem mentibus addunt, / Euryale, an sua cuique deus fit dira cupido?*", 184–85, M 243–46). Euryalus demands to go with Nisus, Ascanius blesses the expedition with the promise of gifts, and in the carnage that follows, first Euryalus is killed, then Nisus in his efforts to save him.

In an authorial aside to his readers following the deaths of Nisus and Euryalus, the narrator exclaims:

> Fortunati ambo! si quid mea carmina possunt
> nulla dies umquam memori vos eximet aevo
> dum domus Aeneae Capitoli immobile saxum
> accolet imperiumque pater Romanus habebit.[15]
>
> (446–48)

> Fortunate pair! If there be any power
> within my poetry, no day shall ever
> erase from you the memory of time;
> not while Aeneas' children live beside
> the Capitol's unchanging rock nor while
> a Roman father still holds sovereignty.
>
> (M 592–97)

These are shocking words. What could be "fortunate" about this unfortunate pair, both of them dead in an expedition of dubious merit at the outset? To be sure, Vergil is claiming here the power of his poetry, a power about which now he has little doubt. But why is it *this* episode that evokes such passionate protests?

The Nisus-Euryalus episode has invited a spirited variety of interpretations. The spectrum ranges from seeing the episode as an unqualified example of ideal heroic action to seeing it as evidence of Vergil's deep suspicion of an outmoded and dangerous heroic code. Much of our reading of the episode depends upon how we view its associations with the other ancient texts upon which Vergil drew. The great theologian Karl Barth advised that one should always read the Bible in one hand with the morning newspaper in the other. Similarly, one cannot read the *Aeneid* without Homer at hand and, in the case of the Nisus-Euryalus episode, without Euripides, Plato, and Catullus as well.

Scholars have long made the connection between this episode and the similarly dangerous nighttime mission in the *Iliad*. There, Diomedes volunteers for a secret expedition into Troy after Nestor offers both fame and a gift of sheep as prizes. Diomedes chooses the cunning Odysseus to venture into the danger with him. As they depart, Odysseus prays to Athena for glory upon their return (*Il.* 10.281–82). This Homeric precedent offers a paradigm of the successful search for enduring reputation and social status (*kleos* and *timé*). In addition, Odysseus' piety is evidenced by his proper prayer to Athena at the outset of the mission.[16]

The *Iliad*, however, is not the sole model for the Nisus-Euryalus episode. Less noted but perhaps equally formative is Euripides' tragedy *Rhesus*, which deals with the same theme. Euripides' treatment of the story, unlike Homer's, implies a deep pessimism about all human activity. This pessimism appears, for example, in the way Athena provides extensive help to the Greeks and once takes the form of Aphrodite to keep Paris from pursuing them. Here the human actors are all but puppets, not independent agents as were Diomedes and Odysseus in the *Iliad*.[17] In the *Rhesus*, Dolon requests from Hector an absurdly grand reward for his mission—the horses and chariot of Achilles—a prize that Hector readily grants and yet confesses he would like for himself.[18] Glory thus has an appetitive dimension that cannot be read as admirable.

Barbara Pavlock has shown how both epic and tragic models contributed to form a new and peculiarly Vergilian version of heroic action. In her reading, Homeric glory yields in the *Aeneid* to Euripidean cynicism, and everlasting fame gives way to greed. Pavlock notes that the excessive rewards Ascanius offers to the young men encourage the materialism that leads Euryalus to disaster and ultimately both men to their deaths. When Euryalus pursues human slaughter and a lust for personal possessions, his twin obsessions for fame and booty come together.[19]

Anthony J. Boyle's reading of Book 9 is perhaps even more pessimistic, for he sees in this episode—and indeed in Vergil's work as a whole—a pervading, almost sinister irony. For him this is evident partly through the simultaneity of Books 8 and 9: while Aeneas is visiting the site of Rome in its Arcadian setting and receiving from his mother Venus a new shield with its image of Rome's glorious future—a gift he embraces even if he does not know its full meaning (8.731)—the "fortunate pair" are butchering Rutulians in ways that violate the very image in which Aeneas is rejoicing.[20] When Nisus and Euryalus die, moreover, they enter into the casualty list caused by the savagery of Trojans and Italians alike in Books 9–12, the sort of human loss that Boyle calls the most unendurable of losses—the annihilation of the young. The deaths of the pair are the first of a long list that will include also Lausus, Pallas, Camilla, and finally Turnus himself.[21] Here, Boyle argues, and many times elsewhere in the *Aeneid*, the human costs far exceed the proper claims of empire: "Wastage of such proportions nullifies the glory of battle. Momentarily, the imperial process is revealed to all as the creator of emptiness, suffering, despair."[22]

John F. Makowski's more sentimental reading of the passage places the Nisus and Euryalus episode squarely within the tradition of homosexual love as set out in Plato's *Symposium*, a dialogue in which the speaker Phaedrus portrays Achilles and Patroclus as lovers whose actions in battle are directly related to their erotic passion for one another. This paradigm undergirds Makowski's argument that the Nisus-Euryalus episode presents a positive, not negative or ambiguous, view of their heroism and thus accounts for Vergil's aside to his readers, calling Nisus and Euryalus fortunate and blessed by a fame, if his song can make it so—a fame that will be coextensive with the Roman empire. In this interpretation, it was Vergil's genius "to suffuse the raw material of Homer and the *eros* of Plato and so to fashion the second greatest love story of the *Aeneid*."[23]

Pursuing the erotic motif, Michael C. J. Putnam offers a far different, more nuanced and elaborate reading of what he calls "a strand of eroticism that runs carefully through the poem, knotting its beginning and end together."[24] He reminds us that Juno's possessiveness is couched in sexual terms at the opening of the poem (she bribes Neptune with six nymphs of great beauty to work her will, 1.71–73). This theme is underscored in the second invocation to the muse in Book 7, offered (otherwise unaccountably) to Erato, muse of erotic poetry (7.37–38). It is sustained most of all in what Putnam sees as the clearly erotic relationship between Aeneas and Pallas, with its numerous verbal echoes of the Aeneas-Dido relationship.[25] In this reading the conclusion of the epic does not revolve around grand political causes but rather exemplifies the power of personal passions. The victory of Aeneas does not look "to any newfound sense of order which might have been reached from an ethical use of arms leading to reestablishment of order but to the life of Aeneas' final victim suffering the ultimate indignity of death."[26] If the relationship between Aeneas and Pallas is sexual, that between Nisus and Euryalus is more explicitly so. The episode in Book 9 is not a misplaced set-piece by a probably homosexual poet,[27] but is thoroughly interwoven into the emotional and narrative fabric of the *Aeneid*. Its consistency with the end of the epic, Putnam would argue, is profoundly meaningful.

For my part, I would point out that two similes within the Nisus-Euryalus episode, the first having to do with violence, the second with sensuality, may adumbrate further Vergil's ambivalence about conven-

tional forms of heroism. In a passage strategically placed between Nisus'
battle madness and that of Euryalus—and thus applicable to both of
them—the two are compared with a ravenous lion:

> impastus ceu plena leo per ovilia turbans
> (suadet enim vesana fames) manditque trahitque
> molle pecus mutumque metu, fremit ore cruento.
>
> (339–41)

> For even as a starving lion, raging
> through crowded sheepfolds, urged by frenzied hunger,
> who tears and drags the feeble flock made mute
> by fear and roars with bloody mouth . . .
>
> (M 451–54)

The simile has a model in the slaughter of Rhesus and the Thracians in the
parent episode in *Iliad* 10.485–86. There, however, Homer's simile is
straightforward: "As a lion advancing on the helpless herds unshepherded /
of sheep or goats pounces on them with wicked intention . . ." The reader will
note that in the *Aeneid* Vergil adds the details of the lion's maddened hunger
and, more strikingly, the terror of the victims. Once again Vergil shows the
consequences to the vanquished of the superior power of the victor.

The second passage is a double simile, one of the most arresting
sections of the *Aeneid*. Finally recognizing that the battle mania has
gotten out of bounds, Nisus persuades Euryalus to leave the scene of the
slaughter—but not until the younger man has plundered a few more
spoils, including the plumed and polished helmet of Messapus, which he
straps on. Because of the glitter of the helmet, Euryalus is detected by
approaching enemy forces with Volcens in command. Although Nisus
tries desperately to save his friend by deflecting the attackers to himself,
Euryalus is laid open by a spear and dies. Vergil describes his death:

> purpureus veluti cum flos succisus aratro
> languescit moriens, lassove papavera collo
> demisere caput pluvia cum forte gravantur.
>
> (435–37)

> . . . even as a purple
> flower, severed by the plow, falls slack in death;

> or poppies as, with weary necks, they bow
> their heads when weighted down by sudden rain.
>
> (M 578–81)

The second component of Vergil's comparison recalls the simile in *Iliad* 8.306–7, attached to the death in battle of Gorgythion, one of the sons of Priam: "He bent drooping his head to one side, as a garden poppy bends beneath the weight of its yield and the rains of springtime." Catullus (80–50 B.C.), the great love poet and Vergil's compatriot from northern Italy—with whom he shares a deep sense of pathos if not historical sensibility—made his own use of this Homeric simile in his poem 11. Catullus is bidding a bitter farewell to his faithless mistress Lesbia, who has treated him with no more concern than a plow that cuts down a wildflower at the edge of a meadow (11.22):

> nec meum respectet, ut ante, amorem,
> qui illius culpa cecidit velut prati
> ultimi flos, praetereunte postquam
>   tactus aratro est.

> nor does she have any regard for my love,
> as before—she who through her guilt killed it,
> just as a flower at the edge of a meadow after it's
>   nicked by a passing plow.[28]

The context of Catullus' simile is different from Vergil's, but the erotic tone is unmistakable. In a reckless excess, perhaps psychologically not unlike that of Euryalus, Catullus has reversed traditional gender codes and made himself the fragile flower rather than plow, just as Vergil makes Euryalus the delicate victim rather than the dauntless spearman.[29]

For W. R. Johnson, this simile is definitive for understanding the episode. He suggests that the Nisus-Euryalus story invites a variety of responses: We may feel sympathy for the young men, even while we do not admire their intelligence. We may even decide that the two men have been sentimentalized in a deliberate travesty of the Homeric precedent in order to undermine epic heroism itself.[30] But because of Vergil's conflation of Catullan with Homeric imagery, we can no longer see these deaths as necessarily and profoundly tragic.[31]

One more simile during the fierce fighting inside Aeneas' camp late in Book 9 may denote the poet's distrust of unalloyed battle rage. Here, as Turnus seizes the young Lycus and tears him from the safety of the Trojan walls, Vergil portrays Turnus as an eagle seizing a hare or swan and also as a wolf seizing a lamb:

> qualis ubi aut leporem aut candenti corpore cycnum
> sustulit alta petens pedibus Iovis armiger uncis;
> quaesitum aut matri multis balatibus agnum
> Martius a stabulis rapuit lupus.
>
> (563–66)

> As when the eagle, armor-bearer of Jove,
> while soaring toward his eyrie has swept up
> some hare or snow-white swan in his crooked claws,
> or when the wolf of Mars has snatched a lamb
> out of the fold, its mother searching long,
> with many bleatings.
>
> (M 747–52)

Once more Vergil's simile incorporates more than is necessary into the characterization of Turnus as a ravening warrior. Lycus may quite appropriately be seen as the seized lamb, but at no point does the lament of the bereft mother intersect with the substance of the narrative.

What we see, I think, in all these cases is Vergil's profound ambivalence about traditional forms of martial heroism as a necessary or absolute good. I believe this in part because Vergil rarely fails to register his awareness that there are consequences to violence and, further, that it is mothers by whom these consequences are commonly borne.

COMPASSION FOR MOTHERS: LAMENT OF THE MOTHER OF EURYALUS

Carolyn Heilbrun writes of the tendency of men longing for the honor of a past culture to fail to mention the costs of that culture to women.[32] Vergil is the clear exception who does not forget. In every book of the *Aeneid*, whether in simile, allusion, or narrative detail, the persistent laments of mothers bear witness to the importance of human attachments and the consequences of violence to those bonds. Vergil affirms the private claims of the close community, of family and maintenance of the cycles of life, as inseparable from the heroic achievements of history and Rome.

The culmination of the Nisus-Euryalus episode and functionally the centerpiece of Book 9 is the lament of the mother of Euryalus upon learning of her son's death. We know little about her, only that she alone of the mothers among the Trojan survivors was prepared to see the journey through to the end while the others remained in Sicily. She does not know Euryalus had left—reminiscent of Telemachus' departure on his dangerous mission in the *Odyssey* without telling Penelope—when the rumor first comes of his death. She is weaving at the time, and the shuttle drops from her hands and the yarn comes unwound. Mindless of the dangers of the battle line she runs to the walls with a woman's wild scream (*femineo ululatu*, 477).

Several details in this passage echo the earlier grief of Dido, another woman who paid the price for someone else's quest for power. At Dido's suicide in Book 4, the town resounds with the wild cries of women, *femineo ululatu* (4.669), a term that appears twice earlier in the same book (168, 606). Like Dido at 4.590, the mother of Euryalus tears her hair in despair (478). Euryalus' mother—who is never named and therefore perhaps more generally represents all bereaved mothers—is called ill-fated (*infelix*, 9.477, M 633), the term frequently attached to Dido in Book 4. Some of these similarities may be inadvertent; taken together, they probably are not.

In her lament over Euryalus, the mother's grief poses the questions that can never be answered:

> "hunc ego te, Euryale, aspicio? tune ille senectae
> sera meae requies, potuisti linquere solam,
> crudelis? nec te sub tanta pericula missum
> adfari extremum miserae data copia matri?
> heu, terra ignota canibus data praeda Latinis
> alitibus iaces! nec te, tua funera, mater
> produxi pressive oculos aut vulnera lavi,
> veste tegens tibi quam noctes festina diesque
> urgebam, et tela curas solabar anilis.
> quo sequar? aut quae nunc artus avulsaque membra
> et funus lacerum tellus habet? hoc mihi de te,
> nate, refers? hoc sum terraque marique secuta?"
>
> (481–92)

"Euryalus, is this the way I see you?
You, evening peace of my last years, cruel son,
how could you leave me here alone? Sent out
on such a dangerous task, you did not even
let me, your mother, in my misery,
say last farewells. You lie in a strange land,
the prey of Latin dogs and birds. And I,
your mother, did not follow you—your corpse—
or close your eyes, or wash your wounds, or wrap
your body in the clothes that I was weaving—
I, hurrying by night and day to finish
before my death, consoling with the loom
the cares of an old woman. Where shall I
go now to find you? For what land now holds
your limbs, your severed loins, your mangled corpse?
My son, is there no more than this that you
can now bring back to me? Is it for this
I followed you by land and sea?"

                                   (M 638–55)

In the first line of this passage the adjacency of the Latin pronouns for
"I" (*ego*) and "you" (*te*) is especially poignant: *hunc ego te, Euryale,
aspicio*? These two words appear together seven times in the *Aeneid*,
four times in contexts in which separation by death has occurred or is
pending. In 4.333 Aeneas begins his final address to Dido with *ego te*; in
6.692 the shade of the dead Anchises addresses Aeneas in the same
terms; finally, in a scene closely paralleling the grief of Euryalus' mother,
Amata in Book 12 implores Turnus not to resist the Trojans further
(*Turne, per has ego te lacrimas . . . unum oro*, 12.56, 60, M 77–83).
Amata, too, had hoped that Turnus would provide security for her old
age. The proximity of the pronouns in each case makes more emphatic
the break in the relationship.

Among the stages of the grief process is negotiation.[33] For a moment
the mother of Euryalus engages in the "if only" questions of her loss, the
final one of which is this: Why could she not have covered her son's
body with the cloak she had been weaving for him? In the ancient
world, gift-giving between or among men was a public transaction, as in
the case of the gifts to be awarded to Rhesus or to Nisus and Euryalus
for their heroic exploits. In the *Aeneid*, gifts given by women extend the

sphere of the private domain. Among men, the status of individuals is at stake with the gift. Women's gifts replace competition with community. One form of gift-giving manipulates power. The other repairs the social fabric.[34]

Thus, in this episode, Vergil maintains parity between family and fame, between human bonds and the public achievements that promise enduring reputation. The two do not merge, their coexistence is not even peaceful—it cannot be—but the claims of one on the other are powerful and exacting. I see the lament of Euryalus' mother, if not the death of the pair of lovers, as tragic in the highest sense.

Any assessment of Book 9 requires close attention also to the similes. Here again the details argue for a more problematic reading of Vergil's treatment of traditional heroic action. In a passage in the first section, Turnus is compared with a wolf stalking a sheepfold for prey, while the Trojans, following the orders of the absent Aeneas, hover inside the walls. The wolf rages at the lambs just out of reach, maddened by prolonged hunger and thirst:

> ac veluti pleno lupus insidiatus ovili
> cum fremit ad caulas ventos perpessus et imbris
> nocte super media: tuti sub matribus agni
> balatum exercent, ille asper et improbus ira
> saevit in absentis, collecta fatigat edendi
> ex longo rabies et siccae sanguine fauces.
>
> (59–64)

> Even as
> a wolf who waits outside the sheepfold
> will howl beside the pen at midnight, facing
> both wind and storm; beneath their dams the sheltered
> lambs keep on bleating; fierce and desperate
> with rage, the wolf is wild against his absent
> prey; after such long famine now the frenzy
> for food, his dry and bloodless jaws torment him.
>
> (M 74–81)

The simile is familiar from Homer. In *Iliad* 11.458–55, Ajax is compared with a hungry lion, harrying the oxen fenced in their pens. Corresponding similes are attached to Menelaus (*Il.* 17.657–64), Sarpedon (*Il.* 12.299–

306), and the Myrmidons (*Il.* 16.156–63). In the *Odyssey* at 6.130–34, Odysseus is compared with a lion stalking oxen or sheep. In none of these cases, however, does Homer make any mention of mothers or their young. All other components of Vergil's simile here are precedented in their Homeric models except the bleating of the lambs under their mothers. Vergil never for very long separates conquest from compassion.

An argument can further be made that this passage is consistent with Vergil's handling of grief throughout the *Aeneid*. Through a careful comparison of Euryalus' mother with Mezentius, the father of Lausus who is killed by Aeneas in Book 10—some fifteen similarities in all—R. B. Egan concludes that the mother's lament as well as the episode that caused it is fully integrated into Books 9–12 and cannot, therefore, be dismissed as anomalous or merely showy pathos.[35]

With a handful of lines in an otherwise sentimental poem, "The Mother on the Sidewalk," Edgar A. Guest captures precisely Vergil's assessment of the cost of war to the "brave and loyal mother of the boy who goes away":

> There are days of grief before her; there are hours
>   that she will weep;
> There are nights of anxious waiting when her fear
>   will banish sleep;
> . . . .
> And no man shall ever suffer in the turmoil of the fray
> The anguish of the mother of the boy who goes away.[36]

In the *Aeneid*, the good of Rome imposes enormous costs on those who cherish community and the bonds of human affection. By the detail he lavishes in his poetry on the mourning of women, Vergil compensates for the losses that in life can never be made right.

WAYS OF READING BOOK 9

One respectable way of reading this book is to take it at face value. Aeneas' showdown with Turnus begins here, even though the provident Aeneas is away gaining allies for his cause. We see the ferocity of Turnus and know that he must be defeated so that *pietas* will ultimately prevail. Turnus' attack on the Trojan camp ends with ships metamorphosing into nymphs, a touch that places Vergil squarely in the tradition of Homer.

The young Ascanius exercises his fledgling wings of command in his dealings with Nisus and Euryalus. This is appropriate, too, because the *Aeneid* is always looking toward another father and son pair, Caesar and Augustus. The nighttime sortie of the two close companions is another heroic touch, one that evokes the mission of mighty Odysseus at Troy. A new Troy is aborning on the Tiber.

If the mother of Euryalus grieves too much, well, let us recall Andromache's keening on the wall at the death of Hector and mark this scene down to Vergil's occasional softer side.

By removing Aeneas physically from the scene of Book 9, however, Vergil also invites more problematic readings. In part because Aeneas is absent, Vergil is able to assess more thoroughly the human toll that the hero's eventual triumph will impose. Here he explores the underside of the heroic system and the costs it imposes on victor and victim alike, as well as on the women who share their lives. The deaths and dilemmas that Aeneas avoids in Book 9 are the very ones he will experience in the remainder of the epic, including in its final lines.

On the narrative level, the *Aeneid* is about Rome—its founding, its perils, its possibilities. On a metaphorical level, the poem is an extended construction of Vergil's view of the world—a world that is intractably complex even for the victors. Book 9 elaborates these complexities by its place in the structure of the epic, its pointed ambivalence about the nature of heroism, and its elaboration of the particular costs of warfare to women and the young. Throughout Book 9 Vergil demonstrates the tension of his imaginative worldview, always hovering between hope and despair. In that very perplexity, however, he holds close to the heart the countless truths of what it means to be human.

CHAPTER 10

EPIC VIOLENCE, EPIC ORDER
Killings, Catalogues, and the Role of the Reader in *Aeneid* 10

Denis Feeney

By the time we reach Book 10 we have read three quarters of this very long poem and we still have not yet seen what the first words of the epic promised us—*arma uirumque*, "arms/man," the epic hero in the quintessentially epic action of warfare.[1] As a young poet, in his first poetic work, the *Eclogues*, Vergil had apparently already wanted to compose an epic and sing of "kings and battles" (*reges et proelia*, *Ecl.* 6.3) but had found himself derailed by the intervention of Apollo into verse of a nonmartial variety. Now, even when he has taken up again this long-deferred epic project, it appears that he still finds it difficult to deliver the epic apparatus of war. In the first half of the poem we have had a love story, much wandering, a tale of inglorious sack, some funeral games, a trip to the Underworld. As the second half of the poem begins, Vergil announces that at last he is moving into a higher gear, with "a greater theme, a greater labor" (*maior rerum . . . ordo, maius opus*, 7.44–45, M 54–55): at last, he says, he will "tell of dreadful wars" (*dicam horrida bella*, 41, M 50–51). Yet we are still kept waiting, with more preliminaries (Book 7) and yet another detour, to the site of Rome and the future (Book 8).

Of course, none of this is accidental. As epic narrators so often do, Vergil self-consciously comments on the way his story is unfolding, repeatedly calling attention to the deferral of the expected epic action. At the beginning of Book 9, for example, when Iris is sent by Juno to incite Turnus to attack the Trojan camp in Aeneas' absence, she says, "Why hesitate? Enough delays!" (*quid dubitas? . . . rumpe moras omnis*, 9.12–13, M 14–15).[2] Even this promising impulse to epic carnage fizzles out dismally, with the transformation of the ships into sea-nymphs abruptly stalling Turnus' assault. It is only three hundred lines from the end of Book 9 that we finally have an epic invocation of the Muse (525–28) and a narration of the exploits of Turnus. After that tantalizing snippet, Book 10 opens with the supreme god, Jupiter, complaining that war has started against his will. Even though the epic slaughter has hardly begun, and even though the epic hero, Aeneas, has still not been seen in action, it appears that Jupiter would rather not witness a continuation or repetition of the *Iliad*: "Now it is time to stop," he tells the assembled gods (*nunc sinite*, 10.15). What Jupiter wants is "a league of peace" (*placitum . . . foedus*).

The last three books of the poem, then, are a frenzy of violence, yet we are repeatedly reminded that none of it need have happened or been narrated: it could have been a very different story. Our reaction as readers is going to be a complex one. Do we really want that "different story"? As epic readers would we have been satisfied and pleased if Jupiter's league of peace had been enforced at the beginning of Book 10, with the poem ending 2,500 lines early, Turnus still alive, a wedding-song to round it off? What Vergil's technique does here is reveal to us our complicity in the violence he is narrating, as he acts out his narrative choices and makes us acknowledge our narrative preferences. One of the most important issues we must address in reading this first book of dedicated epic violence is the kind of pleasure and satisfaction such narratives give. The precious verse artifact here turns to the task of describing how men have their arms chopped off and heads split, their abdomens pierced and their entrails poured out on the ground; and Vergil's commentary on his own deferral of that task has reminded us that we would have felt somehow cheated if he had not delivered on the promise of epic fulfillment. What kind of readers is this poem trying to turn us into?

Book 10, then, is a good place to examine the problem of the aesthetics of violence. It is also a good place to examine the self-referential nature of Vergil's narrative, as he makes his action of narrating and our action of reading part of the text, alluding continually to the choices that he and we are making as we progress. Finally, as we wonder about why epics do the things they do, Book 10 is a good place to examine the conventional nature of epic: Why do epics all have to have the same old things—poured-out entrails, invocations, divine councils, catalogues? Are these conventional features of the *Aeneid* simply the inert inheritance of the past, or are they earning their keep in their new surroundings? At the close of this chapter I shall look at what would appear to be the most obviously tired piece of epic baggage in the book—the fifty lines of the catalogue of Etruscan ships and troops.

First, the aesthetics of epic savagery. The colossal violence of this genre is regularly explained away as being the inheritance of tradition. Commentators on the later books of the *Aeneid* will often helpfully direct you to the Homeric prototypes for particular physical catastrophes, as if such precedent were sufficient explanation. Yet this procedure does not get us very far, not least because, as we shall see, the problem of how we linger over exquisite artistic representation of unbearable pain is already a problem in Homer anyway. If Vergil is famous for anything it is for the beautiful artistry of his verse, and that beauty does not disappear when the verse starts dealing with vile subject matter. Even if you do not read Latin, you can appreciate some of the care and craft lavished on the evocation of unimaginable suffering in this book.

Take one of many deaths in the book, that of Dryops:

> Hic Curibus fidens primaevo corpore Clausus
> advenit et rigida Dryopem ferit eminus hasta
> sub mentum graviter pressa, pariterque loquentis
> vocem animamque rapit traiecto gutture; at ille
> fronte ferit terram et crassum vomit ore cruore.
>
> (345–49)

> Now, confident in his young body, Clausus
> of Cures comes to face the landing party:
> from far he casts his stiff lance, striking Dryops
> with full force underneath the chin, piercing
> his throat: he robs him, even as he speaks,
> of life and voice; and Dryops' forehead hits
> the earth; he vomits thick gore from his mouth.
>
> (M 478–84)

There is a balanced symmetry here between Clausus' act of violence and its result: Clausus "strikes" (*ferit*) Dryops in the second line of our extract, and exactly the same word is used when the dying Dryops "strikes" the ground in the last line. The spear "is driven with heavy force up under his chin," and the poet delivers a weighty line to mimic that weighty pressure, alerting us to his procedure with the adverb *grauiter*, "heavily," which is applicable to the inexorably weighty force both of the thrust and of the verse's heavy spondaic movement at this point. Dryops is saying something as he is hit, and if you read out loud the words that tell us that

Clausus robs Dryops of life and voice at the same time, you will feel the back of your throat laboring to reproduce the cluster of gutturals that imitate Dryops' last sounds: *pariterQUe loQUentis / uoCem animamQUe rapit traieCto Gutture.* Dryops strikes the ground and vomits gore with vivid alliteration of *f* (*Fronte Ferit*) and *c* (*Crassum . . . Cruorem*). The end of our extract is graced with one of Vergil's frequent assonances in '*or*,' *ORe cruORem.* The word *ore* ("mouth") is subsumed in the word *cruorem* ("gore"); since we have just been told that Dryops has no breath or voice anymore, this beautifully sounding phrase mimics the hideous fact that his mouth is now indeed nothing but gore.

The beginning of Book 10 includes a passage that appears to comment directly on the dilemmas of such aestheticized moments in the midst of carnage and chaos. As the Latins attack the Trojan camp, the Trojans man the walls, and in the middle of them is Aeneas' son, Ascanius, who is in command during his father's absence:

> ipse inter medios, Veneris iustissima cura,
> Dardanius caput, ecce, puer detectus honestum,
> qualis gemma micat fulvum quae dividit aurum,
> aut collo decus aut capiti, uel quale per artem
> inclusum buxo aut Oricia terebintho
> lucet ebur; fusos cervix cui lactea crinis
> accipit et molli subnectens circulus auro.
>
> (132–38)

>   In the thick
> the Dardan boy himself, the favored one
> of Venus, handsome head uncovered, glitters
> just as a jewel set in tawny gold
> as an adornment for the neck or head,
> or gleaming ivory inlaid with skill
> in boxwood or Orician terebinth.
> His milk-white neck receives his flowing hair
> encircled by a clasp of pliant gold.
>
> (M 187–95)

In yet another self-referential moment, we see a beautiful object of contemplation set in the middle of the battle-narrative being compared to a beautiful object of jewelry set in the middle of its surround. Ascanius' head is like something enclosed in a piece of art, and it is "itself," in this eddying moment of the poem, something enclosed in a piece of art (note *per artem*, "by means of art," in line 135, referring at once to Vergil's and the jeweler's art). This jewel-like moment holds apart the material on either side, "dividing" it, as Vergil puts it in the third line of our extract (*dividit*). The precious and beautiful head of Aeneas' son, on which so much depends, commands our aesthetic attention in the middle of the chaos.

In this way the image discharges a function similar to that of one of its Iliadic models, an elaborate simile comparing blood from a wound on Menelaus' thigh to dye on a piece of ivory (4.141–47). In the *Iliad*, as Susanne L. Wofford well puts it, "this simile . . . makes the audience or readers briefly take the point of view from which the war seems painful but beautiful, a figurative move that deflects attention to the epic distance, displacing the violence and transmuting the war scene into a source of aesthetic contemplation."[3] It is characteristic of Vergil that he should add an important historical dimension to the already rich Homeric effects, for the artifacts described here are of the kind in circulation in the imperial court of his own time: the simile opens up a perspective forward in time, illustrating the cultural and historical results of the narrated action. The simile reminds us that the horrors of the narrative will one day result in a social order that will produce a supremely beautiful work of art to commemorate them.

Wofford's general point about the aesthetic and ideological dilemmas of the *Iliad* is a fruitful starting point for discussion of the same dilemmas in the *Aeneid*: "The poem . . . tells the costs of heroic struggle—and makes apparent the difficulty of giving social or aesthetic meaning to such action—in the very moment in which it transforms that struggle into a work of art that precisely does carry such supplementary value."[4] The poem describes the establishment of imperial order through violence, becoming a test case for the view recently expressed by the historian of ancient religion, Walter Burkert, that "all orders and forms of authority in human society are founded on institutionalized violence."[5] We need to ask whether the poem's art valorizes or jeopardizes the order that is founded on this violence, for it is precisely this order that makes possible the pro- duction of works of art such as the *Aeneid*. The genre of epic makes vio- lence unavoidable, and so does the establishment of empire: as is shown by the title of David Quint's *Epic and Empire*, for the Romans and their inheritors epic is *the* imperial genre. We have already observed Vergil's authorial reluctance to engage in the violence necessary to carry the epic and the empire through to fulfillment, and there are moments in the poem, such as Jupiter's prophecy of eternal peace to Venus in Book 1, where Vergil appears to hope that the power of empire can contain indefinitely the chaos of Furor. Yet the poem's narrative trajectory runs counter to this hope, enmeshing us more and more in martial rage, so that it appears to many readers that the poem may serve to illustrate the truth of Walter Benjamin's dictum: "There is no document of civilisation which is not at the same time a document of barbarism."[6]

These are difficult issues, which are often dealt with too briskly by modern critics on both sides of the debate. All readers of the book should take the opportunity to reflect upon how and why they read these terrible scenes: Do we loathe Aeneas as he runs amok (517 ff., M 707 ff.)? Do we loathe ourselves if, even in part, we admire the gladiatorial death of Mezentius (856 ff., M 1175 ff.)? In particular, how do we feel about our instinct to keep reading on, our urge to be satisfied by the completion of the reading task? The important studies of Peter Brooks have alerted us to the power of what he calls "narrative desire," a term he uses to capture the way in which "the reading of plot" is "a form of desire that carries us forward, onward, through the text."[7] Whenever we are reading we have a compulsion to achieve the satisfaction of getting to the end, and when we are reading an epic this compulsion may lead us to tolerate or embrace forms of narrative that are appalling. Aristotle spoke of the particular, characteristic pleasure of both tragedy and epic (*Poetics* 1459a21, 1462b13–14), and it is important as readers of the *Aeneid* to be honest with ourselves about the kind of pleasure we want and get from this kind of poem.[8]

At this point we may turn to the second major topic of the chapter, for Vergil himself, as I remarked at the beginning, keeps commenting on the way in which his narrative is unfolding and thereby keeps involving us as readers in being self-aware about our choices and preferences. This feature of narrative has been variously termed "metanarrative," "metafiction," "self-reflexiveness," "self-referentiality." All of these more or less ugly labels describe the capacity of fiction to provide "within itself, a commentary on its own status as fiction and as language, and also on its own processes of production and reception."[9] This may happen in many different ways. We have already seen, for example, how Vergil informs us that he is delaying the onset of epic warfare. This obsession with delay heightens as the poem goes on. One device after another is deployed to

delay the final encounter of Turnus and Aeneas, with each device marked
by some self-referential moment. Right at the poem's end, when Turnus'
sister Juturna finally has to abandon him, she asks *qua tibi lucem / arte
morer*? (12.873–4). Mandelbaum gives us "By what art can I / draw out
your daylight?" (M 1159–60), where the verb translated as "draw out" is
built on this same word "delay": the poet and the character alike have
taken the art of delay as far as it will go. Fifteen lines later, as Aeneas
closes in on Turnus at last, Aeneas' taunt caps Juturna's lament: *quae nunc
deinde mora est*? ("Now what / delay is there?", 12.889, M 1180–81).

Studies of self-referentiality in Latin poets have also devoted much
attention to "poet-figures," characters in the text who in some way or
another embody some aspect of the master-poet's task, or act as a foil to
him. The Sibyl, then, prophesies wars and a replay of Homer's *Iliad*
(6.83–94, M 117–31); Vulcan's team works on formless subject matter and
hammers into shape a harmonious representation of imperial and cosmic
order (8.445–53, M 582–91); *Fama* spreads a mixture of fact and fiction,
flying over the lips of men (4.173–95, M 229–59). Again, we find pieces of
ecphrasis, images of artistic creation that call attention to the parallel but
distinct kind of artistic creation that is the poem: the simile of Ascanius'
head is a clear example in our book. Related both to the poet-figure and to
ecphrasis is the remarkable moment when Juno makes a counterfeit image
of Aeneas in order to lead Turnus away from the battlefield; here we see a
cluster of language that calls attention to the fact that—as an ancient literary
critic would have put it—the entire poem is itself an "imitation," a piece of
mimesis, something insubstantial that deludes us into thinking it real:

> tum dea nube cava tenuem sine viribus umbram
> in faciem Aeneae (visu mirabile monstrum)
> Dardaniis ornat telis, clipeumque iubasque
> divini adsimulat capitis, dat inania uerba,
> dat sine mente sonum gressusque effingit euntis,
> morte obita qualis fama est volitare figuras
> aut quae sopitos deludunt somnia sensus.
>
> (636–42)

> Then out of insubstantial mist the goddess
> fashions a phantom, thin and powerless,
> that has Aeneas' shape (astounding sight)
> and wears the Dardan's arms: she imitates

> the shield and helmet of his godly head
> and gives it empty words and sound that has
> no meaning, and she counterfeits his gait;
> like forms that—it is said—hover when death
> has passed, or dreams that cheat the sleeping senses.
>
> (M 875–83)

As a character, Juno is fabricating something that imitates Aeneas; as a poet, Vergil is fabricating something that imitates Homer, for it is from Homer that he has taken the model for the phantom-Aeneas (*Il.* 5.449– 50).[10] Vergil's boldness is impressive at this point, for he reminds us of the fundamentally illusory nature of poetry's mimetic art even as he distances himself from the falsehoods of Juno's competing illusionism. He is striving to invest his own fictions with power and lasting weight, yet acknowledges here that they are fictions, as he conjures up the terrible risks of artistic failure.

Juno's intervention is most unusual for the battle books. Normally the gods observe and reflect, and we may conclude our discussion of self-referentiality with a consideration of the watching gods' role as a figure for what the author and the readers are doing. In particular, we shall concentrate on the crucial moments of plot decision, crises of judgment, when gods, poet, and reader are observing the alternative future paths of the plot and deciding which one they want to follow. There are numerous divine scenes in the *Aeneid* where gods look down on the action, react to it, and talk about which way it ought to go: these scenes have their origin in Homer, and the metanarrative function of such scenes also goes back to Homer, in whom the "divine audience" is a supple metaphor for the responses of the human audience.[11]

At the beginning of Book 4 of the *Iliad*, after the apparent victory of Menelaus in his duel with Paris to settle the fate of Helen without general war, Zeus goads the divine enemies of Troy with the prospect that the Greeks may sail peacefully home with Helen (4.13–19):

> "So, the victory now is with warlike Menelaos.
> Let us consider then how these things shall be accomplished,
> whether again to stir up grim warfare and the terrible
> fighting, or cast down love and make them friends with each other.
> If somehow this way could be sweet and pleasing to all of us,
> the city of lord Priam might still be a place men dwell in,
> and Menelaos could take away with him Helen of Argos."

After our earlier discussion of Jupiter's intervention at the beginning of *Aeneid* 10, Homer's evocation of ethical and narrative conflict in the audience will be familiar: do we really want a peaceful and premature end to the epic, or will we be complicit with the goddess Hera's vindictive wish to obliterate the city, in accordance with tradition? At the beginning of *Aeneid* 10, when Jupiter says he wants the fighting to stop, and desires a "league of peace," the dilemma is even more acute, for we know that the eventual end of the war will indeed be a "league of peace": the tradition of the Trojan arrival in Italy is not that they devastate the cities of the locals but intermarry and found their own new city. To choose the path of war is urgently compelling, from a generic and ideological point of view; but Vergil's Homeric technique here lays open the alternatives and forces us to accept responsibility for acceding to the continuation in the way we do.

Book 10 has two crucial scenes in which Jupiter and another god look down at the action together and contemplate possible outcomes. Both these scenes are indebted to an Iliadic diptych, a pair of scenes in which Zeus and a goddess discuss the impending doom of a mortal who is dear to Zeus. In the first of these, in *Iliad* 16, Zeus and Hera watch as Patroclus attacks Sarpedon, the son of Zeus (431 ff.). Zeus says that he is torn between rescuing Sarpedon and allowing his fated death to take place, whereupon Hera remonstrates with him, pointing out that he cannot overturn fate without ruinous consequences for the future order. Zeus does not disobey her but weeps tears of blood to honor his doomed son. In the second scene, in *Iliad* 22, all the gods watch as Achilles chases Hector around the walls of Troy (166 ff.). Zeus acknowledges the piety of Hector, and invites the gods to choose whether to rescue him or allow Achilles to kill him. Athena gives a short version of what Hera had said in Book 16, and Zeus allows her to descend to earth to ensure Hector's death. In both of these related scenes (particularly in the more intense and elaborate Sarpedon scene in Book 16), the open canvassing of options is one way of fixing the audience's terrible reaction to the contemplation of these two men's deaths; we cannot bear it to happen, yet we know that it must happen and that we will endure its narrating.

Both of these Iliadic scenes are important to keep in mind when we examine the two scenes in *Aeneid* 10 in which Jupiter and another god contemplate possible outcomes as a favorite is endangered. In the first of these scenes, Pallas prays to Hercules as he comes face to face with Turnus.[12]

Hercules in response can do nothing but groan and weep (464–65); as a recently enrolled god, only a few years before a human guest of Pallas' father, he suffers the all-too-human reaction of helpless grief as he watches the young man coming to the premature end of his life. Jupiter, however, has a far more detached view, as he, in effect, quotes to his son Hercules the lesson he had learnt in the *Iliad* from Hera, when he had had to face the death of Sarpedon; his mention of Sarpedon is at once a personal memory and a poetic allusion to the Homeric model:

> "stat sua cuique dies, breve et inreparabile tempus
> omnibus est vitae; sed famam extendere factis,
> hoc virtutis opus. Troiae sub moenibus altis
> tot gnati cecidere deum, quin occidit una
> Sarpedon, mea progenies; etiam sua Turnum
> fata vocant metasque dati pervenit ad aevi."
>
> (467–72)

> "Each has his day; there is, for all, a short,
> irreparable time of life; the task
> of courage: to prolong one's fame by acts.
> For under Troy's high walls so many sons
> of gods have fallen; even great Sarpedon,
> my own child, lost his life together with them.
> And Turnus, too, is called by his own fates;
> he has reached the border given to his years."
>
> (M 648–55)

Once, in his Homeric manifestation, the supreme god was a far more involved reader of the action; now he has a new and newly chilling detachment, a truly "god's-eye view," which is dramatically highlighted by its juxtaposition to the far more emotional reaction of the novice divinity, Hercules. "These few lines represent a shattering collision of human and divine perspectives, as the most human of the gods is told by the father of the gods how to regard the action. Every reader has to try to be open to these two perspectives."[13]

The Iliadic scene used as a model here is even more systematically reversed less than 150 lines later, when, instead of seeing Hera upbraiding Zeus for wishing to save a favorite, we see Jupiter allowing Juno to rescue

Turnus only for a time, warning her that his eventual fate is sealed. If all
she wants, says Jupiter, is *mora* ("delay"—that word again), that is one
thing, but then he carries on:

> "sin altior istis
> sub precibus venia ulla latet totumque moveri
> mutarive putas bellum, spes pascis inanis."
> et Iuno adlacrimans: "quid si, quae voce gravaris,
> mente dares atque haec Turno rata vita maneret?
> nunc manet insontem gravis exitus, aut ego veri
> vana feror. quod ut o potius formidine falsa
> ludar, et in melius tua, qui potes, orsa reflectas!"
>
> (625–32)

> "But if beneath your pleas is hidden
> some other favor and you think that all
> the war, with this that I now grant, is shifted
> or altered, then you feed on empty hopes."
> Then Juno, weeping, answered: "And what if
> your mind should grant me what your voice denies,
> and Turnus' life continue after all:
> For as things are, a heavy death awaits him
> though he is guiltless—or I am brought far
> from truth. But I should rather be deluded
> by empty terrors if you would improve
> what you have planned for him—for you can do that."
>
> (M 860–71)

Even though, as first readers, we do not know in detail the outcome of the
plot, it appears that the outcome is indeed fixed, at least in the minds of
the poet and his double, Jupiter. Juno's devastated acknowledgment of the
fact that Turnus must be doomed is coupled with a desperate wish that
perhaps, somehow, by some plot-turn or other, he might be saved. And her
twistings here act out the way in which we, as readers, in part want this
better outcome also, for we know that she is correct in the last words she
says in the passage: "you [that is, Jupiter and Vergil] can do that."

Although the similarity is not complete, the gap between the poem's
divine and mortal characters is very like the gap between the reader and
the poem's characters. Just as the gods are involved, yet ultimately

detached by virtue of their immortality and invulnerability, so we as readers are passionately involved in the action, yet ultimately detached by virtue of the fact that we know, in the end, that we are reading a fiction. Vergil crystallizes this similarity for us in two lines that describe the way the gods view the epic action of Book 10:

> di Iovis in tectis iram miserantur inanem
> amborum et tantos mortalibus esse labores.
>
> (758–59)

> The gods inside Jove's palace
> take pity on both armies' pointless anger;
> they sorrow at the trials of mortal men.
>
> (M 1042–44)

Once again, as in his description of the Aeneas-phantom created by Juno, Vergil uses technical language of literary criticism to reinforce his point. "Pity," ever since Aristotle's *Poetics*, had been the quintessential aesthetic response to the events of tragedy and epic.[14] Here the gods are emotionally involved in a strange way, feeling pity even though they regard the anger of the mortals as *inanem*, literally "empty." Mandelbaum translates this difficult word as "pointless," and S. J. Harrison's commentary here aptly points out that, together with the word *mortalibus* ("mortal men"), *inanem* stresses "the futility in divine eyes of the strivings of mortals."[15] The gods feel pity even though they regard the objects of their pity as being ineffably distant from their own status—so far distant that their emotions seem "pointless," "empty."

The gods here are a metaphor for our parallel observation of the epic action, for we too feel pity, even as we know (*at some level* and *in the end*) that what we are pitying is the poet's fictional construction, and therefore *inanem* in the terms of the *Oxford Latin Dictionary*'s definition §11: "having appearance without reality or substance, false, illusory." We are passionately involved (or if we are not we might as well stop reading); yet we are, ultimately, at a remove from the actions of the invented characters. Modern criticism is no closer than ancient criticism to solving the mystery of how fictions move and instruct an audience who are continually being reminded of the fictive status of that which moves and instructs them.

As first readers of the epic, then, we are involved spectators, just like the lesser deities. We know that the text is fixed in advance and that

Jupiter/Vergil will not tell us in advance what the exact form of the text's working-out is going to be. As vital plot-turns come along, we are acting also as critics, judging where the text should go, deciding what it is going to mean, and deciding how willingly we are going to go along with the direction it does in the end take. The massive narratological and ideological power of these moments has a dynamic afterlife, which readers may wish to trace through the very different artistic, social, and religious environments of Vergil's successors. One might begin with the opening of Ovid's *Metamorphoses*, where we see a divine council deliberating whether to kill off the human species and the poem before they have really begun; most memorably, Vergil's dialogues over destiny and choice are rewritten by Milton in a Christian frame in the divine debates that open the second, third, and eleventh books of *Paradise Lost*.

Let us conclude this discussion of epic norms with an examination of an epic convention that few would rank high on their list of favorite poetic set-pieces: the epic catalogue. All epics appear to need a catalogue. Our epic has two—one at the end of Book 7, describing the Latin enemies of the Trojans, and one near the beginning of Book 10, describing the ships of the Etruscan allies of the Trojans. Introducing and interrupting the chaos of warfare are two little emblems of order, with everyone all lined up and itemized—possibly even to the extent of having some alphabetical order in the line-up.[16] As a provisional first point, then, we might see the epic catalogue as an element in tension with the mayhem that follows when the tidily itemized groups collide and try to annihilate each other; as we have already seen, the relationship between order and violence is an epic and imperial obsession.

But we want to find out more than this: after all, what is a catalogue really *for*? Harrison points out that "the original purpose of the epic catalogue of warriors was to identify the major participants in the forthcoming action (thus 125 of the 140 named in the two catalogues of *Iliad* 2 reappear in the poem)."[17] Homer, then, manages to reproduce 89 percent of the listed characters somewhere else in his poem; but, as Harrison goes on to say, "in the *Aeneid* this is true of the Latin Catalogue of book 7 (all but three of the fifteen listed reappear), but not of this Catalogue of Etruscans (only three of the eight listed are heard of again)." Only three out of eight? Surely a literate poet ought to be able to attain a better statistical coverage than an oral one? This cannot be an accident, for Vergil even jokes about it, hailing two of the men in the catalogue with the phrase "Nor shall I overlook you . . . or you" (*non ego te . . . transierim*, 185–86, M 260–62);

it is bad enough that these two (Cunerus and Cupavo, if you want to know their names) are not mentioned in the subsequent narrative, but even in the catalogue Vergil "overlooks" them, telling a little story about Cupavo's father instead.[18]

But the case is even worse than this, for two of those three-out-of-eight are only mentioned again later in order to be swiftly despatched: Abas survives for a mere 250 lines, while Aulestes remains unmentioned until he is killed by Messapus early in Book 12 (290, M 395). One solitary individual is named in the Etruscan catalogue who also plays a part worth considering in the subsequent narrative—Asilas (and we shall return to him in a moment). This is not a catalogue but a not-catalogue: it does not serve to tell us the names of the characters who are going to be important later in the action, because they are not going to be important at all—most of them are not even going to be *there*. Harrison is quite right to observe that "the Etruscan catalogue is generally composed of nonentities who play no significant part in the *Aeneid*."[19] So why has Rome's greatest poet devoted fifty lines of Rome's greatest poem to a parade of nonentities?

If only one of the men in the Etruscan catalogue plays any part in the subsequent narrative, let us have a careful look at him:

> tertius ille hominum divumque interpres Asilas,
> cui pecudum fibrae, caeli cui sidera parent
> et linguae volucrum et praesagi fulminis ignes,
> mille rapit densos acie atque horrentibus hastis.
>
> (175–78)

> Third in line, Asilas,
> interpreter between the gods and men—
> whom cattle entrails and the stars of heaven
> and languages of birds and lightning flashes
> of prophesying thunder all obey
> has brought with him a thousand, close arrayed;
> their spears are bristling.
>
> (M 246–52)

What this man does is communicate between gods and men by means of all the various media available in Vergil's own day: he is a master of what was known as "the Etruscan discipline" (*Etrusca disciplina*). The Etruscan *haruspices* were particular experts in inspecting the insides of sacrificial animals and were summoned from Etruria for this purpose on special occasions. This individual, Asilas, represents an element of Etruscan culture that survived and was maintained in Vergil's day as a self-consciously non-Roman way of doing things. The character Asilas in the catalogue, in other words, has actually left a resilient and distinct trace in the contemporary world of Vergil and his readers, and that is why he leaves a trace in the subsequent narrative—otherwise (according to Vergil's presentation) Etruscan culture has vanished.

With the exception of their religious lore, the Etruscans' function in the poem and in history is to be swallowed up, along with the other Italians and the Trojans themselves, as part of the process of Romanization: that is why they are under the command of a foreigner and that is why their parade turns out to be a narratological damp squib. The continual amalgamation of diverse groups into a ceaselessly evolving Roman *civitas* is one of the great themes of Roman history and therefore one of the great themes of the *Aeneid*. In Asilas we see this process in action—not only in the fact that his skill survives as an element of historical Roman culture, but also in the extraordinary precision with which Vergil organizes the company he keeps in his reappearances later in the narrative. It is a remarkable fact that every single time Asilas is mentioned after the catalogue his name is bracketed with Latins and Trojans, as if to give us an emblem of the eventual amalgamation of the three main ethnic groups who clash in this moment of origin—*Latini . . . Troes . . . Asilas* (11.618–20, M 813–16); *et genus Assaraci Mnestheus et fortis Asilas / et Messapus equum domitor, Neptunia proles* (12.127–28, M 171–74: that is, a Trojan, Asilas, a Latin); most strikingly, at the climax of the final battle, just before Aeneas meets Turnus in single combat, we see swept up together in an anticipation of their future unity all the Latins, all the Trojans, Mnestheus (the same Trojan as in our second passage), Serestus (another Trojan), Messapus (the same Latin as in our second passage), *Asilas and the phalanx of the Etruscans*, and the Arcadian cavalry:

> totae adeo conversae acies omnesque Latini,
> omnes Dardanidae, Mnestheus acerque Serestus
> et Messapus equum domitor et fortis Asilas
> Tuscorumque phalanx Evandrique Arcades alae.
>
> (12.548–51)

> Now all
> the troops rush back into the struggle—all
> the Latins, all the Dardans: Mnestheus and
> the brave Serestus, and Messapus, tamer
> of horses, tough Asilas, and the Tuscans,
> and the Arcadian squadrons of Evander.
>
> (M 738–43)

In literary criticism you can often go a long way by saying, if someone brings up a problem, "Yes, that's the point." So here, if someone says "this is a very funny catalogue: the men in it just disappear," we say, "Yes, that's the point."

If we reread the catalogue, we see that the important theme of amalgamation is already sounded when Vergil mentions the place of origin of one contingent, Mantua. This is where Ocnus comes from:

> fatidicae Mantus et Tusci filius amnis,
> qui muros matrisque dedit tibi, Mantua, nomen,
> Mantua dives auis, sed non genus omnibus unum:
> gens illi triplex, populi sub gente quaterni,
> ipsa caput populis, Tusco de sanguine vires.
>
> (199–203)

> Ocnus,
> the son of prophesying Manto and
> the Tuscan river; Mantua, he gave you
> walls and his mother's name—o Mantua,
> so rich in ancestors and yet not all
> of one race; for you are the capital
> of peoples rising from three races, each
> the rulers of four towns; but you yourself
> have drawn your chief strength from your Tuscan blood.
>
> (M 279–87)

The crucial theme of blending and merging under a dominant capital is here already sounded. If we are alert to moments of self-reference, we might also care to pause over the resonance of a place that is named for prophecy, deriving its name from a "fate-speaking" (*fatidicae*) woman, someone whose name comes from the Greek word for "prophet" (*mantis*). Asilas, the sole survivor of the catalogue, is also acquainted with the fates; perhaps another fate-speaking person of Etruscan ancestry needs to be seen in connection with the mention of Mantua, although his actual name has been passed over—Vergil himself, who was born in this place of significant name.

CHAPTER 11

AENEID 11

The Saddest Book

William S. Anderson

I have long admired a short essay entitled "The Dullest Book of the *Aeneid.*"[1] It intelligently analyzes Book 3 and the reasons, partly designed by Vergil, partly due to unwise audience expectations, for the sense of boredom and weariness afflicting Vergil's characters and consequently many of the book's readers. In this chapter I shall treat Book 11, which also has few passionate admirers, as the "saddest book of the *Aeneid.*" The word "sad" at the start should have all its connotations, covering the range from genuinely pathetic to artistically and/or practically incompetent. That understanding encourages us to ask some questions. Has Vergil carefully explored the sadness of this war in Italy, the sadness of the combatants on both sides, and the griefs of the noncombatants, and has he then communicated to us in the audience the prevailing sadness of this kind of warfare, so that we feel his and his characters' sense of sadness, so that the sadness of Book 11 rightly becomes ours? Or is there somewhere an inadequacy that makes this book sadly unsatisfactory?

The preoccupation with sadness in Book 11 is not my own invention, as even a cursory reading demonstrates. In his recent commentary on this book, K. W. Gransden calls attention to "the most striking example of repetition in Book XI," namely, the dense usage of the Latin word *maestus*, "sad."[2] He provides statistics for the number of times the word appears in the book and in the entire poem: fourteen times in the first eight books; more frequently, that is nine times, in Books 9, 10, and 12; but most frequently, eleven times, in this present book. We should be cautious in what we make of a single word. But it is tempting to infer that Vergil did have the theme of sadness at heart in writing Book 11. We are aware of some scenes that in our experience occasion sadness, which Vergil has emphatically rendered as sad: Aeneas' speech over Pallas' corpse, the description of the funeral cortege, and the lament of the forlorn father Evander. Vergil packs these sad scenes with many words, in addition to *maestus*, that crowd the contexts with pathos. Characters within the poem—and this is particularly true of Aeneas—weep, groan, and desperately grieve over what has happened to them and their loved ones, and Vergil's famous subjective style quickly engages our feelings too. If Aeneas weeps, with the poet's sympathy, how can we not share the sadness?

It is a curious fact, however, that Vergil has concentrated his use of *maestus* within a relatively short portion of Book 11. Eight of the eleven occurrences come in the space of roughly 160 lines, between 26 and 189, that is, from the first mention of dead Pallas to the description of the general funeral for the Trojan fallen. Six of those are especially concentrated within sixty-seven lines that deal exclusively with the preparations of Pallas' corpse for departure and Aeneas' tearful speech of farewell (26–92). To judge from that distribution, Vergil places predominant stress on the sadness that Aeneas, the Trojans, and their Arcadian allies feel. The three other instances of *maestus* apply to the Italian situation: the sadness of the legates who return from Diomedes with gloomy news (226); the tearful dismay of Italian fathers at the prospect of more sons' deaths as Aeneas renews his offensive (454); and the hopelessly pathetic appeal of Italian mothers to Minerva to stop Aeneas dead in his tracks (482). But these episodes are not packed with sadness; they involve undistinguished groups of people, and the sadness functions more as foreshadowing than as a comment on a particular corpse or death, such as that of Pallas. Vergil, by his choice of situation and language, seems to have concentrated sadness among the Trojans. Has he thus engaged our bias for their sadness?

This leads us to the question of whether Vergil has rigged his narrative and our responses to produce unfair propaganda. In this respect it is useful to make some distinctions. Some situations in this book are intrinsically sad, and Vergil has developed and emphasized them as such: for example, Pallas' funeral. Remember the famous photo of the Frenchman weeping as German troops entered Paris? That image said it all for the sadness of the moment. But there are situations, too, which do not openly state their feelings, which, by their very self-restraint, have the potentiality of stimulating sadness in sensitive observers or readers. Almost any picture of John F. Kennedy, and now of Jacqueline, has that potentiality. We implicitly feel the sadness of life expressed in the person of someone who, despite all his or her vitality, was doomed to die prematurely. Vergil, I think, can do

something similar: use scenes of reduced or even ignored sadness to stim-
ulate the active empathy of the attentive audience. Thus, in its expression of
grief for both Trojans and Italians, this is the saddest book throughout.

Book 11 opens with dawn, on the day following the battle depicted in
the previous book. Vergil divides the presentation into three parts. The
first features Aeneas and the mainly sad aftermath of the conflict. Aeneas
sends off the cortege of Pallas, and he agrees to a twelve-day truce for the
burial of the dead on both sides. Another dawn is noted at 182, which
could be the following day or a few days later, when the public funerals
are performed. The opening of the second part blends with the end of the
first (225), but Vergil has transferred his attention to the Italians and the
political assembly called by Latinus. Bad news has come that Diomedes
refuses to join them against Aeneas, and the king feels obliged to deter-
mine how his leaders now feel about the war. This part features the fierce
hostility of Drances, an unscrupulous politician, and Turnus the hot-
headed hero. Neither rouses much confidence. Before a decision can be
made, however, the assembly proves to be abortive, when the report that
Aeneas and his troops are advancing for battle requires immediate action.
Apparently, the twelve days of truce are over. The third part covers the
resulting battle, which is another disaster for the Italians. Turnus lays an
ambush for Aeneas and encourages the Volscian woman-warrior Camilla
to lead the cavalry against the Trojan horse. She does so and performs
numerous feats before succumbing to a treacherous spearcast; and Turnus
leaves his ambush just before he could have caught Aeneas and presum-
ably inflicted much damage. He rushes back to the scene of defeat and
plans to engage Aeneas' men, when nightfall ends combat. Vergil may not
lavish the adjective "sad" on these events, but it clearly has been a terribly
grim day for the Italians.

PART 1

The opening scene of the first part might be viewed as a test case of
Vergil's technique of understated sadness. At first view, in the construc-
tion of the picture and in the words of the speaker Aeneas, we see and
hear only of a magnificent victory, due honor to the gods in ritual that
anticipates later Roman practices, and complete confidence about the
future because of the victory over Mezentius. Everything is said and seen
exclusively from that perspective of Trojan triumph, until finally Aeneas

transfers his attention to dead Pallas and the sadness in store for his father
and city. Now such exclusive emphasis may seem odd after the memorable
way Vergil built up to the ending of Book 10 and the tragic feelings of
Mezentius before his death. No matter what Aeneas and the Trojans do or
say the next day, can we, after Vergil's presentation of those earlier actions
and words, rest content with a unilateral Trojan self-satisfaction? I once
claimed about the conclusion of Book 10: "The humbled words of Mezen-
tius have tragic depth (846 ff.). At the end, when he welcomes Aeneas'
death stroke, he has but one request: to be buried with Lausus (906). Vergil
does not report Aeneas' answer. We are left to decide whether the warrior,
like the poet, would have been generous."[3] I believe Vergil obliges us to
wonder how Aeneas would and should have responded to Mezentius' last
words. When we watch and hear Aeneas proudly exult over his victory, with
not the slightest notice of his foe, Vergil flagrantly ignores an expectation
that he has created. This produces dissatisfaction with Aeneas as well as
with the poet; or, to put it differently, with Aeneas because the poet has
shown him in ungenerous exultation. But Vergil does more: he reveals what
Aeneas' response to the father's appeal must have been through the details
he slips in about the armor of Mezentius adorning the proud trophy on
display.

To produce a Roman trophy, a tree was cut down and worked so that it
served a function similar to a modern headless store dummy: the trunk
represented the human torso, and two branches, with ends lopped off,
served as the site of human shoulders and the beginning of arms. The victor
then dressed this tree-dummy in the armor taken from the corpse of his
victim and set up the ensemble, now a "trophy," as a display of his prowess
and, in some cases, as here, in honor of the war god Mars. The tree trunk
replaced the once-vital human being who wore that armor. Thus, here the
trophy stands for the tragic father who spoke so movingly and meant so
much to Vergil and us. The armor undeniably tells us exactly how Aeneas
rejected his appeal. The helmet crest drips with blood; the breastplate has
been "smashed and pierced through twice-six times." Although the blood
on the crest could have come from the fatal wound in the throat that Aeneas
dealt him, I am doubtful. The twelve rough gashes in his breastplate did
not come from Aeneas or from any opponent who faced Mezentius in life.
They *have* to be evidence of hateful enemy abuse of the corpse—what
Mezentius asked Aeneas, in full dignity, to spare him so that he could be
united with his son Lausus. After Aeneas drove his sword into the throat of
his willing victim, then, we can reconstruct the sequel: Etruscans came up

and vented their fury, with Aeneas' permission, on their hated former king, plunging spears and swords into the corpse and totally disfiguring it. Such detail increases the sadness of Mezentius' end and casts a pall on the heroic rhetoric of the Trojan.

Most of this first part concentrates on the Trojans' and especially Aeneas' deep grief for the death of Pallas. The antithesis is obvious: on the one hand, exultation over the bloody trophy that Mezentius has become, wherever his body is, however disfigured; on the other hand, heavily emphasized sorrow, subjectively presented by Aeneas and sympathetic poet, for the dead youth Pallas. Aeneas has fought and killed enemy, including both Lausus and Mezentius, in the battle; and he has a right to speak about this war and war in general. He knows that war is a dissatisfying mix of "glorious" success and intolerable loss, and he spends far more time on his grief than on his exultation over Mezentius. Some critics believe he blames himself for Pallas' death, but this is not clear from Vergil's presentation, I believe; he has ample grounds for grief in the contrast between what enthusiastic Pallas expected to achieve before returning home in triumph and what has in fact happened. Aeneas weeps as he announces the plan to prepare the cortege (*inlacrimans*, 29), weeps again as he begins his funeral speech by the corpse (*lacrimis obortis*, 41), and is still weeping as he falls silent (*deflevit*, 59). Vergil then devotes another thirty lines to the organization of the cortege, and again he lets Aeneas speak briefly as it departs for Evander's city: "The same frightful fate of war calls me from this / to other tears. I hail you now forever, / great Pallas; and forever, my farewell." In this moment of sadness, war is nothing but "tears."

Vergil enhances the sadness of Pallas' death by adding lamenting women to the scene. Passing into the tent or pavilion where the corpse is laid out, Aeneas finds it attended by "mourning Ilian women, hair disheveled" in standard grieving fashion. Where did these Trojan women come from? Did not Aeneas leave them all behind in Sicily, because they were a drag on the Trojans' heroic purposes? But when it comes to expressing grief, how can you do without women? So Vergil has created some for this occasion. (Remember how he did the same to make the death of young Euryalus more affective in Book 9.)[4] Vergil will soon remind us of the Italian womenfolk and their desperate grief; here, he unexpectedly contrives weeping women for the Trojan side, too.

More sadness is conveyed in the simile about Pallas and the special funeral gift that Aeneas finds for him. Here is Mandelbaum's version of the simile that conveys how the poet sees the boy's corpse (90–94): "just as a flower of gentle violet / or drooping hyacinth a girl has gathered; / its brightness and its form have not yet passed, / but mother earth no longer feeds it or / supplies its strength." He resembles a cut flower, lovely for one last precious moment. But even more, Pallas has been given the descriptive details that belong more aptly to a virgin at the moment of marriage people used to call metaphorically "deflowering" or "defloration." Greek and Latin poetry loves to place the marriageable maiden, the virgin, amid flowers, which she is plucking or is urged metaphorically to gather. A virgin has plucked this flower, and Pallas is dead; the ultimate sexual assault has robbed him of the pleasures of marriage and family, of the happy future that Evander hoped for him. We should be awake to this theme in Vergil's poem, that death deflowers young warriors, men like Pallas and later Turnus, and women, as we shall see, like Camilla.[5]

The connection of war-death and violence to virgins at the time of marriage is bolstered by the reference to "mother" earth, no longer performing her maternal role for the cut flower. The virgin's mother loses her role, too, after the wedding. In that latter sense, the gift of Aeneas is significant: he has passed on a present from dead Dido, a robe richly woven with gold and purple threads by her own loving hand, which she vainly offered him as a token of love that he could not and would not indulge. This gift to Pallas has to awaken a sense of ironic sadness even if Aeneas has put it aside. Pallas and Dido, deprived of life and love, have much in common. When Aeneas veils Pallas' head with this symbolic gift (*obnubit*, 77), Vergil refers to the veil that regularly stands for the virgin's deferential role in the marriage ritual. Pallas' wedding is going to be his funeral, and the pyre will consume this gorgeous robe of loving Dido and the fair hair of Pallas that it veils.

Aeneas' negotiations with the Latin ambassadors support the illusion of time passed while the cortege covers the distance to Evander's city. It is a tearfully sad arrival (139 ff.), with the principal stress of course on Evander's grief, but with no small emphasis, too, on the feelings of the Arcadian women and the sounds of lamentation that fill the "sad city" (*maestam urbem*, 147). Vergil turns away from that scene to the next, I presume, dawn, which in his affective terms brings kindly light to wretched mortals (*miseris mortalibus*, 182). The mass funerals of the Trojans, definitely sad and tearful (*maestum*, 189, *lacrimis*, 191), and of the Italians, also full of grieving (*luctus*, 214, *maerentum*, 216) are juxtaposed. But in the latter case Vergil can concentrate on the noncombatants, the wives, sisters, children, and parents of the dead Italians who curse the war and pick out Turnus as the scapegoat.

PART 2

The second part, which involves the abortive Council of the Italians (225–444), explores more fully the feelings of the Italian males, warriors, and noncombatants, and the extent to which they reflect the passionate war-hating grief of the women, children, and aged recorded above. Treading a cautious tightrope, Latinus reacts to the loss of the hoped-for alliance with Diomedes by emphasizing the little hope they realistically have in their own strength (309–13) and proposing to settle with Aeneas. Drances, quick to seize an opportunity, jumps in with his comments, which are aimed, the poet tells us, to belittle Turnus, the warrior he hates from personal, not patriotic, motives (336–75). In his invidious speech, though he says some things that are true and potentially useful, his bias is obvious, calculated to cause trouble and negate the utility of his words. The real issues—the wretched deaths and the apparent futility of this war—are lost. Caught in a pattern of political vituperation and dishonest rhetoric, Turnus lacks the self-control and broad understanding to restore the focus to the main issues. Even at the end, when he has appealed to the manly courage (*virtus*) of his audience, he cannot help reverting to his anger against Drances and his civilian "cowardice." The result of this mutual sniping is indecisive: the sadness of the Italians has been left unsatisfied, and the cursed war resumes.

Large numbers join in the militant fervor of Turnus, and Vergil briefly records the grief and grumbling doubts of the older male noncombatants, the fathers (*flent maesti mussantque patres*, 454). Their sadness, for all its validity, has no chance of gaining a hearing amid the warlike confusion in Latium. Now, the women and children appear on the walls, to be of use in this ultimate crisis (475–76). Other women accompany Queen Amata to the temple of Minerva, to pray in vain for help in their struggle against Aeneas, whom they hatefully call the "Phrygian pirate" (484). And finally the poet turns his and our attention to their heroic leader Turnus, as he wildly (*furens*, 486) arms himself and then dashes down from the citadel, all "golden" (*aureus*, 490)—an exaggerated adjective to go with his wildness and the irrational enthusiasm of his warriors. Here a simile captures the complex nature of Turnus, so attractive in his energy and drive, so sad

in his crazed reliance on wildness. When Greeks and Romans compared
human beings to animals, they knew that they might be magnifying human
physical qualities, but they were definitely minimizing their rational con-
trol. To make his comparison even more effective, Vergil borrows a
memorable simile from Homer's *Iliad*, which applied first to Paris, then to
Hector, to define their respective moments of irresponsibility:[6]

> exsultatque animis et spe iam praecipit hostem:
> qualis ubi abruptis fugit praesepia vinclis
> tandem liber equus, campoque potitus aperto
> aut ille in pastus armentaque tendit equarum
> aut adsuetus aquae perfundi flumine noto
> emicat, arrectisque fremit cervicibus alte
> luxurians luduntque iubae per colla, per armos.
>
> (491–97)

> He is delirious with courage,
> his hope already tears the enemy:
> just as a stallion when he snaps his tether
> and flies off from the stables, free at last
> to lord the open plains, will either make
> for meadows and the herds of mares or else
> leap from the stream where he is used to bathing
> and, wanton, happy, neigh, his head raised high,
> while his mane sweeps across his neck and shoulders.
>
> (M 649–57)

Like most translations, this one has made some arguable decisions. In
the first line, "delirious" is too strong for Vergil's verb, which is the basis
of our word "exult"; and "courage" is too specifically heroic and human
for the Latin word that I would render "high spirits." Vergil describes the
youthful exuberance of Turnus in words that are also thoroughly appro-
priate for the horse who will now appear in his simile. It seems to make
sense that Turnus in his delirium should "already tear the enemy," but
since such action does not adapt easily to the simile's horse, we might
suspect that Vergil did not quite say that. His Turnus "already in his hope
catches the enemy ahead of time" (*spe iam praecipit hostem*, 491). No
tearing or wounding, simply overtaking. But that is exactly what the
simile wants: the horse is heading for either of two destinations. Thus, we

must change Mandelbaum at line 655. He pictures the second alternative as follows: the horse leaps from the stream after bathing and prances about neighing and sweeping his mane picturesquely over his neck. But that is not it. Here is what the horse joyously imagines and hopes to achieve: *either* he will join the female horses in the pastures, to make love not war, *or* he will flash forward to a familiar stream, where he has been accustomed to bathing. Bathing is a different sensuous pleasure the stallion might pursue after breaking free, again noticeably different in kind from Turnus' militant hope.

Homer's point was that the horse had escaped and was following its natural instincts, not what men had trained it to do, which was to serve men obediently in war. The Homeric horse is regularly part of a pair drawing a chariot into battle and giving a hero quick access to the enemy. The Vergilian horse more often serves as a cavalry animal. Turnus is about to rush wildly away, not only from the orderly Council of State, but also from the cavalry battle that follows immediately on his departure, to lay an abortive and inglorious ambush for Aeneas. Mandelbaum's "free at last" (652) is accurate for the Latin, but the words, so closely now identified with Martin Luther King Jr., have a special irony that Vergil did not envision. The freedom of the stallion and of Turnus, quite unearned, is obvious irresponsibility. That last picture, then, of the horse as it neighs, its head held high, swishing its mane over neck and shoulders, refers to it not in a position of standing still but as moving spiritedly toward either of its destinations, mares or stream. To picture Turnus rushing into war irresponsibly like an escaping animal is an exciting image but also a sad one. How different from Aeneas who hates war and equates it with tears, for himself and both sides involved; he engages in it reluctantly, from a sense of duty. Turnus regards this battle as the means by which he escapes all the public responsibilities that limit his "freedom." His motives rob the Italian cause of valid purpose and seriously compromise its leader.

PART 3

Vergil, although living in the highly prejudiced culture of Rome and writing within the limits of that cultural bias has nevertheless created in the female figure of Camilla a powerfully sympathetic, even heroic, representative of the Italian people. I think that sensitive male poets in Rome—such as Vergil and Ovid, to name but two—were aware of the cruder cultural bias against women and made creative efforts to break that bias down. Just as Vergil let what I called "understated sadness" emerge effectively in his description of the battered, bloody trophy that replaced Mezentius' mutilated corpse at the beginning of this book, I believe he has produced an understated representation of Camilla that is neither chauvinistically triumphant nor pornographically defective. I now argue for that point of view. Much of what I shall advance has been anticipated by Grace Starry West.[7]

The Camilla Vergil introduces as the final entry in the Catalogue of Italians of Book 7, a most dramatic conclusion to that book, is (at least to the internal audience of the epic) a highly attractive compound of feminine militancy.[8] She is a *bellatrix* (warrior) (805) who has rejected the normal woman's role of weaving, and, paradoxically, though a virgin, associates herself with rough battles. Yet Vergil chooses to emphasize her swiftness and light agility, so that we picture her racing gracefully over the fields, not pursuing or attacking an enemy; and he makes her the focus of admiring women, who pick out her regal attire with their eyes and notice nothing of her menacing militarism. These women are mothers (813), and we can well imagine that they think of her longingly as a possible mate for their sons.

The Camilla we get to know in Book 11 is not wholly the same woman; Vergil has not exactly changed her, but he reveals new details about her that suggest the admiring Italian women were perhaps premature in their judgments. Understanding this more complex Camilla, then, involves not only perceiving her thematic function but also exploring afresh the way Vergil presents this female figure.

I start from the new information about Camilla that Vergil introduces as Turnus departs for his ambush and leaves her in command of the cavalry engagement before the city (532–84). The attractive woman of Book 7 received an elusive description as one who did not participate in domestic tasks but engaged in warfare, looked queenly, ran swiftly, carried a quiver and a spear tipped with myrtle (a favorite symbol of Venus). In the work of Vergil's great successor, Ovid, virgins regularly make a choice, that is, either preparing for matrimony and domesticity or dedicating themselves to virginity; this choice can be represented as either weaving or hunting, working for Minerva or for Diana. But the virgin who devotes herself to warfare does not fall into a recognizable pattern other than that of the exotic Amazon. In Vergil's account in Book 11, Diana gives a sympathetic narrative that presents Camilla as a unique kind of temporary devotee, who then has left off hunting for warfare, with the goddess's sad permission. Diana is not angry with her and has no intention of punishing her for abandoning her sacred duty; on the contrary, the goddess, knowing that Camilla is doomed, announces ahead that she will do all she can to ennoble her death (590–94).

The reasons for Diana's special feelings for Camilla are indicated in the background narrative about her father, her narrow escape from death, and the peculiar way in which she became a devotee of Diana. She has not consciously chosen virginity over marriage; her background readily suggests why she is above all a *bellatrix*. Her father Metabus was a cruel and hated king, much like Mezentius, who fled from an uprising and escaped only with his baby daughter. To save the girl, he prayed for Diana's help and dedicated Camilla to the goddess as a servant; the Latin word *famula* (558) is a synonym for the word *camilla* that gives her her name. Metabus hid in the mountains, far from political and social advantages, and Camilla grew up as a kind of "wild girl," drinking the milk of wild animals (571–72) and toting around spear, bow, and arrows once she could walk (573–80). She served Diana devoutly, as virginal huntress, and Diana loved her more than all others (537, 586).

Vergil has carefully used Diana as a sympathetic narrator to influence our response. She does not treat Camilla's decision to become a warrior as a sinful lapse that merits punishment. She respects and honors Camilla's departure as sadly heroic: it is not the treachery of the lapsed (or raped) virgin (like Callisto). Metabus' daughter would inevitably learn about warfare, armies, and regal politics from him in addition to hunting; the royal attire she flaunts from her horse (7.814–15) and the title of "queen" that the poet confers on her during the battle (*regina*, 11.499, 703, 801) may well indicate that she claims her inheritance. Her status also suggests how she could raise and command a cavalry unit. Like Lausus, son of exiled king Mezentius, she respects her father, works to recover his throne, and devotes herself to the military role her ambition and loyalty necessitate. Vergil, however, has altered the Mezentius pattern by removing Metabus from the scene: Camilla seems an independent warrior, fighting for her own goals, superior to Lausus and the other young hero, Pallas on the Trojan side. Though Vergil does not stress her patriotic and political purposes, his use of Diana to introduce her period of heroism is designed to make her a positive paradigm.

In view of this preparation, we should look closely at her victories to see whether in fact Vergil has made them appropriately heroic. Camilla's *aristeia* includes victories over undistinguished foes, but what else could she do? Mezentius, Aeneas, and Turnus kill inferior men also; and frequently Vergil makes their killings far more self-assertive and bestial than those of Camilla. There is no reason to take exception to her first conquest of Eunaeus: his death is ugly, but Vergil does not say anything of Camilla's aims or reactions, and the ugliness reflects that of war in general. Seven more deaths follow without giving us insight into the victorious woman (670–75), before we come to the cloddish hunter trying to be a soldier, Ornytus. Vergil's narrative focuses on the unusual uniform and gigantic size of the man, not on his personality, and his ill-suited manner makes Ornytus an easy mark for Camilla. The killing is not described in detail, but it is colored by Camilla's vaunt (685–89). She speaks with enmity, sneering at him as a hunter out of his element, which is ironically revealed by his death at the hands of a woman! This does not mean that Vergil presents Camilla as a man-hater, a fanatic virgin. Nothing of the sort. Camilla is on friendly terms with Turnus, who thinks it good strategy to put her in command of his male cavalry leaders. There is no chauvinism among the Italians, and Vergil allows little to be expressed by their foes against Camilla. Her vaunt over Ornytus epitomizes the difference between his incompetence and her complete success in changing from hunter to warrior.

Camilla's victories over the two Trojan warriors, Orsilochus and Butes, who also dwarf her in size and apparent strength, are legitimate military exploits, with no negative qualification, no boasting from Camilla (690–98). Then comes the Ligurian son of Aunus. He casts at her the disparaging charge that she is a weak woman whose superiority is only due to her horse's strength (705–6), but Vergil disarms that criticism by his earlier accounts of her victories and by his characterization of the man as a coward. The sneering insult of this man has its effect on Camilla, who rages with anger and hurt pride (709), but she acts decisively to make him eat his words. She leaps down from her horse to fight him hand-to-hand, and, when he thinks he has secured his escape, she runs down his galloping horse and brings the coward to the ground dead. Thus, she emerges his superior, as the falcon-simile demonstrates; his use of *femina* was merely an illicit verbal tactic.

Last we come to Chloreus, the final victim Camilla marks for herself, but does not get, and to Arruns, her killer. I have reviewed numerous commentaries, articles, and books on this episode, but the only person, to my knowledge, who comes right out and says that Chloreus is a eunuch is G. S. West.[9] Modern editors tend to follow the main manuscript tradition and give a text that introduces Chloreus as "sacred to Mt. Cybelus" (*sacer Cybelo*, 768), which means that Vergil indirectly made him a devotee of the goddess Cybele, whose home was that mountain. As devotee of Cybele, Chloreus had to be a eunuch, and Vergil has exaggerated the effeminacy associated with eunuchs by detailing his horse's special mantle, the gold decorations of his armor, the saffron chlamys, and the exotic Cretan arrows he shoots from a Lydian bow. Like Ornytus earlier, Chloreus is a garishly ridiculous figure. He is really a "half-man" out of his element, a sure victim for a real warrior like Camilla, a source of victor's spoils. Had Vergil shown her killing Chloreus and proceeding on to another combat, there would have been no problem. Instead he chose to make this a triangular situation and include Arruns, depriving Camilla of her easy victory over an exotic eunuch and instead giving Arruns a coward's advantage, the opportunity to kill her from ambush.

In his provocative article on heroism in Book 11, T. G. Rosenmeyer suggests that Vergil presents a different standard of heroism from the reality of his own day: "At the court of Augustus, Arruns would have been decorated for his efforts."[10] I am not convinced by that claim: Augustus never decorated an ordinary soldier who claimed to have killed an enemy general.[11] Even in Augustus' day, the most heroic deed was the killing of the enemy general by the Roman general, in hand-to-hand combat; and there was much discussion about the reward for such achievement, the *spolia opima*. Vergil, while stressing the unheroic qualities of Arruns' attack from hiding, also gives him some trappings of piety. When he throws his fatal spear, he prays to Apollo and styles himself a devotee of a special cult on Mount Soracte near Rome, where the worshippers walk on fiery coals (787–88). He prays to eradicate the disgrace (*dedecus* 789), this foul disease (*haec dira pestis* 792) represented by Camilla's superiority over her opponents. Apollo grants that prayer, without necessarily agreeing with the pejorative terminology, but he distinctly deprives Arruns of the chance to enjoy his success at home, which was also part of the prayer. Apollo's sister, then, proceeds to punish him with a lonely death. The last we see of him, he is groaning out his final breaths in a field, and his companions have no idea where he is or what has happened to him. As far as Vergil and his audience are concerned, that is a just death, as Opis states (849). Nobody weeps for Arruns: his victory is inglorious. Sadness is the exclusive property of Camilla in this triangle.

Camilla never gets to confront Chloreus, the effeminate priest of the Trojan cult of Cybele; if given that chance, she would surely have killed him, Vergil makes us believe. Here is where all that golden effeminate finery on Chloreus becomes an unintended weapon. Vergil expresses ambivalence about her feelings (778–79) and aims: whether to dedicate the splendid armor in a temple or to dress herself in the captured gold. If the first, she would have acted as Aeneas himself did at the start of this book (a veritable Roman);[12] if the second, she would have resembled Euryalus, whose greed cost him his life, or Turnus, whose pride in stripping Pallas will ultimately be punished by Aeneas. In fact, though, because she never gets to kill and spoil Chloreus, we and Vergil never can decide the question. But it is striking that Vergil emphasizes her incautious focus on Chloreus' glittering appearance: as Mandelbaum has it, "fearless, with a female's love / of plunder and of spoils, she raged through all / the army" (M 1038). Some readers have read this use of the term "female" (*femineo*, 782) as pejorative. But what exactly does Vergil mean here?

The Latin, literally rendered, does produce what Mandelbaum gives us: *femineo praedae et spoliorum ardebat amore* (782). The adjective "female" and its noun "love" frame the entire clause, with the seemingly pejorative "female" setting up everything that follows. We might assume Vergil's point to be that it is just like a woman to lust for plunder and spoils in war, but this interpretation is not consistent with his general portrayal of Camilla, especially after Vergil's telling us that Camilla's desires were unsure and otherwise giving us no woman-warrior as a paradigm. (And the greed of Euryalus, who was no woman, refutes the claim.) We must, I think, separate the adjective "female" and its prejudicial implications of "just like a woman" from the words "booty" and "spoils" and restrict it to its noun "love." I suggest a translation along these lines: "she burned with desire for plunder and spoils; she blazed with a woman's passion." Female passion is the point, not what she desired; this we already know from the case of Dido. The passion of the aptly named Amata, devoid of materialism, is also highly feminine and fatal. Blind, heedless pursuit of one's goal, fits the Greco-Roman stereotype of the passionate woman, and it belongs to the decorum of epic and tragedy, regularly disastrous, if not fatal.

It is true that Vergil explains Camilla's death as due to her heedless passion, but he does not ask us to scorn that passion. She differs from Euryalus and Turnus not in her desire for spoils, but in her careless pursuit of them, which costs her her life before she could take them. Against the foils of eunuch Chloreus and cowardly fanatic Arruns, Camilla stands high and heroic.[13] Some might wish that the poet had not referred to woman's passion here; this is the only time when he associates Camilla with love of any kind. This love seems distorted, a sad indication of wasted femininity. But the context arouses reactions too complex for us to focus exclusively on this deficiency, and the sadness of Camilla's death colors the remainder of the book. As she dies, she has no thought for her lost spoils or her lost future: she speaks like a commander, concerned that Turnus act to avert a crisis. Vergil gives an affective description of the way her limbs grow cold and relax, and then he assigns her his version of the Homeric line used for Hector's death, the same line that will record Turnus' death and grimly end his poem in 12.952: "and with a moan, her life, resentful, fled to Shades below" (831, M 1101–102). This is a heroine's premature death. It is the saddest and most significant death of Book 11. Camilla's heroism affects the Italian women, who are inspired to die defending their city walls (895). The cruel pathos of her end takes us back to the deaths of Mezentius and Pallas, which were the focus of the book's opening. Thus, in the course of this book, the poet powerfully engages the reader's sympathy for both sides in this civil and thus saddest of wars.

CHAPTER 12

AENEID 12
Unity in Closure

Michael C. J. Putnam

The twelfth book of the *Aeneid* is the longest and in certain respects most complex of the epic. This is the case not least for the diverse acts of closure that it must complete, with careful bows to earlier, crucial moments in the poem, to Vergil's previous writing, to epic's past. The book's first word, "Turnus," sets up one such pattern. It is with Aeneas' prime opponent that the tale's final chapter both begins and ends as, in the poem's last line, Turnus' life relegates itself to the world of the shades. Likewise it is on Aeneas' doomed antagonist that Vergil lavishes, at the start, a rhetorical gesture unique in the poem. This is the epic's only book initiated with a simile. Such positioning draws the reader's attention to the simile's metaphorical richness and to the way Vergil takes multiple advantage of it for allusion to earlier contexts with powerful bearing on events soon to unfold.

We watch Turnus:

> Poenorum qualis in arvis
> saucius ille gravi venantum vulnere pectus
> tum demum movet arma leo, gaudetque comantis
> excutiens cervice toros fixumque latronis
> impavidus frangit telum et fremit ore cruento: . . .
>
> (4–8)

> . . . as a lion on the Punic plains
> when hunters wound him gravely in the chest,
> at last awakes to battle and is glad,

> and shakes the hairy mane along his neck,
> and, fearless, snaps the robber's shaft and roars
> with bloody jaws: . . .[1]

Turnus has twice before in the epic been compared to a lion (9.792–96, 10.454–56) and Vergil would have well known the Iliadic tradition where Homer favors Diomedes, Hector (twice), and Achilles (whose opponent in this instance happens to be Aeneas) with the same analogy.[2] But there is one major difference between the simile that opens *Aeneid* 12 and parallel earlier examples, however much Vergil may have drawn on them for individual details. In his own past usage, as in Homer's, a warrior, when identified with a lion, is involved in a literal conflict during the heat of battle. The wound that Turnus here suffers, however, is figurative and metaphysical, not physical. It is on the hero's inner, psychic circumstances that Vergil concentrates as he introduces the final reach of his epic, not on any external attributes of strength or martial vigor.

But we must be still more specific. The setting of the simile, "on the Punic plains," reminds the reader of Dido, and the next line confirms the reference by repeating, in the phrase *saucius gravi vulnere*, vocabulary of the opening lines of Book 4 (1–2): *At regina gravi iamdudum saucia cura / vulnus alit venis* . . . ("But the queen, stricken for a long time with grievous care, nourishes the wound with her veins . . .")[3] We will see these plural hunters become singular robber reappear later in the book when Aeneas is compared to a hunter hound (*venator canis*) who has trapped Turnus as frightened stag. In being reduced from fearsome to timid in the animal kingdom, Turnus suffers humiliation at the same moment that Aeneas, in his last simile in the epic, is bestialized (749–55).[4] Here at the opening the poet has us concentrate on the emotional "wound" with which Turnus is stricken, which is to say on the eroticism that plays an important part in what follows. The association with Dido suggests that matters do not bode well for Turnus. But, even though Vergil has expanded our horizon from a situation of personal hurt anticipating suicide to one where *eros* and *eris*, love and strife, complement each other in the public struggles of politics and war, nevertheless the poem's ending, as we will see, comments strongly more on the power of private passion than on any larger sphere of conflict. When the figurative wound of line 5 becomes literal, five lines before the poem's conclusion, as Aeneas kills his opponent, we still are made to focus on spiritual demons, this time of the titular hero himself as he performs his final deed.

The simile ends with one symbolic detail whose retrospective function likewise has bearing on what follows. In having the lion Turnus "roar with bloody mouth" (*fremit ore cruento*), Vergil adopts a phrase he employed twice elsewhere in the epic. He applied it to Nisus in Book 9, also compared to a lion, as he plunges into the excess of slaughter that will prove his undoing (9.341), but he used it initially in Book 1 at the first of the three major instances in the poem where he casts our thoughts ahead to the reign of Augustus. At that time, in Jupiter's words, the Gates of War will be closed and:

> "Furor impius intus
> saeva sedens super arma et centum vinctus aenis
> post tergum nodis fremet horridus ore cruento."
> (1.294–96)

> "Within, unholy Rage
> shall sit on his ferocious weapons, bound
> behind his back by a hundred knots of brass;
> he shall groan horribly with bloody lips."
> (M 414–17)

Furor is *impius* because it is emblematic of civil war in which *pietas* is forgotten at a time when brother kills brother. Though suppressed in Jupiter's idealizing vision of the Augustan principate, madness lacking piety is on the loose as we begin Book 12.

These two main subjects of the simile, the complementarity of eroticism with the struggles of war and the imminence in particular of civil strife, personified here in Turnus, remain active elements both in what immediately follows and at the book's end. As the narrative commences we find Latinus attempting to soothe the *violentia* of Turnus with the admission "I took up impious arms" (*arma impia sumpsi*, 31). The king realizes that his share in causing the forces of Turnus and Aeneas to be pitted against each other makes him guilty of impiety not only for going against the fated wishes of the gods but also by fostering what is implicitly fraternal strife. Those guilty of "having followed impious arms" (*arma secuti impia*) are condemned in the Underworld to eternal torture (6.612–13).

The result of this battling, in the striking image Vergil allots to Latinus, is that the Tiber grows warm with "our" blood and that the huge fields whiten with bones (35–36, M 48–49). Vergil appropriates the red-white contrast shortly thereafter in the description of Lavinia blushing at her mother's mention of Turnus. When red suffuses her features it is as if, in the poet's simile, someone had "stained" (*violaverat*) ivory with bloody (*sanguineo*) purple, or lilies grew crimson when mingled with roses (67–69). Lavinia's blush, through Vergil's paronomasia, is intimate with Turnus' *violentia*. His violence forces blood to her face just as the aggressiveness of war, in which he shares, brings about the Tiber's reddening with blood.

Once more sexuality and war are closely conjoined. The Tiber's incarnadine flow and Lavinia's red glow are mediated by Turnus' avowal to Latinus that "blood follows from our wound" (*nostro sequitur de vulnere sanguis*, 12.51). His direct meaning is that blood will flow from a wound that he inflicts, but the reader understands an anticipation of his own deadly wounding by Aeneas. The act of wounding is a synecdoche of the general horrors of war that have engulfed Latium, but, in Turnus' case, it is intimately linked with the *amor* he feels for Lavinia. For him the violence that love inflicts is complicit with war's violence, and both conspire to bring about his death. But few of Vergil's characters are immune from his vision of the destructive power of eroticism, and at the epic's conclusion we will see the titular hero himself become prey to an emotionality not dissimilar to Turnus' here, as he prepares to deliver the final death thrust of the poem.

In fact, as the narrative continues, both Turnus and Aeneas are associated with aspects of the irrational. Turnus is said to be "driven by these furies" (*his agitur furiis*) as he verbally attacks Aeneas and is compared to a bull preparing for battle, thrusting anger into his horns (101). Aeneas in turn we see "fierce in his mother's weapons" (*maternis saevus in armis*) and stirring himself in anger (107). We assume, however, these gestures to be preliminaries for the hand-to-hand combat between the two heroes called for by the treaty between Trojans and Latins, which both sides stand ready to implement. But the narrative of preparations for a systematic conclusion to hostilities is interrupted by the appearance of Juno, the epic's prime embodiment of irrationality, urging Juturna to save her brother by aborting the treaty.

The dialogue thus fomented between order and disorder continues as we return to the treaty confirmation and to speeches by Aeneas and Latinus aimed at assuring its durability. Vergil centers our attention on two aspects of the proceedings. One is the origin of Latinus' scepter, which is strongly personified. Once possessed of a mother in the woods, it now is decorated in bronze to be used by the Latin fathers in their deliberations. Artistry here, like the treaty that the scepter is to help seal, in taking us from alive to dead, from the sylvan world of mothers (regularly an object of suspicion in Vergil's mental universe) to patriarchs about their juridical tasks, seems to shift us from nature to culture, to the bringing of civilization out of wildness tamed.[5] Such is also the potential of the prospective duel.

A second aspect of the treaty-sanctioning on which Vergil concentrates is the need for animal sacrifice as part of the ritual. We hear early on of a pig and sheep led to the altars. At the conclusion of the ceremony, and of Vergil's description, we are told, graphically, of their throat-cutting and evisceration, while still alive. Vergil would seem to be varying the themes he suggested in his depiction of Latinus' scepter. Animals must be offered to the gods in sacrifice to replace the human victims that a treaty makes superfluous, and, in particular, violence has to be done to nonhumans to avert anything parallel in the world of men.

The theme suffers an adroit metamorphosis in what follows as the narrator focuses on the figure of Turnus, venerating the altar "in the role of a suppliant" (*suppliciter*, 220). Juturna, in the guise of Camers, soon takes note of the altars at which he "dedicates himself" (*se devovet aris*, 234). But she begins her disruptive speech with a subtle appeal: "O Latins, are you not ashamed to let / this giant army stake all on one life?" ("*non pudet, o Rutuli, pro cunctis talibus unam / obiectare animam?*," 229–30, M 310–11). Vergil has her words echo those of Neptune in Book 5, forewarning Venus that he will ask for one individual's life in recompense for the Trojan fleet's final progress toward Italy (5.814–15). Juturna would have us envision her brother as placed in a similar position to that of the helmsman Palinurus, as if he were somehow an offering for the survival of his people, replacing the treaty's animal victims. But Turnus is not tendering himself in an act of Roman *devotio* for the victory of his army, nor, as we shall see, is it as a victim on behalf of his people that he is finally sacrificed. There are more personal reasons behind the sacrificant's final deed.

Juturna-Camers continues her deranging work. She sends an omen, misinterpreted as favorable by the augur Tolumnius who hurls the first spear to renew the battle. The narrator comments on the perverse quality of the result. Near the beginning of the present action we are told that the one love that possesses all is to make decisions by the sword (282, M 383–84), and at the end, in one of Vergil's most effective images, we watch the "iron sleep" (*ferreus somnus*) that encloses the fallen warriors in its grip.[6] In the world of war life's ordinary round is perverted, as quotidian repose yields to the sword's final slumber and death's everlasting night.

At the center of the renewal of fighting is the death of Aulestes. He trips backward over the altars and is killed by Messapus who remarks: "He has it; / I give to the great gods a better victim" (*"hoc habet, haec melior magnis data victima divis,"* 296, M 402–3). Once more the notion of human sacrifice comes forward, now formally executed, as the breaking of the compact turns the plot's course away from treaty-making, and the deflection of human violence from man onto animal yields to full-scale battling and to man killing man.

Aeneas attempts to intervene and halt the fight at what is one of the book's major moral nubs. We see him unarmed, stretching forth his hands in appeal to keep the treaty intact. He remarks on the rise of *discordia* (here and elsewhere often tantamount to civil war) and urges all to restrain their anger (*o cohibete iras*!, 314–15). This is the last occasion in the epic at which Vergil has Aeneas styled *pius*, and it is for a purpose (311). We know from the beginning of the epic that *pietas* and *ira*, piety and anger, are regularly antithetical elements. Lines 9–10 of Book 1 contrast Aeneas, outstanding for his piety (*insignem pietate*), with Juno and her anger, and the epic's opening simile pits Neptune, as a man "heavy with piety" (*pietate gravem*), against the fury of the winds, envisioned as an unruly mob, that she has stirred up (1.151). The allegory is clear enough, and its abstractions make their presences explicitly felt here for the final time in the poem, as Aeneas-Neptune gestures for calm. When we reach the epic's conclusion, with Aeneas acting in anger against a fallen warrior stretching forth his hands in prayer, it is well to remember that the last occasion when he was given his standard epithet, which demands of its adherent loyalty and respect toward gods and humans alike, found him in a closely corresponding position to his suppliant antagonist there.

But order is not restored. Aeneas is wounded by an unknown assailant and forced to retreat from battle, giving Turnus his final chance for an expansive moment of individual heroism. Here, too, characterization is significant. We see him *fervidus*, blazing with the hope of victory, the last adjective Vergil also allots his titular hero as the poem ends (325, 951). He is likewise labeled *superbus*, proud, as he enters battle, and here, again, Vergil asks of his reader to prepare for a major paradox of the epic's conclusion (326). Our attention has been readied for both these moments by two earlier texts. One is the concrete reminder of how the narrator apostrophizes Turnus in Book 10 as *superbus* because of his immoderation after the killing of Pallas (10.514). The second is Anchises' abstract dictum given in the Underworld to his son whom he addresses as *Romane*, epitome in his immediate future of patterns of behavior that should typify the Roman race to come: "to spare defeated peoples, tame the proud" ("*parcere subiectis et debellare superbos*," 6.853, M 1137). Vergil is setting the stage for the not long distant moment when Aeneas will confront, in Turnus whom he himself has forced to his knees, an example of pride, as it were, warred down, and the moral dilemma this posture generates.

At the moment, and for the poem's next episode, Turnus is at the peak of his powers. Vergil compares him to Mars whom black Fear, Ambushes, and Angers accompany into battle. In the simile Mars is called bloody (*sanguineus*) and soon after its conclusion we learn of the "bloody dews" (*rores sanguineos*) that the hooves of Turnus' horses scatter as he careens along (339). Once more Vergil would have us observe, through potent metaphor, how war contorts nature, twisting the creative and the usual into something ugly and brutal. But the image has particular point. It recalls the close relation we saw at the poem's opening between blood, the outbreak of war, Turnus' violence, and Lavinia's blush.[7] It also anticipates one of the poem's more graphic descriptions of the results of war's ferocity when Turnus, as the fighting proceeds, cuts off the heads of twin enemies, hangs them from his chariot, and carries them along "dripping blood like dew" (*rorantia sanguine*, 512). If we survey the battle books as a whole, we find that only the savagery of Aeneas in Book 10 after the killing of Pallas exceeds Turnus' barbarity here.

Aeneas himself, meanwhile, through his mother's intervention, is cured of his wound. "Hurry and bring arms for the man" ("*arma citi properate viro*," 425) shouts the physician Iapyx, forewarning us that we are about to witness the last, and most morally crucial, conjunction of *arma virumque*, of a hero and the weapons that lend him invincibility, for which the poem's opening line has long since prepared us.[8] Aeneas then urges his son to learn courage and the truth of hardship from him, (good) fortune from others, shaping words ominously akin to those that Sophocles gives to Ajax shortly before his suicide (Soph., *Aj.* 550–51) and once more allowing Vergil to offer his readers a further opportunity to ponder the ambiguities in Aeneas' epic career as it draws to a close.

Elements of ambiguity also hang over the simile that Vergil uses to distinguish his hero as he returns to battle. He is likened to a storm cloud moving landward, at whose advent:

> . . . miseris, heu, praescia longe
> horrescunt corda agricolis: dabit ille ruinas
> arboribus stragemque satis, ruet omnia late . . .
>
> (452–54)

> . . . luckless farmers, seeing it far off,
> shudder within their hearts, for it will bring
> destruction to their orchards, kill their crops,
> and cut down every planting; . . .
>
> (M 607–10)

Vergil models his simile on one in *Iliad* 4 where the followers of the Ajaxes are compared to a cloud driven by the west wind from which a frightened goatherd and his flock take shelter (*Il.* 4.275–79). Vergil alters his original, as critics have pointed out, by changing goatherd to farmers and by adding, in accordance with his usual *sympatheia*, the descriptive adjective *miseris*, and the interjection *heu* by means of which poet has narrator enter into the scene itself of the simile to express pity for the helpless sufferers.[9] (Homer's particular shepherd can protect his flock. Vergil's farmers, as a group, watch the coming of disaster in vain.) Aeneas is imagined as a destructive, elemental force, but one also of particular moment to a student of the Vergilian intellectual past. As Vergil taught us in the *Georgics*, it is the role of man, in the guise of farmer, to bring order to his world and tame the wildness of nature, whether animate or inanimate, outer or inner. Vergil has his hero, as he enters into the final battle, adopt an ungeorgic stance, which is to say that now he, too, appears to represent malevolent nature instead of the prospects of civilization for which the farmers' efforts stand.

This attitude finds confirmation in events soon to follow. Turnus' sister continues to deflect her brother from the final confrontation. As Aeneas pursues, he narrowly escapes a second wounding. At this point, in the words of the narrative, angers rise up inside him (*adsurgunt irae*, 494) and with this goes all self-control:

> iam tandem invadit medios et Marte secundo
> terribilis saevam nullo discrimine caedem
> suscitat, irarumque omnis effundit habenas.
>
> (497–99)

> at last Aeneas charges into battle;
> and terrible, with Mars behind him, he
> awakens brutal, indiscriminate
> slaughter, he lets his violence run free.
>
> (M 670–73)

Aeneas' battle fury is likened to horses freed from restraint, animality on the lose. Vergil will appeal again to parallel language to characterize his hero's behavior during the epic's final moments. Turnus, too, proceeds on his own spate of slaughter. Both heroes now are likened to ruinous forces of nature and both, again, are subject to anger (521–25, 527).

At this point Vergil adds an episode that is gratuitous as far as narrative line is concerned and therefore serves as commentary on matters of significance beyond its immediate context. Instead of bringing his two combatants together for the final clash the poet has Venus, trenchantly styled Aeneas' "most beautiful mother" (*genetrix pulcherrima*), put into his mind the destruction of Latinus' city, and he urges his men on to the task (554). The passage is riddled with ironies. One detail can serve to exemplify part of the poet's larger objective. In his speech of exhortation to his fellow soldiers Aeneas apostrophizes them as *cives*. It is in their roles as citizens, Roman citizens, that Aeneas asks his Trojan warriors to commence their work of devastation. The last "civic" goal that Aeneas, founder of Rome, contemplates before the conclusion of his epic is the ruination of the city of his opponents, a city nearly incapable of defense.

A further level of irony is added here by Vergil's self-allusions. At two points in the action that follows, as Aeneas leads the attack, the poet's language looks back to the moment in Book 2 where the Greeks, in their devastating course into Troy, reach its core, the palace of Priam. The phrase *primosque trucidant* ("and they slay [the guards] in front") is used in Book 2 of the Greeks breaking their way through the palace doors (12.577, 2.494), and the words *ipse inter primos* ("himself among the first"), used here of Aeneas, are in Book 2 applied to Pyrrhus, son of Achilles, as he heads the charge (12.579, 2.479). Aeneas, in indirect speech, excuses his superfluous violence on the grounds that the Latins twice violated the treaty aimed at bringing peace through single combat. But Vergil's language, by implicitly comparing Aeneas' men to Greeks and Aeneas himself to Pyrrhus, tells another tale. Not only do the Trojans, as their supremacy becomes assured, suffer metamorphosis into destructive Greeks, in the process they perpetrate on others what they themselves suffered. Aeneas, Pyrrhus *redivivus*, is leader of the attack.

The dynamic simile that concludes the episode helps pull many of these strands together. Aeneas, threatening to level the city to the ground, is compared to a shepherd (*pastor*) who has tracked (*vestigavit*) bees to their lair and begins the operation of smoking them out. Aeneas has twice elsewhere in the epic been compared to a shepherd. In Book 4 he is a *pastor nescius*, a shepherd trailing a deer, blind to the wound he has inflicted on Dido, and in Book 2, as the collapse of Troy begins, he is seen as a shepherd who, unaware (*inscius*) of what he is witnessing, hears from a distant crag the sound of a torrent on the rampage (4.71–72, 2.308). In both these earlier instances Vergil calls attention to the ignorance of the shepherd about the harm that is bring wreaked, whether by nature or by himself. He is either passive before events or acts unwittingly. In Book 12 the purposive force of *vestigavit* must not be minimized. We are not dealing with a "shepherd" of bees, like Aristaeus in the fourth *Georgic*, or with an ordinary farmer who must use smoke to make his way into the bees' "august dwelling" and reap the harvest of honey (*G.* 4.317, 228–31). Rather *pastor* Aeneas here is an enemy on the attack, a shepherd in the alien territory of the georgic world, to which he brings unexpected turbulence. As in the case of the antigeorgic storm-cloud simile in the preceding episode, Aeneas, through metaphor, appears to corrupt and debase his world, the unfostering, antipastoral shepherd who brings hurt to the farmer's living, the city-founder who seeks to maim creatures who, as the earlier simile describing the building of Carthage suggests, are one of the standard emblems of a city's civilizing order.[10]

The gradual isolation of Turnus begins now with the suicide of his supporter Amata and with the realization that he must indeed face Aeneas. In lines of great potency Vergil pinpoints Turnus' emotional predicament:

> . . . aestuat ingens
> uno in corde pudor mixtoque insania luctu
> et furiis agitatus amor et conscia virtus.
>
> (666–68)

> In his deepest heart there surge
> tremendous shame and madness mixed with sorrow
> and love whipped on by frenzy and a courage
> aware of its own worth.
>
> (M 888–91)

The tensions that the narrator outlines secure our impression, as we enter the epic's final segment, of Turnus as a tragic figure, both rational and irrational, only partially capable of controlling his own actions. And in fact Vergil has twice before alluded to Orestes, one of the great figures of Greek drama, in similar terms. In Book 3 he is said to be "stimulated by the furies of his crimes" (*scelerum furiis agitatus*, 3.331) and in Book 4 Dido is compared to Orestes "driven about the stage" (*scaenis agitatus*) for whom the Furies lay waiting (4.471). Aeneas, as we will see, is allotted not dissimilar language, with good reason, in the poem's concluding lines.

As the final confrontation nears, Vergil unleashes a series of similes that both differentiate and unite the two heroes. Turnus is compared to a huge boulder released from a mountainside by rain or age. Father Aeneas, by contrast, is a mountain itself, not subject to time, whether Athos or Eryx or *pater Appenninus*, the backbone of Italy. Both men are also bestialized. In one simile they are likened to bulls who must battle it out for control of a herd. In another, which I mentioned earlier, Aeneas is a hunter hound who has trapped a stag, the stronger animal (pointedly called *vividus*, very much alive) poised to vanquish the weaker (749–55). The "Punic" color of the feathers used to frighten the deer is a further reminder of the connection between Turnus and Dido who, we remember, was also a doe fatally wounded by the shepherd Aeneas. The hound is also called Umber, once again giving Aeneas an Italian analogy that exactly locates his domination and control as his new destiny evolves. But the gist of the simile takes us in another direction as well. Vergil would have us think, here and often in the lines that follow, of the combat between Achilles and Hector in *Iliad* 22 where the Greek victor is the hound and the Trojan loser a stag (*Il.* 22.189–92). Aeneas may be Italianized, as he gains the upper hand in an essentially civil conflict, but he is also no longer the passive Trojan, enduring what comes his way, but an Achilles, triumphant Greek, killer of Troy's noblest hero and begetter of Pyrrhus, who would be a prime instigator of the city's fiery doom.

The process of Italianization for Aeneas and the Trojans continues as the scene shifts to Olympus and to a dialogue between Jupiter and Juno. Jupiter announces that Aeneas is *indiges*, that is, a quasi-divine native hero who is owed to heaven, and forbids his consort to make further trouble. Juno in turn requests that the Latins, in the peace to follow, not be forced to become Trojans but that Troy should pass away in favor of Latium. Jupiter, noting Juno's anger (*irae*) and urging her to forgo her *furor*, agrees to her request: "mixed together in stock only, the Trojans will sink down [into the mass]" (*commixti corpore tantum / subsident Teucri*, 835–36). What will remain in the ascendant, in Juno's words, is "Roman stock strengthened with Italian valor" (*Romana potens Itala virtute propago*, 827). In other words, in this, the most critical of the poem's idealizing moments, where the divine world seems ready to serve as foil for the human scenario that follows, Juno will allow her anger and fury to relent at the same time as the Trojans renounce their individuality in favor of absorption into the Latin mould. The result will be a race, according to Jupiter's penultimate, hyperbolic words, that will surpass both humankind and the gods in *pietas*.

However diverse the details, the moral universe the two gods project makes for a consistent whole. The assimilation of Troy into Latium presumably diffuses the possibility of further civil strife (now and in any putative future moment) as the potential conflicts implicit in duality yield to the harmony of homogeneity. This means, in turn, that the *impia arma* that Latinus had taken up, and that define the internecine aspect of the *Aeneid*'s battling, will give place to a society where *pietas*, the very Roman multivalent quality of respect among men and between men and gods, will be the commanding abstraction. Complementing this new ethical departure and essential for the resultant civic unity will be the loss of individuality and in particular the renunciation of *ira* and *furor*, the anger and madness that have typified Juno and those under her spell since the opening moments of the poem. It is against this intellectual background, posited as pattern for mankind in the omnipotent realm of the gods, that we must measure the performance of the human actors in the drama as it reaches its climax and Aeneas kills Turnus. What wins out in the end, we must ask, private vendetta or public self-effacement, the rage and savagery of the singular mortal or its opposite, the *pietas* that would seem to bring unanimity to society and urge on the race that cherishes it to equality with the gods?

Jupiter now proceeds to the final isolation of Turnus by sending down one of his servant Furies to prohibit Juturna from giving further aid to her brother. Carried along like a brisk whirlwind, she flies to earth, the equivalent in simile to a poisoned arrow. Her appearance, flitting before the warrior's face, produces the desired effect. Turnus is now left alone to face his foe who has the power of Jupiter behind him. Turnus is also fully aware of his probable doom, announcing that he is not frightened by Aeneas' fervid words of mockery but by "Jupiter, my enemy" (*Iuppiter hostis*, 895).

Omnipotence lies with the king of the gods and his terrestrial favorite, but the poet turns the reader's sympathy deftly toward Turnus. As his vitality begins to fail, Vergil compares him to someone dreaming. I quote the simile in full:

> ac velut in somnis, oculos ubi languida pressit
> nocte quies, nequiquam avidos extendere cursus
> velle videmur et in mediis conatibus aegri
> succidimus; non lingua valet, non corpore notae
> sufficiunt vires nec vox nec verba sequuntur: . . .
> (908–12)

> Just as in dreams of night, when languid rest
> has closed our eyes, we seem in vain to wish
> to press on down a path, but as we strain
> we falter, weak; our tongues can say nothing,
> the body loses its familiar force,
> no voice, no word can follow: . . .
> (M 1209–14)

Vergil has once again chosen a model from *Iliad* 22, but he has changed it in two important ways. In the *Iliad* simile the dream centers on two people, one who cannot grasp his prey, the other who cannot elude the pursuit (*Il.* 22.199–200):

> endless as in a dream . . .
> when a man can't catch another fleeing on ahead
> and he can never escape nor his rival overtake him . . . [11]

Vergil concentrates on Turnus alone, the Hector figure. He also focuses our attention by a usage of first-person plural verbs unique in the epic. Elsewhere he has his narrator make occasional recourse to second-person verbs at special moments—to enter the thoughts of Dido facing Aeneas' departure, to join the reader with Aeneas contemplating Vulcan's shield, in the battle books to thrust briefly forward warriors about to die—but in no other instance does he persuade us as we read not only to feel compassion for a character but actually to become his equivalent. We are Turnus, as any strength he might muster for the final confrontation ebbs away.

In this position of powerlessness Vergil has Turnus twice hesitate (916, 919), but it is to Aeneas, and in particular to his spear, that our attention is now directed. Its roar is compared to rocks hurled from a catapult against city walls or to a thunderbolt, while its flight is like that of a black whirlwind. The final two analogies further the link of Aeneas with Jupiter, first, as all-powerful nature god, second, as the unleasher of a Fury who also not long before had sped earthward against Turnus like a whirlwind. The first metaphorically renews his role as city-destroyer, with Turnus now standing in for the people whose leader he is (and whose independence will presumably be lost along with his life). The resultant wound, however, unlike that which Achilles inflicts on Hector, is not fatal, allowing Vergil to prepare his hero to face a moral dilemma that has no parallel in the *Iliad* but whose resolution possesses far-reaching consequences for Aeneas and Rome.

Turnus' subsequent speech, as actions yield momentarily to words, serves several purposes. It publicly proclaims Aeneas' victory. In one line (936) Turnus announces "you have won" (*vicisti*) and professes himself conquered (*victum*). He also offers Aeneas the opportunity to spare his life (*et me, seu corpus spoliatum lumine mavis, / redde meis*, "return me or, if you prefer, my body devoid of light to my people," 935). It is not fortuitous that in his accompanying prayer for mercy Turnus reminds him of his father Anchises, for it was Anchises, we remember, who in Book 6 had pronounced the famous dictum that should serve as major moral touchstone for his son's behavior here. As paragon for his race to come, he should consider clemency for the defeated a salient ethical concern. The theoretical framework laid down at a point of climax halfway through the poem finds its moment of practical application at its conclusion. Proud Turnus has been beaten down in combat, the *superbus* has been made *subiectus*.

Turnus rephrases Aeneas' opportunity through his final words: "do not press further in your hatred" (*ulterius ne tende odiis*, 12.938). In analyzing his request we can draw on Cicero's definition of *odium* as *ira inveterata*, anger that has become chronic (Cic., *Tusc Disp.* 4.21). Turnus offers his victorious opponent the chance not only to relent in his longstanding anger but to embrace what we have regularly seen, in Vergil's ethical universe, to be its opposite, namely *pietas*. Piety here, the duty of son to father, therefore preaches both the abstention from anger and its complement, a clemency that, in sparing suppliants, exemplifies the restrained use of power.

Turnus' words seem, for a moment at least, to win the day. Aeneas
rolls his eyes—always a sign for Vergil that the person in a quandary has
not come to a decision—and he hesitates (*cunctantem*), replacing Turnus'
hesitation before facing death with his own hesitation before inflicting it.
His words begin to "bend" Aeneas, but the sword-belt of Pallas, booty of
Turnus' deadly victory, "appeared" (Vergil's astonishing word) on his
shoulder. It reminds Aeneas of the "savage grief" (*saevi doloris*) he suffered
from the youth's death. "Set aflame by furies and terrifying in his wrath"
(*furiis accensus et ira / terribilis*, 946–47), he speaks to Turnus (947–49):

> ". . . tune hinc spoliis indute meorum
> eripiare mihi? Pallas te hoc vulnere, Pallas
> immolat et poenam scelerato ex sanguine sumit."

"Are you, clothed in the spoils of my own, to be snatched hence
from me? Pallas, Pallas sacrifices you with this wound and exacts
punishment from your criminal blood."[12]

And thus the epic ends (950–52):

> hoc dicens ferrum adverso sub pectore condit
> fervidus; ast illi solvuntur frigore membra
> vitaque cum gemitu fugit indignata sub umbras.

Saying this he buries his sword under the chest of his enemy,
blazing; but [Turnus'] limbs are undone with cold and his life with
a groan flees, indignant, under the shades.

The calculated dissatisfactions of this ending are many, especially by
contrast to the epics of Homer and Apollonius, or to what we can presume
of Roman historical epic. Odysseus' desire for further vengeance is sup-
pressed by the gods as his epic ends, and the *Iliad* concludes with funeral
games for Hector, after the reconciliation scene between Achilles and
Priam has brought about the ransom of the latter's son and the return of
Achilles to humanity. We expect some rational explanation for Aeneas'
violence—piety toward Pallas' father Evander, for instance—especially
when he contravenes his own father's injunction for *clementia*. Nor does
Vergil offer any gesture of accommodation to a future including Aeneas'
marriage with Lavinia or union between Trojans and Latins. Rather the

poem ends with exactly the opposite of what the preceding dialogue between Jupiter and Juno had led us to believe, with a savage gesture of self-expression on the part of the Trojan chief. It is well to look at the ramifications of that gesture and of the epic's final words, bestowed on conquered, not conqueror.

We have examined before the antonymical relation between *ira* and *pietas* that the poem's opening develops. *Saevitia* and *dolor*, savagery and resentment, also form part of the complex of negative abstractions that motivate the Trojan's arch-enemy, Juno, as the epic starts. As the poem reaches its conclusion, one of Vergil's most ironic gestures of unity is to impute much the same motivation to Aeneas who has gained full command of his destiny. Circularity implies a continuity of human violence, however the actors may change over time. The phrase *furiis accensus* performs a parallel function. It is used only once elsewhere in the poem, to identify the Latin mothers who have been "set aflame by furies" (*furiis . . . accensas*, 7.392) as Juno and her Fury Allecto arouse the Latins against the newly arrived Trojans. The rounding-off of the second half of the epic reinforces the larger circularity of the poem as a whole, further presupposing a certain persistence of Junonian irrationality in the climactic deed of Aeneas himself.

Then there is the sword-belt of Pallas, sight of which triggers Aeneas' violence. We associate it with the narrator's accusation of pride when Turnus dons it after killing Pallas. But Pallas' death also initiates the ugliest surge of brutality in the epic where, among other acts, Aeneas takes eight captives to be human sacrifices, kills Magus, who had begged for mercy in the name of Anchises, and Haemonides, like the Sibyl, a priest of Apollo and Diana. Vergil connects this episode with the poem's final lines through his only usages of the verb *immolare*, to offer in sacrifice. It is applied to the future and present deaths of the eight captives and of the priest (10.519, 541). It is also, as we saw, put into the mouth of Aeneas as he prepares to kill his antagonist. Turnus is, in Aeneas' infuriate understanding, another human victim to be offered to Pallas, as the rush of violence continues on.

The two episodes are also connected by the belt itself, which Turnus strips as spoils from the body and which Aeneas now sees. It contains on it, according to the narrator's brief ecphrasis, the "foul" murder on their wedding night of the helpless sons of Aegyptus by the daughters of Danaus. The crimes of eros become war's ugly massacre. But the analogy suggests a particular, apposite slant. The Danaids killed their cousins and therefore in the context of the *Aeneid* their deed stands as emblematic for the impious murder of civil war. The ecphrasis suggests a resemblance between Aeneas' two bouts of killing and the use of *impia arma* as touched on by Latinus at the book's opening. It sparks a continuing vendetta that, like the iteration of *immolare*, promises repetition of violence, not the restraint of anger on which clemency is based. The memory of Pallas' loss elicits from Aeneas an act of irrationality that suppresses recollection of any larger, humane concerns.

The *furiae* we witnessed at work on Turnus near the start of the book have given place at the end to the furies of which Aeneas is, finally, the passive victim. The concluding lines also urge our thoughts back, once again, to the opening of the poem. The phrase *solvuntur frigore membra* ("his limbs are undone by cold"), applied to Turnus here, is strikingly echoed from Book 1 where the limbs of Aeneas suffer the same phenomenon, as he faces the storm that epitomizes Juno's savagery (1.92).[13] Though matters are now reversed, the echo is consequential. He who had been the sufferer of someone else's violence now inflicts the workings of his own inner demons on his victim. The wrath of Juno, based on sexual deprivation and jealousy, is internalized in Aeneas as he performs his final deed.

The verb that Vergil selects for Aeneas' last action, *condere* (to bury), also plays a part in this circularity. It occurs twice in the epic's opening lines, first in connection with the establishment of the city of Rome, second with the founding of the Roman race (1.5, 32). At the end the creation of grand institutions gives place to the singular burial of the seemingly omnipotent hero's sword in the chest of his opponent. But this turnabout is also in its way a climax as well. In Book 12 we have watched Aeneas commence the destruction of Latinus' city, and, nearer to hand, the spear thrust with which he wounds Turnus, we recall, was compared to a rock launched from a catapult against a city's walls. In terms of a future "plot" that Vergil does not mention, the killing of Turnus might mean that all opposition to the creation of the community of Rome has been cleared away. In terms of the irony that Vergil generates, the manner of Turnus' death, in some deeply metaphysical way, is a synecdoche for the death, not the birth, of cities, for violence that is as ethically ruinous as it is repetitive, however changed the manifestations, in human existence.

The last line of the poem bolsters the idea of repetition but from another angle. From Vergil's earliest commentators on, it has been noticed how the line is echoed from the death scene of the warrior maiden Camilla in Book 11.831. Iteration of language, it would seem, mimics the recurrence of deaths in epic. Recourse to Vergil's model in the *Iliad* will also help further to elucidate Vergil's purpose. We have already seen something of how Vergil appeals to Homer in the grand gestures of bringing his poem to its unparalleled closure. Here we must look at a particular instance of emulation. Vergil bases the line he uses twice on two that Homer also employs twice: "And his soul, flying from his limbs, went to Hades, lamenting its fate, relinquishing manhood and youth." Homer's usages of the line are linked, first, with Patroclus slain by Hector, then, six books later, with the death of Hector at the hands of Achilles (*Il.* 16.856–57, 22.362–363). Without doubt we are meant to dwell on the latter connection as Aeneas and Turnus are for the last time matched with Achilles and Hector. The idea of vengeance and vedetta is also in the air. Just as Hector's killing of Patroclus was avenged when he was dispatched by Achilles, so Aeneas exacts requital for Pallas' death by the concluding slaughter of Turnus. Homer's repetition asks us to dwell on the connection.

But the idea of repetition is also paramount in a more general way. There is no specific linkage between the deaths of Camilla and Turnus, as there is, say, between those of Patroclus and Hector. All that can be said for unity is that both in a larger sense are Italians who die opposing the fated domination of Aeneas and his colleagues in Latium. Rather, as we observe Vergil bowing twice directly to lines that Homer repeats, we are forced to ponder the notion of death's iteration, within the *Iliad* and from the *Iliad* to the *Aeneid*, as a constant in epic poetry and therefore in the histories of which it tells, which is to say in the more expansive saga of mankind as well.

Several details in Vergil's final line are interesting for the variations they bring to their Homeric prototype. For instance, the phrase "relinquishing manhood and youth" is reduced to the single participle *indignata* ("indignant"), a word that appears in the last line of the description of Vulcan's shield where it is applied to the river Araxes, resentful at Rome's attempt to master it. But two other alterations, that of "flying" to *fugit* and of "to Hades" to *sub umbras* have special bearing on the last form of circularity I would like to look at, namely that of the sweep of Vergil's allusions to his own poetry.

A form of *umbra* is the final word of Vergil's first *Eclogue* as it is of his epic, and the technical use of the verb *fugere*, "to suffer exile" (often by force majeure) is used prominently near the beginning of that same poem as it is at the end here (*fugimus, Ecl.* 1.4). There the poet is concerned with the distinction between the idyllic condition with which the singer-shepherd Tityrus has been blessed and the realities of expatriation that civil war has necessitated for his colleague, Meliboeus. Here it is the resentment of Turnus' life turned to death that Vergil chooses to be our final object of attention.

The poet has carefully prepared the way for the comparison. The phrase *nos patriae / nos patriam*, for instance, which appears in anaphora at the start of *Eclogue* 1 and in close conjunction with *fugimus* (*Ecl.* 1.3–4) recurs, in Book 12 in the words of Juturna-Camers. Turnus, according to her, may die a hero's death to gain deserved immortality (236–37):

> "nos patria amissa dominis parere superbis
> cogemur, qui nunc lenti consedimus arvis."

> ". . . we, our homeland lost, shall be compelled
> to yield before insulting masters—we
> who sit today taking our ease on the fields."[14]

The doom that Juturna conjures up for her fellow Latins as the outcome of war is not so much exile but total loss of their homeland, resulting in domination by the "haughty" Trojans.

Twice also, during the episode in which Aeneas prepares to demolish Latinus' city, Vergil evokes the first *Eclogue* for his readers. The first instance is a reference to smoking rooftops. In *Eclogue* 1, as the poem reaches its equivocal conclusion, Tityrus reminds the departing Meliboeus of the landscape that he might possess for one final night (*Ecl.* 1.82–83): "and now the tops of the villas' roofs are smoking and greater shadows fall from the lofty mountains" (*"et iam summa procul villarum culmina fumant / maioresque cadunt altis de montibus umbrae"*). Aeneas turns a similar phrase as he threatens ruin for Latinus' city (569): "I will raze [it] and I will place its smoking rooftops level with the ground" (*"eruam et aequa solo fumantia culmina ponam"*).[15] For the fortunate and naive shepherd, Tityrus, the smoking roofs betoken the calm contentment of a peaceful countryside at nightfall. For readers of the *Aeneid*, however, absorbing the import of Aeneas' minatory words, they ominously recall the landscape from which Meliboeus is exiled as both he and his setting suffer the ravages of civil war. We, and perhaps Meliboeus too, understand this. Tityrus may see only the perfection of pastoral, but readers of the epic sense that moral corruption is as present at the start of Vergil's career as at its conclusion.

Nor is it accidental that *umbras* is the epic's last word. The "greater shadows" (*maiores umbrae*), which conclude *Eclogue* 1, extend the daytime arboreal shelter from the sun's glare, so crucial according to the poem's opening lines to the production of pastoral song, into night's more all-embracing gloom. Yet night, at least in Tityrus' version of pastoral, will, we presume, soon give way again to dawn. At the epic's end, by contrast, the phantom residue of Turnus' humanity is left to join the other shades and perpetually to endure the continuous night of death, bringer of the greatest shadow of all and the final, logical figure in the progression that the first *Eclogue* itself initiates from pastoral dream to the ravages of civil war.

The second reminiscence of *Eclogue* 1 in this passage from *Aeneid* 12 supports the ambiguous suggestiveness of the first. In *Eclogue* 1 Meliboeus' concluding speech characterizes the Roman soldier, soon to occupy his fields, as *barbarus* and *impius*, uncivilized and lacking piety both because he has no care for the inhabitants who worship their acreage and because what has come his way was the consequence of civil war. This thought elicits from Meliboeus the mordant exclamation: "behold whither discord has brought pitiable citizens" (*en quo discordia civis / produxit miseros*, *Ecl.* 1.71–72). The phrase *discordia civis* recurs in *Aeneid* 12, in the narrator's description of the discord that arises within Latinus' city, centered on how to respond to Aeneas' behavior (583). But, as the echo from *Eclogue* 1 implies, the citizens' response is one small part of a larger picture that makes of the particular episode, and of the war in general, a civil conflict.

As we come full circle in the career of Vergil we bring the dialogue of Tityrus and Meliboeus with us into the *Aeneid*'s finale. Tityrus' happiness, assured by a beneficent young god in Rome, is based on constancy of setting and song, as nature daily renews itself in an arcadia allowed to exist untouched by reality. Shade is an essential element of the idyll, protection against the sun during the day, a symbol of night's arrival after the sun has run its course, to sequester this eden from life at large.[16] The shades to which Turnus descends, at the epic's end, remind us more of the harsh truths of Meliboeus' experience, for it is the language of Meliboeus (or the way he would find deeper connotations to Tityrus' smoking villas) that haunts *Aeneid* 12. It is his world, of history and its grand spans of time, of the particular oppression of war, of movement away from the stable center of song, that dominates our thoughts as we contemplate the *umbrae* of death that Turnus joins.

The *Aeneid* has its Tityran side where on focal occasions an idealized existence during a future golden age under Augustus is presaged. But our final vision, ambiguous at best, is of a concatenation of anger and violence engendering for its victim the final exile of death. It is the sadness of Meliboeus and the indignation of Turnus, of those who must suffer the constraints of Rome, that round to completion the Mantuan's magisterial art.

CHAPTER 13

THE *AENEID* AS FOUNDATION STORY

Gary B. Miles

DEFINITIONS AND REFLECTIONS

Foundation stories constitute a subclass of stories about beginnings.[1] I define a foundation story as a narrative about the origins of a particular human community that is perceived from the outset as one among several communities. In this sense a foundation story is different from a creation story, which I define as concerning the origins of the entire human race. The story of Adam and Eve, for example, is a creation story; it is set within the context of the divine creation of the cosmos; Adam and Eve are characterized by attributes that apply to all peoples: they are masters of all the animal kingdom; they are beholden to God, their creator; their loss of innocence compromises the relation of all humankind to God, and his punitive reaction to their initial sin determines the conditions of necessity under which all subsequent humans must toil.

Foundation stories, by contrast, typically focus on the primacy of human initiative and agency. Even when natural or divine powers play a central role in foundations, these narratives are nonetheless concerned with the creation of a particular community and call attention to some aspect of that community's distinctiveness. Several ancient communities, for example, attributed their origins to Hercules. For each of them the identification, generally, with the more culturally "advanced" Hellenism that Hercules represented and, more specifically, with a "hero" consti- tuted the basis for a certain superiority to surrounding communities.[2] More exclusive is the identity perpetuated by the Athenians' idea of auto- chthony. Believing they were sprung spontaneously from the soil itself, the Athenians defined themselves as a people timelessly attached to a specific place. From the perspective of this story, one cannot become an Athenian: one is either descended from those who sprang from Athenian soil, or not.

These two examples illustrate how foundation stories concern the circumstances that set one community apart from others. The stories of Hercules focus on certain cultural traits that confer (at least to certain audiences) status: his foundations embody the ideal of civilization associated in the ancient world with Hellenism. The story of Athens focuses rather on race or ethnicity. The difference between the two types of story is significant. A community defined by culture is potentially open: one may become a member of that community by acquiring its culture. A community defined by race or ethnicity, on the other hand, is accessible only to those who are born to existing members of the requisite group. In practice, of course, the two often overlap: race and ethnicity may be associated with certain qualities and vice versa. In either case, foundation stories help to define who is in, who is out, and whether membership is open or closed.

The interests and needs of communities change over time, and communities' perception of themselves alter accordingly. A changing sense of identity calls for reassessment of original foundation stories, for their modification or replacement by new stories to match or justify new self-perceptions. Foundation stories are typically generated not at the time of foundation, but after the fact, in an effort to address changes in self-perception associated with other changes in the community. They may be efforts to inhibit change, calls for return to essential values in danger of being lost, efforts either to support innovation by presenting it as a return to traditional values, or to redefine the community by claiming to displace a false story of foundation with "the true story." Similarly, because foundation stories concern the essential identity of a community and who can belong to it, a great deal is at stake in these stories, and they are often highly contested. Consequently, a community's foundation stories may not only proliferate over time; several of them may compete for acceptance at any given moment, especially during times of intense political, social, or cultural disturbance.

Let me illustrate these points by reference to "America." I put "America" in quotes here because the notion of what constitutes "America" is in fact a matter of dispute. Some would define it as "the Americas," a new community, however loose and diverse within itself, that began with Columbus' discovery of "the New World"—"new", that is, from the perspective of Europeans, not from that of the peoples who preceded the arrival of the Europeans. For others "America" is above all the United States. This "America" may have its origins, variously, with the first colony of European settlers, with the arrival of the Pilgrims, with the "American Revolution," or with the signing of the Constitution, depending on whether one wishes to emphasize America's Anglo-Saxon heritage, its tradition of religious toleration, its commitment to the principles of political and economic self-determination, or the broader humanitarian and constitutional principles enunciated in the Constitution.

All of the foregoing events achieved their status as foundation stories not at the time of their occurrence but sometime after the fact: George Washington was hailed as "father of his country" only after his death; others among his contemporaries had to wait much longer for inclusion in the canon of "Founding Fathers," a category that remains vague and unstable today. Fourth of July celebrations did not achieve wide popularity and a regular character until the generation after 1815, and only a generation later became "secularized," that is, occasions criticized for excess whether in eating, drinking, and revelry, or in the bombast of speakers who exploited them for partisan ends.[3]

The "American" foundation stories to which I have referred remain current today, although each receives varying degrees of emphasis in different contexts and has enjoyed different degrees of prominence at different periods of our history. Contemporary private militias call attention to the "right to bear arms" articulated in the Constitution and see themselves as heirs to the citizen militias of the Revolution. The story of the Pilgrims becomes important in relation to ongoing questions of religious freedom and toleration or the issue of the separation of church and state. The Founding Fathers were early associated with the Declaration of Independence, although interest in that document seems to have changed from a focus on the iniquities of King George III before the 1790s to interest, later, in the broader philosophical principles laid out in the preamble.[4] Today, however, the Founding Fathers seem most often to be evoked as guarantors of one or another interpretation of the Constitution. The character of Columbus and his status as the discoverer of "America" have recently been questioned in conjunction with an emerging effort to redefine "America" as a multicultural rather than a Eurocentric community. The intensity of emotions surrounding debate about Columbus reflects the very real issue at stake: who can claim to be "real" Americans?

ELEMENTS OF THE FOUNDATION STORY IN THE *AENEID*

The *Aeneid* takes us back to the moment when the formation of Roman identity began. In fact the poem identifies that moment alternately as the murder of Turnus, when the Trojans secured their position in Italy and thus set in motion the long process of imperial expansion that would come to embrace the entire world, or as the fall of Troy and the circumstances that impelled Aeneas to abandon the traditional, Greek ideal of heroism and seek a new destiny. In the latter case, the *Aeneid* views Rome in terms of an idea or ideal, one that defines heroism in terms of service to the community rather than single-minded pursuit of one's own reputation for martial prowess; in the former, in terms of an actual community that begins with the elimination of the first great obstacle to the union of Trojans and Italians.[5] In both cases the poem focuses on defining aspects of the community and on the question of who belongs to it. Further, the first half of the poem calls attention to the qualities that define Romanness in its contrast between Aeneas' Trojans, the bearers of those nascent qualities, and others who do not share them, for example, the Trojans who elect to stay behind in Sicily (5.604–754, M 795–993).

When we first see Aeneas it is as he laments that he could not die the traditional hero's death as did others, both Greek and Trojan, in the world that he has left (1.94–101, M 133–43). This, it turns out, is part of the process by which he learns that his ruling virtue must be Roman *pietas*, obedience to the claims of ancestors and community, rather than Greek *arete*, the display of personal prowess. Aeneas' account of the fall of Troy (Book 2) focuses as well on another traditional Roman virtue, *fides*, "trustworthiness, reliability," again through contrast with others. This time the contrast is not between Aeneas and the whole heroic world, but between the generous-spirited Trojans and the duplicitous Greeks. Such contrast between Romans and treacherous others was a commonplace among Vergil's contemporaries: Hannibal and the Carthaginians who had once invaded Italy, for example, were well known for their *Punica fides*, "Carthaginian [bad] faith."[6] By virtue of such contrasts, we come to know the Romans as a unique people, distinct from others.

Vergil, however, does not deny all connection between Roman identity and the world of Greek heroic achievement. Aeneas, after all, does come from that world, even if he must learn a new hierarchy of values. His own status rests in part on his divine ancestry and in part on his participation in the heroic fight for Troy. Both aspects of his heritage play a role in his pursuit of Roman destiny. The gods take an active interest in him: he benefits from their protection and guidance, even as he suffers the hostility of Juno; memory or report of the Trojan War and his part in it often assure him a sympathetic welcome as he makes his way to the destined shores of Italy. His heroic temper and prowess reassert themselves ever more powerfully as he is drawn more and more into renewed hostilities in Italy.

As the first half of the poem progresses, the idea of Romanness is refined by contrasts between Trojans and peoples that they meet on their journey to Italy. Prominent among these are Dido's Carthaginians, who seem to have everything that Aeneas is seeking except the fact of having achieved it for himself and his own people. But not the least of those from whom Aeneas and his followers are differentiated are those Trojans who do not have the heart to press on to the final destination that has been decreed by fate and where there await *bella, horrida bella* ("wars, horrid wars," 6.86, M 122; 7.41, M 51). Such events help to define further what is distinctive about the Romans.

Other passages reinforce and expand our appreciation of Roman identity. Here, too, the emphasis is on Roman uniqueness. Thus, in Book 1, Jupiter promises universal Roman *imperium*, a condition that necessarily differentiates Romans from all others. In what are perhaps the poem's most famous lines, Anchises advises Aeneas that it is the Romans' destiny to rule, while others will be more productive in rhetoric and the arts (6.847–53, M 1129–37). Any Roman would have understood this contrast as applying particularly to all those whom the Romans regarded as "Greeks," that is, all the Hellenized peoples of the eastern Mediterranean. These explicit contrasts are important in their own right and also because they confirm the other, dramatized contrasts that help define the Romans' uniqueness.

If Roman identity is to be fulfilled, however, it must be more than an idea. It requires a community that will embody Roman virtues and destiny and will realize its potential. This is the theme of the second half of the poem, the story of how Aeneas finds a place for his people. The place is, significantly, not the city of Rome; settlement of Rome will come later. Rather, it is Latium, which in time will incorporate all Italy and, of particular importance, all Italians. As the decisive encounter between Aeneas and Turnus nears, Aeneas swears that if he fails, he will retreat to Evander's town and be content with it (12.183–86, M 246–51). That is, he will be content with the site of what was to become the city of Rome. If, however, he should be successful, Aeneas promises that he will not subordinate Latins to Trojans, but rather treat them as equals (12.190, M 258), join with them in eternal alliance (12.191, M 258), even name his settlement Lavinia in honor of his Latin wife (12.194, M 263).

This vision of a union between Trojan and Latin is ratified and developed even further at the end of Book 12. There Jupiter finally persuades Juno to relent in her opposition to Aeneas and his followers. He offers her in exchange the prospect of a single people who will honor her above all others (12.840, M 1117). Trojans will not only give up their name and share power as equals with the Latins; they will also give up all separate identity. They will first merge into the race of Latins, then of all Italians:

> sermonem Ausonii patrium moresque tenebunt,
> utque est nomen erit; commixti corpore tantum
> subsident Teucri. morem ritusque sacrorum
> adiciam faciamque omnis uno ore Latinos.
> (12.834–37)

> For the Ausonians will keep
> their homeland's words and ways; their name will stay;
> the body of the Teucrians will merge
> with Latins, and their name will fall away.
> But I shall add their rituals and customs
> to the Ausonians', and make them all—
> and with one language—Latins.
> (M 1107–13)

While the immediate union will be specifically with the Latins, in time it will lead to a cultural and racial union with the Ausonians, that is, with all Italians. In this context Aeneas' determination to withdraw to Evander's Palatine community only if he fails against Turnus is particularly important: it makes emphatically clear that Rome's essential identity is bound up less with the actual city of Rome than with Italy and the Italian peoples.[7]

Vergil presents the ultimate union of these peoples as the culmination of a process that is inevitable. In Book 7 we are told again and again that the union of Trojan and Latin that will lead to the larger union of Trojan and Italian is not a matter of choice but of fate. Thus at lines 50–51 (M 62–63), for example, we hear that "the edicts of the gods had left Latinus /

no male descent" (*filius huic fato divum prolesque virilis / nulla fuit*); at line 58 (M 73–74) we are told that "the omens / of gods with many sinister alarms" (*variis portenta deum terroribus*) stand in the way of the proposed wedding between his only child, Lavinia, and Turnus. This warning is reiterated by the god Faunus who appears to Latinus, forbids the marriage of Turnus and Lavinia, and promises instead new sons-in-law whose blood

> ". . . qui sanguine nostrum
> nomen in astra ferant, quorumque a stirpe nepotes
> omnia sub pedibus, qua sol utrumque recurrens
> aspicit Oceanum, vertique regique videbunt."
>
> (7.98–101)

> ". . . will raise our name
> above the stars; and their sons' sons will see
> all things obedient at their feet, wherever
> the circling Sun looks on both sides of Ocean."
>
> (M 124–27)

This is followed by Aeneas' own recognition of an omen signaling the Trojans' arrival at their destined home, and his exclamation, "Welcome, my promised land! [land owed to me by the fates]" (*salve fatis mihi debita tellus*, 7.120, M 153). At lines 241–42 (M 313–17) Aeneas' companion, Ilioneus, informs Latinus that "we were driven forward by the fates / of gods and their commands to seek your lands. / . . . Apollo / has urged us on by high decrees to find the Tuscan Tiber" (*huc repetit iussisque ingentibus urget Apollo / Tyrrhenum ad Thybrim*). His words recall to Latinus' mind the oracles of Faunus and what the fates had foretold regarding his future son-in-law (7.254–58, M 332–38). Eventually even Juno, the wife of Jupiter, concedes that "I cannot keep [Aeneas] from the Latin kingdoms: / so be it, let Lavinia be his wife / as fates have fixed" (*non dabitur regnis, esto, prohibere Latinis, / atque immota manet fatis Lavinia coniunx*, 313–14, M 414–16).

As the narrative of the second half of the *Aeneid* progresses, it becomes increasingly clear that Italy's fated role in the Trojans' destiny cannot be accidental. Despite the intense hostilities that arise between Italians and the Trojan immigrants, there are important affinities between the two peoples. To begin with, we learn that the Trojans actually trace their ancestry back to Italy; Italy is their home, as much and in some cases, perhaps ironically, even more so than it is the home of those who oppose their return: Latinus himself recalls a distant tradition that Dardanus, Troy's founder, came originally from Latium (7.205–11, M 272–79). Ilioneus, recalling Aeneas' own words to Dido, reminds Latinus of this fact (7.240, M 315; cf. 3.167, M 222–24).[8] We learn that Turnus, on the other hand, is descended from the Greeks of Mycenae (7.371–72, M 492–95; cf. 7.409–11, M 545–47); Evander, ruler of the Palatine community where the city of Rome will eventually be founded, was a refugee from Greek Arcadia (8.155–62, 333–36; M 204–12, 434–37) and was himself preceded by the Golden Age of Saturn, who settled there after Jupiter drove him from Olympia (8.319–20, M 418–20).

In fact, what Aeneas finds in Italy is a fusion of the best from the Greek world with indigenous traditions that Vergil's contemporaries would have recognized as central to their ideal vision of themselves. Thus, for example, the Palatine community perpetuates the memory and worship of Hercules, who, following his role as civilizer, eradicated the last vestiges of the Titans' primitive barbarism when he killed the monstrous Cacus (8.184–275, M 242–360). And yet Hercules brings nothing of Eastern luxury or decadence to Evander's well-regulated kingdom. Rather, in Vergil's description, repeated contrasts between the modesty of Evander's kingdom and the grandeur of imperial Rome reflect a view common among his contemporaries that Rome owed its greatness to virtues inherited from a simpler past, virtues for which Italians claimed to be the guardians. Similarly, in the description of Latinus' palace, Vergil's contemporaries would have recognized the origins of institutions central to their own society and government:

> hic sceptra accipere et primos attollere fascis
> regibus omne erat; . . .
>
> . . . .
> quin etiam veterum effigies ex ordine avorum
> antiqua e cedro . . .
>
> . . . .
> multaque praeterea sacris in postibus arma,
> captivi pendent currus curvaeque secures
> et cristae capitum et portarum ingentia claustra
> spiculaque clipeique . . .
>
> (7.173–86)

> Here Latin kings received their scepters, here
> beneath its auspices first took their fasces;
>
> . . . .
> Here, too, carved images of their forefathers
> were carved in ancient cedar . . .
> . . . Beside them many weapons
> hang from the holy doorposts: captured chariots
> and curving battle-axes, helmet crests
> and massive bars of gates and shafts and shields . . .
>
> (M 228–45)

The practice of taking the auspices, the fasces as a symbol of public authority, the formal display of ancestral busts in one's entrance hall, and the display of military trophies on household doorposts were all to become distinctive marks of Roman political life. Attention to such aspects of the world that Aeneas encounters on his arrival in Italy makes it clear that the Italians are neither mere victims of the Trojans, nor obstacles to be swept aside as the Trojans press forward on their path to becoming Roman. They are, rather, essential contributors to and partners in the realization of that destined end.

In light of all this—the Trojans' primeval ties to Italy, the virtues they share with the Italians, the qualities and institutions they owe to them— above all, in light of the inevitability of union between the two peoples, the bitter conflicts that precede that union seem especially tragic. They are in an important sense conflicts not between alien peoples but among a single people. Many passages invite us to think of these battles as civil wars. When Juno finally concedes that she is powerless to stop the eventual realization of Roman destiny and determines at least to delay it by stirring up hostility between the Trojans and Italians, she prays, "Let the son- and father-in-law pay / for peace with their own peoples' death" (*hac gener atque socer coeant mercede suorum*, 7.317, M 419–20). This, of course, refers most imme- diately to Aeneas and Latinus, who propose to join in a marriage alliance. But the idea of civil war as a conflict among relatives is an obvious meta- phor and one well established at Rome.[9] Consequently Juno's choice of words here has a larger, more ominous ring. When Allecto reports to Juno the successful completion of her mission, her language makes unambiguous her understanding that the resulting conflict is a civil war: "See the discord I made ripe / for you in bitter war," ("*en, perfecta tibi bello discordia tristi*,"

7.545, M 718–79). "Discord" here is a translation of the Latin *discordia*, a term that by Vergil's age had come specifically to distinguish civil from foreign conflict.

Paradoxically, this "civil war" between Trojans and Italians is essential to the two peoples' eventual union. It is the vital bridge that leads from the simple alliance between Trojans and nearby Latins that Aeneas first pursues to larger engagements between Trojans and Italians. These larger engagements look forward, in turn, to the eventual fusion of Trojans and Italians that Jupiter prophesies to Juno. The bitterness of Amata whose plans for her daughter are thwarted, the anger of the Latins over the murder of their pet deer, the resentment of Turnus over a broken alliance with the king of the Latins—these all-too-human rivalries and jealousies are catalysts that set the fateful wars between Trojans and Italians in motion. The wars themselves are the price the Italians must pay for partnership in the glories of Roman destiny, just as they are the price the Trojans must pay to attain the leavening of Italian virtue and custom that will make them, finally, into Romans. As Vergil observes in the introduction to his poem, "It was so hard to found the race of Rome" (*tantae molis erat Romanam condere gentem*, 1.33, M 50).

THE *AENEID* IN HISTORICAL CONTEXT

Contemporary concerns lie behind the ways in which questions of identity and membership are framed in the *Aeneid*.[10] As I have noted, one of the most important ways in which the character of the Romans is defined in the poem is through contrasts with the Greeks. Concern about the relation of native Roman virtues and character to Hellenistic culture had long been a conspicuous element of public discourse in Rome. As early as the mid-second century B.C., Cato the Elder made anti-Hellenism a defining aspect of his own self-presentation and a basis from which to discredit his rivals. Cato notwithstanding, the acquisition of Hellenistic goods (objets d'art, books, slaves) and the adoption of Hellenistic fashions (in dress, education, language) became increasingly widespread. This was especially significant among members of the Roman and Italian aristocracies. For them the trappings of Hellenistic culture came to play a central role in their rivalry for distinction through conspicuous display. This guaranteed that the relationship between essential Roman character and Hellenistic culture remained a highly charged issue in Rome, one that was

frequently negotiated in terms of day-to-day political life (the charac-
terization of someone as a collector or even connoisseur of Greek statuary,
for example, in order to discredit that person politically).

Political developments during and immediately preceding the years
when Vergil began composition of the *Aeneid* lent a particular urgency to
the question of Rome's rulers in relation to Greek and Roman identity.[11]
The principal contenders in the civil wars for control of Rome sought
increasingly to advertise their preeminence by identifying themselves
with Hellenistic models of charismatic leadership (above all Alexander
the Great) and by representing themselves in the symbolic language of
those models. Thus, Pompey lay claim, early in his career (81 B.C.), to the
Hellenistic tradition of heroic, supra- constitutional, and incontestable
leadership by choosing for himself the cognomen *Magnus*, "The Great,"
in obvious imitation of Alexander the Great; his portraits stressed physical
similarities between himself and Alexander, and, in keeping with the
Hellenistic tradition of heroism, he presented himself as the descendant of
a divine parent, Venus. Other eminent leaders such as Mark Antony and
Julius Caesar also claimed divine or heroic ancestry.

This sort of behavior, of course, raised serious questions about the
integrity of traditional republican government and values among Rome's
leaders. Octavian seems to have attempted an adroit middle course: using
Hellenistic conventions to advertise his superiority while simultaneously
presenting himself as a defender of Roman identity against the Helleni-
zation of his rivals. As relations between himself and Mark Antony
worsened (36–32 B.C.), he made much of the fact that Antony had (for
good tactical reasons) made Egypt, not Rome, his center of operations and
that he had identified himself with that most un-Roman of Greek gods,
Dionysus—an image that seemed to confirm Antony's reputation for
drunkenness and sexual license. Octavian himself enjoyed the ancestry of
Venus through Julius Caesar, his father by adoption, but during his conflict
with Antony he stressed particularly not his descent from Venus but, more
modestly, his protection by the more sober Apollo. In his portraits he grad-
ually evolved a style that bypassed the Hellenistic models of his rivals and
harkened back to the more distant models of fifth-century classicism.[12]
Still, even in his most patriotic moments, Octavian/ Augustus could take
Alexander the Great as a model. Pliny the Elder (A.D. 23/4–79) tells us that:

> at Rome [the painter Apelles'] Castor and Pollux with Victory and
> Alexander the Great are much admired, and also his figure of War

with the hands tied behind him, with Alexander riding in triumph in his chariot. The deified Augustus with restrained taste had dedicated both pictures in the most frequented parts of his Forum [the Forum of Augustus]. (*Natural History* 35.93–94)[13]

This figure of War must certainly be the inspiration for the image to which Vergil gives such a striking place in the prophecy of Roman greatness that Jupiter offers in *Aeneid* 1.293–96 (M 412–417). In this, as in other ways, the essential ambiguity of Aeneas as an embodiment of Romanness (distinct from the Greeks, but still part of their world) is echoed in the *Aeneid* and is acknowledged as an aspect of Augustus' and Vergil's own age— assertions of Roman uniqueness notwithstanding.

The question of who could be a Roman likewise had a particularly contentious history in Vergil's age.[14] Tradition recorded that the Romans were almost constantly at war with their Italian neighbors during their first centuries as an independent community. During the fifth, fourth, and third centuries B.C., Romans gradually consolidated control of the Italian peninsula through a succession of alliances and conquests that established Rome at the center of a series of bilateral relationships with other Italian communities. As in the *Aeneid*, these relationships were established first and were most fully developed with the Latin communities closest to Rome both spatially and culturally. With time Roman alliances extended further afield. Rome's victory over foreign invaders of Italy during the third century confirmed her dominance in Italy beyond dispute and determined the basis for the extension of Roman *imperium* beyond Italy in the generations that followed: Roman leadership supported by Italian auxiliary forces.

However, the Italian allies, or *socii* as the Romans called them, grew dissatisfied with this arrangement. After a few isolated rebellions, a great many of the *socii* joined together to oppose Roman domination in what became known as the Social Wars. These extended from 91–87 B.C., with the main fighting in 90–89 B.C. We possess no firsthand explanation for the Italians' discontent, but it is not difficult to imagine some of the considerations that probably influenced various groups and classes of Italians. Although members of the Italian aristocracies had their own records of local achievement and could boast of their own distinguished ancestries, they were generally excluded from holding office at Rome. This meant exclusion from the positions of highest prestige. It also meant exclusion from real power, including the opportunity to serve as commander. This position carried not only additional prestige but also the right to distribute booty, a means to political influence and the development of client followings, as well as to personal wealth. Similarly, the rank and file of the Italian auxiliary forces long were subject to separate and sterner discipline than their Roman counterparts. While this complaint was addressed before the outbreak of the Social Wars, it is likely that the auxiliary forces continued to receive a smaller share of booty than Romans. We also hear of occasional, but probably not atypical, cases of Roman haughtiness toward their Italian junior partners in empire.

Whatever their actual motivations, most Italian communities joined a federation, established their own capital at Corfinium, minted their own coins (showing the Italian bull goring the Roman wolf), and sought to establish their independence from Rome. Their rebellion was as short-lived as it was because the outnumbered Romans adopted a policy of divide and conquer. In exchange for peace, the Romans made offers of full Roman citizenship, first to those Italians closest to them, the Latins, but gradually further afield. Still, some Italians, especially the Samnite hill tribes of the central Apennines, could be reduced only after protracted and bitter struggle. In 89 B.C. Rome agreed to incorporate into the citizen body virtually all free Italians, although actual enrollment of Italians in the Roman census might not have taken place until 70 B.C.[15]

The process of integrating Roman and Italian remained far from complete, however, and continued through the next generation on several fronts. Three of the most important were the following. Even after formal enfranchisement of the Italians, Romans retained tight control over access to Roman political office. Italians such as the elder Cato, Marius, and Cicero who did achieve high office in Rome did so only through the patronage of Roman aristocrats and were so uncommon as to be called *novi homines*, "new men." The de facto barriers that excluded Italians from Roman office-holding did not finally come down until Octavian's victory at Actium in 31 B.C. brought an end to a succession of civil wars that had begun in 88 B.C. After 31 B.C. Octavian/Augustus' virtually complete control of government made it both possible and expedient for him to draw on the Italian aristocracy in order to replenish a ruling class that had been decimated by the civil wars. Second, competition for client followings among the rivals in the Roman civil wars made it desirable for them to extend the process of enfranchisement beyond the limits included in the settlement of the Social Wars to include new areas, most notably the Transpadine region of northern Italy. Finally, regional differences among

Italian communities, each with its own historical relationship to Rome and often with loyalties to one or another rival politician, undoubtedly contributed to the shape and course of the civil wars themselves. For example, in the civil war of 82 B.C. between Sulla and the younger Marius, Marius found his chief support among Samnite hill people who had been among the last holdouts against Rome in the Social Wars and had been treated with particular harshness by Sulla. Their ill-fated decision to side with Marius, then, was undoubtedly influenced by resentments held over from the Social Wars. Defeat of the Marians only led to the Samnites' renewed suffering at Sulla's hands. It seems reasonable to assume, therefore, that when the young Julius Caesar presented himself as the guardian of Marius' memory and a champion of the Marians, he did so not only because his aunt had been Marius' wife. He was also appealing to Marius' Samnite followers, and they must have constituted a significant presence in his military and political followings.

By contrast, Caesar's chief rival, Pompey the Great, drew much of his support from another quarter of Italy. His father had championed the extension of partial rights to Italians who lived north of the Po River. Pompey began his political career by serving under his father, an unpopular but effective leader in the suppression of Italian rebels during the Social Wars. Later he recruited three legions from among his father's clients and with them he supported Sulla against the younger Marius. Thus, the eventual conflict between Caesar and Pompey undoubtedly involved regional as well as personal loyalties. It carried with it the memory of differences that went back to a time when Romans and Italians were two separate peoples at war with each other.

Vergil's characterization of the wars between the Trojans and Italians as civil wars reflects, as I have suggested already, the irony of the wars' final outcome, the forging of a single people from these two adversaries. In the context of recent Roman history, however, it might equally serve to remind his audience that the civil wars were in important respects a continuation of the conflict that came to the surface with the Social Wars. It was not until Augustus that a final resolution of the relationship between Romans and Italians seemed a real possibility. A central element of his political program was finally to unite Romans and Italians as a single people behind his leadership. In preparation for the battle of Actium, Octavian (not yet Augustus) had called upon all Italy to swear personal allegiance to him.[16] After victory at Actium, as Augustus, he sought to consolidate his position constitutionally. He did this in part by sponsoring the admission of Italians into the Roman Senate. In this way he redefined Rome's political aristocracy as pan-Italic, while securing the personal loyalties of those Italian families who owed to him their new position at the center of Roman society and power.

THE *AENEID* AS ONE OF SEVERAL FOUNDATION STORIES

This brief sketch of Roman history cannot begin to do justice to the range and intensity of conflict and change that characterized Vergil's age. Nonetheless, it is sufficient to suggest that Vergil's account of Roman origins took its place among a variety of views about Roman cultural identity and in the debate over who were the true Romans. Even before Vergil's age Romans were familiar with a multiplicity of stories about the foundation of their community. One scholar has counted at least twenty-five basic Roman foundation stories.[17] The literary survivals of Vergil's own age suggest a concentration on two of them: the stories of Aeneas and of Romulus. Each basic version, however, received quite different interpretations at the hands of different authors.

Let us begin with the Italian-born Romulus, founder of the city of Rome. In one of his early poems Horace, for example, evoked the memory of Romulus not as the heroic founder of the city, but as the murderer of Remus, an act that stood as the emblem and starting point for all subsequent civil wars at Rome (*Epode* 7.17–20):

> Sic est: acerba fata Romanos agunt
> scelusque fraternae necis,
> ut inmerentis fluxit in terram Remi
> sacer nepotibus cruor.

> So it is: bitter fates pursue the Romans
> and the crime of a brother's murder,
> since the gore of undeserving Remus flowed into the earth
> a curse to his descendants.[18]

Another contemporary of Vergil, Dionysius of Halicarnassus, offered a quite different perspective. Writing as a Greek and in Greek for a Greek audience, he emphasized the continuities between Rome and the Greek world. For him, Aeneas was thoroughly Greek; Romulus, although born on Italian soil, perpetuated a Greek ideal of heroism in his distinguished ancestry and in his role as founder not only of the city of Rome but also of virtually all its essential institutions. Romulus was depicted as a thorough-going Greek even in his culture, for according to Dionysius the most reliable version of the twins' story is that they were not exposed on the banks of the Tiber River but that substitutes were exposed in their place; the twins themselves were spirited off to the nearby city of Gabii "in order to receive a Greek education" (*hos Hellada paideian ekmathoien*, Dion. Hal., *Ant. Rom.* 1.84.5).

Romulus is central to another, yet more subtly nuanced alternative to Vergil's account of Roman origins. This is the monumental history authored by Vergil's contemporary, Livy.[19] Although Livy acknowledges a tradition that Aeneas brought his Trojans to Italy, he treats it cursorily. His real interest is in the series of institutional developments that begin with Romulus. For him Romulus is the first of six individuals whom he iden-tifies with the title *conditor*, "founder," a title Livy does not confer upon Aeneas. Each of Livy's six founders is associated with a particular act or institution: Romulus with establishing the physical city, Numa with laying the foundations of Roman piety, Servius Tullius with instituting the essen-tial organization of the political state, Brutus (who expelled the Tarquin kings) with founding Roman *libertas* by instituting an annual consulship in place of monarchy, and Camillus with establishing the institution of refoundation that allows the city to survive and recreate itself after disas-ters. In that sequence of "founders," we find Augustus identified as "founder and restorer of all the temples" (*templorum omnium conditorem ac restitutorem*, 4.20.7), a reference to his ambitious campaigns to rebuild Rome and revive traditional religion at the end of the civil wars. Thus, although the personal and moral qualities that occupy Vergil are also important to Livy's conception of Roman identity and development, they take their place in Livy's narrative beside an equally central focus on the development of specific institutions.

Livy is also much more insistent than Vergil on the uniquely Roman origins of Roman character and greatness. In presenting his account of Romulus as Rome's first real founder, Livy consistently expresses skep-ticism about the fantastic elements in Romulus' story: the rape of his mother by Mars, for example, or his rescue by a wolf. On the other hand, he emphasizes how the exposed infant grew to maturity among shepherds, totally cut off from his ancestors, how he owed his character to the demanding conditions of his rustic upbringing, and how both his assassination of his evil uncle, Amulius, and his founding of Rome were achieved entirely through his own resources (Livy 1.3.10–7.3). The independence of Rome from Greek culture is implicit in this emphasis upon Romulus' nature as essentially native and self-made. This idea is developed more directly in Livy's portrait of Rome's second king and founder, Numa Pompilius. There Livy goes out of his way to refute a tradition according to which Numa owed his wisdom to Pythagorean teaching. He concludes:

> Suopte igitur ingenio temperatum animum virtutibus fuisse opinor magis instructumque non tam peregrinis artibus quam disciplina tetrica ac tristi veterum Sabinorum, quo genere nullum quondam incorruptius fuit.

> Therefore I think rather that his mind was governed by virtues because of his own disposition and was educated not so much by foreign arts as by the stern and austere discipline of the old Sabines; no race has ever been more uncorrupted. (1.18.4)[20]

It is for this native wisdom, learned among the Italian Sabines, that the Roman elders summon Numa to rule their city.

This emphasis upon native, self-made virtues contributes to a second theme central to Livy's portrayal of Rome's founders: their role as precedents for "new men" who were pressing their claims for inclusion among the Roman political leadership during the late Republic. Technically "new men" were individuals who were the first in their families to hold the highest elected positions in Roman government. Many of them came from Italian aristocracy. Their small numbers reflected the exclusionary policies of a traditional Roman aristocracy that were not effectively challenged until the turbulence of the civil wars and the patronage of Julius Caesar and Augustus.

The idea that the kings of Rome constituted a precedent for recognizing the qualifications of "new men" is developed explicitly in Livy's narrative of the early political struggles that ultimately shaped the Roman constitution. Here, in a striking anachronism, the plebeian tribune, Canuleius, protests the exclusion of plebeians from political office by a general appeal to the example of "the best of the kings, new men" (*optimis regum, novis hominibus*, 4.3.17). Canuleius goes on to evoke the example of Servius Tullius in language that is particularly noteworthy because it applies almost exactly to the earlier representation of Romulus as well:

Enunquam creditis fando auditum esse, . . . Ser. Tullium . . .
captiva Corniculana natum, patre nullo, matre serva, ingenio,
virtute regnum tenuisse?

You do believe what you've heard people say, don't you, that . . .
Servius Tullius . . . born of a captive woman from Corniculum,
with no father, his mother a slave, held the kingship through his
natural abilities, his excellence? (4.3.10–12)

The references here to *ingenium*, "natural abilities," and *virtus*, "excellence," recall the arguments of "new men" such as Cicero that they were no different from the founders of the *nobilitas* who first established their families' preeminence at Rome on the basis of their own talent and virtue, not of birth.[21] The characterization of Rome's "best kings" as "new men," then, provides the strongest kind of sanction for the "new men's" arguments.

The foregoing examples show a precedent for drawing upon Italian outsiders for Roman leadership. Livy addresses the relationship among Romans and Italians in many other ways as well. While he details the long history of their varied conflicts, he also presents Romans as being conscious from the very first that their own survival and attainment of greatness depend on a policy of incorporating and assimilating Italians. Romulus acts on this policy at the outset of his reign. First, he sets up a place of asylum that attracts a motley crowd of Italian refuges who, like himself, come from the margins of society (1.8.1, 8.6; 2.1.4). Later, the sequence of events that leads to the abduction of the Sabine women and to Rome's consequent union with the Sabines begins with a realization that "due to a dearth of women, the greatness [of Rome] was only going to last one generation" (*penuria mulierum hominis aetatem duratura magnitudo erat*, 1.9.1).

This theme is expressed implicitly throughout much of Livy's narrative and is developed at some length in the eighth book of his narrative. There, one of the leading statesmen of his day raises the question of what policy Rome should adopt toward rebellious Italians, arguing that there are really only two possible choices: they must either be treated with clemency or obliterated. He concludes:

Voltis exemplo maiorum augere rem Romanam victos in civitatem
accipiendo? materia crescendi per summam gloriam suppeditat.
Certe id firmissimum longe imperium est quo oboedientes
gaudent.

Do you wish to follow the example of our ancestors and augment Rome by accepting into citizenship those who have been defeated? The means of growing to the highest glory is to hand. Without doubt that *imperium* whose subjects delight in it is by far the most secure. (8.13.16)

Thus, where Vergil emphasizes the tragic, if inevitable character of Roman-Italian relations, Livy focuses more on the essential contribution that Italians make in Rome's rise to greatness and on the laudable pragmatism of the earliest Romans who fight when they must, but consciously choose a policy of assimilation rather than forcible subjugation wherever they can.

CONCLUSION

It is tempting for us in retrospect to see how the different views of Roman origin that I have surveyed here may reflect in part the different circumstances of their authors. None of them was a "real Roman." Dionysius, of course, was a Greek, and, as I suggested above, wanted to minimize differences between his people and their Roman masters. Horace was the son of an ex-slave from Apulia, not far from the instep of Italy's boot. His hometown, Venusia, had joined the Italian rebels during the Social Wars and he had himself fought in Brutus' army when it was defeated by Antony and Octavian at Philippi in 42 B.C. His reference to Romulus' murder of Remus occurs in a poem that most likely was written while the last of Rome's civil wars was still in progress, before Vergil and Livy had begun their works. It reflects a disillusionment that is appropriate to an outsider who found himself caught up on the losing side in wars among Roman warlords.[22]

Vergil and Livy had a slightly different relation to Rome. They were likely closer to native aristocracy than was Horace, but both of them came from Transpadine Italy, an area that had only received full Roman citizenship during their own lifetimes, and neither the *Aeneid* nor Livy's history was made public until after the decisive battle of Actium promised a new, if still not clearly defined, era in Roman history. Both authors construct a distinctive Roman identity, particularly in contrast to Hellenism. Vergil's Aeneas redefines the Greek heroic tradition, even as he remains an intermediary between important aspects of that tradition and Rome: he brings with him divine ancestry and tutelage, his reputation from the Trojan War, and a sense of obligation to live up to that moment. Livy's self-made heroes mark a more radical break with Greek tradition: they derive their strength and character from the austere conditions of their way of life rather than from the lofty eminence of the gods, and their energies are realized in the creation of distinctively Roman institutions as well as in their prowess on the field of battle. Both authors also share the view that Italians are necessary participants in Roman destiny. Vergil presents the story of their unification with Rome as simultaneously glorious and tragic but, in any event, beyond the power or even full comprehension of its agents. Livy records the long history of conflict between Romans and Italians fully, but he prepares for the ultimate union of the two peoples as the consequence of a sustained and deliberate policy of assimilation, a policy that expresses the Romans' explicit awareness that their own greatness positively requires the infusion of Italian virtue and manpower. What all of these authors have in common is their determination to isolate the essential elements of Roman identity by tracing them to their origins. In so doing they claimed definitive authority for their own visions of Rome during a period when critical aspects of Roman identity and membership were hotly contested and the stakes were high.

CHAPTER 14

THE WOMEN OF THE *AENEID*
Vanishing Bodies, Lingering Voices

S. Georgia Nugent

The "constant changeability" that Vergil's Mercury predicates of "woman" (*mutabile semper / femina*, 4.570) might well be applied to the *Aeneid* itself. For readers' understanding of the poem continually evolves, reflecting changes in historical circumstances, cultural mores, and critical fashions. Essays in this volume discuss ways in which the elusive meaning of Vergil's epic has been quite differently understood, for example, by readers for whom the sun never set on their national empire and by readers whose nation was embarked on a war they believed to be unjustified and unjust. Not surprisingly, just as Victorian imperialism or the Viet Nam War inflected, in their time, readers' understanding of the *Aeneid*, so has the political and intellectual movement of feminism in recent decades led some readers to look at the *Aeneid* in a different way, to ask new questions of the text, and to reevaluate its significance.

In the context of widespread critical reappraisal and reevaluation of the role of women in literary texts, it is worthwhile to examine female characters and their deployment in the *Aeneid*, for they figure importantly in almost every book of the epic.[1] The history of critical attention to the female figures of the *Aeneid*, however, is marked by paradox. There is no doubt that the *Aeneid* is profoundly centered around men, their aspirations and relationships with one another. And yet the divine figure of Juno and especially the human figure of Dido have always elicited great interest among readers. Both characters, it is true, have been largely perceived as fascinating obstacles in the path of the inevitable (and male-identified) mission of Aeneas. But that is not the whole story. While Juno has been seen in an almost unrelievedly negative light,[2] Dido has been understood both as the most dangerous threat to the Roman project and as an enormously sympathetic tragic figure.

St. Augustine provides perhaps the most stirring example of the emotional impact of Dido's tale, admitting in a well-known passage of his *Confessions* that he wept over her death when she was abandoned by Aeneas, although he did not weep for the death of his own soul when he had abandoned God. The great German classicist Richard Heinze called Dido "the only character created by a Roman poet to pass into world literature."[3] Much more recently, in her exploration of "gender and the politics of reading Virgil," Marilynn Desmond notes that "to many readers, the Dido story eclipses the plot of the *Aeneid* as a whole."[4]

Thus Dido, who seems to present the greatest threat to the eventual founding of Rome that is the subject of the *Aeneid*, also emerges paradoxically as the focus of readerly sympathy and even, perhaps, as the most memorable creation of Vergil's epic. I shall argue here that this representational strategy, which casts the woman both as what must be rejected—even destroyed—and as what remains most indelibly present, is not unique to Dido, but characterizes Vergil's representation of other women in the *Aeneid* as well. This essay will explore three aspects of the depiction of women that contribute to this construct, all of which are dramatically exemplified in the case of Dido: the centrality of female suffering and its distinction from Vergil's portrayal of male suffering; the resistance female characters offer to what has been called the "dominant voice" of Vergil's poem; and, finally, women's frequent tendency in the poem toward (self-) destruction and/or disappearance. Even as they disappear from the narrative surface of the poem with alarming regularity, women remain deeply inscribed as traces in the Vergilian text.

TAKE IT LIKE A MAN

As one contemporary scholar has written, "Dido's suffering lingers in the mind long after Aeneas' plotting and piety have faded."[5] The centrality, the defining quality of suffering in the perception of Dido's greatness is surely no accident. The experience of loss and its painful memory— *lacrimae rerum*—lie at the heart of the *Aeneid*, even if the celebration of empire-founding beckons on its horizon. In the bleak and shadowy landscape through which the men and women of the *Aeneid* pass on their way to that promised empire, they endure great hardship and pain, both physical and spiritual.

As readers of the *Aeneid*, we are led to understand immediately, from his first appearances in the poem, that Aeneas is a character haunted by the anguish of suffering and loss, yet also deeply marked by a sense of responsibility to master (even, if necessary, to mask) that anguish for the sake of others. Early in Book 1, when Aeneas' ships have found refuge from the storm at Carthage, the poet tells us explicitly that Aeneas' words of encouragement are crafted for his men, to "put a good face on things," while the leader suppresses within himself his own grave concerns:

> Talia voce refert curisque ingentibus aeger
> spem vultu simulat, premit altum corde dolorem.
> (1.208–9)

> These are his words; though sick with heavy cares,
> he counterfeits hope in his face; his pain
> is held within, hidden.
> (M 290–92)

In the figures of Aeneas and Dido, Vergil has created characters who differ dramatically from one another along a multitude of dimensions. But perhaps their differing capacity for absorbing and conferring meaning upon suffering is one of the most significant of those dimensions, not only for understanding the continuing tragic appeal of the Carthaginian queen, but also for understanding broader implications of the roles of women in the epic. Women in the *Aeneid* suffer greatly, but not well. The men seem capable of performing a marvelous alchemy that trans-mutes the seemingly senseless pain endured and inflicted for an elusive future goal into the fine stuff of heroism and civic virtue. But women possess no such philosopher's stone. Rather than absorbing and some-how transforming pain, the women of the *Aeneid* very often simply reflect it back into the community. Sometimes they do this in the form of outrage or even violence (as in their burning of the ships in Book 5 or seizing makeshift weapons in Book 11). More often they do it in the form of weeping and wailing, the onomatopoeic ululation of women's lamentation that sounds continually at the periphery of the poem.[6] And not infrequently, a woman reflects back into the community the pain she cannot endure by destroying herself, making of her own death an unmistakable message.

Compensating to some extent for the prevalence of pain and sorrow in the *Aeneid*'s moral universe is the father/son relationship, which—it is clear—grounds the more extensive systems of mutual commitment and obligation through which not only familial but civic order may be forged and preserved by men. It is not at all clear, however, that women are capable of participating successfully in the social relationships like those bonding father to son and comrade to comrade in a way that can confer meaning upon and in some sense transcend or redeem suffering.

While it is by no means primarily women who endure hardship or suffer grief in the *Aeneid*, yet Vergil represents women, by contrast to men in pain, as suffering extravagantly, without measure, often without dignity, and without sublimation to a higher purpose. This gendered distinction is well illustrated in the tightly packed sequence of tragic events in Books 9–11, which includes the death of Euryalus and the reaction of his mother, the death of Lausus and the reaction of his father Mezentius, and the death of Pallas and reaction of his bereaved father Evander.

Focusing not on the pathos *experienced* by these young men in meeting their untimely ends but on the pathos of *reception* as a parent is informed of tragic death, the clearest comparison may be made between Vergil's representation of Euryalus' mother and of Pallas' father, as they learn that their respective sons are dead. It is worth noting at the outset several fundamental distinctions between these characters. One lies in their identity or fullness of being in the text. Euryalus' mother is not a figure whose narrative significance extends, as does Evander's, through the course of the *Aeneid*, yet Book 9 confers considerable attention upon her—without conferring a name. Her presence in the Trojan camp is first alluded to by Nisus, a presence that comes as a surprise, since it contradicts the reader's understanding that at the conclusion of Book 5 all of the Trojan women have elected to stay behind in Sicily. In this passage, in which Nisus and Euryalus discuss taking on a dangerous reconnaissance mission, Euryalus' father is immediately named, but his mother is simply called (proleptically) by Nisus, *mater misera* ("wretched mother," 9.216). When the two friends, having made their pact, present their plan to Ascanius, Euryalus asks only that Ascanius see to the welfare of his mother, should he not return, noting also that he could not bear to tell her of his departure. Ascanius responds emotionally that she will be like his own mother to him, lacking only her name. In fact, here and later, Euryalus' mother lacks *any* name. Vergil's choice to leave her unnamed inevitably renders her a more contingent figure than Evander. She enters into the text not as a subject but as a topic of men's discussion, an object of their concern—to be sure—but also an object for their disposition.

In addition, the two parents, we realize from Euryalus' words, are distinct in the matter of agency. While Evander in fact sent his son off to war with Aeneas, Euryalus' mother not only had no say in her son's fatal decision, she was not even informed of it. Thus, Evander's suffering is an outcome to which he has, in some sense, given prior consent, even authorized, by sending his son into war with Aeneas.[7] At the moment of his son's departure Evander offers fervent prayer for Pallas' protection, but the premonition of disaster is clearly present, as he suddenly fails and faints at the moment of leave-taking (8.572–84, M 745–60). The possibility of bereavement for Euryalus' mother is also foreseen in Vergil's text, but only by others—Nisus, Euryalus, Ascanius. The woman herself is kept ignorant of the potentially tragic events transpiring. That ignorance is suddenly and horribly ended by the sight of her son's head, dripping gore, affixed to an enemy spear. Confronted with this sight, Vergil explicitly describes her as "out of her mind," (*amens*, 9.478), as she rushes to the wall of the Trojan camp, tearing her hair and wailing "like a woman" (*femineo ululatu*, 9.477), filling the air with her screams of lamentation.

Evander, like Euryalus' mother, is alerted by Fama ("rumor") to the approach of his son's remains.[8] The sight he encounters, however, is far different from that (*visu miserabile*, "awful to see," 9.465) which confronts the mother of Euryalus. Approaching Evander's city is a funereal procession, flanked by torchlight, bearing home the bier of Pallas. Although unable to accompany the corpse himself, Aeneas has made elaborate arrangements for this procession, decreeing that a thousand men accompany the fallen soldier home and himself wrapping the body in cloth of gold and purple. It is to this body, carefully and appropriately composed, that Evander clings in mourning. Unquestionably, the father is deeply grieved by this terrible loss (*lacrimansque gemensque*, "crying and groaning," 11.150), but—equally clearly—he is not driven mad (*amens*) by it, as Euryalus's mother is represented.

The words of mourning uttered by the two parents diverge in an equally dramatic way. Euryalus' mother begins with a harsh reproach to the dead (*crudelis*, "cruel one," 9.483), for leaving her thus alone.[9] Lamenting that she has not even been able to perform the appropriate funeral rites for her son's corpse nor wrap it in the clothing that she has been weaving for him, she reaches a crescendo of grief with the apparently perverse plea that, if the Rutulians have any *pietas*, they should manifest it by running her through with their spears and swords (9.493–94). An alternative prayer to Jupiter to cast her into the Underworld (9.495–97)[10] concludes the words allotted to her in the text before, at a signal from Ilioneus and Ascanius, she is seized and carried away:

> Illam incendentem luctus Idaeus et Actor
> Ilionei monitu et multum lacrimantis Iuli
> corripiunt interque manus sub tecta reponunt.
> (9.500–502)

> As her grief kindles,
> so Actor and Idaeus, at a word
> from tearful Iulus and Ilioneus,
> lift her and bear her homeward in their arms.
> (M 664–67)

What is portrayed, then, in the case of Euryalus' mother is a suffering that is at once deranging, that lashes out and accuses the other, that culminates in the purely negative desire for self-destruction,[11] and that also apparently threatens to enlist others in its nihilistic force—since the motivation for the woman's physical removal from the scene seems to be the debilitating effect her words are having on Ascanius' men.

> Hoc fletu concussi animi, maestusque per omnis
> it gemitus, torpent infractae ad proelia vires.
> (9.498–99)

> Her wailing moved their minds;
> a moan of sorrow passed through all; their force
> is broken, numbed for war.
> (M 662–64)

Though presented with precisely the same overmastering tragedy in the loss of his son, Evander's reaction to that loss—and its effect—are diametrically opposite to the grieving of Euryalus' mother. The father acknowledges at once that he realized the possibility (*haud ignarus eram . . .* , "I was not ignorant," 11.154) of this sad outcome—in sharp contrast to the mother who was not even aware of her son's perilous undertaking. Then, rather than cursing the dead boy as cruel (*crudelis*), Evander pronounces a blessing upon his wife, fortunate, in her death, to have been spared this tragedy. Again in direct contrast to the reproachful words of Euryalus' mother, Evander explicitly absolves his Trojan allies of blame in this calamity, reflecting philosophically that this sorrow was simply his lot in life:

> nec vos arguerim, Teucri, nec foedera nec quas
> iunximus hospitio dextras: sors ista senectae
> debita erat nostrae.
>
> (11.164–66)

> But I cannot blame you, Trojans, or
> our treaties or the right hands we have joined
> in friendship, for this was the chance assigned
> to my old age.
>
> (M 212–15)

Indeed, going further, Evander explicitly praises his son's death in a worthwhile cause and takes pleasure in the appropriate honor that has been shown him by Aeneas. Though he reflects briefly at one point that it would have been better had *he* been the one to die, Evander expresses this wish only as a contrary-to-fact conditional, in contrast to the multiple imperatives calling for death that conclude Euryalus' mother's speech. Evander concludes on a note that could hardly be more different. Reproaching himself for even having detained the Trojans briefly from battle, he urges them to fight with renewed vigor and—far from seeking death—pledges to remain alive expressly so that he may see his son's killer, Turnus, dead and the Trojans victorious. In pointed contrast to the mourning of Euryalus' mother, which had broken the men's spirits for further battle, Evander receives the news of his son's death in such a way that his lamentation actually turns into a rallying cry.

The representation of the mother's sorrow renders it accusatory, self-pitying, irrational, and excessive in a way that is so directly harmful to Aeneas' cause it must be silenced. But the father's sorrow is measured, reflective, and supportive—even appreciative—of the martial and civic ties that bind men and mitigate such sorrows (even if, implicitly, they are also contributing causes). Evander's suffering, far from undermining

Aeneas' project, is supportive of it in every way and even reinvigorates it, adding urgency and purpose to renewed battle by including the explicit motive of vengeance. The destructive urge resulting from Evander's loss is appropriately channeled and directed against the enemy other—and it is also accompanied by constructive aspects, reaffirming the importance of established bonds, shared purpose, and cooperative effort. But the raging grief of Euryalus' mother lacks a constructive dimension, and its destructive force is turned back, ineffectually, upon the self.

The tragic narratives of *Aeneid* 9–11 of course present another case in which a bereaved parent—in this instance, a father—reacts to loss by seeking death. Vergil's treatment of Mezentius and his son Lausus is complex and many-faceted, yet even the suffering of this father, in many ways an explicitly evil figure in the poem, finds a positive resolution that we do not see exemplified in women's suffering.

Mezentius' status as an exemplar of evil is immediately established with his introduction into the poem as *contemptor divum* ("disdainer of the gods," 7.648, cf. 8.7). Also highlighted immediately is his paternal relationship to Lausus, who "deserved a better father" (. . . *dignus patriis qui laetior esset / imperiis et cui pater haud Mezentius esset*, 7.653–54). The monstrous behavior that has led to Mezentius' overthrow by his own people is later vividly described by Evander to Aeneas (8.481–503), and the man's brute, virtually inhuman strength and force are displayed in a sustained epic *aristeia* in Book 10, in the course of which he is compared to a huge boulder buffeted by the sea (10.693), a wild boar (10.708), a hungry lion (10.723), a whirlwind (10.763), and Orion (10.763). But hinted at as well is a tenderness between father and son, as Vergil briefly notes Mezentius' gift of battle spoils to his son (10.700–701) and his boast that Lausus shall also have Aeneas' armor as a trophy (10.774–76).

When, rather than taking Aeneas, the old man is wounded by him, Lausus rallies at once, slipping under Aeneas' spear to protect his father's retreat and ultimately, predictably, falling to the experienced warrior's greater force. Lausus' death turns immediately to pathos, as even his killer Aeneas is overwhelmed by the enormity of what he has done.[12] Mezentius, like Evander and Euryalus' mother, suffers the experience of his son's untimely death. The result, in this case, is utterly transformative.

Although no Fama alerts him to the tragedy, Mezentius intuits the awful truth (10.843). Like Achilles mourning the death of Patroclus, he defiles himself with dirt in his mourning and blames himself for his son's demise.

This heretofore vicious individual at once articulates an understanding of his past transgressions, their repercussions upon his son, and the debt he owes his own people (10.851–56). He proclaims his intention to ride to his own death at Aeneas' hands.

At this point, Vergil pulls out all of the emotional stops, depicting the supposedly heartless Mezentius not only as ready and willing to sacrifice himself to atone for the death of his son, but also as emotionally attached even to the animal kingdom, when he lovingly addresses his faithful horse Rhaebus. Vergil then exploits this figure's narrative potential by making the horse both Aeneas' direct victim and the indirect killer of Mezentius, as it is pierced between the temples by Aeneas' spear and then pins in its fall its unfortunate master. Thus trapped, Mezentius offers no resistance but rather an unflinching acceptance of the inevitable. Essentially, his submission to death at the hands of Aeneas proclaims an acceptance of his own failures, of the warrior's code, and of Aeneas' mission.

The death of Mezentius unmistakably and—I would argue—unequivocally confers nobility upon this contemnor of the gods who has, himself, perpetrated acts beneath contempt. The quintessential Roman virtue of *pietas* typically entails an appropriately reverential recognition of one's place in a "great chain of being," stretching from the divine father through the senatorial "fathers" of the Roman state to one's own father and on into the endless future of Rome through one's own son, with corresponding obligations, responsibilities, and privileges at each link in the chain. In the character of Mezentius, however, Vergil has boldly severed this chain, separating its lower, merely mortal reaches from its supernatural span. Mezentius is repeatedly identified with the stock epithet of *contemptor divum* (7.648, 8.7), explicitly claims that he has no concern for the gods (10.880), and at one point declares his own right hand his god (10.773); yet at the moment when he learns of Lausus' death he spreads his hands to heaven in a gesture recognizably that of Roman prayer,[13] and the extraordinary power of his love for and sense of obligation to his son is not just ennobling but ultimately salvific.

Confronted with the death of his beloved son, Mezentius, like Euryalus' mother, wishes to die. But Mezentius courts that death in a way that Vergil's text sanctions and in fact validates, using it as a means of redeeming this formerly despicable character. The same does not hold true for the female mourner. Rather than enlisting her in some larger project on behalf of Aeneas' mission and the Roman state's values, her suffering is represented as pointless and destructive. As Vergil represents it, women's grief is a dead-end confrontation with limitless sorrow, lacking the power either to redeem the self or to edify others. Men's grief, by contrast, provides not disillusionment but a reason for perseverance.

THE GRAND REFUSAL

The model for male, heroic, Roman comportment that Aeneas enacts is one of assent. However confusedly, however reluctantly, however misguidedly, Aeneas accepts and endures. Told that his mission is to "seek your ancient mother" (*antiquam exquirite matrem*, 3.96), he repeatedly misinterprets the injunction, yet persists. Confronted with the necessity of abandoning Dido—and explaining to her his need to do so—he pleads that his will is not his own: *Italiam non sponte sequor* ("It's not of my own volition that I'm setting out for Italy," 4.361). When his goddess mother, Venus, presents him with a miraculous shield on which is depicted the future history of Rome, though he cannot understand what he sees, nevertheless he admires it and takes pleasure in the images (*miratur rerumque ignarus imagine gaudet*, 8.730). Aeneas assents—to the burden of destiny and, often, to the will of others (even, apparently, to Dido's desire to detain him and love him). The great female characters of the *Aeneid*, by contrast, refuse. They refuse, in various ways, their traditional roles of passivity, domesticity, and subordination; they refuse the mission of Rome; they even refuse to give credence to the pronouncements of the gods.

The implicit assumption that Dido's leadership of her people is paradoxical and fundamentally unnatural—in some sense a refusal of the female's appropriate role—is what gives point to the brief tag *dux femina facti* ("they made a *woman* their leader," 1.364).[14] The way in which Dido's highly unusual choices in how she lives her life are seen by those around her as specific *rejections* of more normal roles is made explicit both by Iarbas' outraged allusion to her rejection of his advances (*conubia nostra / reppulit*, 4.213–14) and by her sister Anna's attempt to bring her round to more sensible ways:

> solane perpetua maerens carpere iuventa
> nec dulcis natos Veneris nec praemia noris?
>
> (4.33–34)

> . . . are you to lose
> all your youth in dreary loneliness,
> and never know sweet children or the soft
> rewards of Venus?
>
> (M 39–42)

Even further outside the boundaries of feminine decorum is the warrior maiden Camilla, a young girl inured to harsh battle, whose distinctiveness is initially presented as a negation of feminine norms: *non illa colo calathisve Minervae / femineas adsueta manus, sed proelia virgo./ dura pati* ("she did not accustom her girlish hands to weaving but instead, a virgin, she endured harsh battle" 7.805–7, my translation).

Dido and Camilla present extreme examples of nontraditional female behavior. But women who play the more typical roles of wives and mothers also refuse at various points throughout the poem to remain confined within those roles. Explicitly inspired by the courage of Camilla, for example, the Italian mothers fight in desperation to fend off the Trojan invaders and save their city:

> ipsae de muris summo certamine matres
> (monstrat amor verus patriae, ut videre Camillam)
> tela manu trepidae iaciunt . . .
>
> . . . .
> . . . primaeque mori pro moenibus ardent.
>
> (11.891–95)

> Even the mothers
> along the walls, remembering Camilla,
> are rivals in their eagerness to cast
> their shafts with anxious hands; true love of homeland
> points out the way . . .
>
> . . . .
> each burns to die first for her city's sake.
>
> (M 1180–86)

The Trojan mothers in Book 5, frustrated and discouraged by the fruitless voyages on which Aeneas has led them in search of "the ancient mother," violently signal their refusal to continue by setting fire to the ships on which they have traveled.[15] Euryalus' mother, as we have seen, seems clearly to overstep her proper bounds in the lamentation for her dead son and is forcibly removed from the public space of the camp and reconfined to an interior space appropriate for women (9.498–502). Such acts dare to question the inevitability and inherent rightness both of the state-founding mission on which Aeneas is embarked and of the women's duty to support that mission.

Indeed, although Aeneas affirms that he is on "a mission from god," Dido openly questions this claim, noting with sarcasm that she doubts very much the gods are troubling themselves about him (4.376–80). While Dido rejects Aeneas' *claim* of prophetic guidance, at other points females more directly refuse to accept the will of the gods. The *contemptor divom* is a stock figure in epic, a hubristic, megalomaniacal character who refuses to recognize the gods as superior to himself. The women in the *Aeneid* who refuse to capitulate to divine will, however, do so not out of hauteur but out of desperation. Amata, for example, cannot accept that her daughter must be married to a foreign invader rather than to Turnus, the bridegroom Amata has chosen for her. In part, Amata's ultimately frenzied opposition to Lavinia's fated union is caused by the intervention of Juno, via the insinuation of the Fury Allecto into the queen's very body. Yet Vergil makes it clear that Amata has fixed upon refusal of fate's course *before* Allecto appears on the scene (7.344–45) and that she clearly articulates her reasons before the Fury's poisons take effect (7.356–58).

Another notable example of a woman's resistance to fate is the case of Juturna, Turnus' sister—who, as a recompense for rape by Jupiter, has been transformed from a human being into an immortal nymph. Throughout the final book of the *Aeneid*, Juturna acts to aid her brother, although Juno has made it clear to her that Turnus' fated day is upon him. Juno, it must be said, also urges the nymph to undertake the futile effort on Turnus' behalf, a last-ditch attempt to thwart (or at least delay) the inevitable. Yet, despite Juno's original instigation, Juturna's brilliant and resourceful interventions are very much her own. So much so that Juno explicitly circumscribes her role in the episode (12.813–17), and her own retreat from the arena does not effect Juturna's as well. Finally, Jupiter must summon what seems to be the ultimate weapon of horror, the Dira, to drive Juturna from the field of combat. Her brother Turnus has, we learn late in the book, cannily recognized his sister throughout, despite the inventive disguises she assumes. He perceives just as clearly that what is at stake is Juturna's persistent but futile defiance of what has been fated:

> iam iam fata, soror, superant, absiste morari;
> quo deus et quo dura vocat Fortuna sequamur.
>
> (12.676–77)

> "Sister, fate has won; do not
> delay me; let us follow where both god
> and cruel fortune call."
>
> (M 900–902)

Whereas Aeneas, Anchises, Evander, and Latinus yield unquestioningly to the exigencies of fate, female figures such as Dido, Camilla, Amata, Juturna, and others suggest the possibility of choice and independent volition. By refusing what has been spoken (*fatum*) by the gods, scripted by their society, or chosen for them by others, the strong women of the *Aeneid* assume a tremendous narrative burden for the poem: acting as a counterpoint to *pius*, passive Aeneas, they serve as signposts to the road not taken. It may seem surprising that this exploration of independent judgment should be allotted to the women of the *Aeneid*. It is less surprising, however, when we note the regularity with which the memorable female characters of the *Aeneid* die—or wish to die. While representing alternatives to the "dominant voice" of the *Aeneid*, women also indicate and play out in the text the failure of these alternatives. In contemporary critical terms, one might employ the Lacanian notion of being "under erasure." That is, Vergil's representational strategy enables him to show, often through women who question, refuse, or reject dominant ideological tenets of the *Aeneid*, that alternative modes exist. Yet, to the extent that they fail, they do not in fact exist as *viable* alternatives. Both these women's choices and—as we shall see—they themselves are under erasure in Vergil's text, a presence that (quite literally) becomes an absence.

ALL THAT IS SOLID MELTS INTO AIR

Contemporary scholarship has shown the way in which classical texts, in the representation of women, draw heavily upon a cultural imagination that constructs woman as deeply embedded in a body, paying particular attention to the rounded forms and surfaces of that body and attending as well to the mysterious inner spaces in which unborn progeny or thoughts or words may be harbored.[16] This construction is almost entirely absent from Vergil's poem. Indeed, the opposite is true—women in the *Aeneid* seem transient sojourners in the material world, drawn inexorably toward incorporeality, toward disappearance, toward nonbeing.

The woman's tenuous hold on physical presence and corporeality is well exemplified by the fate of Creusa, Aeneas' first wife.[17] As he relates in Book 2 the story of Troy's last night and his own confused attempts both to fight and to flee, Aeneas thinks of Creusa a number of times (2.562, 597, 651, 666). Yet from the moment the decision is made to set out for exile—and the Roman destiny—Aeneas' wife becomes oddly tangential. In the physical configuration of his family that the hero constructs as he plans their escape from the besieged city, the superfluity, the nonessential nature of Creusa's presence is starkly visible: Aeneas carries his father on his shoulders, takes his son by the hand, and has his (unnamed) wife follow at a distance (*et longe servet vestigia coniunx*, 2.711). This vignette physically embodies the patrilineal relation and accurately represents the woman's marginal relationship to it.[18] First moved in this way from her position in the center of the home to the margins of the filial group that Aeneas is intent on saving, Creusa soon vanishes altogether.

As Aeneas reconstructs the story (for the narrative of the fall of Troy takes place entirely as a "flashback" related at the court of Carthage), he realizes that Creusa must have fallen behind as he ran erratically through the streets of the falling city. Given the circumstances, in the panic of flight, it may not be surprising that he fails to remark her absence. Yet even after he has arrived at safe haven, it seems as if this loss impinges on Aeneas in an oddly mediated and impersonal way, virtually as the result of an inventory:

> . . . hic demum collectis omnibus una
> defuit, et comites natumque virumque fefellit.
> > (2.743–44)

> . . . here
> at last when all were gathered, she alone
> was missing—gone from husband, son, companions.
> > (M 1001–3)

Having realized that "one was missing," Aeneas turns his steps back to the burning city. In doing so, he enters an urban landscape that itself seems elusive or surreal. The destruction of Troy is presented to Aeneas' gaze as

in a film or a dream: fire races from threshold to roof and structures collapse, yet the city is eerily silent; Aeneas' shouts of Creusa's name echo
through the empty streets. Strangely arrested within those streets—and in
one of Vergil's rare unfinished lines—is a group of women and children:

> pueri et pavidae longo ordine matres
> stant circum.
> (2.766–67)

> . . . and Trojan boys
> and trembling women stand in a long line.
> (M 1034–35)

While this group is present to Aeneas' sight, it seems not to share the
same existential plane; he sees them as one might see creatures trapped in
amber.

Creusa is not among these women, but when she appears to Aeneas a
few moments later, it is clear that she too now belongs to a different ontological order. In recounting thirty-five lines earlier the story of her loss,
Aeneas had said that after setting out from their household he never laid
eyes on her again: *nec post oculis est reddita nostris* ("nor, after this, did
she ever return to my sight," 2.740). Yet, when he reenters the city, the
image of Creusa does in fact appear before him:

> infelix simulacrum atque ipsius umbra Creusae
> visa mihi ante oculos et nota maior imago.
> (2.772–73)

> . . . the effigy
> and grieving shade of my Creusa, image
> far larger than the real.
> (M 1041–43)

No longer living and yet not dead, Creusa seems to exist in some
interstitial niche between the human and the divine. As she explains to
Aeneas, the gods did not see fit for her to accompany him into exile, nor
to be taken as a captive Trojan slave to Greece; rather, the Magna Mater
has "detained her on these shores" (*sed me magna deum genetrix his
detinet oris*, 2.788). Having accurately foretold the wanderings, war, and

wife that the future will hold for Aeneas, she dissolves into thin air,
bidding him farewell:

> "haec ubi dicta dedit, lacrimantem et multa volentem
> dicere deseruit, tenuisque recessit in auras.
> ter cognatus ibi collo dare bracchia circum;
> ter frustra comprensa manus effugit imago,
> par levibus ventis volucrique simillima somno."
>
> (2.790–94)

> "When she was done with words—I weeping and
> wanting to say so many things—she left
> and vanished into transparent air. Three times
> I tried to throw my arms around her neck;
> three times the Shade I grasped in vain escaped
> my hands—like fleet winds, most like a winged dream."
>
> (M 1065–70)

Creusa has been translated to some other realm of being; we might
think of it as the realm of ideas. For throughout her representation in the
book, Creusa seems to have been to Aeneas less of a being than an idea.
Even before her disappearance, she comes into Aeneas' thoughts not as a
fully encountered person but rather as a concept, a sign—of his familial
responsibilities and of the home to which he must return. If Aeneas will
fulfill his destiny in the act of founding, Creusa seems to fulfill hers
through a process of etherealization, an abstraction from the flesh-and-
blood of an embodied woman to a disembodied concept or relation. This
apparent tendency toward incorporeality and etherealization, first encoun-
tered in Creusa, is by no means unique to her.

Vergil is never a deeply carnal poet. Yet he takes full account of the
bodiliness of male characters. In his many poignant depictions of male
deaths, Vergil leaves readers not only with the keen sense of life profli-
gately lost but also with the pitiful remains of heroic sacrifice, the too, too
solid flesh. Aeneas' moment of epiphany as he contemplates the lifeless
features of Lausus is unforgettable. The disposal of the bodies of Pallas,
of Mezentius, of Nisus and Euryalus is explicitly cause for concern in the
text. But females tend, in various ways, to waft away. While the bodies of
fallen male warriors may be variously retrieved by their comrades, pitied
and provided for by their slayers, or even intentionally and quite explicitly

defiled by the enemy, the body of Vergil's lone female warrior, Camilla, is miraculously transported through the air at the behest of her patron goddess, Diana (11.593–94). Presumably, from the point of view of mere human warriors, Camilla, lying lifeless on the battlefield one moment, simply disappears the next moment.

Another female death striking for its elusive quality is that of Amata, Latinus' queen, who—mistakenly believing that her champion, Turnus, has already been killed—suddenly hangs herself from a roofbeam within the palace:

> purpureos moritura manu discindit amictus
> et nodum informis leti trabe nectit ab alta.
> (12.602–3)

> . . . she is ready
> to die and tears her purple robe and fastens
> a noose of ugly death from a high beam.
> (M 808–10)

This suicide, as Vergilian commentators note, is clearly modeled on Greek tragedy and particularly Sophocles' Oedipal cycle, in which no fewer than three women hang themselves—Jocasta in the *Oedipus Tyrannos* and, in the *Antigone*, both Antigone and Creon's wife Eurydice. In each of these instances, however, the body of the hanged woman appears in the text—famously and horribly so in the case of Jocasta, as Oedipus pierces his eyes with the brooches he has torn from the lifeless body of his wife and mother (*Oedipus Tyrannos*, 1264–74). Haemon embraces the hanging body of his lost love Antigone (*Antigone*, 1221–25) and, just a few lines later, the body of Creon's wife Eurydice is revealed to him by the chorus (1293).

Vergil follows and even outdoes these tragic models in the swiftness of his female character's suicidal action. But he completely elides its result: the lifeless body. Although Lavinia, Latinus, and indeed an entire entourage (*turba*, 12.607) of Latin women seem to learn immediately of the queen's death, how they do so is unspecified. Certainly, there is no mention of a body. Instead, within the space of five lines, Amata—or at least her death—has been transformed into *fama*, "a tale," "a rumor" (12.608). In the Sophoclean texts the body itself signifies, the corpse of the woman becoming in a sense her ultimate statement. But in Vergil the woman's body vanishes, it takes flight at the earliest opportunity, leaving behind a meaning expressed not corporeally but verbally.

Perhaps the clearest example of this phenomenon, the distillation of the woman's body into pure signification, is that of Caieta, Aeneas' nurse, alluded to in the opening lines of Book 7, as Aeneas' ships reach the spot that bears her name. The physical presence of this woman whose body nourished that of the infant Aeneas is elided: of her we learn nothing except that, in dying, she left behind an undying name:

> tu quoque litoribus nostris, Aeneia nutrix,
> aeternam moriens famam, Caieta, dedisti;
> et nunc servat honos sedem tuus, ossaque nomen
> Hesperia in magna, si qua est ea gloria, signat.
>
> (7.1–4)

> In death you too, Aeneas' nurse, Caieta,
> have given to our coasts unending fame;
> and now your honor still preserves your place
> of burial; your name points out your bones
> in broad Hesperia—if that be glory.
>
> (M 1–5)

While Caieta may present the most extreme example of passing from substance to sign, it is a pattern exemplified by many women in the *Aeneid*, their significance becoming all the more powerful the more evanescent their bodies.

Dido too, despite her erotic valence in the poem, remains remarkably unembodied and intangible. She is never visually realized. Vergil's introductory description of her, however powerful, relies solely on the suggestion that her presence among her people somehow resembles Diana processing with her nymphs (1.498–504). The queen is *forma pulcherrima*, "beautiful in form" (1.496), and that is all. To the extent that her body is represented at all by Vergil, it is a site not of *eros* but of *pathos*. Subject to the arrows, the torches, and the poisons of ill-fated love, Dido's body seems less a presence than a space, a laboratory in which the gods may undertake their experiments on the emotions.

And Dido, like Creusa and Camilla, disappears. Her corporeality is first burned away through cremation and then transmuted, in Aeneas' final encounter with her in the Underworld, into a luminous mirage, a sliver of the new moon glimpsed—or perhaps only imagined—through a scrim of clouds. Like Creusa, but in more complex ways, Dido is transformed ultimately into a sign. When the Carthaginian queen takes her own life, climbing onto the funeral pyre she has deceptively prepared for her suicide, she will be physically changed into mere ashes. The fire and smoke of Dido's cremation, of course, as we know from the opening lines of *Aeneid* 5, are in fact perceived by Aeneas and his men as they sail away. Willfully ignorant of her demise, however, Aeneas receives this sign but does not interpret it: *quae tantum accenderit ignem / causa latet*, "the cause which had enkindled such a great fire lay hidden" (5.3–4).

In addition to sending this smoke signal, however, Dido will become in the Roman future which lies beyond the narrative time of the poem that embodiment of pure speech, the curse. For Vergil and for his readers, Dido comes to represent, in essence, the undying hatred that she proclaims in her terrible curse upon Aeneas and his descendants (4.607–29, M 838–68), the enmity between the peoples of Carthage and Rome that will culminate in the Punic Wars. In her embodied form, the affect Dido holds for Aeneas remains inscrutable; but when her whole being has been concentrated upon the hurling of a curse, refined into pure language, there is no question of its power.

FURTHER VOICES/WHOSE VOICES?

Scholars of the *Aeneid* continually emphasize the multiple voices of Vergil's text, its undecidability and open-endedness. While it is a commonplace that many great literary works invite multiple, varying, and even contradictory readings, the *Aeneid* seems uniquely open and unceasingly contested. The representation of women in the *Aeneid* plays a substantial role in this textual polyvalence. In various ways, at a number of significant points, women present an oppositional point of view—through their choices, their words, and their acts they question what has been called the dominant voice of the epic, they resist. The evaluation of that resistance is not clear. Although women raise opposition, the alternative views they present seem largely discredited by their own failure. They are shown to be lacking in authority, their counterclaims are repudiated, their personal passions are discredited, and they die ingloriously.

And yet, Vergil has not only raised a specter of doubt through his female characters but often done so with extraordinary sympathy—particularly in the cases of Dido or Camilla. If one associates these female figures with certain values that appear to run counter to the Authorized Roman Version of cultural life—such as romantic love, the preservation of life over honor, fidelity to the self rather than to the state—these values seem, through their appearance in the epic, duly considered and ultimately renounced. Yet the questions raised in some ways resonate more than the answers given. Female figures of the *Aeneid* fail dramatically in terms of their represented life histories, but they triumph resoundingly in the language of the poem, transmuted from body to word. While they do not seem aligned with the overt values of the work, female figures nevertheless become identified with poetic language itself and indeed with the voice of the poet.

CHAPTER 15

VERGIL AND APOLLONIUS

Charles Rowan Beye

Traditional criticism of the *Aeneid* has concentrated on the relationship between Vergil's poem and earlier epic poetry both Roman and Greek. Although the early Roman epics, most notably those of Ennius and Naevius, survive in mere fragments, it is obvious that the strong historical emphasis in the *Aeneid*, the patriotic sense of things Roman, the idea of destiny created from depicting what was future to Aeneas in the narrative as established fact for the first-century B.C. reader, had their roots in these epics. The surviving texts of the *Iliad* and *Odyssey*, on the other hand, have made it possible for critics to trace their large influence in story, style, and ideology on the narrative of the Roman poet. In addition, Vergil critics have traditionally noticed that the love affair in Book 4 between Aeneas and Dido shows the influence of the third century B.C. epic poem the *Argonautica* by the Alexandrian Greek poet Apollonius.

The fame of the third book of the *Argonautica* stems perhaps from the ancient critic Servius' note: "Apollonius in writing the *Argonautica* introduced Medea in love in his third book, from which almost the whole of this book [i.e., Book 4 of the *Aeneid*] is brought over." The observation is not exactly accurate since the detailed account of the growing love between Jason and Medea (or perhaps better, Jason's attempted seduction of Medea and her clear-eyed negotiation with Jason) is only hinted at in the *Aeneid*. Dido's angry response to Aeneas' determination to leave, on the other hand, while modeled to some extent on Medea's outburst in the fourth book of the *Argonautica* (not in the third), comes much more from the response of Euripides' Medea to her spineless consort's cheery estimation of the long-range benefits to them both in his abandoning her. What is more, Vergil's portrait of the lovesick and abandoned Dido—a victim, perhaps, as some would argue, sacrificed on the altar of Rome's inexorable progress to imperial greatness—is utterly foreign to Apollonius' conception of the strong and ambitious Medea whose misfortune is to have been made to fall in love by divine design with the weak and cowardly Jason.

Readers of the *Aeneid* will benefit, however, from paying close attention to the entire *Argonautica* for its relation to the Roman poem, if for no other reason than that it is the major surviving piece of Alexandrian literature and Vergil's poetic circle was immediately engaged with the heritage of the Alexandrian literary movement. What for Roman authors of the first century B.C. was a most exciting literary movement has not always been treated with the same attention and respect by critics of the last few centuries. In the annals of western literary history the Alexandrian period has generally been under the shadow of fifth-century Athens or late Republican and early Imperial Rome. Among the many reasons for this is one that in the late twentieth century ironically enough has given Alexandrianism the lustre it deserves, and that is its obsessive preoccupation with its literary heritage. For centuries scholars have dismissed what they perceived as mere copying, whereas in fact the Alexandrians were engaged in a lively reimagining. Like the international high modernism of the first half of the twentieth century, Alexandrianism produced creative artists who reconstituted the works of their tradition so as to give them a sensibility that was contemporary. Both periods and movements share in a strategy of equaling or surpassing the inheritance of their acknowledged masters by reworking the legacy. Any student of twentieth-century literature will remember Ezra Pound's "Only make it new!" and can perceive how the principle manifests itself in that poet's *Cantos*, a clear evocation of ancient epic, or in T. S. Eliot's *The Waste Land*, a veritable compendium of western literary motifs, conceits, and ideas, or in Picasso's series of drawings of the Minotaur, which among so many other "antique" themes in the painter's work constantly evokes the Mediterranean of ancient Greece and Rome. Twentieth-century modernism is characterized by the wholesale appropriation of the past, especially Greek and Roman antiquity, lovingly recreated in so strong a fashion as to make high modernism at once completely new and entirely timeless.

Alexandria was founded by Alexander to be an advance post of Greek culture in his relentless cultural aggrandizing. From the surviving fragments of the Alexandrian poet Callimachus it is possible to piece together what seems to have been the reigning artistic credo—a third-century B.C. version of "Only make it new!" In a fragment of his *Aitia* the poet advises:

"Drive your chariot / not on the tracks of others, not on the wide road / but on untrod roads, even if the path is narrower." Callimachus' aesthetic, like that of his contemporaries, was clearly shaped by the presence in Alexandria of the Library, the creation of Egypt's new ruler, Ptolemy Soter I. When Alexander died, his military general in Egypt, Ptolemy, seized power and set himself up as absolute ruler, successor to the Pharoahs and to Alexander, creating a dynasty that was to last until 31 B.C. when his descendant Cleopatra VII killed herself rather than submit to the conquering Roman leader, Octavian Caesar (to whom within six years the Roman Senate would grant the title of Augustus). Ptolemy was intent upon creating a city, society, and culture that would rival fifth-century Athens and at the same time advertise itself as Athens' successor. His most brilliant innovation was to import Demetrius of Phaleron who had helped establish a library in mainland Greece. Together they worked to make a collection of papyrus rolls that finally amounted to some seven hundred thousand (as a gauge to size: the *Iliad* filled twenty-four rolls), the greatest repository of Greek literature in the world.

Many of the scholars who worked on the library collection were also the poets of the age. At the library they worked to classify and to authenticate manuscripts, and they carried these preoccupations over into their poetry. The Alexandrian aesthetic is therefore dominated by ideas of categories or genres and of authorial convention. The Callimachean emphasis on novelty more often than not inspired creations that mirrored or refined genre or convention as much through perversity and omission as through outright imitation. One may say that Alexandrian literature is in constant dialogue with its models. This is a major change from the literature of fifth-century Athens.

While familiarity with modernism has helped contemporary scholars appreciate the third-century B.C. Egyptian literary scene for the outstanding creative period it was, traditional *Aeneid* criticism until very recently[1] continued to scant the Apollonian influence (except in the case of Book 4) because most critics were unwilling to take the *Argonautica* seriously. The stumbling block to appreciating the Alexandrian or the Apollonian in the *Aeneid* has always been wit, or irony, or the hint of the absurd that abounds in Alexandrian writing. Scholars habituated to the high seriousness of the classical period of Greek literature resist these attitudes. Hence, the traditional devaluation of the *Argonautica*.[2]

Influence is of course a tricky proposition. Will we speak of allusion or borrowing? The latter term comes from what I would call the "cut and

paste" school of Vergilian criticism, as old and honorable and authoritative
as its original proponents, Servius and Macrobius, who wrote the first
surviving commentaries some four centuries after the *Aeneid* was com-
posed. These critics look upon borrowings as though the Roman poet were
a teenaged hot rod enthusiast cannibalizing parts in an auto junk yard to
make his souped-up dream car. Allusion, on the other hand, requires one to
identify a literary technique never once described by ancient literary critics,
not to mention surrendering to the intentional fallacy on the theory that the
poet intends that his reader notice the parallel with the paradigm passage.[3]
In any case, "intertextuality" is perhaps the better term for the strategy of
reading demanded here, rather than "allusion." When classicists use the
word "intertextuality," they are generally referring to the reader's engage-
ment with two or more texts, more specifically the interpretation of a later
text from the allusions to a previous one. The *Aeneid* does seem to authorize
the kind of close intertextual reading upon which allusion is grounded. To
take a minor but illustrative example, in the seventh book list of Rutulians
marching into battle, where alphabet dictates placement, the name Mes-
sapus appears out of alphabetical order (7.691). This seeming anomaly
demands that the knowledgeable reader know the connection of Messapus
with the name Cycnus in myth and substitute in his or her mind the alpha-
betically correct Cycnus in the otherwise unalphabetic position of Mes-
sapus.[4] Nothing, by the way, could be more Alexandrian!

But the author makes an even stronger claim for interpreting the text
through allusion in the first scenes of the poem. When Aeneas stands
gazing at the mural paintings in the temple to Juno, he sees, as the narrator
says, Achilles "selling the body of Hector" (1.484), an allusion to the scene
in the *Iliad* when the aged Priam comes to Achilles to retrieve his son's
body. Priam, as the *Iliad* narrator tells us, has been told to bring gifts, as
befits the visit to a great king from whom one seeks a favor. This is, of
course, not a "sale." Centuries before Vergil, however, the gift-exchange
mechanism had been filtered through the anti-Homeric bias of Plato, who
introduced the notion of commerce. Vergil's reader, therefore, has an array
of choices for a reading. He or she can remember the scene as Homer
narrates it and decide that the mural painter is passing judgment, or that the
Aeneid narrator is passing judgment, or that Aeneas, loyal to the Trojan
cause, or perhaps revealing the finer instincts (in the eyes of a Roman
narrator for a Roman reader) of someone about to become Roman, judges
the event himself. It is not therefore the allusion *per se* that matters, but
rather the reading or interpretation that it encourages in the later text.

The simile at *Aeneid* 8.22 ff. comparing Aeneas' anxious mind to light flickering on water is an example of how Vergil is able to play off Apollonian material to inspire his reader into more complicated interpretations than the surface meaning might dictate. This simile comes from *Argonautica* 3.756 ff. where it describes Medea's anxious concern for Jason. Neither borrowing nor allusion is the point so much as how the reader may make a reading or interpretation by comparing the two texts. Here is the Apollonian sensibility at work. It effects an incongruity when applied to Aeneas that in Alexandrian terms tends to deconstruct the text, to reveal a kind of indeterminacy so dear to the hearts of the postmodernist critics. It is this very quality that makes the passage objectionable to modern commentators; for instance, Conington says of the passage: "It must be owned that the comparison is more pleasing when applied, as it is by Apollonius, to the fluttering heart of Medea, than to the fluctuating mind of Aeneas."[5] But let us consider contexts. The scene in Book 8 in which the simile occurs with its description of night ("it was night and deep sleep held all the weary animals . . ," *nox erat et terras animalia fessa per omnis / alituum pecudumque genus sopor altus habebat,* 8.26) recalls by virtue of the repetition of language Dido's sleepless night ("it was night and tired bodies took their pleasure in sleep," *nox erat et placidum carpebant fessa soporem / corpora,* 4.522) just before she embarks on the last scene in her tragic drama of involvement with Aeneas. Dido's sleepless night is, of course, Medea's sleepless night, which is described in the *Argonautica* right before the simile in question. In the *Aeneid*'s version of this scene Dido resolves to die. In the *Argonautica* Medea also resolves to die and then moderates this into a resolve to give Jason all the aid he needs. This change in resolution, we might say, is in fact a kind of self-destruction since to help Jason is to destroy herself as a daughter of the family of Aeetes.

The description of night and the simile in Book 8 recall to the reader the situations of Dido and Medea in Aeneas' own nocturnal mental turmoil and indecision, but because of the incongruity—he is a male, a resolute leader, they are women, lovesick, vulnerable, and doomed—Aeneas' circumstance is highlighted more completely. He is not a woman struggling with sexual desires and potential or already established dependency, he is not a woman being manipulated by the gods through sexual desire (which the ancients understood to be a powerful physical sickness that raced through and contorted the body no differently from malaria or typhoid fever). Aeneas is a male, captain of his own fate, by virtue of his *pietas* and his identification with Roman/Trojan destiny, which is to conquer and dominate the Italian peninsula.

That this scene is crucial for the narrative is established through the Dido and Medea contexts, yet in *his* night scene Aeneas, instead of being left alone with confused and anguished thoughts, is visited by Tiberinus. The god vouchsafes to him that he will emerge triumphant on Latin soil, commands him to ally himself with Evander for the coming battle, and suggests that the gods' hostility has abated and that prayers to Juno will finally end her wrath. Tiberinus' words signal a major change in the direction of the narrative of the poem, the beginning of the end, so to speak. Dido and Medea's decisions also establish a point of no return, a crucial turning point that in the *Aeneid* passage is recreated in Tiberinus' words. The potential incongruity that arises from assigning to Aeneas the emotional state of the two women compels the reader to enter the narrative to resist the incongruity, hence to assess Aeneas' maleness as culturally defined—he is a leader and a patriarch—which highlights his healthiness and their sickness. It also presents a contrast: he is beloved of the gods, in this instance guided and encouraged by Tiberinus, whereas they are so much used by gods.

The fundamental instability of the glancing light described in the simile builds in the somewhat hysterical musings of Medea, whereas it is checked and overcome by the commanding and supporting words of Tiberinus. Therein lies a vast difference, which the use of the simile emphasizes. Aeneas is portrayed in strength whereas the two women are finally victims of gods, psychologically or, more particularly, physically victims of desire, victims of the men they are attached to by virtue of their dependency, and victims of a society that cannot tolerate powerful women and thus finds their destruction aesthetically and morally satisfying. It is satisfying and at the same time altogether tragic. And yet there remains underneath the Roman leader's nighttime scene an unsettling hint of an *equation* of Aeneas with the two women, since the reader might perceive him also as someone who has surrendered to and has become dependent on or a victim of his destiny and the deities who typify it, just as these women have capitulated to love and to a man.

Apollonius makes great demands on his reader. He emphasizes disparities and incongruities between his own poem and the Homeric epics in order to reinforce his poem's uniqueness even as it nonetheless is subsumed into the epic genre. In effect the poet asks that a Homeric feature appearing in his *Argonautica* will have its context implied or understood by the reader. To the degree the reader recognizes that the feature has become distorted in its new context or is alien to its new context, he or she is reinforced in understanding the Homeric model text or reads the Homeric model text with new understanding, at the same time reading the Apollonian passage with a greater appreciation of its essential difference from the Homeric ethos and manner.

A variety of passages in the *Aeneid* suggests that Vergil was looking back at the Homeric epics through the lens of the Apollonian view of them. The ideal Vergilian reader therefore must be someone who has the whole of Greek and Roman literature at his or her command. The *Aeneid* is so rich, so far-ranging that it can honestly be said to be in dialogue with the whole of the literary culture that precedes it, to be the one great ecumenical poem, true to the imperial dimension of the political world that gave it birth. What is particularly original about the *Aeneid* is that the narrator, by constant allusion or borrowing, directs the reader to a realm of intertextuality where he or she will make meaning that transcends or departs from the immediate text and forges in combination with remembered other texts a poem finally of the reader's imaginings. This is why more than any other poem in the Western canon the *Aeneid* can mean so many different things to so many people.[6]

The reader of the *Aeneid* can get some idea of the complexity with which the Apollonian Vergil is working through examination of his characterization of Aeneas. Apollonius had been most original in his construction of an epic hero. His Jason is a hero and the "hero" of the *Argonautica* narrative, yet no reader would confuse him with Achilles or Odysseus. An aura of something weak, or tentative, or unsuccessful hovers about him. It has been argued that Apollonius is original in creating an epic poetic narrator who is willing to betray the poem's central character by violating the epic conventions used to describe a hero.[7] Specifically, the Apollonian narrator humiliates Jason by undercutting his appearances in a variety of ways. For example (one of many), early in the poem there occurs an assembly scene into which Jason enters. The practiced reader is startled when the narrator flouts Homeric convention by interrupting a description of Jason's movement toward the waiting group in order to note the arrival of some latecomers who divert their attention. The reader whose attention is similarly diverted from Jason is thus complicit in the violation of the Homeric ethos. Shortly thereafter, Jason calls for the election of a leader for the enterprise. At this point the reader's conventional expectation is shattered and the central figure further diminished when the assembly in one voice calls out not for Jason but for Heracles. The reader is used to the Homeric poet, maker of what is often called "praise-blame" poetry, who introduces strong characters whose forceful actions may be blamed or praised but remain forceful always. The archaic epic poet, relentlessly defending and adulating his central character, would never betray him. In the *Aeneid*, on the other hand, there sometimes surfaces a hint of Apollonius' narrator in Vergil's presentation of Aeneas, certainly in the earlier books. Although Aeneas is far more "Homeric" than Jason, from the traditional epic perspective there are interesting faults in the construction of the hero. (These the critic might suggest are there so as more fully to dramatize Aeneas' triumph in the latter half of the poem.)

Several interesting narrative maneuvers in the *Aeneid*'s opening books make the reader question Aeneas in his role as conventional male epic hero. One is the moment when the shipwrecked Aeneas reconnoitering the unknown shores of North Africa encounters his mother Venus, disguised as a young girl of the neighborhood (1.314 ff.). The practiced reader will enter into the several intertextual ironies constructed here. In the Homeric *Hymn to Aphrodite*, on the very occasion of Aeneas' conception, Aphrodite, similarly disguised, first presents herself to the about-to-be father Anchises, the unsuspecting teenaged country rube minding the sheep (no matter that he is a prince of Troy). In Vergil's version, Aeneas' instant suspicion that this girl is a goddess ("You don't have the face of a mortal; oh, madam, certainly you are a goddess!", *namque haud tibi vultus / mortalis, nec vox hominem sonat; o dea certe*) echoes his father's suspicions (*Hymn to Aphrodite* 921 ff.). The goddess in both versions is quick to insist that she is only a mortal girl.

In the context of this scene, the reader will also recall Odysseus' encounter with Nausicaa (*Od.* 6.149 ff.). Because Venus is dressed as a hunter, Aeneas imagines the girl to be Diana in disguise and proceeds to supplicate her. The reader will remember how Odysseus uses the Artemis ploy with Nausicaa even though he surely knows that she is mortal. But because Nausicaa has just been compared to Artemis by the *Odyssey* narrator, Odysseus with his Artemis/Nausicaa equation ironically matches the narrator in his simile-making, succeeding momentarily to the narrator's role and gaining power over the narrative not usually vouchsafed a character. Odysseus is deliberate and manipulative in talking with Nausicaa; the Phaeacean princess responds by inviting the hero home. Aeneas, by contrast, gets nowhere with his Diana comparison.

Also in this context the reader will remember the scene in which Athena presents herself to Odysseus (13.221 ff.) as he awakens on the shore of his native Ithaca. She, too, is in disguise, and the landscape, misted over by the goddess, is unrecognizable to the hero. He is a stranger in the landscape just like Aeneas, and also confronting a stranger. When asked to identify himself Odysseus lies to Athena. Athena responds to the lies (which she of course knows are lies) with complete approval, reveals herself as a goddess, and lifts the mists from the landscape. Aeneas, however, simply tells the truth, but the telling brings on further ironies. His speech (1.371 ff.) has the rhetorical tension of Odysseus' when he rises to speak at the court of the Phaeacians (*Od.* 9.2 ff.). Just as Odysseus reveals his name only after some delay and lingers over seventeen lines of peroration, possibly to make his audience, already ablaze with curiosity, positively tingle, Aeneas is six lines into his reply before he abruptly announces *sum pius Aeneas*. That he says this all unknowing to a goddess who knows well enough everything he has to say demonstrates perfectly the power and control of the Achaean wayfarer and the inherent vulnerability of the Trojan prince.

What follows is not exactly suitable to the meeting between a country girl and a shipwreck: "I come bringing with me the household gods, snatched from the enemy / I who am known by reputation to the heavens above" (*raptos qui ex hoste Penates / classe veho mecum, fama super aethera notus*, 1.378–79). The close of the second line belongs more to the ages, that is, to the reader's knowledge of Aeneas' coming stardom in history's annals, than to this chance meeting on the road. More particularly it has come to Aeneas from the mouth of Odysseus ("I am Odysseus, son of Laertes, known to all men for my cunning and deceit, and my fame goes up to the heavens," *Od.* 9.19 f.) at a moment fraught with the high expectation of an audience that has been waiting about seven hundred lines for this information. Odysseus' storytelling skill, his sense of glamour, his well-developed capacity for self-congratulation are all reflected in the lines.

Here in the countryside of North Africa, however, extravagant language between a man and a maid seems—at least realistically—to be unlikely, or it makes Aeneas out to be more than a little pompous. One would like to excuse him by saying that Vergil's early imperial audience would accept such high rhetoric out of the mouth of the principal totem of their culture, were it not for the curious fact that the hero is severely undercut almost immediately. After only six more lines of his speech, Venus can tolerate no more (*nec plura querentem / passa*). She then dismisses him with something like: "Whoever you are, it looks as if the gods are on your side, or you would not have made it to Carthage alive. Just go on and get to the queen's palace."

The reader is reminded of a character in the *Argonautica*, the ogrelike king Aeetes, Medea's father, who will not tolerate a similar supplicating introductory speech from Jason, interrupting him harshly with "Stranger, why do you have to go through every little detail without restraint?" (*Arg.* 3.401). Jason, rebuffed by Aeetes before he really has time to introduce himself, is yet again betrayed as he pretends to the style of his heroic predecessors. Aeneas in the first important encounter in the poem is similarly rebuffed in his attempt to portray himself as heroic and consequential in a scene so resonant with other important encounters. The expectations of the practiced reader are thwarted or subverted, and that sense of betrayal translates to the hero. That his goddess mother, who only moments before was beseeching Jove on his behalf, can stop him from offering his heroic bona fides suggests that his rhetoric has failed him.

There is a stunning recapitulation of this idea at the close of Book 1 when Dido is entertaining Aeneas at a banquet. When she asks him to tell his story the reader is reminded of the final scene of Book 8 of the *Odyssey* when Alcinous asks Odysseus to identify himself: in a banquet setting a poet sings, after which the host asks the guest to tell about himself. The song of Troy that Demodocus sings causes Odysseus to cry, prompting Alcinous to ask his identity. This motivates the travel narrative of the next several books. Here at Dido's banquet the moment arrives for the Roman hero to rival Odysseus. Instead, the narrator betrays Aeneas' first- person account of the fall of Troy and his travels, the subject of the second and third books of the *Aeneid*, even before Aeneas can begin.

At Dido's banquet Iopas finishes his song, the audience applauds, but the queen, the narrator suggests (note his *nec non*, 748), has not even been listening. She is talking to her guest. His identity she knows, she wants details. And yet, as the narrator specifically says, Dido is really not interested; her motive is only to keep the Trojan prince with her longer ("unhappy Dido prolonged the night with one conversational ploy after another, asking many questions, about Priam, about Hector," *vario noctem sermone trahebat / infelix Dido . . . / multa super Priamo rogitans super Hectore multa . . .* , 1.748 f.) It is passion that drives her interest in Aeneas, not curiosity over what he has to say. As the narrator remarks, she is getting drunk on love (*infelix Dido longumque bibebat amorem*). It is also possible that Dido is unaffected by Iopas' song not only because she is sick with passion, but because she is a woman. Songs such as these are for male company.[8] Because her persistent questioning, which leads to the response that fills books 2 and 3, is motivated by her desire to keep Aeneas at her side, it is perhaps fair to say that she has no interest in masculine heroic exploits either. Like Hypsipyle who is duplicitous in getting Jason into her bed (because she wants a baby for which she needs a male), Dido feigns an interest and Aeneas is taken in.

In addition to these smaller moments in the narrative the very structure of the *Aeneid* occasionally seems a bow to the Alexandrianism of Apollonius. Perhaps the most important example is the unusual postponement of the exordium at the beginning of Book 7. Instead of occupying the conventional place of the first lines of the book, it appears at the thirty-seventh line. The structure of the divide between Books 6 and 7 is momentous for its implications: travels end and the struggle for Italy begins; saga ends and history begins; exile ends and homecoming begins; some would say the *Odyssey* ends, the *Iliad* begins. The postponement is a significant advertisement of the poet's allegiance to the Apollonian aesthetic. It has been argued that Apollonius made dramatic book divisions that highlighted the novel aesthetic feature of dividing continuous narrative into books. It is assumed that Alexandrian librarians had only recently divided the Homeric texts into twenty-four segments for purposes of classification and storage.[9] Vergil seems to be advertising his allegiance to the Apollonian aesthetic in responding to this device, for while, on the one hand, the poet employs a traditional exordium and apostrophe to a helper deity, thus creating a monumental form that stands, as it were, as the gate into the rest of the poem, he delays introducing this commonplace piece of epic machinery until the thirty-seventh line. It seems to have been enough of a departure from convention to cause Servius to remark upon it (ad 7.37), saying "now we have the beginning of the rest of the work; for what has been said before this point belongs to the material that came before."

The thirty-six lines preceding the exordium situate the reader in varied places. First, the narrator speaks to Aeneas' nurse, Caieta, who has died at that moment in the narrative, recounting how her name is given to the harbor of Gaeta. The narrator effectively breaks the narrative by going outside it to call upon a third party. What is more, the narrator, in calling out to Caieta, has broken the narrative plane at a moment in which the form, itself, breaks the plane. For the book division is itself an intellectualist imposition upon the depiction and flow of so-called reality. When the exordium begins the narrator will call upon Erato to help him with the story; this introduces another plane apart from the narrative one. The matter is further complicated because in one rupture the narrator speaks to a character from the story (Caeta) who lives on in history, in the other he speaks to a supernatural figure (Erato) who lives eternally in the realm of myth and poetry. The separation between these two narrative interruptions contains a marvelously naturalistic geographical description of the sailing from Gaeta past what is now Circeo San Felice up to the mouth of the Tiber and into the exordium, as if to mark the opposition between "realism" and "artificiality" as fully as possible. The aggressive play with form seems stunning, powerful, and entirely Apollonian.

The narrator's apostrophe to Erato, the muse of erotic poetry, strikes some critics as problematic, since gore rather than love seems the key motif in the latter half of the poem. It becomes less problematic when the reader recalls that Apollonius called upon Erato to help him with Jason and Medea's love story in the latter half of his poem. Vergil uses Erato to establish that his narrative shares in the same sensibility, although it is more Odyssean: that is, Aeneas gets the girl, kills her suitor, and, by implication, lives happily ever after. Such an ending is characteristic of comic narrative, and a twentieth-century critic could say that the *Aeneid* is therefore comic, not tragic, Odyssean, not Iliadic. By extension he or she might say that Aeneas, the comic hero, wars with and finally vanquishes Turnus, the tragic hero. One could expand the notion to say that comic, future-oriented, linear Roman historical thinking triumphs over tragic, cyclical Greek historical thinking, or, in a display of belatedness, that the older man, Aeneas, a stand-in for the older, wiser, Roman civilization triumphs over the younger, adolescent, Turnus, stand-in for the much younger, infinitely less matured civilization of the Homeric epics.

The ending of the *Aeneid* is unsatisfying or problematic to many.[10] Some would argue that Aeneas kills whom he should spare, ignoring his father Anchises' advice to him that a Roman should "spare the conquered" (*parcere subiectis*, 6.853), thus occasioning many a suspicion of Vergil's own dissatisfaction with the Roman imperial enterprise. Read as an Alexandrian poem, however, the *Aeneid* could end no other way. And the poet plays one last Alexandrian verbal game, an Apollonian strategy that will allow for Turnus' death as a satisfying event. At the beginning of Book 12 King Latinus tries to stop Turnus from fighting by appealing to a logic that defies the convention of death-oriented, death-celebrating tragic epic poetry. Since he will settle with the Trojans once Turnus is dead, says

Latinus, Turnus should go home now, find another woman, and, although Latinus does not really say this, live happily ever after. To this offer to come aboard the comic narrative of life, Turnus can only reply "let me barter for fame with my death." It is the cliché of glory that has animated all the doomed young men of this poem, the motive behind praise-blame poetry to begin with, indeed, the motive that has fueled so many of the unspeakable acts of western history. But it is the appropriate response of a male set into a tragic context.

So as to establish Aeneas as a noncommittal nemesis the narrator endows Turnus the tragic hero with hubris, rendering it beautifully in the young man's fatal misreading of Homer that only a reader practiced in intertextuality will notice. Turnus boasts that "[Aeneas'] mother won't be around this time, to cover his escape with a cloud that only a woman would use and conceal herself in phantom shadows" (52–53). Turnus, however, confounds *Iliad* 5.311 ff. where Venus uses her *gown* to shield Aeneas with *Iliad* 5.344 and 20.321 where Apollo and then Poseidon rescue him in a *cloud*. Furthermore, the attentive reader will remember that in this last passage Poseidon declares that he is saving Aeneas for later glory. What, of course, can this be but to found the Roman race and the opportunity to star in his own epic poem? While Turnus knows the *Iliad* well enough to allude to those scenes, he seems in getting the details wrong not to understand that this is not a "mama's boy" he confronts on the field of battle but the man protected and preserved for this very moment by two of the principal male deities of the Homeric universe. It is another of Turnus' delusions, his inability—fatal from an Alexandrian perspective, as well as supremely tragic—to read epic and saga (which is, after all, his history) correctly.

As is often remarked, Alexandrian literature is first and foremost about literature, nowhere more so than in the case of Apollonius' *Argonautica*.[11] Here at the very close of the *Aeneid*, literary imperatives clash, and for every reason the tragic sensibility (Turnus) must yield to the comic sensibility (Aeneas). Whether Vergil understood "comic" and "tragic" as they are being used here is another matter. Aristotle defined them in terms of social class, but later on the first century A.D. text of the pseudo-Longinus speaks of the *Odyssey* as a comedy in the sense we have appropriated for the word. In the later fourth century one Evanthius wrote that "Homer made the *Iliad* as a tragedy, the *Odyssey* as a comedy," and also that "tragedy was a repudiation of life, just as comedy was a grasping of life" (*in tragoedia fugienda vita, in comoedia capessenda*). One would like to think that Vergil understood this; but, nonetheless, the *Aeneid* seems to be a monument to the idea expressed by Evanthius, even if not yet perfectly understood and conceptualized. In ending his poem with a battle between the comic and the tragic, Vergil shows himself to be a true heir to the literary values established in Apollonius' poem.

CHAPTER 16

FIVE HUNDRED YEARS OF RENDERING THE *AENEID* IN ENGLISH

William S. Anderson

The development of the printing press, which ended the need for Latin manuscripts and enabled readers to buy texts of Vergil easily and cheaply, was also the stimulus for translations of the Latin. That pioneer English printer, William Caxton, brought out in 1490, shortly before his death, a work in prose purporting to summarize the *Aeneid* faithfully. In fact it was essentially a translation of a French work of 1483, which catered to popular tastes for a romanticized story of Aeneas. In reaction to what he felt was Caxton's unscrupulous tendency to alter or ignore major episodes of the Latin original, Gavin Douglas, the scholarly Scottish bishop, passed his exile in England during the years 1512–1513 by conscientiously translating every line of Vergil's poem.[1] Naturally, he used the Scottish dialect, but his work counts as the first poetic translation of the *Aeneid* in English, and it has many admirers today. Douglas did not publish the work either in England or Scotland. In his own day and for years after the plague in London killed him in 1522, Douglas's translation was unknown and so exerted no influence on subsequent translations. After his death, the manuscript was found, but because it was in Scottish and unprofitable, no London publisher took the risk of printing it until 1553.

During the 1550s, before the published version of Douglas's translation could gain a foothold, a second translation was in the works, in true English and in a lively new meter very popular at the time. Using fourteeners, Thomas Phaer began his rendition of the *Aeneid* and had completed Book 9 and started 10 when he died in 1560. The incomplete version was published posthumously and won instant success, and it is no surprise that another enterprising scholar-poet, Thomas Twyne, decided to finish the last three books in the same general style. The full translation of the entire *Aeneid* appeared in 1573, and it enjoyed immediate and long success with the British audience.[2] For a century it survived all challenges, moving through repeated printings. During the Restoration, as the heroic couplet started to become the favorite verse form, a number of translators tried to outmaster Phaer and Twyne. Their efforts are largely forgettable, because they were eclipsed by the magnificent version of John Dryden, who, it can be shown, quarried his less able predecessors for phrases and rhymes and yet created a product that was distinctly his own.[3] Dryden's translation, published in 1697, dominated all potential rivals for two centuries.

World War I, although it raised questions for British poets and writers about heroic warfare, did not provoke a popular new translation of Vergil in an idiom different from the heroic couplet. Those who tried simple prose were too far off base to win many adherents. It took the tense times of World War II in Britain to concentrate attention once again on the *Aeneid* and its special kind of unromantic heroism as a parallel for the savagery and stress of modern warfare. For this era, the poem found its ideal translator and a fresh spirit in C. Day Lewis and its first ideal medium in BBC radio. Lewis read successively, day after day, his version of Vergil's twelve books, to which the hearts of the hard-pressed Britons, struggling to survive and hold firm against Hitler's greatest successes and imminent threats, especially the heavy bombings of their island, deeply responded. The United States went through World War II with its own rhetoric, without the self-reflection that made Vergil and Lewis's version strike such deep chords in England.

After the war ended, however, a special situation developed in American education that gave people on their side of the Atlantic an opportunity to profit from Lewis and from a series of subsequent translators. In the 1950s, a significant boom occurred in high school and college courses that emphasized the classics of literature, the Great Books, or, as developed by ambitious departments of Classics, introduced students to classical civilization, to Roman history and literature, or even to such rich genres as ancient epic. General education meant that students should graduate having acquired some knowledge of Greek and Roman history and literature and some appreciation for the similarities and differences between ancient and modern cultures, resulting in better understanding of our common humanity. American teachers quickly realized that students would rebel against Dryden and any other translator who used stylized vocabulary, dated concepts, and the long-discarded heroic couplet. What students wanted was something clear, readable, and interesting, if not at the first reading, then at least after the first class and the helpful introduction devised by the instructor. Thus came into existence a major impetus for new translations and phenomenal profits for the translator and publisher who produced the version of Homer, of the Greek tragedians, or of Vergil that was available, competitive, and chosen for these countless new courses and thousands of new readers. The first successful translation was that of Rolfe Humphries, which appeared in 1951 and was frequently reprinted thereafter. It was followed by Lewis's in 1952 and by numerous others, at least one good version a decade. Notable are those of F. O. Copley (1965), Allen Mandelbaum (1971), and Robert Fitzgerald (1983). At this point in the final decade of the century, it is still too early to name the next major translation, but there are writers and publishers who compete for that title right now.

Having surveyed the major trends and translations of the past five hundred years and the various circumstances that stimulated them, we can now focus our attention on these translations, first on their choice of poetic form and second on their preconceptions and achievements as responsible interpretations of the Latin original. Poetic translations of Greek and Latin have generally attempted to make the ancient text appeal to the translator's times by evoking the style of contemporary speech. This was the express purpose of Dryden: "to make Virgil speak such English as he would himself have spoken, if he had been born in England, and in this present age." Lewis approved and subscribed to this creed. While it is true, of course, that no translation can ever perfectly transfer the poem of another time and language to an alien culture, it is also apparent, as Steiner shows, that the practical theory of poets such as Dryden and Lewis needs some refining, to include the factor Steiner calls "compensation" or "restitution."[4]

Vergil used a poetic meter that had been appropriated by narrative and didactic poetry in Greece since Homer's epics and the admired works of Hesiod. The first Roman epics were composed in native Italian meter, but as soon as Roman writers became sensitive to the superiority of Greek forms, the Greek hexameter of Homer and his successors was also adapted for Roman epic. Quintus Ennius was the first to write Latin epic in hexameters. His epic poem the *Annals* was a chronicle of Roman glory from the time of Aeneas and the legendary founding of Rome right down to the contemporary military achievements of Roman generals at the beginning of the second century B.C. Ennius' epic struck his readers as so magnificent, as such a grand Latin rival to Homeric epic, that all epic thereafter used and developed his hexameters as the requisite poetic form. But until Vergil's poem was published, no poet had challenged Ennius' success. Vergil and Horace had to study and memorize the *Annals* in school; very soon after the *Aeneid* appeared in 17 B.C., students studied only Vergil. Metrically and thematically, Vergil had put his predecessor in the shade.

The hexameter, as used by Homer and later Greeks, then adapted by Ennius, Vergil, and later Romans, was a versatile poetic vehicle, ideal for serious narrative and speeches, such as we find in the *Aeneid*. It based itself on six metrical feet (as its name implies), the primary unit being dactylic. A dactyl consisted of three syllables, of which the first, receiving the stress, was naturally long, and the second and third were short and unstressed. Poets were permitted to substitute for the dactyl a foot of two long syllables called a spondee (also stressed on its first syllable). Thus, depending on the amount of permissible substitution, a single hexameter line would always have six stresses, but the number of its syllables and therefore its relative speed or heaviness could vary considerably. In Latin, as the poets explored the opportunities of the hexameter, it became increasingly easy and attractive to write dactyls and produce a smoothly flowing narrative. They varied their pauses within the line, and they were free to move, when they chose, from one line to the next without a break—what we call enjambment or run-on—so that short sentences and longer periodic statements could be effectively combined.

In English, the dactylic hexameter has never found a comfortable home or a warm reception. The native Germanic verse forms did not resemble the Latin, and the early English poets, though many knew Latin and much fine Latin poetry, continued to prefer their own traditions. There are exceptions, however. Henry Wadsworth Longfellow was spectacularly gifted in such versification: his *Evangeline* (1847) and *The Courtship of Miles Standish* (1858) provide excellent examples of his virtuosity but also suggest why others did not choose to imitate him. Here are some early lines from the introduction to *Evangeline*:

> This is the forest primeval; but where are the hearts that beneath it
> Leaped like the roe, when he hears in the woodland the voice of the huntsman?
> Where is the thatch-roofed village, the home of Arcadian farmers—
> Men whose lives glided on like rivers that water the woodlands,
> Darkened by shadows of earth, but reflecting an image of heavens?

(7–11)

Somehow, the dactylic hexameter makes the line too long for the ear in English. Poets and their audiences preferred something shorter. And the dactyl, with its initial beat, at the beginning of every line, strikes us as unnatural.

The verse form behind Douglas's translation was the pattern so brilliantly used by Geoffrey Chaucer at the end of the fourteenth century, most notably in *The Canterbury Tales*. Chaucer wrote in pairs of basically rhyming iambic pentameters. The lines do not form couplets, as later with Dryden and Pope, but the meter and rhymes do give some expected shape to the lines, and the shorter narrative unit—ten syllables instead of up to seventeen—was more congenial to the English style of speech. Here is Chaucer introducing the proud rooster Chauntecleer in *The Nun's Priest's Tale:*

> A yeerd she hadde, enclosed al aboute
> With stikkes, and a drye dych withoute,
> In which she hadde a cok hight Chauntecleer.
> In al the land of crowyng nas his peer.
>
> (27–30)

Notice how the first sentence runs to three lines and ends forcefully on the resonant name of the cock; then a fourth independent line tells us something important about this "hero" of the story. This freedom to develop the narrative in appropriate amounts allows the translator of Latin to be more responsive to the variable units of Vergil. He is not forced, as Dryden later will be by his heroic couplet, to come to a temporary stopping point every two lines. On the other hand, it is not easy to capture the sense of the longer lines of Latin, which also had the advantage of its inflected forms (obviating the need for prepositions, which are necessary in English), without considerably expanding the number of lines.

FROM DOUGLAS TO FITZGERALD: FORMAL CONSIDERATIONS

In this section, I shall review translations in chronological order, from Douglas to Fitzgerald (1981), drawing on Book 11 (discussed in my earlier chapter in this volume) for examples.

In his 1513 version, Douglas aimed to capture all the Latin of Vergil—and more. Here is the way he opens Book 11 and deals expansively with what Vergil put in three tight lines:

Duryng this quhile [while], furth of the sey [sea] dyd spryng
The fresch Aurora with the brycht dawyng.
Ene [Aeneas], albeyt [albeit] hys hasty thochtfull curis [cares]
Constrenyt hym, as twyching [touching] sepulturis
Of hys folkis new slane [slain] and berying,
Forto provide a tyme mast accordyng,
And gretly eik [also] in mynd he trublyt was
For the slauchtyr and ded corps of Pallas . . .

(1–8)

Vergil wrote:

Oceanum interea surgens Aurora reliquit;
Aeneas, quamquam et sociis dare tempus humandis
praecipitant curae turbataque funere mens est . . .

(1–3)

I translate this passage literally: "Meanwhile Dawn rising left the ocean. Aeneas, although his grief urges him to take time to bury his comrades and his mind is upset by death . . ."

Douglas's eight lines convey a mournful mood for the start of the book. But almost every adjective serves as a supplement to the scene, and in the last quoted line he gratuitously restricts and focuses Aeneas' grief for the general loss of life in the previous day's battle to sorrow for young Pallas alone. That prepares us nicely for the speech that the Trojan will tearfully deliver over the boy's corpse, but Vergil did not put it that way. Obviously, Douglas does not cut back on Vergil's account—far from it. He resonates to the sadness of the scene and renders three effective Latin lines in eight of his Scots English. With line 3, he begins a long sentence that continues beyond 8 to end at line 12. He has pairs of rhymes, but definitely not heroic couplets.

It is unlikely that Thomas Phaer knew of Douglas's version (published posthumously in 1553) as he started his translation. Yet he chose to abandon the Chaucerian metrical pattern for heroic narrative, ten-syllable sets of iambs, and to adopt a form called the "fourteener." It consisted again of a series of essentially iambic feet, every other line rhyming, but now there were seven feet instead of five, fourteen syllables instead of ten. This was the meter chosen by Arthur Golding for his 1567 translation of Ovid's *Metamorphoses*, so much admired and quarried by William

Shakespeare. And Thomas Twyne was well advised to finish up the work of Phaer and publish the complete epic in fourteeners in 1573. To Twyne, then, we owe the version of Book 11. He comfortably renders the first three lines of the Latin now in four:

> The dawning day thiswhile ye Ocean sea had clerely left.
> Aeneas though some Time on those whom warres of lives had reft,
> His care constraines hime to employ, their graves for to prepare,
> And now his minde and senses all on funerals fixed are . . .

It can be quickly said that Twyne almost exactly captures Vergil's first line, end-stopping it as did the original. With the second, he starts on the dependent clause ("though"), which does not end until line 4 of the Latin. He correctly captures the general sense of "funerals" and does not limit it by a gloss to the needs of dead Pallas. There might be a hint that Twyne has seen Douglas in line 3 ("his care constraines hime . . . for to"; cf. Douglas 4–6). If so, he has tightened up his predecessor's translation. This version feels more like the Latin, and in Twyne's time it looked and read like current English.

A different verse form, the heroic couplet, reached a stage of perfection at the end of the seventeenth and opening of the eighteenth centuries in the poetic works of Dryden and Pope. As a combination of rhyming iambic pentameters, it appears to be a more disciplined form of the heroic meters of Chaucer and Douglas. While it returns to the shorter narrative line that is congenial to English, it encapsulates its units within each couplet, where the rhymes are significant and the ideas are pointed and often witty. Choosing the most effective rhymes and rendering the meaning in the most memorable way became major goals, to punctuate the narrative and bring heroism under cool, often ironic scrutiny. Nine different translations of individual books or of the entire *Aeneid*, each in heroic couplets, appeared in the seventeenth century between 1622 and 1687. Although it is possible that Dryden did not know the earliest, it is quite evident that he possessed copies of most of them and worked ingeniously from them as he produced his own version. He appropriated lines, half lines, and especially end rhymes from five of his predecessors who published up to 1660, and he worked closely from the unpublished text of the Earl of Lauderdale, which he borrowed while working on his *Aeneid*.[5] Dryden's systematic search in the versions of his "rivals" for the right final words and rhymes illustrates the importance of the couplet closure in the heroic meter he was perfecting.

Here is the way Dryden opens his Book 11:

> Scarce had the rosy Morning rais'd her head
> Above the waves, and left her wat'ry bed;
> The pious chief, whom double cares attend
> For his unburied soldiers and his friend,
> Yet first to Heav'n perform'd a victor's vows:
> He bar'd an ancient oak of all her boughs;
> Then on a rising ground the trunk he plac'd,
> Which with the spoils of his dead foe he grac'd.

Like Twyne, Dryden renders Vergil's first three lines in four. His product, however, is very different. He expands the single Latin line about dawn into an effective couplet, with its allegorical rhymes "head" and "bed" that offer us a vivid picture of Aurora rising from the bed of her mate Tithonus, as known from familiar myth. Vergil did not choose to dwell on such comfortable domestic details: he simply had the day dawn. Yet Dryden's expansion has its poetic effect in the implicit contrast between the uninterrupted pleasures of the gods and human misery, on which the poem will now concentrate. Even though Dryden sacrifices some details from the Latin as he generalizes about the twin cares of Aeneas, he adds new emphasis. Vergil named Aeneas without qualification at the start of line 2, and we saw that both Douglas and Twyne followed his model. Dryden chooses the heroic mode, noun plus epithet, and foreshadows the action before the trophy of Mezentius that will occupy our attention, styling the "chief" as "pious." The rhyme with which he closes the second couplet looks forward, too, to the grief over Pallas; in this interpretation he limits Vergil, but agrees with Douglas. Gone is the spacious narrative style, with its mellifluous alliterations, that the fourteener allowed Twyne. Dryden has an energetic, rhetorically effective, and pointed style.

The twentieth century has abandoned the heroic couplet, restless with its pointed rhymes and its insistence on bringing the narrative development to a halt every two lines so that the audience can savor rhyme and closure. In its place, poets have substituted a more natural narrative technique and a looser metrical system.[6] Lewis worked out a six-beat line that resembled a Latin hexameter, except that he used two-syllable iambs and trochees rather than the Classical dactyls, and he liked to end the line with an unstressed syllable. With the space provided by his longer line, Lewis was thus intent on, and regularly succeeded in, giving a line-for-line version of Vergil's original. His first four lines of Book 11, then, equal four Latin lines:

> Night came and went. Aurora rose up, leaving the ocean.
> Aeneas, although he felt a pressing duty to make time
> For burying his friends, and was greatly distressed by the death of Pallas,
> First, at daybreak, fulfilled the vows he had made for victory.

This is a highly faithful version, with considerable metrical flexibility. The third line achieves its length by substituting an anapest (three syllables, short, short, long) for the more common iamb and by ending with a short syllable. The low-key narrative makes a striking contrast to the declamatory style of Dryden.

Humphries aimed also to keep close to Vergil's line numbers and to get rid of the rhyming heroic couplet, but he chose to retain the general feel of the iambic pentameter, loosening it up as Lewis did so that an unaccented syllable could follow the final iamb. That allowed much more natural diction at the line end, unlike the more artificial end-stopping practiced by Dryden and his contemporaries. In his opening four lines, Humphries crowds a fraction more than four lines of the original:

> Meanwhile Aurora, rising, left the ocean.
> Aeneas' heart was troubled—so much dying,
> So great a need for funeral rites,—but first
> Vows must be paid for victory. At dawn . . .

The first line is an exact translation of Vergil: six words for five because of the article required by English. It merely marks the time. In the second and third lines, Humphries structures the two "troubles" of Aeneas by his anaphora of "so," and he correctly keeps the funeral rites general (not focused on Pallas), but he is forced to abbreviate the Latin words. He turns into a passive the active verb that Vergil used to depict his hero in decisive movement to deal first with the most important religious duty, which weakens somewhat our sense of Aeneas. Still, Humphries achievement is remarkable and has influenced the choices of subsequent translators.

In the next decade, the translation of Copley subscribed to principles similar to those of Humphries: a fairly regular iambic pentameter, though allowing an unaccented syllable to end the line, and an effort to make the lines of English correspond to those of Latin. His first four lines, then, closely resemble in their strategies those of his predecessor:

> Meanwhile the Dawn rose up and left the sea.
> Aeneas knew deep concern—the press of time—
> the need to bury his men—dark thoughts of death.
> But first for victory he must thank the gods.

The short clauses and sentences imply the difficulty faced by Copley in dealing with the longer, more complex sense-units of Vergil. Probably it was an artistic error to try to render the more flexible Latin line for line into English.

In the two major translations that appeared in the 1970s and 1980s, Mandelbaum's and Fitzgerald's, it ceased to be a desideratum to make the line numbers of English and Latin exactly correspond. Although both versions continue to adopt the iambic pentameter in its permissive form, as Humphries used it, they are more interested in rendering the full sense of the original than in equaling its length. Here, first, is Mandelbaum's version of the opening of 11:

> Meanwhile Aurora rose; she left the Ocean.
> Aeneas—anxious though he is to give
> his comrades rapid burial, and though
> his mind is much distressed by Pallas' death—
> first pays the gods a victor's vows beneath
> the morning star.

That covers four Latin lines. Fitzgerald does much the same:

> When Dawn came up from Ocean in the east,
> Though Pallas' death had left Aeneas shaken,
> And duty pressed him to give time
> For burial of the dead, he first
> In early light discharged his ritual vows
> As victor to the gods.

Fitzgerald has proceeded with even greater freedom than Mandelbaum, both in meter and in his version of Vergilian structure and emphasis. His third and fourth lines, in fact, have only four beats. (Periodically throughout he permits himself this variation, often for effective emphasis.) He turns these opening lines into one long period by means of dependent temporal and concessive clauses. He changes Vergil's and other translators' insistence on Aeneas as the first word of line 2 and main subject of the sentence, and he pulls up to the forefront and specifies as "Pallas' death" what Vergil left implicit and others at least properly relegated to the second of the leader's cares. "In the east" (1) and "in early light" (5) felicitously expand the Latin: Fitzgerald has added his own poetic touches to Vergil. Both translations read well to the Latin-less, and we may predict that increased freedom in metrical and poetic form will be the practice for some years to come.

CULTURAL CLASHES

The choice of poetic form, as we have seen, is determined by changing goals and stylistic preferences within a cultural period, as well as by individual poets' perceptions of the most apt aesthetic in English for rendering epic. It is similarly true that the interpretation of Vergil and his views of heroism varies with the cultural constraints of successive eras in British and American history and with the peculiar consciousness of the different poets who have essayed the daunting task of translating the *Aeneid*. The proud Scots Bishop Douglas differed widely from the disappointed and impecunious Roman Catholic Dryden, whose struggles began after the Stuarts and their Catholic cause had been discredited and stripped forever of royal power. He in turn, with his nostalgia for a pious leader, was miles apart from his distant rivals in the times of and just after World War II, accustomed to a constitutional regime and a royal figurehead or no king at all, for whom heroism arose not from inherited nobility but from personal achievement and innate moral worth. As rhymes and couplets and artful rhetoric yielded to more open meaning and simple, natural metrics, so the power of Vergil's passages came to depend on their essentially complicated significance, not on external poetic display. I shall look at some particular episodes in Book 11, about which readers still disagree today or over which they struggle to win consent. How have translators over the past five hundred years treated the complex Aeneas, who is both a leader and a human being with feelings, and how have they interpreted Vergil's presentation of the Italian enemy, especially of Turnus and of the one woman, Camilla, who, for a while, successfully fought the Trojans?

The most ready to bias the portrait of Aeneas was Dryden, who, as we saw, at the start of Book 11 intruded the epithet "the pious chief" for the simple name. He volunteered "the pious man" soon after, when Aeneas looks at the corpse of Pallas and laments. Even when the Latin does refer to the gods, Dryden worded it in language that echoed the English Bible: so Aeneas warns his men to be ready "at Heav'n's appointed hour," much as Jesus warns his disciples. Dryden's Aeneas was a Christ-figure. Interestingly enough, the reverend Bishop Douglas did not emphasize that side of the Trojan: he was drawn instead to the emotional, sympathetic Aeneas. At every opportunity early in Book 11, where Vergil refers to Aeneas' tears and laments, Douglas magnified them. Where the Latin merely uses a participle "weeping over" (11.29), Douglas offered: "wepand salt terys our his face." Where Vergil talked of "tears welling up" (41), Douglas wrote: "with terys brystand [bursting] from hys eyn [eyes]." At the end of his second speech of farewell to Pallas, in the Latin Aeneas simply heads back to camp, but Douglas could not refrain from adding "with terys of ennoy." This extremely tearful Aeneas did not appeal to later times, especially our modern era. Twyne let Vergil be his guide on weeping Aeneas, but his liking for alliteration in his long sixteener produced an emphatic line to back the Trojan's grief at 11.28: "A dire and dismold day hath drencht full deepe in deadly lake" [i.e., Pallas].

The twentieth century searched for a new paradigm for Aeneas.[7] In the context of World War II in Europe, Lewis viewed the Trojan as an ideal commander of men. The scene where the soldiers collect in front of the trophy of Mezentius evokes a modern situation following a successful engagement with the enemy. Aeneas, therefore, "musters" "his field commanders" and begins "a rousing speech" by addressing them as "gentlemen." Aeneas is no longer a distant, pious king. Humphries did not visualize the scene quite as a gathering of the British command: his Aeneas does not capitalize on the analogy with World War II situations. He addresses his men rather improbably as "my heroes." Although Humphries overstressed the pathos of Pallas' death for his father Latinus, he radically muted the tears that Vergil attributed to Aeneas (at 29, 41, 59), omitting the last reference entirely.

Copley saw Aeneas once again as a commander-in-chief. He gathers his "generals" for his first speech and calls them "men" in the familiar American sense. He has only "a tear" when talking of Pallas (39), and "tears welled up" as he addresses the corpse with these tepid words: "I'm sorry, son!" Although Vergil emphasized the continuity of the tears throughout the speech, Copley weakened them to "this sad eulogy." Aeneas is a stiff-upper-lip Roman such as Hollywood likes to imagine, but rather different from Vergil's emotional hero. Mandelbaum also saw the military situation of the opening: his Aeneas addresses "the crowding company of his commanders" with a hearty "Men." But in the pathetic scene with Pallas' corpse, Aeneas weeps and sheds more than one tear: he is true to Vergil's description. In different words but with a very similar interpretation, Fitzgerald presented Aeneas. In short, it seems we need not be embarrassed any longer by the hero's tears.

The chief Italian opponent of Aeneas, Turnus, plays a key role in the Council that is held in Book 11 to deal with the series of setbacks the Italian side has suffered. He fails to exert the kind of leadership we have seen in Aeneas, angrily defends a policy of continuing the war, with less apparent concern for Italian misery than for his hurt pride, and ends by breaking off discussions with the excuse that immediate military needs take priority. Vergil assigns him a moment of ironic glory and an exciting horse-simile that captures the animal magnetism of the man and also his wild irresponsibility. This scene (486–97), analyzed in my earlier chapter in this volume, again brings out the cultural and temporal differences between translators.

When the Council breaks up, Turnus wildly arms himself and then he rushes down from the citadel, his armor glittering, his head as yet bare of helmet, imagining that he has already caught Aeneas. Here is the Latin, followed by a literal translation:

> cingitur ipse furens certatim in proelia Turnus.
> iamque adeo rutilum thoraca indutus aenis
> horrebat squamis surasque incluserat auro,
> tempora nudus adhuc, laterique accinxerat ensem,
> fulgebatque alta decurrens aureus arce
> exsultatque animis et spe iam praecipit hostem.
>
> (486–91)

Raging, Turnus arms himself fiercely for battle. And now, having put on his reddish breastplate, he made the bronze scales shake roughly; he had wrapped his calves in gold greaves; and, while still bare-headed, he had strapped his sword to his side. He gleamed with gold as he ran down from the summit of the citadel; and he

exults in his heart and in hope he imagines ahead of time catching
up with the enemy.

Douglas saw this ferocity, but rather emphasized the fearsome effects
of his armor. And then he refused to have Turnus race wildly down the hill
to his troops. Instead, he pictured how he "fast can glide / throw [through]
out the palyce ryall [royal] heir and thar, / reiosyt [rejoiced] in his mynd,
as thocht [though] he war / in ferm beleif fortill [for to] ourset [over-
throw] his fo: / and on sik wys gan walkyng to and fro." This conveys
stately and heroic movement in royal surroundings, such as were familiar
to Douglas, but it gives to Turnus a controlled heroic quality that fails to
prepare us for the simile. Vergil rightly wanted us to see the man dashing
down from the citadel, much like a runaway horse.

Twyne was also reluctant to imagine Turnus as Vergil saw him. He
gratuitously called him "Kinge Turnus" as the scene opens. Turnus then
buckled on "his brave Rutilian armour"; the adjective, not in the Latin,
wrongly builds up the situation. Then,

> All glittring bright he shines, and from the pallaice forth he goes
> Triumphing in his minde, and whole in hope hath foyld his foes.

Twyne, too, imagined a palace rather than a citadel as the center of activity,
and he wilfully changed the force of Vergil's verb in order to depict a stately
regal appearance, not a wild dash downhill of an ambitious man (no recog-
nized king). Turnus' triumph is a figment of his mind and his vain hopes,
which would have emerged more ironically if matched by the correct verb
for his movements. Twyne also attenuated the picture of the runaway horse
that has broken its tether: for him, it is simply a "noble horse that from the
stable is start away," a fit analogue in its nobility for kingly Turnus.

Dryden also magnified the appeal of Turnus while muting the implicit
Vergilian criticism of his irresponsibility. Dropping the key Latin word
furens ("wild," 486), he gave a picture of a hero arming himself, then went
on:

> Nor casque, nor crest, his manly features hide:
> But bare to view, amid surrounding friends,
> With godlike grace, he from the tow'r descends.
> Exulting in his strength,, he seems to dare
> His absent rival, and to promise war.

Not a word in these five lines catches Vergil's irony, and the expansions and choice of language force us to identify with Turnus rather than to perceive his serious flaws. Dryden changed the locale from palace to tower, but it is a noble descent from the tower that we imagine, like the royal processions suggested by Twyne and Douglas before him. It is no surprise, then, to find that Dryden also altered the simile in Turnus' favor.

The translators of the twentieth century have been far less indulgent of Turnus, more responsive to Vergil's complexity than were the three earlier masters. Most of them catch the thematic word *furens* that Vergil uses to characterize the wild way in which Turnus arms himself: he is "enraged" (Lewis); "all impatience, hot for action" (Humphries); he "made furious haste" (Copley); was "furiously on edge for battle" (Fitzgerald). Mandelbaum alone weakens the idea with "as quick as any." The same four agree that Turnus ran down from the citadel or fortress, whereas Mandelbaum seems to moderate the action with "he hurries from the high fortress." And they develop the simile accordingly. Vergil did engage the audience's sympathies for Turnus—he was not simply an evil enemy—but modern translators appear to have come closer to the grand but irresponsible character that emerges in the Latin.

The last problematic character of Book 11 is Camilla, the warrior-queen. As she triumphs over one Trojan after another, her threat to masculine achievement grows. Her final victory, over a Ligurian who tries to trick her into dismounting from her horse so that he can suddenly ride away to safety, is still so easy that she is compared to a falcon swooping down on a helpless dove and disemboweling it in the air (721–24). Then, Vergil prepares us for her death from a treacherously thrown lance. She spots a warrior-priest, Chloreus, who wears glittering gold armor and robes of rich golden thread. In her eagerness to win these items as spoil, Camilla fails to exert due caution and thus becomes an easy victim to Aruns, who shoots her down like a hunter in ambush. The complicated triangular situation constructed by Vergil, involving priest, Camilla, and Aruns, does not offer a simple interpretation to the audience. But still, I believe, the poet expected us to privilege the warrior-queen over her intended victim and over her killer.

A key passage that poses difficulty for translators is Vergil's summary of the situation just before Aruns launches his spear. Why is Camilla acting with such fatal carelessness? The poet offers two alternatives: either she intends to dedicate the golden armor to the gods or she plans to wear it herself (778–80). Here is the Latin followed by a literal translation:

hunc virgo, sive ut templis praefigeret arma
Troia, captivo sive ut se ferret in auro
venatrix, unum ex omni certamine pugnae
caeca sequebatur totumque incauta per agmen
femineo praedae et spoliorum ardebat amore.

(770–82)

It is this man [Chloreus] that the maiden pursued, whether to set
up the Trojan armor in a temple for all to see or to adorn herself in
the captured gold. A huntress, she followed him alone of all the
enemy in the battle, blindly and carelessly over the entire line,
and she burned for plunder and spoils with a woman's love.

As argued in my previous chapter, I do not think that line 782 prejudices
us into believing that she had decided to take the armor for herself, but it
surely raises questions about the way Camilla's "love" operates.

In dealing with this episode, translators have always faced a series of
hurdles. Douglas, for example, was taken with the fact that Chloreus was
a priest, and he did not pay attention to what kind of priest he was, nor
how ironically Vergil described him. Spontaneously, he added to Vergil's
bare language that Chloreus was a "spiritual man blissyt [blessed] and
consecrat." He lavished detail on the priest's armor, conveying the sense
that it was rich but warlike, which is not Vergil's point. What is a priest so
gleamingly armed in gold doing in this scene, scattering arrows around?
Douglas and others after him missed the poet's implication that this priest
was a eunuch of Cybele, inclined to effeminacy and attracted to gold
finery. So when Camilla spots and desires all that gold, is she not perhaps
more worthy of it, especially since she has the warlike ability to take it
from the weak, arrow-wielding eunuch? Douglas described her without
attenuation: "Blynd in desire this Troiane to assay, / In womanly appetyt
ardent of this pray."

Twyne, like Douglas, favored Chloreus, not as a priest, but because he
was a male warrior. He introduced him as *Sir* Chloreus, and he, too, saw
his armor and weapons as virile. Chloreus has "sturdy" thighs; his armor
is "brave." Those adjectives, added to the Latin, misread and thus misin-
terpret Vergil for the reader.[8] For Camilla, however, Twyne had less sym-
pathy. He worded the Latin of 782, "With greedy woman's lust of spoyles,
she flies the field about." As Aruns unseen readies his spear for the throw,
he makes a speech, which takes the form of a prayer to Apollo. Twyne felt

and made us feel the solemnity of that speech. Thus, as I read it, he reversed the Vergilian view of this triangular situation, leading readers to favor Chloreus and Aruns over Camilla.

Dryden would not allow this prejudice against Camilla, though he, too, was mistakenly attracted by the description of Chloreus. The eunuch has a "brawny chest," and supposedly "with deadly wounds he gall'd the distant foe" [i.e., as he shot his arrows]. However, when he came to Camilla, Dryden decided simply to eliminate 782 from his translation. Thus, without any chauvinistic overtones, he merely remarked on her heedlessness: "Blind in her haste, she chases him alone, / And seeks his life, regardless of her own." This at least is a positive heritage for future versions.

The twentieth-century translators have not been so overwhelmed by a view of Chloreus the priest or the priest-warrior as to exaggerate the Latin, but they have not seen the reality of this eunuch and his finery as Vergil meant it to be sensed.[9] His unconventional masculinity receives no stress, while Camilla's unconventional femininity cannot escape. Lewis imagined her potential goal "to strip off his [Chloreus'] gold and wear it herself," a gratuitous addition to the Latin; and he worded the ambiguous 782 "on fire with a woman's desire for another's finery," refusing to see that she desired what male warriors pursue, plunder and spoils. Lewis then understated her fatal wound and limited our sympathies: "the spear went into her body, just under the naked breast, and stuck there, / deeply drinking the maiden blood where it lodged." Vergil makes it clear that the spear pierced her breast beneath the exposed nipple.

Humphries agreed closely with Lewis's bias. He found nothing wrong with the outlandish, effeminate display of Chloreus or with his useless archery. But he knew exactly what was wrong with Camilla: "she was a huntress / in blind pursuit, dazzled by spoil, a woman / reckless for finery." No, she was a genuine warrior, easily capable of killing Chloreus, and typically eager for a victor's spoils. Humphries then cut radically back on Vergil's description of the effect of Aruns' spear: it "went to its lodging / in the bare breast and drank the maiden's blood." These versions suffer by their attenuations.

Copley seemed to sense the outlandishness of Chloreus, priest playing warrior. He added a parenthesis to the picture of this eunuch astride "a foaming horse caparisoned in mail (like some big bird of bronze and gold)"; this suggests a tone of irony. Camilla, eager to despoil him of that gold, is also closer to Vergil's heroine: "blind and incautious she trailed him through the host / with a woman's burning love to win that wealth."

And the fatal spear seems indeed a tragic parody of the baby Camilla will never fondle: "the spear point struck her naked breast / and sank and clung and drank her virgin blood."

Mandelbaum retreated from any irony about Chloreus, whom he called "dear to Cybele" without apparently realizing that "dearness" would require emasculation. Hence, his description does not convey the significance of that display of gold and exotic dress or of the bow and arrows. His Camilla, "fearless, with a female's love / of plunder and of spoils, [she] raged through all / the army." He, too, gave the accepted picture of her fatal wound: "the shaft drove in below her breast, / held fast and drank deep of her virgin blood." There are touches in Fitzgerald's Chloreus that invite us to picture the travesty of this gilded eunuch warrior sporting his Eastern tunic and trousers. And he modified the chauvinism in defining Camilla's flaw: "she rode on / through a whole scattered squadron recklessly, / in a *girl's* love of finery." But the description of her wound, making two sentences of it, weakens Vergil's focus: "the javelin swooped and thudded home / beneath her naked breast. There, driven deep, / the shaft drank the girl's blood."

Five hundred years of translations, as represented by the eight I have chosen, have illustrated some of the cultural differences among the periods of Vergil's major English translators, even while giving credit to their active poetic genius in experimentation with meter, language, and heroic rhetoric. The translators of the twentieth century have flattened out the meter and style into a more natural expression, and they have benefited from years of scholarship on Vergil's poem. Even so, as I have tried to show, it remains a demanding task to catch the full significance of the roles of such characters as Aeneas and Turnus in such complex situations as those developed in Book 11, and Camilla the woman-warrior-queen has so far defied the efforts of the exclusively male translators.

NOTES

EDITOR'S INTRODUCTION

1. Classicists as well might find fresh and valuable insights, since all contributors to this volume are professional scholars of the Classics.

2. Horsfall 1995, 1–25.

3. See Miles in this volume for discussion of the Social Wars (i.e., with the *socii*, the allies). Dissatisfied allies banded together to oppose Roman domination. Although the Social Wars proper lasted only from 91 to 87 B.C., the process of integrating Roman and Italian remained far from complete as Vergil composed the *Aeneid*. See also Toll 1997.

4. Shakespeare, *Antony and Cleopatra*, 5.2.

5. Nagy 1990, 11.

6. See Horace, *Epistles* 1.2: Homer sets forth "what is noble, what is base, what useful, what not, more clearly and better" than philosophers.

7. Cairns 1989, on the other hand, has argued for the centrality of the *Odyssey* as a model throughout. Other structures have been seen: a wave structure of alternating light and dark books; a structure of thirds, where Books 1–4 are Dido's tragedy, Books 5–8 the discovery of Italy and Rome, Books 9–12 Turnus' tragedy. A progression toward Rome is climaxed in Book 8, as Aeneas arrives first on Italian shores in 6, in Latium in 7. Aeneas' descent to the Underworld in Book 6 has been read as a moral or philosophical turning point.

8. Bloom 1973 and 1975. See Lyne 1987, who refers to "a productive irony" in what he calls Vergil's "designed intertextuality"; Vergil's use of allusion is never merely "typological," that is, to suggest that Aeneas is a better example of the hero than Achilles or Odysseus (114). For other discussions of Vergil's use of his literary models, see esp. Beye, Boyle, and Hexter in this volume, Conte 1986, and Farrell 1991, 1–25.

9. Certain events narrated in the *Aeneid* come not from Homer, but from the cyclic epics, composed after the Homeric poems (probably seventh to sixth

centuries B.C.). These are now fragmentary or exist only in summary. The account of the wooden horse and fall of Troy come from the *Little Iliad* of Lesches and the *Sack of Troy* of Arctinus; the story of Penthesilea from the *Aethiopis* of Arctinus.

10. For a discussion of Alexandrianism and the *Argonautica*, see Beye 1982 and in this volume. For the relationship of Hellenistic authors to their literary past, see Bing 1988.

11. Goldberg 1995, 43.

12. Barchiesi 1994, 109: "la presenza del dolore unisce e divide gli attori dell'epica, questa communità di inuguali che devono continuamente conoscersi e separarsi: uomini e dei, amici nemici."

13. See Nagy 1981, 265–75, on the Greek epic tradition of Aeneas.

14. In the *Aeneid*, Anchises does not reach Italy.

15. Vergil and Livy, expounding what became the canonic version, interpolate a line of Alban kings between the fall of Troy (traditionally dated at 1184 B.C.) and the founding of Rome (753 B.C.), in order to preserve the line of common chronology. See Gruen 1992, 5–51, for a detailed overview; Horsfall 1987; and Galinsky 1992.

16. A more extensive discussion of Vergil's innovations in the Dido story may be found in Hexter 1992, esp. 338–40, and Horsfall 1973–74.

17. Feeney 1991, 152.

18. Stahl 1981, 157.

19. My survey will be focused on the Augustan or anti-Augustan question. For a more exhaustive listing of *Aeneid* scholarship see S. J. Harrison 1990, 1–20. For other histories of *Aeneid* reception, see Johnson 1976, 1–22, and R. D. Williams in S. J. Harrison 1990, 21–36. See Wlosok 1973 for discussion of German studies of the *Aeneid* from 1915 to 1973.

20. *Quid enim miserius misero non miserante se ipsum et flente Didonis mortem, quae fiebat amando Aenean, non flente autem mortem suam, quae fiebat non amando te, deus, lumen cordis mei? . . .* ("What can be more pitiful than an unhappy wretch unaware of his own sorry state, bewailing the fate of Dido, who died for love of Aeneas, yet shedding no tears for himself as he dies for want of loving you, my God and my Life?") (*Confessions* 1.13.21, trans. Pine-Coffin, 1961). Cf. Dryden: "In the meantime I may affirm, in honor of this episode, that it is not only now esteem'd the most pleasing entertainment of the *Aeneid*, but was so accounted in his own age . . . for which I need produce no other testimony than that of Ovid" ([1697] 1944, xxxvii).

21. Dryden [1697] 1944, ix.

22. Ibid., xxi.

23. Ibid., xx.

24. Ibid., xxi.

25. Eliot 1944, 54.

26. Ibid., 70–71.

27. Ziolkowski 1993, 119–28, 133.

28. Ibid., 193.

29. For the phrase *anima naturaliter christiana*, see Tertullian, *Apol.* 17.6.

30. Vergil seems to have anticipated this possibility. In *Eclogue* 9, for example, two poets in contrasting circumstances (old vs. young, hopeful vs. hopeless) quote fragments of a third, master, absent poet. Each poet cites fragments consistent with his own frame of mind, with the result that the one absent poet's work generates two opposed (optimistic vs. pessimistic, one might say) readings. This disparity in readings might support Kennedy's contention that it is the conditions of reception rather than the text itself that determine readings (1992, 41).

31. Aeneas then would show development from a more primitive Homeric heroism to selfless Roman dedication (*pietas*). Wlosok 1992 describes precedents in late antiquity for reading the difficulties of Aeneas' travels from Troy to Rome as a spiritual trajectory, on the Odyssean model of progression toward ethical enlightenment, and later, in Christian readings, as an ascent from earthly troubles to knowledge of God.

32. Pöschl [1950] 1962, 15. See Wlosok 1973 for a discussion of studies by German scholars: Heinze 1915, Klingner 1967, Pöschl 1950, Büchner 1958, Buchheit 1963, Knauer 1964, and Binder 1971. The term "optimistic" does not, of course, occur in her review of their work, for it is the assumption of all these scholars that the *Aeneid* endorses Aeneas, Augustus, and the Romans' progression toward world dominion as the reflection of fate and divine will. Wlosok restricted her discussion to studies in German and English because, she said, these were the source of the most important new work on Vergil (130). In the present time Italians such as Conte (1986) and Barchiesi (1984, 1994) are producing influential work.

33. Johnson 1976, 9. Among these readers Johnson (6) numbers: Klingner 1967, Büchner 1955, Pöschl 1962, and Buchheit 1963. For his traditional/Augustan reading the American Otis belongs in this group as well. To these may be added Cairns 1989, Hardie 1986, Stahl 1981 and 1990, and Galinsky, esp. 1988 and 1994.

34. Johnson 1976, 11.

35. Ziolkowski 1993, 26.

36. Ibid.

37. Johnson 1976, 7.

38. Analogously, deconstruction and related movements have made it possible to read the *Aeneid* as undecidable or indeterminate and without ultimate unity. Classical scholars have traditionally assumed unity in texts.

39. Boyle 1993, 93.

40. Johnson 1976, 20.

41. Hardie's later studies (e.g., 1993) reflect a more "pessimistic" reading.

42. Galinsky 1996, 251

43. Ibid., 229, 231.

44. Ibid., 250.

45. Ibid., 248.

46. Ibid., 251.

47. Servius' reading (ad loc.) has affinities with Barchiesi's (1994, 119–22) and Quint's (1993), for he sees the contrary pressures of *pietas* and *clementia*. He concludes that Aeneas' moral conflict enhances his stature, because both his inclination to pity and his loyalty to duty are to his credit.

48. See, e.g., Redfield 1975 or Crotty 1994.

49. Austin 1971, ad 1.257 ff. Similarly R. D. Williams 1990 [1967]: "Jupiter's answer [i.e., the prophecy to Venus] sheds a radiant and optimistic light over the whole of the gloom and uncertainty [of the opening passage], and the long toil which will be necessary to found Rome is seen to be worth whatever it involves" (22).

50. Martindale 1993, 45.

51. O'Hara 1990, 98 and 130. Johnson's study of the poem's closing scene makes a similar argument about Jupiter (1976, 114–54). Lyne 1987, 61–99, argues that the gods represent no moral force in the poem; Feeney 1991 reads the gods as more than simply allegorical figures or extensions of human qualities, but rather, in the interpretive/ontological difficulties they pose, as figuring the terrifying inscrutability of the Vergilian universe.

52. Feeney 1991, 140–55.

53. Ibid., 155.

54. Lyne 1987, 216.

55. Conte 1986, 161.

56. Ibid.

57. G. Williams 1983, 3–16.

58. S. J. Harrison 1990, 5.

59. Otis 1964, 319.

60. Ibid., 350.

61. Ibid., 356.

62. Eagleton 1983, 120. Cf. Smith 1968, 120: "We might wonder, for example, if the spectator in a theater who rushes on the stage to disarm the villain is any

more naïvely and improperly deluded than the reader who believes, when he is reading Donne's 'Holy Sonnets,' that he is eavesdropping on the poet's private meditation."

63. Wofford 1992, 102.

64. Hardie 1993, 92.

65. Conte 1986, 168–69.

66. Not all of the original participants in the NEH institute were able to contribute to this volume, and some chapters were commissioned subsequent to the institute.

67. Adherence to this suggestion was not always feasible.

68. Discussions of Homer's influence on the *Aeneid* occur throughout the volume.

69. Martindale 1993, 28: "A classic becomes a text whose 'iterability' is a function of its capacity . . . for continued re-appropriations by readers." Martindale's definition of the classic as a text continually available for new readings is implicitly at variance with Eliot's (1957), which suggests that the classic, as it is "mature," is stable, magisterial, eternal.

70. For other introductions to Vergil and the *Aeneid*, see Anderson 1989, Camps 1969, Miles and Allen 1986, and Griffin 1986. Anderson and Camps provide comprehensive introductory studies of the *Aeneid*, the former proceeding book by book, the latter by topic. Griffin provides a brief, suggestive overview of all of Vergil's works. Miles and Allen combine critical observations with careful placement of Vergil's texts in their historical context.

CHAPTER 1. "*AENEID* 1: AN EPIC PROGRAMME"

1. I limit consideration of intertexts to Homer for the most part. For Apollonius, see Beye 1982 and in this volume.

2. Cairns 1989 has argued that this binary view of the poem is inadequate, that "the *Aeneid* as *Odyssey*" (chap. 8, 177–214) is a more accurate conception.

3. My interest here is in observing the defining features of comic and tragic epic as they are established in the *Odyssey* and the *Iliad*, Vergil's primary intertexts. It may be a commonplace of literary history that most comedies end with the marriages, and most tragedies with the deaths, of the protagonists (Smith 1968, 118), but this formula does not quite fit the Homeric poems. The *Odyssey*, which ends with the renewal of the wedding of Penelope and Odysseus and with reconciliation between antagonists in Ithaca, fits this formula for comedy precisely; the *Iliad*, which ends not with the death of either Achilles or Hector, but

rather with the ransoming of Hector, his burial, and, finally, the laments for him, evidently does not fit this formula for tragedy. As Roberts 1993, 573, points out and as Vergil would have seen, Greek tragedies end, as a rule, not with death and disaster but with aftermath and reaction. That is, death or disaster is followed by some episode of vision, interpretation, or redemption. Greek tragedy, therefore, follows the Iliadic model more closely than does the *Aeneid*. See further Hardie 1993, 88, on the *Odyssey* and *Iliad* as comic and tragic, respectively.

4. While Homer establishes the model for favorable and unfavorable gods, Hardie 1993, 58, observes that Vergil innovates by introducing a "radical dualism."

5. Dante understood Vergil's vision as tragic, and therefore he made his Vergil refer to the *Aeneid* as "*l'alta mia tragedia*" (*Inf.* 20.113), while he himself wrote a redemptive Christian *commedia*, predicated on faith in the justice of God. See the editor's introduction for further discussion of Dante's reading of Vergil. Nevertheless, I believe (and argue further below) that the *Aeneid* continually straddles the comic/tragic divide, adhering wholly to neither model. In particular, the ending of the poem fits neither the comic nor tragic model of Homer. This formal suspension between the tragic and comic model allows Vergil to problematize his own text's representation of the moral quality of experience.

6. Feeney 1991, 32, observes that Juno's soliloquy is like a *tragic* prologue. For my purposes, this would further contribute to the tragic character of the poem's opening.

7. The violation of Cassandra in Athena's temple by the Locrian Ajax, son of Oileus, was a tradition of the epic cycle.

8. Note that Servius ad 1.27 points out that Aeneas has no share in any guilt relating to the Judgment of Paris.

9. Lucretius 3.833–37, Livy 29.17.6, cited by Feeney in S. J. Harrison 1990, 342, n.12.

10. Juno's role as antagonist of the Romans has multiple and profound levels: Juno is historically identified with the chief Carthaginian goddess Tanit from at least 500 B.C. The Romans' fear that Juno was disaffected was a problem the Senate had to confront in the prosecution of the Punic Wars (Livy 21.62.8 and 22.1.17). The poetic tradition is divided about when Juno gave up her hostility to the Romans. She may have played a hostile role in Naevius' epic, but Ennius' Juno (according to Servius on 1.281) was placated during the Second Punic (Hannibalic) War (218–10 B.C.) and began to favor the Romans at that time. This discrepancy is significant for the *Aeneid*, since Juno allows Jupiter and the reader to infer that she will cease to hate the Romans at the end of the *Aeneid*. Inasmuch as her hostility is perceived to endure several centuries more (through one or more of the Punic Wars), her reconciliation with Jupiter in Book 12 would be

either only anticipatory or partial. Juno's antipathy to Rome figures in works of Ennius, Vergil, Horace, Ovid, and Silius, each of whom attributes her final reconciliation to different circumstances, thus showing that the tradition continued to vary on that question. Further, the Greek Hera (= Juno) was imagined to be etymologically related to *aer* (the wet element) and in that capacity was associated with storms, as is thematically apt for the Juno of Book 1, who instigates precisely the storm that constitutes the poem's first episode. On Juno in the *Aeneid* see Feeney in S. J. Harrison 1990, 339–62, and Feeney 1991, 116–50.

11. Contrast Spence 1988, 11–51, who suggests that the text is as concerned with Juno's exile as it is with Aeneas' voyage (23). Juno represents the universal repressed irrational forces that Vergil valorizes to the degree that he represents her pain. In either case her powerful presence dominates the poem. Cf. Johnson 1976: the anger of Juno comes "close to being the central theme of the *Aeneid*" (14); and Feeney 1991: "the disorderly goddess is the poem's principal force for structural cohesion" (150).

12. Quint 1993, 8–10 and passim.

13. See Pöschl 1962, 13–24, and Otis 1964, 227–34, for these symbolic oppositions. In the poem's conclusion these terms assume a different relationship to each other. See Putnam 1966, 151–201, and in this volume.

14. There seems to be an assimilation here of the image of the imprisoned winds to that of the imprisoned Titans in Hesiod's *Theogony* (729 ff.). Thus the *furor* and storm of this opening episode share in the motif, pervasive in the *Aeneid*, of the "Gigantomachy, a myth that concerns the struggle between cosmos [order] and chaos at the most universal level" (Hardie 1986, 85) or, as the *Aeneid* represents it here, of *furor* versus *pietas/imperium*. The war between the Titans (or Giants) and the Olympian gods, which resulted in the triumph of the gods and the original creation of the cosmos, served as the mythological representation of the eternal conflict between disorder and order. Visual artists and poets availed themselves of this myth to represent the outcomes of contemporary military or political conflicts as triumphs of good over evil, civilization over barbarism. See Hardie 1986 for a meticulous study of the Gigantomachy theme in the *Aeneid*, with its implicit equation of "cosmos and imperium." Hardie 1993 (perhaps modifying Hardie 1986) observes that "Virgil's dualistic scheme already contains its own contradictions and tensions of such a kind that final stability is never attained" (58).

15. Contrast Cicero, *Clu.* 138: *ex quo intellegi potuit id quod saepe dictum est: ut mare, quod sua natura tranquillum sit, ventorum vi agitari atque turbari, sic populum Romanum sua sponte esse placatum, hominum seditiosorum vocibus ut violentissimis tempestatibus concitari* ("from which [event] the truth of what is

often said was corroborated: that as the sea, which is by nature tranquil, is agitated and disturbed by the violence of the winds, so the Roman people, placid of its own accord, is aroused by the voices of seditious men as if by very violent storms") (my translation).

16. Regrettably, for my purposes, Mandelbaum translates 1.54 in such a way that no precise equivalent for *imperium* occurs.

17. Aeneas conceives of Dido as "pious" because of her generous welcome of the Trojans (1.603), to whom she is bound neither by nationality nor blood.

18. Camps 1969, 24–25; Galinsky 1969, chap. 1.

19. *Pietas* was a political slogan of Octavian in his pursuit of vengeance against the murderers of his adoptive uncle Julius Caesar (Syme 1971, 157). Quint 1993 describes *pietas* (expressed as vengeance) and *clementia* (clemency) as opposing ways of controlling the past.

20. Austin 1971, ad loc. For descriptions of *pietas* similar to those of Austin on the part of some German scholars, see summaries in Wlosok 1973 and 1983.

21. *Iliad* 2.144–52 shows the inverse: Agamemnon (testing the men) rouses the crowd, which is then compared to the sea.

22. By political I mean relating to the *polis*, i.e., the city or state.

23. Pöschl 1962, 13–33.

24. Stahl 1990 and Galinsky 1988 argue that some *furor* is good and legitimate. Therefore they would say that my equation of Aeneas' ("good") *furor* with, for example, Juno's bad *furor*, is illegitimate. Whether *furor* has a consistent or a variable ethical valence throughout the poem is a critical interpretive question for readers.

25. See Boyle 1986 and in this volume.

26. Discussion of these speeches is indebted to Clausen 1964. See also Anderson 1989, 13–16, on Aeneas as "passive" hero.

27. Stahl 1990, 201 and 201 n.36, has another reading: Aeneas means that he wishes he had died fighting.

28. Clausen 1964, 76. See also Hardie 1993, 118, on *oppositio in imitando*.

29. On Aeneas' despair, see E. L. Harrison in Wilhelm and Jones 1992, 123–25: Aeneas' gesture of prayer is not, in fact, accompanied by prayer; neither is he subsequently shown in religious observance in Carthage.

30. See Beye 1982 and in this volume.

31. This story allows an integration of the old legend of Romulus and Remus with the otherwise independently developing story of Aeneas. See the editor's introduction for further discussion.

32. For example, Livy 1.7; see Feeney 1991, 112, and Johnson in this volume.

33. See Gruen 1992, 54.

34. Cf. Austin 1971, ad 292: "the implied reconciliation is symbolic of the end of civil war."

35. For many commentators this phrase denotes primarily civil war.

36. E.g., R. D. Williams 1972, ad 1.223–96.

37. Austin 1971, ad 1.257 ff.: "The speech reflects some of Virgil's deepest feelings." Ad 1.264: "Virgil stresses Rome's unique and special gift to the world, as he saw it (*moresque . . . ponet*)." Wlosok 1983 argues that Vergil's Jupiter is his own theological creation: an elevated, particularly Roman conception of the highest god: the all powerful Stoic-cosmic god, joined with Jupiter, god of the Roman state. For varied readings of the gods, see Heinze 1993, 291–318; Feeney 1991, 99–187; G. Williams 1983, 17–39, 125–31; Lyne 1987, 61–99; Quinn 1968, 316–20.

38. See, for example, W. R. Johnson in this volume.

39. See O'Hara 1990, 138–39, on this prophecy as a *consolatio* and 132–63 for a general reading of its overly optimistic claims.

40. See Mack 1978 on the diminishing claims of the prophecies and O'Hara 1990 on their inconsistency and delusive optimism.

41. See Leach 1988, 309–18, and Leach and Boyle in this volume for discussion and references on these ecphrases. Putnam has done extensive work on ecphrasis; see e.g., 1985, 1995a, and 1998.

42. E.g., Hexter 1992, Horsfall 1973–74, and Leach 1988. Or is it a monitory representation of military defeat, a warning to the Carthaginians that they too might be vulnerable to attack, as Barchiesi 1994, 121–22, suggests? Most critics focus on the question of the validity of Aeneas' interpretation of the frieze, but Hexter poses the question of why, in Carthage, a temple to Juno and not to Tanit, and why a frieze of the Trojan war rather than, say, an event from Carthaginian history. For Hexter the occlusion, precisely, of *Sidonian* Dido (the title of his article) is an occasion of "Roman self-blinding" (351), a reflection, as he reads it, of Vergil's nationalist perspective on Roman history.

43. In whose interpretation is Achilles selling the body for gold? The frieze artists'? Aeneas'? While many post-Homeric versions emphasized the cruelty of Achilles, Homer's version of the ransom in *Iliad* 24 illuminated Achilles' generosity and humanity. Priam's own version in *Aeneid* 2.540–43 accords rather with Homer's.

44. Apparently the most common Dido story, current even after Vergil (Macrobius 5.17.5), does not include a meeting with Aeneas, which the traditional chronology of the founding of Carthage (ninth century) would preclude. Rather, Dido, an exile in Africa, kills herself to avoid a second marriage. In Christian writers

(Tertullian, Jerome) Dido appears as the very model of chastity. How might Roman readers of Vergil's day have responded to the idea of Dido's suffering tragically? As founder of Carthage, Dido might not be expected to elicit sympathy from Roman readers, yet she is surely sympathetic in Book 1. First-time readers of the *Aeneid* may have felt some confusion of sympathy, therefore, intensified by the unprecedented pairing of Dido and Aeneas in a love affair (Book 4). Servius ad 5.4 knows of a version in which Anna, Dido's sister, died for love of Aeneas, but Vergil is apparently the first to make *Dido* die for love of Aeneas. She is mentioned in Naevius' *Bellum Punicum*, but her role and character in that work are not known. Horsfall 1973–74, 143, imagines her to have been "evil, treacherous, insidious, a magician," in keeping with Roman prejudices against Carthage. See Horsfall 1973–74, Hexter 1992, and Perkell 1981, 208–9, for summaries of the Dido legend.

45. This event is represented on the kylix by the "Penthesileia painter," Antikensammlung, Inv. 8705, Munich. It seems to represent Penthesilea and Achilles falling in love as he kills her. For reproduction and discussion see Pollitt 1972, 22 (re. fig. 9).

46. Barchiesi 1994, 118 n.16, citing Janko, *Classical Quarterly* 38 (1988): 259–60.

47. Macrobius, *Sat.* 7.1.14, read this learned song as a graceless, laughable choice for a dinner party. Austin 1971, ad 742 ff., saw "no more than a reflection of Augustan intellectual interests."

48. Servius, ad loc.; Pöschl 1963, 150–54; Segal 1971; Kinsey 1979. Arcturus and the Hyades are particularly associated with stormy weather. See Hardie 1986, 52–66, and Dyson 1996a, 210–11, for discussion of Iopas' "scientific" song in relation to those of Demodocus in *Odyssey* 8. For Dyson, Epicurean thought characterizes both Dido and Iopas.

49. Perkell 1989, 139–90.

50. By contrast, Orpheus' song in the *Argonautica* does move on to stories of gods (Kronos, Rhea, the Titans, and Zeus) after it treats the origin of the heaven, sea, and earth (with its mountains, rivers and river nymphs, and "crawling things") and the fixed movements of stars, moon, and sun.

CHAPTER 2. "*DIS ALITER VISUM*:
SELF-TELLING AND THEODICY IN *AENEID* 2"

1. For these terms, see Genette 1983, 185–193; 1988, 72–78.

2. One wonders sometimes at 8.93 ff. and 533 ff. whether Alcinous notices the hero's tears when listening to Demodocus' song not because he alone is

observant but because Odysseus, eager to boast and compete, so positions himself that Alcinous will see his response and thereupon ask him why he is weeping, which will then permit him to "sing his say"; recall his request to Demodocus at 8.486 ff. for "The Lay of the Trojan Horse."

3. See Pucci 1987, 157–64. For useful observations on the frequency of Odysseus' references to himself as compared with Aeneas' more modest percentages in this regard, see Mackie 1988, 63–46.

4. For an interesting recent example, with useful bibliography for symbolic readings, see Miller 1995. For a contrary view of Aeneas as *rhetor* thoroughly in control of his situation of discourse, anticipating accusations of his treasons at Troy with masterful *anteoccupatio*, see Ahl's ingenious descriptions (1989).

5. Genette 1983, 252–54.

6. See O'Hara 1990, 24–26, 30–31, 39, 52–53. According to Cairns, one of these confusions, Creusa's "mistake" about the location of the Tiber (2.780–84), may have been a slip that revision would have taken care of (1977, 112).

7. For the *coniuratio Italiae* in 32 B.C., see Salmon 1982, 143–44.

8. See Feeney 1991, 112–13, 119–20, for the possible role of Naevius in this transformation.

9. See Feeney's chapter on Vergil (1991, 129–87) for a lucid and subtle discussion of the tribal/universal paradox. He sees that this Jupiter is a contradiction in terms, that his perspectives are irremediably incompatible, since he was once partial (as Rome's god and Venus' father and Aeneas' grandfather) and, as the symbol of "Fate, of Time, of history," also impartial; this stark incompatibility, which both Aeneas' narrative and the entire poem reflect, presents us with mere vagueness or with ironic and irresoluble indeterminacies (see, in particular, 153–55). For a meticulous description of an impartial, transcendental Jupiter, see Wlosok 1983, 187–202. For summaries of Klingner and Büchner (and the tradition that Wlosok writes from) see S. J. Harrison 1990, 6. See also Feeney's deft dismantling of an attempted solution (in respect of Iliadic Zeus) of the tribal/universal paradox (1991, 113–44, n.77).

10. The theme of useless or hostile (or even malevolent) deities is, of course, appropriate to the action of Book 2, but the "narrating I" does more than reflect the feelings of the "narrated I" at the time in question; he shares them at the time of his performance: otherwise he would suppress or soften them. Other instances of the *dis aliter visum* theme in Book 2 occur at 54, 247, 257, 320, 326, 336, 351–52, 396, 429–30, 433–34, 515, 641 and 647 (Anchises), 659, 738.

11. Austin 1964, ad loc., notes that the imagery of the "fiendish" gods fits badly with theme of "the ultimate reasonableness of divine purpose and its readiness to respond to *pietas* (the effect of the mismatch "is more than incongruous, it is irra-

tional"). His solution is to suppose that Vergil would have revised the passage. For further comments on Austin's thoughts on this topic, see D. P. Fowler 1990, 49–50.

12. Some of what is unspoken in the poem, some of what "the political unconscious" blurts out, has to do with what happens when we read the poem from what might now be called a postcolonial perspective. What the voice that asks Jupiter that last, anguished question in Book 12 hates (and loves) is not Augustus, but the Roman empire, which Vergil and many of his contemporary readers have recently become part of (they are newly "naturalized" Romans, as the oxymoron has it, they are/were exiles, emigrants, immigrants). In the poem, Trojans and (a few) Italians became mingled according to "god's plan" (see E. L. Harrison in S. J. Harrison 1990, 55–56). So, Romans and Italians would continue to mingle (violently) throughout Roman history until the Augustan solution to the problem of their disunions (for the *coniuratio*, see note 7 above); it is important to remember that "Italians" reduces a complex variety of peoples up and down the peninsula to a tidy entity that means "not Roman". Vergil and his naturalized readers share a perspective where they are at once Roman and Italian (in Vergil's case Cisalpine), but this (desired) hybridity is conflicted, since if they are both, that would mean that, in a sense, they are also neither. After Actium and the unification of Roman Italy, if Italy had indeed become Roman (and Rome had become Italian), much of what had made everyone what they were would have been lost. Vergil's poem meditates, mostly in its undersong, on what those losses meant to those who had suffered them: see Gossage 1961–62, and Momigliano 1987.

CHAPTER 3. "IMITATING TROY: A READING OF AENEID 3"

1. G. Williams 1983, esp. the appendices, "Signs of Changes of Plan in the *Aeneid*" (245–85) and "The Peculiarities of Book 3" (262–78). Book 3 has been well appreciated by a number of scholars, more than my notes and bibliography in this volume can list. For references to earlier treatments, see Cova 1994, cxxiii–xxxii, and the excellent overview of Putnam, "The Third Book of the *Aeneid*: From Homer to Rome," *Ramus* 9 (1980):1–21, reprinted in Putnam 1995*b*, 50–72. Bettini 1997 came to my attention after my contribution to this volume was complete but fortunately before the final copy was due to the publisher; I am pleased that, as I see it, his approach in this essay complements my own.

2. Book 3 has one of the highest concentrations of half lines. Only Book 2 has more half lines (ten) and only Book 5 has as many half lines (seven). The distribution of half lines among the other books is as follows: Books 4, 9, and 10—five half lines; Books 1 and 8—three half lines; Books 6 and 11—two half lines; Book 12—one half line. The most recent and rigorous scholarly treatment

shows convincingly that different half lines suggest different stages of work-in-progress in different cases (Günther 1996). One of Günther's great strengths is that he refrains from guessing what a complete *Aeneid* would look like.

3. For example, Dupont 1994.

4. R. D. Williams 1972, 265.

5. Ibid., 266.

6. Ibid., 265.

7. Cp. Konstan 1991, 24.

8. On the *Odyssey* as a particular model for the *Aeneid*, see also Cairns 1989, 177–214.

9. Putnam 1995*b*, 50.

10. After R. D. Williams 1972, 266.

11. See Most 1989, esp. 24–30.

12. See Hexter 1992.

13. G. Williams 1983, 270–272, suggests another reading of these lines, but his point is to show that they still reflect a compositional stage when the events of Book 3 were narrated by the poet, not Aeneas.

14. The narrating Aeneas has already heard the story of Dido, Pygmalion, and Sychaeus—from Venus no less (1.335–70).

15. On prophecies in the *Aeneid*, O'Hara 1990 is particularly valuable. For an argument that posits a specific link between deceptive language and Vergilian poetry, see Hexter 1990.

16. "*laetam*" *autem propter Pergama restituta*, on 133 (Thilo and Hagen, eds., 1961).

17. Here we have *miro . . . amore* (298). Compare *miratur*, the operative verb describing Aeneas' inspection of Carthage (1.421, 422) and especially of the frieze on Juno's temple there (1.456); on Aeneas' misinterpretations, see Hexter 1992, esp. 353–55, considerably harsher about the implausibility of his inferences than is Konstan 1991, 23.

18. 3.269–71, the verses immediately preceding the two cited in the text above, are particularly rich with echoes of and even translations from the *Odyssey*; cp. R. D. Williams 1962, 109–10. In the schematic chart above, the skirting of Ithaca comprises a literal "excursus," breaking the otherwise predictable pattern of threes and throwing it into particular relief.

19. The close connection between Andromache's tears and the presence of twin altars is not stated, but it relates to her having tragically lost not only her husband Hector, but also their son Astyanax. This seems to me (and not me alone) a better explanation than R. D. Williams 1962, 120, where he refers simply to "the doubling of offerings to the dead."

20. From the Greek *kenotaphion*, from Greek *kenos* ("empty") and *taphos* ("tomb"). The point that Vergil correctly and completely converts the word into Latin here (*tumulum . . . inanem*, 304) is not without significance for his larger argument about the proper Romanization of Greek literature. On *patrio* and *cessisse*, see Bettini 1997, 9–11.

21. Servius on 302 glosses "false" as "simulated" (*simulati*) (Thilo and Hagen, eds., 1961). Subsequent Servian commentary links the use of "false" here with its appearance in the description of Amor in Book 1, when, disguised as Iulus, he has embraced Aeneas "and sated the great love of his false father" ("*et magnum falsi implevit genitoris amorem*," 1.716). For other overtones here, see Bettini 1997, 12–13.

22. On the anachronism of the term "nostalgia," see Bettini 1997, 25–31.

23. Bettini 1997, esp. 16–21, who develops the idea of Buthrotum as *bricolage* and a site of anachronism.

24. R. D. Williams 1972, ad 349–51, contrasts *Iliad* 20.73.

25. This is an economic oversimplification. See Cameron 1995, esp. 363–66, who provides access to earlier bibliography on the relevant metaphorics. On Roman poets and Hellenistic aesthetics, see Hutchinson 1988, 277–354. Of earlier work, Wimmel 1960 remains of signal value. See also Bing 1988.

26. *Odes* 4.2, esp. vv. 5–8: *monte decurrens velut amnis, imbres / quem super notas aluere ripas, / fervet immensusque ruit profundo / Pindarus ore.*

27. [Longinus], *On the Sublime* 9.13 (though an ocean ebbing in the *Odyssey*; the passage is difficult, but the basic comparison is beyond question).

28. In four books, attributed to Lesches of Mitylene. It is open to question whether there is special significance to the fact that the "Little Iliad" is adduced as an example of the cyclic epics. According to our most complete summary of the work, Helenus plays a part of some importance (he is abducted by Odysseus and forced to prophesy the taking of Ilium); and, of course, it told of the Trojan horse and Sinon, presented by Vergil in *Aeneid* 2.

29. Cova 1994, ad loc., might suggest a less brutal translation, substituting "servant" for "slave," but his own note on *servitio* in line 327 supports the stronger wording.

30. The detail permits appreciation of poetic justice: in Book 2, Pyrrhus had killed Polites before the latter's father's (Priam's) eyes as the Trojans sought protection at comparable altars (2.526 ff.). Pyrrhus (= Neoptolemus) then slaughtered Priam.

31. Childlessness is the most telling symptom of the infertility and aridity of nature at Buthrotum. Pyrrhus is childless (so Achilles' line dies out after one generation). Andromache, now that Astyanax has been murdered, is childless.

Though it is a mere inference on my part (I would be delighted if some other reader could find textual support for it), I suspect we are to assume that the arranged marriage of Andromache and Helenus will remain without issue. The very fact that Helenus was not killed, even if this was because he was a priest, suggests that the Greeks regarded him as less than a full man, though there is no suggestion that he was castrated like the priests of some other cults. Moreover, were Helenus to have had a child, especially a son, it would have left a direct descendant of Priam in play. (Hence I can accept Bettini's description of Andromache and Helenus' union as an example of the "levirate" [1997, 9–11] only as deeply ironical—which may explain his use of scare-quotes. The point of the levirate was to give the deceased brother issue. An infertile union would not do so. Moreover, in this case, Hector already had issue in Astyanax, dead though he now is. If it is a levirate, it is an inopportune and infertile one.)

32. In addition to the two passages discussed above (esp. 302–4 and 349–51), with their insistence on acts of calling and naming, there are also the words of Andromache, "who named the plains / Chaonian—all the land Chaonia, / for Trojan Chaon—placing on the heights / a Pergamus and this walled Ilium" (*"qui [Helenus] Chaonios cognomine campos / Chaoniamque omnem Troiano a Chaone dixit, / Pergamaque Iliacamque iugis hanc addidit arcem*," 334–36, M 434–37).

33. *Renovare* is the verb Vergil has Aeneas use in the first line of his narration to Dido, speaking of "sorrow," not of an earlier author. Servius glosses the verb *retexere, iterare*, on 2.3 (Thilo and Hagen, eds., 1961).

34. Putnam 1995*b*, 62, emphasizes the link the name makes with the Achaemenids of Persia, but other echoes can be heard (so, e.g., Cova 1994, 122). Achaemenides is sometimes criticized as in large measure a doublet of Sinon, but Putnam 1995*b*, 65, takes the similarities (and differences) of the episodes, and their placement, to advance an attractive argument about the unity of Books 2 and 3.

35. Gruen 1992, 9–12, 16–21, 30–31, with references to ancient sources and further bibliography.

36. For a valuable survey of the imitative tradition from the ancient world to the Renaissance, see Greene 1982, esp. 28–80.

37. Representative of many such judgments are remarks quoted in Quintilian (10.1.85–86) and Aulus Gellius (9.9).

38. See G. Williams 1983, 262–64, on the episode's shortcomings.

CHAPTER 4. *"VARIUM ET MUTABILE*: VOICES OF AUTHORITY IN *AENEID* 4"

1. The extent to which Dido is Vergil's own creation is discussed by Desmond 1994, 24–28.

2. We know, but she does not, that this love was set in motion by Venus in the first book.

3. Horsfall 1995, 126. For an overview of the Dido question see also Pease 1935, 14–21, and Desmond 1994, 24–45.

4. Here, most notably, see G. Williams 1958, 23–24.

5. Cairns 1989, chap. 2.

6. Quinn 1968, 135; Otis 1964, 267.

7. Perkell 1981, 221.

8. Monti 1981, 76.

9. Studies of the voices in this book and in the epic as a whole have been done by Parry 1963 and Lyne 1987, among others. See Biow 1994 for a provocative analysis of the difficulties associated with determining authority in the epic.

10. Aeneas has been seen to play many roles: foil for Dido, cad, lover, so-called husband, Roman. For a discussion of these roles see Horsfall 1995, 123–34. See also Farron 1980.

11. Feeney 1991, 150, makes a comparable claim about the power of Juno, claiming that the "disorderly goddess is the poem's principal force for structural cohesion."

12. On Vergil's skills in establishing an emotional point of view (the "subjective style"), see Otis 1964, 65–94.

13. For a sensitive treatment of this important simile, see Otis 1964, 72–76.

14. For a superb reading of the role Juno plays in this final section of Book 4, see Johnson 1976, 67–68.

15. Here see Muecke 1983, Moles 1984, Heinze 1993, chap. 3, Pöschl 1962, 60–90, and Quinn 1968, 323–49. On the polyphonic quality of Vergil's text as a whole, see Parry 1963 and Lyne 1987.

16. Translation by Janko (1987). Subsequent quotations of Aristotle's *Poetics* are from the same translation.

17. See Moles 1984; Muecke 1983.

18. Segal 1990, 11–12.

19. This irony is only heightened when we realize that Ariadne, too, fits this mold, and the allusions to Catullus 64 intensify the reader's tragic anticipation. On allusion in Vergil, see also Conte 1986, esp. 141–84.

20. The poem, in effect, begins twice, first in the poet's own voice (*cano*) and then with an invocation to the muse in line 8.

21. It is important here to realize, with Hexter 1992, that Dido is not presented as a representation of the "other," but as, at least initially, similar to Aeneas, upholding comparable "Roman" values.

22. The fact that many identify Dido as a tragic heroine, however, does not mean that she is always absolved from assuming the guilt of the relationship. Austin 1955, xiv, suggests that Vergil sympathizes with and pities her before he discards and condemns her.

23. Another excellent example of this is Monti's observation that Dido, at both the beginning and end of her story, represents Roman ideals (1981, 69).

24. I have shown in Spence 1988 that an important dimension of male authority in speech-making, in addition to the appeal to reason, is embodied in the man's superior physical position, which is then aligned with power.

25. See Greene 1963, 78–85.

26. The curse is clearly modeled on Ariadne's curse in Catullus 64, lines 188–201, and that of Apollonius' Medea, 4.379–83.

27. *Rhetoric* 1.2.3–6 and 2.1.1–4 define the relationship between ethos, pathos and logos; 2.2–11 discusses pathos in depth.

28. Dyson (1996*a*, 215) has recently argued that here "Stoic meets Epicurean in a climactic confrontation," a confrontation made all the more wrenching by the fact that "even as Virgil denies the truth of the Epicurean world view, he recognizes its beauty" (203).

29. Austin 1955, ad 331–61.

30. So Putnam 1995*b*, 67–68.

31. Throughout the text eyes are used as an indication of power. More specifically, Vergil uses *volvens* and *fixus* as two key terms in relation to the eyes: where the eyes roll, uncertainty or hesitation is being suggested; when they are set, control is being asserted.

32. The parallels between Dido and Ajax also include anger, suicide, and madness.

33. For the perhaps counterintuitive concept of power through absence see Spence, forthcoming, where I adduce extensive evidence to support this idea.

34. See Monti 1981, chap. 6, and Putnam 1966, passim, on the ways in which Book 4 adumbrates much of what occurs in the second half of the poem.

35. I would, therefore, have to disagree with Suzuki 1989 who claims that "under the overarching patriarchal order, Virgil's epic narrative subsumes tragedy's interest in the subjectivity of Dido" (112).

CHAPTER 5. "*AENEID* 5: POETRY AND PARENTHOOD"

1. On this point see Dyson 1996*b*.

2. So Aeneas informs Dido at the end of Book 3 (707–15, M 915–27).

3. On this theme in general see Pavlovskis 1975–76, Glazewski 1972–73, and Bertram 1971.

4. The Latin word behind Mandelbaum's "anxious" is *turbidus* (cf. English "turbid"), which seems to me more concerned with the shimmering and frightful appearance of Anchises' ghost than with the spirit's own state of mind.

5. This tableau appears in the poem at 2.706–11 (M 956–61) and 721–25 (M 974–78). It is illustrated over a long stretch of time by any number of ancient sculptures, paintings, and other works of art, most famously, according to Ovid (*Fasti* 5.563–64), by the (lost) statuary group in the sculptural program of the Forum of Augustus.

6. For further development of this point, see Farrell 1997.

7. So argue many Vergilians of note. For a survey of opinions see R. D. Williams 1960, xxiii–xxx. In defense of Book 5, see Galinsky 1968, 157–85, who decisively answers most of the principal charges against the book.

8. Heinze 1915, 145–70 = Heinze 1993, 121–41. Heinze should now be read, whether in German or English, in the light of Barchiesi 1996.

9. On the literary background of this episode see (in addition to Heinze) Poliakoff 1985.

10. Otis 1964, 41–61.

11. Bloom 1973 and 1987; cf. Mandelbaum 1971, v.

12. Putnam 1965, 64–104. The theme of sacrifice in *Aeneid* 5 is reconsidered in Girardian terms by Quint 1993, 83–96; Hardie 1993, 32–33 and 51–52; and Feldherr 1995.

13. Nugent 1992.

14. Ibid., 260.

15. Ibid., 257.

16. Ibid., 267.

17. It cannot be insignificant in this apparently paternalistic book that Acestes' relationship to the Trojans is matrilinear: he is the son of the river Crinisus and an unnamed Trojan mother (5.38–39, M 51–52).

18. On Eryx, Venus Erycina, and the significance of Sicily in the Aeneas legend, see Galinsky 1969, esp. 63–102.

CHAPTER 6. "VIEWING THE *SPECTACULA* OF *AENEID* 6"

1. E.g., Horace *Odes* 1.5 and *Satires* 2.1. Of course these *tabellae* are paintings, probably executed in the mode of popular narrative art, and would not

have been carved on temple doors. However, many Pompeian paintings show *tabellae* placed at the bases of shrines. In allowing Daedalus to make history of his autobiography by preempting a place of public memory, Vergil has created an interesting conflation of the customs of public and private art.

2. All the same, *Georgics* 4, like *Aeneid* 6, contains an account of the journey to the Underworld made by Orpheus, although it is an ultimately fruitless journey, with the object of the quest, Eurydice, forever lost. Since Aeneas does, however, speak of Orpheus as his direct predecessor in the journey, his failure to retrieve Eurydice is worth keeping in mind as one ponders the question of what Aeneas himself may be said to derive from his journey.

3. Segal 1965, 643, associates this with the mythological, as opposed to the historical, side of the book, especially in its emphasis on the subject of personal entanglements.

4. Otis 1964, 280–83.

5. For a word on the paradigmatic value of viewing as an insight into ancient cultural experience, see Goldhill and Osborne 1993, 9–10.

6. In the long run the symbolic death of Misenus standing in for his leader parallels the death of Elpenor that precedes Odysseus' encounter with the shades. This issue of a living encounter with the shades will of course arise later as a test of the divinely favored status of the hero in conversation with the Sibyl; it is preceded by a symbolic death and by the token of the Golden Bough.

7. Fredericksen 1984, 94–99, provides a concise political history, rationalizing accounts by ancient historical writers who do not agree on many points.

8. Parke 1988, 71–99. The tyrant Aristodemus who was ruler at the time when the Tarquins were supposed to have left Rome is a likely candidate for the Sibyl's sponsor, in keeping with his practice of supporting cults as civic promotions.

9. Zanker 1988 and Kellum 1986 are particularly concerned with cohesion among the various monuments.

10. Favro 1993, 230–32. Favro gives particular mention to the interrelationship between author and participating reader of the "urban text."

11. Nichols 1992, 136–43; Putnam 1995*b*, 419.

12. Lessing [1766] 1984, 95–97.

13. D. P. Fowler 1991, 25, attributes the current popularity of ecphrasis to its capacity for raising many of the theoretical issues most pressing in classical and cultural studies.

14. An early example is Lawall's exposition of the embroidered cloak that Athena bestows upon Jason in Apollonius' *Argonautica* (1966, 154–60).

15. Roman rhetorical writers of the Republic and early Empire did not theorize ecphrasis as such and, as Innocenti points out, they did not theorize *descriptio* itself

explicitly (1994). The general aim is to sway the hearer's judgment by showing. Innocenti demonstrates that the hallmarks of "vivid description" are its sharply focused details.

16. Pöschl 1975 first made this point upon which many successive interpretations have capitalized.

17. Otis 1964, 284–85, reconstructs Daedalus' story with a reading based on his own view of Aeneas as a narrative "full of sentiment and passion," inspiring a vicarious pity for a past recalled in its erotic implications; Segal 1965, 642–45, broadens the significance of the individual instance in speaking of art as a paradigm of the human desire to transcend suffering, but W. Fitzgerald 1984, Putnam 1995b, 73–99, and Leach 1988, 356–59, all bring out in one way or another the deceptiveness of an elliptical representation wherein Daedalus omits his own participation in the most incriminating scenes.

18. Segal 1965, 644: "His work as an artist survives him to be sure, but he cannot make a work of what is dearest to him as a man."

19. Leach 1988, 353–60.

20. On the side of their reality is the term "wide-gated" in 571 (eurupules).

21. The Odyssey landscapes were discovered and reported in 1853, but readers will be best served by consulting some of the more recent publications. Von Blanckenhagen 1963, 100–146 and pls. 46–53, provides a full description with considerations of visual sources. Leach 1988, 27–72, also discusses the composition of the landscapes in conjunction with techniques of Vergilian description.

22. Otis 1964, 290.

23. Segal 1965, 650–54.

24. Otis 1964, 292 and 417.

25. Putnam 1995b, 208, puts the point succinctly: "Anchises' pronouncement in book 6 is the ethical center of the poem. It establishes a major norm for Roman behavior, the combination of power with moderation and restraint."

26. Or as Putnam 1995b, 209, notes, in Book 10 where, "Anchises' rules are first put to the test."

27. Reminiscences of the bee-kingdom in Georgics 4 are obvious, but also Bettini 1991, 197–202, sketches briefly a cultural history of beliefs concerning the bee as a symbol for the soul that can relate both the Carthaginian imagery and the imagery here to rebirth.

28. Habinek 1989, 238–54.

29. Habinek 1989, 236–38; Bettini 1991, 142–50, defends the analogy as a procession that involves future promise as well as remembered glory.

30. On the Area Capitolina, Campus Martius, and Library of Asinius Pollio see Richardson 1992, 31–32 s.v. Area Capitolina, 65–67 s.v. Campus Martius, 41

s.v. *Atrium Libertatis*. Eck 1984, 129–68, stresses the increased importance that portrait sculptures assumed as memorials when other opportunities for glory such as triumphs and buildings became restricted.

31. The model post-facto is of course the Forum of Augustus, dedicated A.D. 2, where two hemicycles display atavistic collections pertinent to Augustus: on the one side the line of the Julian house, on the other the *summi viri* ("most outstanding men") of Roman history. These commemorations included extensive textual material, as Zanker 1988, 210–15, explains.

32. For Putnam 1995*b*, 202, the address characterizes Aeneas "not only as one standing for many but as the epitome of Republican Roman moderation."

33. Quint 1993, 62–65.

34. Michels 1981, 140–146.

35. Lines 888–99 open at least two possibilities. First we hear of Anchises' exhortation, then of his practical advice concerning the coming wars in Latium and the strategies Aeneas should use. There follows the ecphrasis of the Gates with its clear allusion to the *Odyssey*:

> Sunt geminae Somni portae, quarum altera fertur
> cornea, qua veris facilis datur exitus umbris,
> altera candenti perfecta nitens elephanto,
> sed falsa ad caelum mittunt insomnia Manes.
>
> (893–96)

> There are two gates of Sleep: the one is said
> to be of horn, through it an easy exit
> is given to true Shades; the other is made
> of polished ivory, perfect, glittering,
> but through that way the Spirits send false dreams
> into the world above.
>
> (M 1191–96)

The phrase following this passage, with the backwards reference "*his . . . prosequitur dictis*," shows Anchises' escorting Aeneas and the Sibyl to the gates and dismissing them through the ivory gates.

36. This question was suggested to me by the volume editor. In my view, the answer to this question, as with other resonant questions in this book, lies with the reader.

CHAPTER 7. "THE BIRTH OF WAR: A READING OF *AENEID* 7"

1. Although *eros* and related words bring to mind erotic love, Archilochus uses the adjective *eratos* to describe what his homeland Thasos is not in poem 18, so it is certainly possible that Vergil could associate *eros* with the Italy he loved.

2. Tilly 1947, 3.

3. As one of the press's readers pointed out, eponymous heroes are common in the *Aeneid* as they are both in earlier and later literature. Book 7 has quite a few.

4. Cf. W. W. Fowler [1916] 1978, 27–28.

5. See McKay 1970, 147–93, on the connections between Aeneas' war and Rome's early wars in Italy.

6. See Gransden 1984, 39–41.

7. Reeker 1971, 60–62, points to other parallels between the opening of *Aeneid* 7 and the *Argonautica*.

8. Moskalew 1982, 136–83.

9. Surely Todd 1931, 217, is wrong when he asserts that the invocation of the Muse ends with "O goddess, help your poet."

10. For a study of sacrifice and scapegoating of females in epic, see Suzuki 1989, 92–149.

11. Erato is female by definition since she is a Muse: the birth imagery makes her gender seem relevant. Celaeno's gender does not seem to matter particularly, but she *is* female and so fits into the group I will discuss.

12. I am indebted to Putnam 1970 for a great deal of my discussion of Circe.

13. Reckford 1961, 266.

14. As one of the press's readers pointed out, Aeneas himself thinks of Lavinia as a city name: "*urbique dabit Lavinia nomen*" ("Lavinia shall give those walls her name," 12.194, M 263).

15. Grimal 1985, 219: "C'est ainsi que l'union d' Enée et de Lavinia aura lieu, sans qu' il l'ait vue, et sans qu'elle-même l'ait aperçu. Ainsi, dans les maisons nobles Romains . . . " ("It is thus that the wedding of Aeneas and Lavinia will take place, without his having seen her, and without her having laid eyes on him. Thus in the noble Roman houses . . .")

16. I, like R. G. Austin, ad 765, take *educet* to mean "she will raise"; Mandelbaum translates it as "she will bear."

17. Conington 1898 [1963], ad loc., disagrees. He thinks that *Laomedontia* here simply means "Trojan," although it conveys reproach at 3.248 and 4.542.

18. Discomfort with the conclusion to Vergil's six books of war is not a uniquely late-twentieth-century phenomenon. Back in 1428 Maphaeus Vegius

found the ending of the poem so unsatisfying that he composed a whole Book 13 in Latin hexameters neatly tying up all the loose ends Vergil had left. In his book the Rutulians surrender to Aeneas, Turnus is buried, Aeneas marries Lavinia, founds Lavinium, and is finally carried up to heaven, just as Jupiter said he would be (1.259–60, M 361–62).

19. On Allecto see Heinze [1915 1972, 182–84 (1993 trans., 148–50).

20. See Lyne 1987, 15 ff., on the erotic nature of Amata's passion. See also Zarker 1969.

21. It should not surprise us that Dido's name, like Amata's, is connected with "love." See Zarker 1969, 24 n.31.

22. According to Anderson 1969, 68–69, Ascanius is not to be blamed for hunting; nevertheless, the hunt reminds us of Aeneas' fateful hunt (real and metaphorical) in Carthage.

23. Compare that other hunt: "that day was the first of death and first the cause of disaster" (*ille dies primus leti primusque malorum / causa fruit*, 4.169–70, my translation).

24. I have often thought that Juno can be reconciled with Jupiter as she seems to be in Book 12 because she has already compromised Roman history to the point that she is not needed.

25. On Camilla see Arrigoni 1982.

CHAPTER 8. "*AENEID* 8: IMAGES OF ROME"

1. Otis 1964, 342.

2. Gransden 1976, 29.

3. Putnam 1965, 150.

4. Otis 1964, 381 ff.

5. Readers will find useful observations on Book 8 in Anderson 1969, Boyle 1986, Gransden 1976 and 1984, Gurval 1995, Otis 1964, Putnam 1966, and Quint 1993. Zanker 1988 has much to say of relevance on the ideological import of the shield.

CHAPTER 9. "THE MAN WHO WAS NOT THERE: AENEAS AND ABSENCE IN *AENEID* 9"

I wish to thank the members of the graduate seminar on Vergil's *Aeneid*, Vanderbilt University, spring 1996, for their assistance in bibliographical research for this chapter.

1. Forms of *absens* appear in Book 9.63, 215, 361, and 389; Book 4.83 (twice) and 384; 7.28; and 10.661. Of the twenty-five repetitions in the *Aeneid* of some form of the words *arma virumque*, seven (or 28 percent) appear in Book 9 at lines 57, 318, 357–58, 376, 462, 620, and 777.

2. See Wiltshire 1992, 189–205.

3. R. D. Williams 1973, 321.

4. The war had been anticipated by Anchises at 3.539–40; Vergil himself announces his intentions at 7.41: *dicam horrida bella* ("I shall tell of dreadful wars").

5. Servius Danielis at 9.81: *vituperabile enim est poetam aliquid fingere quod penitus a veritate discedat, obicitur Vergilio de mutatione navium in nymphas . . .*

6. One young child observed on hearing this story, "Those gods can sure do a lot of tricky things."

7. Hardie, 1994, 9–10, tabulates the main Homeric models for Book 9 as follows:

Aeneid 9	Homer
1–24: Iris, sent by Juno, prompts Turnus to battle.	*Il.* 2.786–810: Iris tells Hector to marshal the Trojan forces. *Il.* 18.165–202: Iris tells Achilles to rescue body of Patroclus.
25–46: Rutulian advance.	*Il.* 3.1–14, 4.422–45: Advancing armies.
47–167: Turnus attacks Trojan camp and camps around the wall at nightfall	*Il.* 8.157–565: Hector routs the Greeks and camps round the wall at nightfall.
77–122: Ships changed into nymphs.	*Od.* 13.125–64: Poseidon changes Phaeacian ship into a rock.
77–97: Invocation to Muses: which god saved Trojan ships from being burnt?	*Il.* 16.112–13: Invocation to Muses: how did fire first fall on the Greek ships?
168–458: Night. Nisus and Euryalus.	*Il.* 10: Night. Doloneia. *Il.* 9: Night. Embassy to Achilles.
459–502: Nisus' and Euryalus' heads carried round Trojan wall; grief of Euryalus' mother.	*Il.* 22.395–515: Hector's body dragged round Troy; grief of Hector's wife.
503–735: Attack on Trojan camp; Turnus enters the camp.	*Il.* 12.35–471: Attack on Achean wall; Hector breaches the wall.

672–755: Pandarus and Bitias.	*Il.* 12.127–94: Polypoites and Leonteus.
756–61: Turnus would have taken the camp.	*Il.* 16.698–701: Patroclus would have taken Troy.
802–5: Jupiter sends Iris to warn off Juno from helping Turnus.	*Il.* 8.397–432: Zeus sends Iris to warn off Hera and Athene from helping Achaeans.
806–14: Turnus retreats under heavy fire.	*Il.* 16.102–11: Ajax retreats from the defence of the ships under heavy fire.

8. This reading to some extent revises that of Anderson 1957, 17–30, who pioneered an Iliadic construction of Books 7–12.

9. Hardie 1994, 8.

10. Fantham 1990, 119.

11. Kingsolver 1995, 162.

12. See Beye in this volume, chap. 15, on Turnus as an imperfect reader of epic.

13. Otis 1964 [1995], 344–45.

14. See Hexter 1990.

15. Hardie 1994, 153: "V. reserves for this young couple the most emphatic authorial intervention in the epic and the only explicit reference to the power of his own poetry." Hardie sees this passage as reflecting a more traditionally Homeric notion, "that in the end the only lasting result of heroic struggle and death is undying *kleos* [fame]."

16. Pavlock 1985, 209.

17. Ibid., 209: "Euripides' play thus totally undermines the positive heroic ideal in Homer's Doloneia. By imitating the *Rhesus* as the second major model, Vergil does not simply invert Euripides' deep skepticism but instead reveals an uneasy tension between Homeric epic and Euripidean tragedy."

18. In the *Aeneid*, Ascanius similarly offers Nisus and Euryalus grandiose gifts, including some that belong to his father and are not properly his to give—for example, a bowl given to Aeneas by Dido (9.266). As Hector promises Achilles' horses to Dolon in the *Rhesus*, Ascanius—son of the "new Hector"—promises Turnus' horse to Nisus and Euryalus in the *Aeneid*. These are not practical gifts but appeals to the arrogant acquisitiveness the Greeks linked with hubris.

19. Pavlock 1985, 212, 215–16.

20. Boyle 1986, 91–92.

21. Ibid., 120, 124.

22. Ibid., 1986, 121.

23. Makowski 1989, 15.

24. Putnam 1995b, 29.

25. Ibid., 37–43.

26. Ibid., 46. (An observant reader of Putnam's prose will notice almost a Vergilian hexameter here.)

27. Certain poems in the Vergilian *Appendix*, including *Catalepton* VII, support such a conclusion.

28. The translation of Catullus is my own.

29. Two details further modify the simile from Homer. Vergil adds the term "by chance" (*forte*) to describe the rains that randomly cause the drooping of the poppies, which diminishes any sense of Euryalus' death as somehow designed by destiny. Second, in a rare usage, Vergil chooses the more colloquial adjective *lasso* to describe the weary neck or stem on which the poppies droop, rather than *fesso*, the metrically equivalent adjective that is more usual in epic. Vergil uses the rarer word also to evoke the pathos of Creusa, who may have stopped to rest on the streets of falling Troy because she was weary, *lassa* (2.739).

30. Johnson 1976, 62: "in order to stress the nature of vainglory and to challenge the foundations of the epic sensibility."

31. Johnson 1976, 62–63. For other interpretations of this episode, see Lee 1979, 77–80, 109–113; Lennox 1977; Duckworth 1967; G. J. Fitzgerald 1972; Goldberg 1995, 21–23.

32. Heilbrun 1979, 135.

33. As identified by Kübler-Ross 1969, who identifies the five stages of the grief process as denial, numbness, anger, negotiation, and acceptance.

34. See Wiltshire 1989, 38–55, for a more extended version of this argument.

35. Egan 1980, 159–63.

36. Guest 1925, 13, 14.

CHAPTER 10. "EPIC VIOLENCE, EPIC ORDER: KILLINGS, CATALOGUES, AND THE ROLE OF THE READER IN *AENEID* 10"

I am much in debt to David Califf, whose paper "The Divine Audience in *Aeneid* 10"—written for my fall 1992 *Aeneid* seminar, University of Wisconsin, Madison—taught me much and inspired me to look again at this old problem.

1. In the *Iliad* there is a good deal of martial action from early on, but we are still kept waiting until Book 20 before we see Achilles, the hero named in the poem's first line, in action.

2. By repeating the phrase *rumpe moras* from an earlier occurrence, Vergil here reminds us that one-third of the epic has passed since Mercury said the same thing to Aeneas in order to force him to break free of the poem's first huge delay, the delay in Carthage (4.569).

3. Wofford 1992, 33.

4. Ibid., 6.

5. Burkert 1983, 1.

6. Benjamin 1968, 258.

7. Brooks 1992, 37.

8. In other words, we need an epic counterpart to Nuttall 1996 on the pleasure of tragedy.

9. Hutcheon 1980, xii. Latinists have done much important work in this area in recent years, particularly on post-Vergilian narratives: Jamie Masters's 1992 study of Lucan, for example, is a tour de force.

10. He imitates with variation, as the Latinists put it (*imitatio cum variatione*), for in Homer a god friendly to Aeneas made a phantom-Aeneas in order to save Aeneas, whereas now the phantom-Aeneas is being made in order to save Turnus, Aeneas' enemy.

11. Griffin 1980, 179–204.

12. See Barchiesi, 1984, 11–54, for fundamentally important analysis of the intertextuality between Homer and Vergil in this scene.

13. Feeney 1991, 157.

14. Or, we should say, it had been *half* of the Aristotelian response, along with "fear": Is it significant that the gods feel only pity and not fear?

15. S. J. Harrison 1991, 254.

16. See ibid., 108, for discussion of this possibility.

17. Ibid., 106.

18. He has already used this joke in the catalogue of Book 7, telling one Oebalus that he will not be absent from his verses (733)—he is never mentioned again.

19. S. J. Harrison 1991, 108. Corroboration of this conclusion is offered by the fact that Aeneas' ship is carefully mentioned as coming *first* (157), without actually being technically part of the catalogue itself, which begins *after* the description of Aeneas' progress.

CHAPTER 11. "*AENEID* 11: THE SADDEST BOOK"

1. Allen 1951.

2. Gransden 1991, 28.

3. Anderson 1969, 86.

4. On these walk-on Trojan women, see Babcock 1992.

5. For discussion of this theme, see D. P. Fowler 1987, especially 195 ff. on Camilla; also Mitchell 1991, who writes of Pallas but not Camilla.

6. Cf. *Iliad* 6.506–11 and 15.263–68.

7. West 1985.

8. On Vergil's creation of the character Camilla, see Horsfall 1988.

9. West 1985, 22–23: "Chloreus is Cybele's Eunuch, and overtones of her sensuous, sexually ambiguous worship appear in the richness of his clothes and horse."

10. Rosenmeyer 1960, 164.

11. Shakespeare has a comparable episode in *Henry IV*, Part 1: The two young heroes, Percy Hotspur and Prince Hal, engage each other on the battlefield at Shrewsbury, and Hal kills Percy. Then, along comes Falstaff, who in ridiculous fashion tries to claim credit for the victory. The poet makes Falstaff's disgrace obvious.

12. Some critics score a few points for Arruns because he expressly abjures the spoils of victory if he should kill Camilla (790–91). But if he were heroic, he might, like Aeneas, have erected a trophy. At the least, he would not have run away, as Vergil puts it, like a cowardly and vicious wolf (809 ff.). His deed is base to the poet.

13. Thus I would not agree with Suzuki 1989, 141, who writes that Vergil's "ambivalence toward her [Camilla] arises from her superior military ability that threatens to make male warriors 'feminine.'" Vergil may stir that innate ambivalence in male translators and critics and then be considered to share it by feminists, but I believe he clearly favors Camilla throughout Book 11, while she is in battle and especially in his construction of the triangle of tension around her death. Arruns and Chloreus only emphasize her grandeur.

CHAPTER 12. "*AENEID* 12: UNITY IN CLOSURE"

1. Translation by Mandelbaum 6–11, with the alteration of "hunter" to "robber" at 10.

2. *Il.* 5.136–42 (Diomedes); 12.41–48 and 16.822–26 (Hector); 20.164–73 (Achilles).

3. The translation is my own.

4. Aeneas is associated with animals twice elsewhere. He is one of two bulls in simile at 12.715–22 and part of a group of wolves in simile at 2.355–58.

5. Vergil's model here is the scepter that Achilles holds and describes at *Il.* 234–39, but the emphasis on mothers and fathers and on artistry is the Latin poet's own.

6. *Aen.* 12.309–10 = 10.745–46 with the change from *clauduntur* to *conduntur*. The surrounding language also alludes to Catullus 5 and 51, furthering the linkage between eroticism and war.

7. *Sanguis* or *sanguineus* occurs at 36, 51, 67, and 79.

8. Among several other examples of the collocation cf. 8.441 where Vulcan prepares to fashion the arms themselves.

9. Cf. R. D. Williams 1973, ad 12.451 f., with further citations.

10. Cf. *Aen.* 1.430–36.

11. Translation is by Fagles.

12. The translations for this and the subsequent quotation are my own.

13. Cf. *Aen.* 12.950–52.

14. The translation is my own. *Lenti* (237) recalls Meliboeus' description of Tityrus as *lentus in umbra* ("at ease in the shade"), also in the fourth line of *Eclogue* 1.

15. The translation is my own.

16. The word *umbra* also serves to unify *Eclogue* 1 itself, appearing in line 4 as well as 83.

CHAPTER 13. "THE *AENEID* AS FOUNDATION STORY"

1. On foundation and charter myths generally, see Doty 1986, MacDougall 1982, and Malinowski 1971, chap. 2.

2. This tradition is alluded to in the story of Hercules' visit to the Palatine in *Aeneid* 8.

3. The formation of a national tradition based on the Revolutionary Age is admirably documented in Kammen 1978, esp. 12, 15–16, 18, 42 (and note 19 on that page), 44, 54–55.

4. Kammen 1978, 45.

5. For a discussion of the *Aeneid* in the specific tradition of Greek colonial foundations, see Horsfall 1989.

6. E.g., Livy 30.30.27; or *Punica fraus*, "Punic bad faith," e.g., Livy 30.22.6.

7. Earl 1967, 67, observes that "the whole theme of the *Aeneid* is the foundation struggle not of a single city but of a unified nation."

8. It is noteworthy, however, that in this, as in so much else, the *Aeneid* does not allow us to take things at face value: at 8.134–43 (M 175–86) Aeneas presents Evander, himself of Greek descent, with a quite different geneology for Dardanus, who now also seems to be descended from a Greek.

9. See, e.g., Horace, *Epode* 7.17–20, translated and discussed in this essay below. In *Aeneid* 1, Jupiter's prophecy of domestic concord at Rome is expressed in terms of harmony between Remus and his fratricidal brother (1.291–93, M 408–12).

10. Due to space constraints I can only offer a brief and highly selective sketch of the poem's historical context. Here I will say little about the poem's relation to Augustus' political and cultural "program," focus of almost all discussions of the poem's historical context. The fullest of these is Hardie 1986; for my own perspective on this issue, see Miles and Allen 1986. In keeping with my specific definition of the *Aeneid* as a foundation story, I will focus, rather, on historical circumstances most closely related to questions of ethnic identity and membership (Romans vis-à-vis Greeks and Italians). On this subject see also Horsfall 1990, Schweizer 1967, and Toll 1991 and 1997.

11. On Republican Roman reaction to Hellenistic culture, see Gruen 1992, esp. chaps. 2 and 6; Miles 1980, chap. 1; Petrocheilos 1974.

12. Zanker 1988, 98–100.

13. The translation is that of Stewart 1993, 366.

14. On the history of ancient Italy and the Social Wars, see also David 1996, Gabba 1973, Keaveney 1987, Klingner 1965, and Pallottino 1991.

15. Brunt 1988, chap. 2, "Italian Aims at the Time of the Social War," and esp. 136.

16. Appropriately, then, the shield forged for Aeneas by Vulcan in Book 8 represents Aeneas going into battle against Antony at Actium, "leading the Italians to battle, / together with the Senate and the People, / the household gods and Great Gods" (*agens Italos in proelia Caesar / cum patribus populoque, penatibus et magnis dis*, 8.678–79, M 879–81).

17. Bickermann 1952; Gruen 1992; Wiseman 1995, "Appendix: Versions of the Foundation of Rome," 160–68.

18. My translation.

19. On foundation stories in Livy, see Miles 1995, esp. chaps. 2 and 4.

20. Here and in subsequent quotations from Livy, the translations are my own.

21. The ideological positions of *nobiles* and *novi homines* vis-à-vis each other are summarized in Wiseman 1971, 107–16. See also Earl 1966, esp. 34–35.

22. Subsequently, of course, he became the friend of Maecenas and Augustus and the veritable poet laureate of the new regime.

Chapter 14. "The Women of the *Aeneid*: Vanishing Bodies, Lingering Voices"

1. In the context of this collection of essays, organized primarily by book, it may be useful simply to list those characters schematically here: Book 1—Dido; Book 2—Dido, Creusa, [Helen]; Book 3—Andromache; Book 4—Dido, Anna; Book 5— the Trojan women; Book 6—Dido, the Sibyl; Book 7—Caieta, Amata, Sylvia, Camilla; Book 9—Euryalus' mother; Book 11—Camilla; Book 12—Amata, Juturna. Of course, the role of goddesses (particularly Juno and Venus) is also of major significance in the *Aeneid*. Consideration of female figures both human and divine, however, is beyond the scope of this brief essay, which will focus specifically on the human women of Vergil's epic. For recent studies that do explore in detail the role of goddesses within epic, see Slatkin 1991, Clay 1983, and Spence 1988.

2. The association of Juno with contrarian forces is perhaps best exemplified in modern readings by Michael Putnam's meticulously philological identification of the goddess with *furor*, the passionate antithesis to Roman and Aenean virtues. Putnam's student, Sarah Spence, presents a more recuperative view of Juno in her 1988 study.

3. Heinze 1993, 133. For a stimulating attempt to read the *Aeneid* through the figure of Dido, taking her complexity as a paradigm of the complexity of the poem, see Hexter 1992.

4. Desmond 1994, 1. Desmond's study usefully foregrounds the ways in which implicit assumptions about gender and class have structured the reading of the *Aeneid*, noting that "the *Aeneid* has generally been read by one segment of the population—the male elite, destined by education and/or birth to occupy powerful positions in a hierarchically arranged social structure" (3) and that "the exclusion of women from the study of classical languages has historically kept women marginalized and socially subordinated within the elite formations of culture" (4).

5. Lipking 1988, 3–4.

6. For a sensitive discussion of the significance of mothers' lamentation in the *Aeneid*, see Wiltshire 1989, chap. 2, "Grieving Mothers and the Costs of Attachment," 38–55.

7. It is also nontrivial that this decision of Evander's is itself apparently authorized by a higher power, since Evander perceives Aeneas' arrival as fulfilling a prophecy (8.477, 495–519).

8. Interea pavidam volitans pennata per urbem
nuntia Fama ruit matrisque adlabitur auris
Euryali.

(9.473–75)

Meanwhile winged Rumor, rushing, flies across
the frightened town with tidings; she glides toward
the mother of Euryalus and reaches
her ears.

(M 628–31)

Et iam Fama volans, tanti praenuntia luctus,
Evandrum Evandrique domos et moenia replet . . .

(11.139–40)

Now Rumor, first to tell of such a sorrow,
races to King Evander, filling all
his house and city . . .

(M 181–83)

9. Such reproachful words to the dead are very common in classical lamentation, perhaps most shockingly exemplified in Euripides' *Alcestis*, where Admetus, *who has solicited his wife Alcestis to die in his stead*, then begs her not to be so harsh as to leave him alone (Euripides, *Alcestis* 280).

10. Compare Dido's similar wish to be cast into the Underworld by Jupiter (4.24–27).

11. Compare the reaction to Euryalus' death of his companion Nisus. He too, mad with grief (*amens*, 9.424) at the death of the boy, not only invokes death but actively seeks it, sacrificing himself to wreak vengeance on Euryalus' killer. Rather than being silenced, as was Euryalus' mother, Nisus (along with Euryalus) is famously apostrophized by Vergil, who asserts that his poetry will preserve the memory of the blessed pair (*fortunati ambo*, 9.446) as long as Rome endures.

12. Aeneas' painful gaze riveted on the dying face of Lausus (10.821–24) resonates eerily with Mezentius' atrocities earlier described by Evander: he coupled the living and the dead, face-to-face (8.485–88).

13. *ad caelum tendit palmas* (10.845)—cf. 1.93 (of Aeneas), 2.688 (of Anchises), 5.256 (of Ganymede's guardians), 5.233 (of Cloanthus), 5.686 (of Aeneas).

14. Cf. Desmond 1994, 15: "Medieval readers of Virgil's text repeatedly categorize Dido as a virago—a woman who performs as a man."

15. For a detailed study of this episode, see Nugent 1992.

16. See, for example, duBois 1988 and Zeitlin 1996.

17. For a thoughtful reading of Aeneas' relationship to Creusa—and its implications for understanding Aeneas' values—see Perkell 1981, 355–77.

18. Cf. Perkell 1981, 358–60.

CHAPTER 15. "VERGIL AND APOLLONIUS"

1. Hunter 1993, chap. 7, "*Argonautica* and *Aeneid*," and more specifically the forthcoming Nelis 1999 begin to give Apollonius his due.

2. Otis 1964, 5–40, is an eloquent statement of this position.

3. See the warning as it applies to modern criticism of Alexandrianism in Nyberg 1992, 16 f.

4. Convincingly demonstrated by O'Hara 1989, 35–38.

5. Conington and Nettleship 1898 [1963], ad 8.22.

6. So well discussed by Kermode 1983, 15–45.

7. Beye 1982, 82–90.

8. Servius' odd argument for the presence of the song (at 742, *bene philosophica introducitur cantilena in convivio reginae adhuc castae*) seems to demonstrate that he is uncomfortable with it.

9. Beye 1982, 35–38.

10. Putnam's 1995*b* collected essays on the poem's ending are brilliant.

11. This is the central argument of DeForest 1994.

CHAPTER 16. "FIVE HUNDRED YEARS OF RENDERING THE *AENEID* IN ENGLISH"

The translations discussed in this essay are as follows (in chronological order):

Douglas, Gavin. 1553, 1710, 1839, 1874, 1951. *The "Aeneid" of Virgil Translated into Scottish Verse*. London, Edinburgh.

Phaer, Thomas, and Twyne, T. [1573] 1987. *The "Aeneid": A Critical Edition*. New York.

Dryden, John. 1697. *The "Aeneid" of Virgil*. London.

Humphries, Rolfe. 1951. *The "Aeneid" of Virgil*. New York.

Lewis, C. Day. 1952. *The "Aeneid" of Virgil*. Oxford.

Copley, F. O. 1965. *Vergil: The "Aeneid."* Indianapolis.

Mandelbaum, Allen. 1971. *The "Aeneid" of Virgil: A Verse Translation.* New York.

Fitzgerald, Robert. 1981, 1983. *Virgil: The "Aeneid."* New York.

1. For Douglas's reaction against Caxton, see his preface and Singerman 1985, chap. 4.

2. See the critical edition of Phaer and Twyne 1987.

3. See Proudfoot 1960.

4. On the theory and practical problems of translating Vergil, see Austin 1956, R. B. W. Lewis 1961 and C. D. Lewis 1969. For a more contemporary theory of translation, see Steiner 1992, chaps. 4–6. Steiner (269–70) cites from Dryden's 1697 preface to his *The Aeneid of Vergil*, as does C. D. Lewis (p. 10).

5. See Proudfoot 1960 and Frost 1955.

6. See Anderson 1969, 101–7, for an analysis of the way three poets of the mid-twentieth century (Humphries, Lewis, and Copley) dealt with the final lines of Book 12.

7. C. D. Lewis 1969, 10–14, indicated that he set himself consciously to replace the dated work of Dryden; Austin 1956, 17–19, criticized him both favorably and severely for what he considered his mixed success at modernization.

8. It has been suggested to me that Twyne was being ironic about Chloreus and that he questioned his knightliness. After further thought, I still believe the language Twyne used suggests genuine respect, not irony.

9. On Vergil's presentation of Chloreus as a eunuch, see West 1985.

COMPREHENSIVE BIBLIOGRAPHY

ABBREVIATIONS

A&A	*Antike und Abendland*
AJP	*American Journal of Philology*
BICS	*Bulletin of the Institute of Classical Studies*
CA	*Classical Antiquity*
CJ	*Classical Journal*
CP	*Classical Philology*
CQ	*Classical Quarterly*
CR	*Classical Review*
CW	*Classical World*
G&R	*Greece and Rome*
HSCP	*Harvard Studies in Classical Philology*
ICS	*Illinois Classical Studies*
JRS	*Journal of Roman Studies*
PCPS	*Proceedings of the Cambridge Philological Society*
PVS	*Proceedings of the Vergil Society*
RE	*Pauly-Wissowa, Real-Encyclopädie der classischen Altertumswissenschaft*
TAPA	*Transactions of the American Philological Association*
YCS	*Yale Classical Studies*
YJC	*Yale Journal of Criticism*

Ahl, F. 1989. "Homer, Vergil, and Complex Narrative Structures in Latin Epic: An Essay." *ICS* 14:1–31.

Allen, A. W. 1951. "The Dullest Book of the *Aeneid*." *CJ* 47:119–23.

Anderson, W. S. 1957. "Vergil's Second *Iliad*." *TAPA* 88:17–30.

——. [1969] 1989. *The Art of the "Aeneid."* Wauconda, Ill.

Arrigoni, G. 1982. *Camilla, Amazzone e sacerdotessa di Diana.* Milan.

Austin, R. G. 1956. *Some English Translations of Virgil. An Inaugural Lecture*. Liverpool.

———, ed. 1955. *P. Vergili Maronis Aeneidos liber quartus*. Oxford.

———, ed. 1964. *P. Vergili Maronis Aeneidos liber secundus*. Oxford.

———, ed. 1971. *P. Vergili Maronis Aeneidos liber primus*. Oxford.

———, ed. 1977. *P. Vergili Maronis Aeneidos liber sextus*. Oxford.

Babcock, C. L. 1992. "*Sola . . . multis e matribus*: A Comment on Vergil's Trojan Women." In *The Two Worlds of the Poet: New Perspectives on Vergil*, ed. R. Wilhelm and H. Jones, 39–50. Detroit.

Bacon, H. H. 1986. "The *Aeneid* as a Drama of Election." *TAPA* 116:305–34.

Barchiesi, A. 1984. *La Traccia del modello: effetti omerici nella narrazione virgiliana*. Pisa.

———. 1994. "Rappresentazioni del dolore e interpretazione nell' *Eneide*." *A&A* 40:109–24.

———. 1996. Review of Heinze 1993. *JRS* 86:229–31.

Becker, A. S. 1990. "The Shield of Achilles and the Poetics of Homeric Description." *AJP* 111:139–53.

———. 1992. "Reading Poetry through a Distant Lens: Ecphrasis, Ancient Greek Rhetoricians and the Pseudo-Hesiodic 'Shield of Herakles.'" *AJP* 113:5–24.

Benjamin, W. 1968. *Illuminations*. Trans. H. Zohn. London.

Bertram, S. 1971. "The Generation Gap and *Aeneid* 5." *Vergilius* 17:9–12.

Bettini, M. 1991. "On the Way: Generational Time and the Review of Heroes in Book 6 of Vergil's *Aeneid*." Chap. 5 in *Anthropology and Roman Culture: Kinship, Time, Images of the Soul*, trans. J. van Sickle. Baltimore.

———. 1997. "Ghosts of Exile: Doubles and Nostalgia in Vergil's *parva Troia* (*Aeneid* 3.294 ff.)." *CA* 16:8–33.

Beye, C. R. 1982. *Epic and Romance in the "Argonautica" of Apollonius*. Carbondale, Ill.

Bickermann, E. J. 1952. "*Origines Gentium*." *CP* 47:65–81.

Binder, G. 1971. *Aeneas und Augustus. Interpretationen zum 8. Buch der "Aeneis."* Meisenheim.

Bing, P. 1988. *The Well-Read Muse: Present and Past in Callimachus and the Hellenistic Poets*. Hypomnemata 90. Göttingen.

Biow, D. 1994. "Epic Performance on Trial: Virgil's *Aeneid* and the Power of Eros in Song." *Arethusa* 27:223–46.

Bloom, H. 1973. *The Anxiety of Influence: A Theory of Poetry*. Oxford.

———. 1975. *A Map of Misreading*. Oxford.

———. 1987. *Ruin the Sacred Truths: Poetry and Belief from the Bible to the Present*. Cambridge, Mass.

Boyle, A. J. 1986. *The Chaonian Dove: Studies in the "Eclogues," "Georgics,"* and *"Aeneid" of Virgil*. Leiden.

———. 1993. "The Canonic Text: Virgil's *Aeneid*." In *Roman Epic*, ed. A. J. Boyle, 79–107. London.

Brenk, F. E. 1991. "Wind, Waves, and Treachery: Diodorus, Appian, and the Death of Palinurus in Vergil." In *Mito/Storia/Tradizione: Diodoro Siculo e la storiografia classica: atti del convegno internazionale Catania-Agira 7–8 dicembre 1984*, ed. E. Galvagno and C. Molè Ventura, 327–46.

Briggs, W. W. 1975. "Augustan Athletics and the Games of *Aeneid* V." *Stadion* 1:267–83.

———. 1981. "Virgil and Hellenistic Epic." In *Aufstieg und Niedergang der römischen Welt*, 2d ser., vol. 31.2, ed. H. Temporini and W. Haase, 948–84. Berlin.

Brinton, A. C., ed. [1471] 1930. In *Maphaeus Vegius and His Thirteenth Book of the "Aeneid."* Reprint, Stanford.

Brooks, P. 1992. *Reading for the Plot: Design and Intention in Narrative*. Cambridge, Mass.

Brunt, P. A. 1988. *The Fall of the Roman Republic and Related Essays*. Oxford.

Buchheit, V. 1963. *Vergil über die Sendung Roms*. Heidelberg.

Büchner, K. 1955/1958. "P. Vergilius Maro." *RE* 8 A1 (1955):1021–264; *RE* 8 A2 (1958):1265–1486.

Burkert, W. 1983. *Homo Necans: The Anthropology of Ancient Greek Sacrificial Ritual and Myth*. Trans. Peter Bing. Berkeley.

Butcher, S. H., trans. 1951. *Aristotle's Theory of Poetry and Fine Art*. With critical notes. New York.

Cairns, F. 1977. "Geography and Nationalities in the *Aeneid*." *Liverpool Classical Monthly* 2:109–16.

———. 1989. *Virgil's Augustan Epic*. Cambridge.

Cameron, A. 1995. *Callimachus and His Critics*. Princeton.

Camps, W. A. 1969. *An Introduction to Virgil's "Aeneid."* Oxford.

Clark, R. J. 1977. "Vergil, *Aeneid* 6.40 ff. and the Cumaean Sibyl's Cave." *Latomus* 36:482–95.

———. 1991. "Vergil's Poetic Treatment of Cumaean Geography." *Vergilius* 37:60–69.

Clausen, W. 1964. "An Interpretation of the *Aeneid*." *HSCP* 68:139–47; reprint with revisions in Commager 1966, 75–88.

———. 1987. *Vergil's "Aeneid" and the Tradition of Hellenistic Poetry*. Berkeley.

Clay, J. 1983. *The Wrath of Athena: Gods and Men in the "Odyssey."* Princeton.

Commager, S., ed. 1966. *Virgil: A Collection of Critical Essays*. Englewood Cliffs, N.J.

Conington, J., and H. Nettleship, eds. [1898] 1963. *P. Vergili Maronis opera*. 3 vols. Rev. F. Haverfield. London. Reprint, Hildesheim.

Conte, G. B. 1986. *The Rhetoric of Imitation: Genre and Poetic Memory in Virgil and Other Latin Poets*, ed. Charles Segal. Ithaca.

Copley, F. O., trans. 1965. *Vergil: The "Aeneid."* Indianapolis.

Cova, P. V., ed. 1994. *Virgilio. Il libro terzo dell'Eneide*. Biblioteca di Aevum Antiquum, 5. Milan.

Crotty, K. 1994. *The Poetics of Supplication: Homer's "Iliad" and "Odyssey."* Ithaca.

David, J.-M. 1996. *The Roman Conquest of Italy*. Trans. Antonia Nevill. Oxford.

DeForest, M. M. 1994. *Apollonius' "Argonautica": A Callimachean Epic*. Leiden.

Desmond, M. 1994. *Reading Dido: Gender, Textuality and the Medieval "Aeneid"*. Minneapolis.

Doty, W. 1986. *Mythography: The Study of Myths and Rituals*. Alabama.

Douglas, G. 1553, 1710, 1839, 1874, 1951. *The "Aeneid" of Virgil Translated into Scottish Verse*. London and Edinburgh.

Dryden, J. [1697] 1944. *Virgil: The "Aeneid": Translated by John Dryden, with Mr. Dryden's Introduction*. Reprint, New York.

duBois, P. 1988. *Sowing the Body: Psychoanalysis and Ancient Representations of Women*. Chicago.

Duckworth, G. E. 1967. "The Significance of Nisus and Euryalus for *Aeneid* IX–XII." *AJP* 88:129–50.

Dupont, F. 1994. *L'invention de la littérature: de l'ivresse grecque au livre latin*. Paris.

Dyson, J. T. 1996a. "Dido the Epicurean." *CA* 15:203–21.

———. 1996b. "*Septima Aestas*: The Puzzle of *Aen*. 1.755–56 and 5.626." *CW* 90:41–44.

Eagleton, T. 1983. *Literary Theory: An Introduction*. Minneapolis.

Earl, D. C. 1966. *The Political Thought of Sallust*. Amsterdam.

———. 1967. *The Moral and Political Tradition of Rome*. London.

Eck, W. 1984. "Senatorial Self-Representation: Developments in the Augustan Period." In *Caesar Augustus: Seven Aspects*, ed. F. Millar and E. Segal, 129–68. Oxford.

Egan, R. B. 1980. "Euryalus's Mother and *Aeneid* 9–12." In *Studies in Latin Literature and Roman History*, vol. 2, ed. Carl Deroux, 157–76. Brussels.

Eliot, T. S. 1957. "What is a Classic?" In *On Poets and Poetry*, 52–74. New York.

Fagles, Robert, trans. 1990. *Homer: The "Iliad."* New York.

Fantham, E. 1990. *"Nymphas . . . e navibus esse*: Decorum and Poetic Fiction in *Aeneid* 9.77–122 and 10.215–59." *CP* 85:102–19.

Farrell, J. 1991. *Vergil's "Georgics" and the Traditions of Ancient Epic: The Art of Allusion in Literary History*. New York.

———. 1997. "The Virgilian Intertext." In *The Cambridge Companion to Virgil*, ed. C. Martindale, 222–38. Cambridge.

Farron, S. 1980. "The Aeneas-Dido Episode as an Attack on Aeneas' Mission and Rome." *G&R* 27:34–47.

Favro, D. 1993. "Reading the Augustan City." In *Narrative and Event in Ancient Art*, ed., Peter Holliday, 230–57. Cambridge.

Feeney, D. C. 1984. "The Reconciliations of Juno." *CQ* 34:179–94; reprint with corrections in S. J. Harrison 1990, 339–62.

———. 1991. *The Gods in Epic: Poets and Critics of the Classical Tradition*. Oxford.

Feldherr, A. 1995. "Ships of State: *Aeneid* 5 and Augustan Circus Spectacle." *CA* 14:245–65.

Fitzgerald, G. J. 1972. "Nisus and Euryalus: A Paradigm of Futile Behaviour and the Tragedy of Youth." In *Cicero and Virgil: Studies in Honour of Harold Hunt*, ed., John R. C. Martyn, 114–17. Amsterdam.

Fitzgerald, R., trans. 1981. *Virgil: The "Aeneid."* New York.

Fitzgerald, W. 1984. "Aeneas, Daedalus, and the Labyrinth." *Arethusa* 17:51–66.

Fordyce, C. J. [1977] 1990. *P. Vergili Maronis Aeneidos libri VII-VIII*. Reprint, Glasgow and Oxford.

Fowler, D. P. 1987. "Vergil on Killing Virgins." In *Homo Viator: Classical Essays for John Bramble*, ed. M. Whitby, P. Hardie, and M. Whitby, 185–98. Bristol.

———. 1990. "Deviant Focalisation in Virgil's *Aeneid*." *PCPS* 36:42–63.

———. 1991. "Narrate and Describe: The Problem of *Ekphrasis*." *JRS* 81:25–35.

Fowler, W. W. [1916] 1978. *Virgil's Gathering of the Clans*. Reprint, New York.

Fredericksen, M. 1984. *Campania*, ed. with additions by Nicholas Purcell. London.

Frost, W. 1955. *Dryden and the Art of Translation*. New Haven.

Gabba, E. 1973. *Republican Rome: The Army and the Allies*. Trans. P. J. Cuff. Berkeley.

Galinsky, G. K. 1968. "*Aeneid* V and the *Aeneid*." *AJP* 89:157–85.

———. 1969. *Aeneas, Sicily, and Rome*. Princeton.

———. 1988. "The Anger of Aeneas." *AJP* 109:321–48.

———. 1992. "Aeneas at Rome and Lavinium." In *The Two Worlds of the Poet: New Perspectives on Vergil*, ed. R. Wilhelm and H. Jones, 93–108. Detroit.

———. 1994. "How to be Philosophical about the End of the *Aeneid*." *ICS* 19:191–201.

————. 1996. *Augustan Culture: An Interpretive Introduction*. Princeton.

Genette, G. 1983. *Narrative Discourse: An Essay in Method*. Trans. Jane E. Lewis. Ithaca.

————. 1988. *Narrative Discourse Revisited*. Trans. Jane E. Lewis. Ithaca.

Glazewski, J. 1972–73. "The Function of Vergil's Funeral Games." *CW* 66: 85–96.

Goldberg, S. 1995. *Epic in Republican Rome*. New York.

Goldhill, S., and Robin O., eds. 1993. *Art and Text in Ancient Greek Culture*. Cambridge.

Gossage, A. J. 1961–62. "Vergil in Exile." *PVS* 1:35–45.

Gransden, K. W. 1984. *Virgil's "Iliad": An Essay on Epic Narrative*. Cambridge.

————, ed. 1976. *Virgil: "Aeneid" Book VIII*. Cambridge.

————, ed. 1991. *Virgil: "Aeneid" Book XI*. Cambridge.

Greene, T. 1963. *The Descent from Heaven: A Study in Epic Continuity*. New Haven.

————. 1982. *The Light in Troy. Imitation and Discovery in Renaissance Poetry*. New Haven.

Griffin, J. 1980. *Homer on Life and Death*. Oxford.

————. 1986. *Virgil*. Oxford.

Grimal, P. 1985. *Virgile ou la seconde naissance de Rome*. Paris.

Gruen, E. 1982. "Augustus and the Ideology of War and Peace." In *The Age of Augustus: An Interdisciplinary Conference Held at Brown University*, ed. R. Winkes, 51–72. Providence.

————. 1992. "The Making of the Trojan Legend." In *Culture and National Identity in Republican Rome*, 6–51. Ithaca.

Guest, E. A. 1925. "The Mother on the Sidewalk." In *Mother*, 13–14. Chicago.

Günther, H.-C. 1996. *Überlegungen zur Entstehung von Vergils "Aeneis."* Hypomnemata 113. Göttingen.

Gurval, R. A. 1995. *Actium and Augustus: The Politics and Emotions of Civil War*. Ann Arbor.

Habinek, T. 1989. "Science and Tradition in *Aeneid* 6." *HSCP* 92:223–54.

Haecker, T. 1934. *Virgil: Father of the West*. Trans. A. W. Wheen. London.

Hardie, P. R. 1986. *Virgil's "Aeneid": Cosmos and Imperium*. Oxford.

————. 1993. *The Epic Successors of Virgil: A Study in the Dynamics of a Tradition*. Cambridge.

————, ed. 1994. *Virgil, "Aeneid," Book 9*. Cambridge.

Harrison, E. L. 1992. "The Opening Scenes of the *Aeneid*." In *The Two Worlds of the Poet: New Perspectives on Vergil*, ed. R. Wilhelm and H. Jones, 109–28. Detroit.

Harrison, S. J., ed. 1990. *Oxford Readings in Vergil's "Aeneid."* Oxford.

———, ed. 1991. *Vergil: "Aeneid" 10*. Oxford.

Heilbrun, C. 1979. *Reinventing Womanhood*. New York.

Heinze, R. [1915] 1972. *Virgils epische Technik*. 3d ed. Leipzig and Berlin. Reprint, Darmstadt.

———. 1993. *Vergil's Epic Technique*. Trans. H. and D. Harvey and F. Robertson. Preface by A. Wlosok. Berkeley.

Hexter, R. 1990. "What Was the Trojan Horse Made of? Interpreting Virgil's *Aeneid*." *YJC* 3:109–31.

———. 1992. "Sidonian Dido." In *Innovations of Antiquity*, ed. R. Hexter and D. Selden, 332–84. New York.

Holt, P. G. 1979–1980. "*Aeneid* V: Past and Future." *CJ* 75:110–21.

Horsfall, N. M. 1973–74. "Dido in the Light of History." *PVS* 13:1–13. Reprint in S. J. Harrison 1990:127–44.

———. 1983. "Camilla, o i limiti dell' invenzione." *Athenaeum* 66:31–51.

———. 1987. "The Aeneas Legend from Homer to Virgil." In *Roman Myth and Mythography, BICS*, suppl. 52, ed. J. N. Bremmer and N. M. Horsfall, 12–24. London.

———. 1989. "Aeneas the Colonist." *Vergilius* 35:8–26.

———. 1990. "The *Aeneid* and the Social Structures of Primitive Italy." *Athenaeum*, ser. 2, 78:523–27.

———. 1995. *A Companion to the Study of Virgil*. Leiden.

Humphries, R., trans. 1951. *The "Aeneid" of Virgil*. New York.

Hunter, R. 1993. *The "Argonautica" of Apollonius*. Cambridge.

Hutcheon, L. 1980. *Narcissistic Narrative: The Metafictional Paradox*. Waterloo, Ont.

Hutchinson, G. O. 1988. *Hellenistic Poetry*. Oxford.

Innocenti, B. 1994. "Towards a Theory of Vivid Description as Practiced in Cicero's *Verrine* Orations." *Rhetorica* 12:355–83.

Janko, R. trans. 1987. *Aristotle: "Poetics" 1*. Indianapolis.

Johnson, W. R. 1976. *Darkness Visible: A Study of Vergil's "Aeneid."* Berkeley.

Kammen, M. 1978. *A Season of Youth: The American Revolution and the Historical Imagination*. New York.

Keaveney, A. 1987. *Rome and the Unification of Italy*. London.

Kellum, B. 1986. "Sculptural Programs and Propaganda in Augustan Rome: The Temple of Apollo on the Palatine." In *The Age of Augustus*, Archeologia Transatlantica 5, ed. R. Winkes, 169–79.

Kennedy, D. F. 1992. "'Augustan' and 'Anti-Augustan': Reflections on Terms of Reference." In *Roman Poetry and Propaganda in the Age of Augustus*, ed. A. Powell, 26–58. Bristol.

Kermode, F. 1983. *The Classic*. Cambridge.

Kingsolver, B. 1995. "Postcards from the Imaginary Mom." In *High Tide in Tucson: Essays from Now or Never*, 158–69. New York.

Kinsey, T. E. 1979. "The Song of Iopas." *Emerita* 47:77–86.

Klingner, F. 1965. "Italien. Name, Begriff, und Idee im Altertum." In *Römische Geisteswelt*, 11–33. München.

———. 1967. *Virgil. "Bucolica," "Georgica," "Aeneis."* Zurich.

Knauer, G. N. 1964. *Die "Aeneis" und Homer*. Göttingen.

Konstan, D. 1991. "The Death of Argus, or What Stories Do: Audience Response in Ancient Fiction and Theory." *Helios* 18:15–20.

Kübler-Ross, E. 1969. *On Death and Dying*. New York.

Lattimore, R., trans. 1951. *The "Iliad" of Homer*. Chicago.

———, trans. 1965. *The "Odyssey" of Homer*. New York.

Lawall, G. 1966. "Apollonius' *Argonautica*: Jason as Anti-Hero." *YCS* 19:119–70.

Leach, E. W. 1988. *The Rhetoric of Space: Literary and Artistic Representations of Landscape in Republican and Augustan Rome*. Princeton.

Lee, M. O. 1979. *Fathers and Sons in Virgil's "Aeneid."* Albany.

Lennox, P. G. 1977. "Virgil's Night-Episode Re-examined (*Aeneid* IX, 176–449)." *Hermes* 105:331–42.

Lessing, G. E. [1766] 1984. *Laocoön: An Essay on the Limits of Painting and Poetry*. London. Reprint, trans., with introduction and notes, by E. A. McCormick. Baltimore.

Lewis, C. D., trans. 1952. *The "Aeneid" of Virgil*. Oxford and New York.

———. 1969. "On Translating Poetry." The Second Jackson Knight Lecture. Exeter.

Lewis, R. W. B. 1961. "On Translating the *Aeneid*: Yif that I Can." *Yearbook of Comparative and General Literature* 10:7–15. Reprint in Commager 1966, 41–52.

Lipking, L. 1988. *Abandoned Women and the Poetic Tradition*. Chicago.

Loraux, N. 1987. *Tragic Ways of Killing a Woman*. Trans. Anthony Forster. Cambridge, Mass.

Lyne, R. O. A. M. 1983. "Vergil and the Politics of War." *CQ* 33:188–203.

———. 1987. *Further Voices in Vergil's "Aeneid."* Oxford.

MacDougall, H. A. 1982. *Racial Myth in English History: Trojans, Teutons, and Anglo-Saxons*. Hanover, N.H.

Mack, S. 1978. *Patterns of Time in Vergil*. Hamden, Conn.

Mackie, C. J. 1988. *The Characterisation of Aeneas*. Edinburgh.

Makowski, J. F. 1989. "Nisus and Euryalus: A Platonic Relationship." *CJ* 85:1–15.

Malinowski, B. 1971. *Myth in Primitive Psychology*. Westport, Conn.

Mandelbaum, A., trans. 1971. *The "Aeneid" of Virgil: A Verse Translation.* New York.

Martindale, C. 1993. *Redeeming the Text: Latin Poetry and the Hermeneutics of Reception.* Cambridge.

Masters, J. 1992. *Poetry and Civil War in Lucan's "Bellum Civile."* Cambridge.

McKay, A. G. 1970. *Vergil's Italy.* Greenwich, Conn.

Michels, A. K. 1981. "The *Insomnium* of Aeneas." *CQ* 31:140–46.

Miles, G. B. 1980. *Virgil's "Georgics": A New Interpretation.* Berkeley.

———. 1995. *Livy: Reconstructing Early Rome.* Ithaca.

Miles, G. B., and A. W. Allen. 1986. "Vergil and the Augustan Experience." In *Vergil at 2000: Commemorative Essays on the Poet and His Influence*, ed. J. D. Bernard, 13–42. New York.

Miller, P. A. 1995. "The Minotaur Within: Fire, the Labyrinth and Strategies of Containment in *Aeneid* 5." *CP* 90:225–40.

Mitchell, R. N. 1991. "The Violence of Virginity in the *Aeneid*." *Arethusa* 24:219–38.

Moles, J. L. 1984. "Aristotle and Dido's Hamartia." *G&R* 31:48–54.

Momigliano, A. 1987. "How to Reconcile Greeks and Trojans." In *On Pagans, Jews, and Christians.* Scranton, Penn.

Monti, R. C. 1981. *The Dido Episode and the "Aeneid": Roman Social and Political Values in the Epic. Mnemosyne* Supplement 66. Leiden.

Moskalew, W. 1982. *Formular Language and Poetic Design in the Aeneid.* Leiden.

Most, G. W. 1989. "The Structure and Function of Odysseus' *Apologoi*." *TAPA* 119:15–30.

Muecke, F. 1983. "Foreshadowing and Dramatic Irony in the Story of Dido." *AJP* 104:134–55.

Mynors, R. A. B., ed. 1969. *P. Vergili Maronis Opera.* Oxford.

Nagy, G. [1979] 1981. *The Best of the Achaeans: Concepts of the Hero in Archaic Greek Poetry.* Baltimore.

———. 1990. *Greek Mythology and Poetics.* Ithaca.

Nelis, D. 1999 (forthcoming). *The "Aeneid" and the "Argonautica."* Papers of the Leeds Seminar, ed. Francis Cairns. Leeds.

Nichols, S. 1992. "The Illuminated Rose: Ekphrasis, Iconoclasm and Desire." In *Rethinking the Romance of the Rose: Text, Image, Reception*, 134–64. Philadelphia.

Nugent, S. G. 1992. "*Aeneid* V and Virgil's Voice of the Women." *Arethusa* 25:255–92.

Nuttall, A. D. 1996. *Why Does Tragedy Give Pleasure?* Oxford.

Nyberg, L. 1992. *Unity and Coherence: Studies in Apollonius Rhodius' "Argonautica" and the Alexandrian Epic Tradition.* Lund.

O'Hara, J. J. 1989. "Messapus, Cycnus, and the Alphabetical Order of Vergil's Catalogue of Italian Heroes." *Phoenix* 43:35–38.

———. 1990. *Death and the Optimistic Prophecy in Vergil's Aeneid.* Princeton.

Otis, B. [1964] 1995. *Virgil: A Study in Civilized Poetry.* Oxford. Reprint, with a foreword by Ward W. Briggs, Jr., Norman.

Page, T. E. [1894, 1900] 1962, 1964. *The "Aeneid" of Vergil.* 2 vols. London. Reprint, New York.

Pallottino, M. 1991. *A History of Earliest Italy.* Trans. Martin Ryle and Kate Soper. Jerome Lectures 17. Ann Arbor.

Parke, H. W. 1988. *Sibyls and Sibylline Prophecy in Classical Antiquity.* New York.

Parry, A. 1963. "The Two Voices of Virgil's *Aeneid.*" *Arion* 2:66–80; reprint in Commager 1966, 107–23.

Pavlock, B. 1985. "Epic and Tragedy in Vergil's Nisus and Euryalus Episode." *TAPA* 115:207–24.

Pavlovskis, Z. 1975–76. "*Aeneid* V: The Old and the Young." *CJ* 71:193–205.

Pease, A. S. [1935] 1967. *P. Vergili Maronis Aeneidos liber quartus.* Cambridge, Mass. Reprint, Darmstadt.

Perkell, C. 1981. "On Dido and Creusa and the Quality of Victory in Vergil's *Aeneid.*" *Women's Studies* 8:201–23; reprint in *Reflections of Women in Antiquity,* ed., H. Foley, 335–77, London.

———. 1989. *The Poet's Truth: A Study of the Poet in Virgil's "Georgics."* Berkeley.

———. 1994. "Ambiguity and Irony: The Last Resort?" *Helios* 21:63–74.

Petrocheilos, N. 1974. *Roman Attitudes to the Greeks.* Athens.

Phaer, T., and Twyne, T. [1573] 1987. *The "Aeneid": A Critical Edition.* Reprint, New York.

Pine-Coffin, R. S., trans. 1961. *St. Augustine: Confessions.* Harmondsworth, Eng.

Poliakoff, M. B. 1985. "Entellus and Amycus: Vergil, *Aen.* 5.362–484." *ICS* 10:227–31.

Pollitt, J. T. 1972. *Art and Experience in Classical Greece.* Cambridge.

Pöschl, V. [1950] 1962. *The Art of Vergil: Image and Symbol in the "Aeneid."* Trans. Gerda Seligson. Ann Arbor.

———. 1975. "Die Templetüren des Dädalus in der *Aeneis* (VI 14.33)." *Würzburger Jahrbucher,* n.s., 1:119–23.

Proudfoot, L. 1960. *Dryden's "Aeneid" and Its Seventeenth Century Predecessors.* Manchester, Eng.

Pucci, P. 1987. *Odysseus Polutropos: Intertextual Readings in the "Odyssey" and the "Iliad."* Ithaca.

Putnam, M. C. J. [1965] 1988. *The Poetry of the "Aeneid": Four Studies in Imaginative Design.* Cambridge, Mass. Reprint, Ithaca.

———. 1970. "*Aeneid* VII and the *Aeneid.*" *AJP* 91:408–30.

———. 1980. "The Third Book of the *Aeneid*: From Homer to Rome." *Ramus* 9:1–21; reprint in Putnam 1995*b*, 50–72.

———. 1985. "Possessiveness, Sexuality, and Heroism in the *Aeneid.*" *Vergilius* 31:1–21. Reprint in Putnam 1995*b*, 27–49.

———. 1987. "Daedalus, Vergil and the End of Art." *AJP* 108:173–98. Reprint in Putnam 1995*b*, 73–99.

———. 1995*a*. "Ganymede and Virgilian Ekphrasis." *AJP* 116:419–40.

———. 1995*b*. *Virgil's "Aeneid": Interpretation and Influence.* Chapel Hill.

———. 1996. "The Lyric Genius of the *Aeneid.*" *Arion* 3:81–101.

———. 1998. *Virgil's Epic Designs: Ekphrasis in the "Aeneid."* New Haven.

Quinn, K. 1968. *Virgil's "Aeneid": A Critical Description.* London.

Quint, D. 1993. *Epic and Empire: Politics and Generic Form from Vergil to Milton.* Princeton.

Raaflaub, K. A., and M. Toher, eds. 1990. *Between Republic and Empire: Interpretations of Augustus and his Principate.* Berkeley.

Reckford, K. J. 1961. "Latent Tragedy in *Aeneid* VII, 1–285." *AJP* 82:252–69.

Redfield, J. M. 1975. *Nature and Culture in the "Iliad": The Tragedy of Hector.* Chicago.

Reeker, H.-D. 1971. *Die Landschaft in der "Aeneis."* Hildesheim.

Richardson, L., Jr. 1992. *A New Topographical Dictionary of Ancient Rome.* Baltimore.

Richlin, A., ed. 1992. *Pornography and Representation in Greece and Rome.* Oxford.

Roberts, D. 1993. "The Frustrated Mourner: Strategies of Closure in Greek Tragedy." In *Nomodeiktes: Greek Studies in Honor of Martin Ostwald*, ed. R. Rosen and J. Farrell, 573–89. Ann Arbor.

Rose, A. 1982–83. "Vergil's Ship-Snake Simile (*Aeneid* V, 270–81)." *CJ* 78:115–21.

Rosenmeyer, T. G. 1960. "Vergil and Heroism." *CJ* 55:159–64.

Salmon, E. T. 1982. *The Making of Roman Italy.* Ithaca.

Schweizer, H. J. 1967. *Vergil und Italien.* Aarau.

Segal, C. P. 1965. "*Aeternum per saecula nomen*: The Golden Bough and the Tragedy of History." Pt. 1. *Arion* 4:615–57.

———. 1971. "The Song of Iopas in the *Aeneid.*" *Hermes* 99:336–49.

———. 1990. "Dido's Hesitation in *Aeneid* 4." *CW* 84:1–12.

Singerman, J. E. 1985. *Under Clouds of Poesy: Poetry and Truth in Reworkings of the "Aeneid" 1160–1513.* New York.

Skutsch, O., ed. 1985. *The Annals of Quintus Ennius.* Oxford.

Slatkin, L. 1991. *The Power of Thetis: Allusion and Interpretation in the "Iliad."* Berkeley.

Small, S. G. P. 1959. "Virgil, Dante, and Camilla." *CJ* 54:295–301.

Smith, B. H. 1968. *Poetic Closure: A Study of How Poems End.* Chicago.

Spence, S. 1988. *Rhetorics of Reason and Desire: Vergil, Augustine, and the Troubadours.* Ithaca.

————. Forthcoming. "The Polyvalence of Pallas and Its Significance in the *Aeneid.*" *Arethusa.*

Stahl, H.-P. 1981. "Aeneas—An 'Unheroic' Hero?" *Arethusa* 14:157–78.

————. 1990. "The Death of Turnus: Augustan Vergil and the Political Rival." In *Between Republic and Empire: Interpretations of Augustus and His Principate,* ed. K. Raaflaub and M. Toher, 174–211. Berkeley.

Steiner, G. 1992. *After Babel: Aspects of Language and Translation.* 2d ed. Oxford.

Stewart, A. 1993. *Faces of Power: Alexander's Image and Hellenistic Politics.* Berkeley.

Suzuki, M. 1989. *Metamorphoses of Helen: Authority, Difference, and the Epic.* Ithaca.

Swallow, E. 1952–53. "The Strategic Fifth *Aeneid.*" *CW* 46:177–79.

Swanepoel, J. 1995. "*Infelix Dido*: Vergil and the Notion of the Tragic." *Akroterion* 40:30–46.

Syme, R. [1939] 1971. *The Roman Revolution.* Oxford.

Tilly, B. 1947. *Vergil's Latium.* Oxford.

Thilo, G., and Hagen, H., eds. [1884] 1961. *Servii Grammatici qui feruntur in Vergilii carmina commentarii.* 3 vols. Reprint, Hildesheim.

Todd, F. 1931. "Virgil's Invocation of Erato." *CR* 45:216–18.

Toll, K. 1991. "The *Aeneid* as an Epic of National Identity: *Italiam Laeto Socii Clamore Salutant.*" *Helios* 18:3–14.

————. 1997. "Making Roman-ness and the *Aeneid.*" *CA* 16:34–56.

von Blanckenhagen, P. H. 1963. "The Odyssey Frieze." *Mitteilungen des Deutschen Archäologischen Instituts (Röm. Abt.)* 70:100–46 and pls. 46–53.

Watt, L. M. 1930. *Douglas' "Aeneid."* Cambridge.

West, G. S. 1985. "Chloreus and Camilla." *Vergilius* 31:22–29.

Wilhelm, R. M., and H. Jones, eds. 1992. *The Two Worlds of the Poet: New Perspectives on Vergil.* Detroit.

Williams, G. 1958. "Some Aspects of Roman Marriage Ceremonies and Ideals." *JRS* 48:16–29.

———. 1983. *Technique and Ideas in the "Aeneid."* New Haven.

Williams, R. D. 1967. "The Purpose of the *Aeneid.*" *Antichthon* 1:29–41. Reprint in S. J. Harrison 1990, 21–36.

———, ed. 1960. *P. Vergili Maronis Aeneidos liber quintus.* Oxford.

———, ed. 1962. *P. Vergili Maronis Aeneidos liber tertius.* Oxford.

———, ed. 1972. *The "Aeneid" of Virgil, Books 1–6.* Basingstoke.

———, ed. 1973. *Virgil "Aeneid" 7–12.* Basingstoke.

Wiltshire, S. F. 1989. *Public and Private in Vergil's "Aeneid."* Amherst, Mass.

———. 1992. "War and Peace in *Aeneid* X." In *The Two Worlds of the Poet: New Perspectives on Vergil,* ed. R. Wilhelm and H. Jones, 189–205. Detroit.

Wimmel, W. 1960. *Kallimachos in Rom.* Wiesbaden.

Wiseman, T. P. 1971. *New Men in the Roman Senate.* London.

———. 1995. *Remus: A Roman Myth.* Cambridge.

Wlosok, A. 1973. "Vergil in der neueren Forschung." *Gymnasium* 80:129–51.

———. 1983. "Vergil als Theologe: Iuppiter-pater omnipotens." *Gymnasium* 90:187–202.

———. 1992. "*Gemina Pictura*: Allegorisierende Aeneisillustrationen in Handschriften des 15. Jahrhunderts." In *The Two Worlds of the Poet: New Perspectives on Vergil,* ed. R. Wilhelm and H. Jones, 408–32. Detroit.

Wofford, S. L. 1992. *The Choice of Achilles: The Ideology of Figure in the Epic.* Stanford.

Zanker, P. 1988. *The Power of Images in the Age of Augustus.* Trans. A. Shapiro. Ann Arbor.

Zarker, J. 1969. "Amata: Vergil's Other Tragic Queen." *Vergilius* 15:2–18.

Zeitlin, F. 1996. *Playing the Other: Gender and Society in Classical Greek Literature.* Chicago.

Ziolkowski, T. 1993. *Virgil and the Moderns.* Princeton.

CONTRIBUTORS

WILLIAM S. ANDERSON is Professor of Latin Emeritus at the University of California at Berkeley. His works include *The Art of the "Aeneid"* (1969), *Barbarian Play: Plautus' Roman Comedy* (1993), and *Ovid's "Metamorphoses"* (text and commentary), Books 1–5 (1996) and Books 6–10 (1972).

CHARLES ROWAN BEYE is Distinguished Professor of Classics Emeritus at Lehman College and at the Graduate School of the City University of New York. Among his books are *Epic and Romance in the "Argonautica" of Apollonius* (1982) and *Ancient Epic Poetry* (1992).

ANTHONY J. BOYLE is Professor of Classics at the University of Southern California and Editor of *Ramus*. His publications include *The Chaonian Dove: Studies in the "Eclogues," "Georgics," and "Aeneid" of Virgil* (1986), translations with commentary of Seneca's *Phaedra* (1987) and *Troades* (1994), and *Tragic Seneca: An Essay in the Theatrical Tradition* (1997).

JOSEPH FARRELL is Professor of Classical Studies at the University of Pennsylvania. He is the author of *Vergil's "Georgics" and the Traditions of Ancient Epic* (1991) and *Latin Language and Latin Culture*, forthcoming from Cambridge University Press.

DENIS FEENEY is Fellow and Tutor in Classical Languages and Literature at New College, Oxford. He is the author of *The Gods in Epic: Poets and Critics of the Classical Tradition* (1991) and *Literature and Religion at Rome: Cultures, Contexts, and Beliefs* (1998).

RALPH HEXTER is Professor of Classics and Comparative Literature at the University of California at Berkeley. He is the author of *Ovid and Medieval Schooling* (1986), *A Guide to the "Odyssey": A Commentary on the English Translation of Robert Fitzgerald* (1993), and coeditor with Daniel Selden of *Innovations of Antiquity* (1992).

W. R. JOHNSON is J. M. Manly Professor of Classics and Comparative Literature Emeritus at the University of Chicago. He is the author of *Darkness Visible: A Study of Vergil's "Aeneid"* (1976), *The Idea of Lyric: Lyric Modes in Ancient and Modern Poetry* (1982), and *Horace and the Dialectic of Freedom: Readings in "Epistles" 1* (1993).

ELEANOR WINSOR LEACH is Professor of Classical Studies at Indiana University. She is the author of *Vergil's "Eclogues": Landscapes of Experience* (1974), *The Rhetoric of Space: Literary and Artistic Representations of Landscape in Republican and Augustan Rome* (1988), and *Roman Painting and Roman Society* (1999).

SARA MACK is Professor of Classics at the University of North Carolina, Chapel Hill. She is the author of *Patterns of Time in Vergil* (1978) and *Ovid* (1988).

GARY MILES is Professor of History and Classics at the University of California, Santa Cruz. He is the author of *Vergil's "Georgics": A New Interpretation* (1980) and *Livy: Reconstructing Early Rome* (1995).

S. GEORGIA NUGENT is Associate Provost and Lecturer in Classics at Princeton University. She is the author of *Allegory and Poetics: The Structure and Imagery of Prudentius' "Psychomachia"* (1985) and is currently completing a comprehensive study of female figures in Roman epic.

CHRISTINE PERKELL is Associate Professor of Classics at Emory University. She is the author of *The Poet's Truth: A Study of the Poet in Virgil's "Georgics"* (1989).

MICHAEL C. J. PUTNAM is MacMillan Professor of Classics and Professor of Comparative Literature at Brown University. He is the author of several books on Vergil, among them *The Poetry of the "Aeneid"*

(1965), *Virgil's "Aeneid": Interpretation and Influence*, and *Vergil's Epic Designs: Ekphrasis in the "Aeneid"* (1998).

SARAH SPENCE is Professor of Classics at the University of Georgia at Athens and Editor of *Literary Imagination: The Review of the Association of Literary Scholars and Critics*. She is the author of *Rhetorics of Reason and Desire: Vergil, Augustine, and the Troubadours* (1988) and *Texts and the Self in Twelfth-Century France* (1996).

SUSAN FORD WILTSHIRE is Professor of Classics at Vanderbilt University. Her books include *Public and Private in Vergil's "Aeneid"* (1989), *Greece, Rome, and the Bill of Rights* (1992), *Seasons of Grief and Grace* (1994), and *Athena's Disguises: Mentors in Everyday Life* (1998).